2024

HOROSCOPES

365 daily predictions for every zodiac sign

PATSY BENNETT

ROCKPOOL

THE MOON'S PHASES FOR THE YEAR

The moon's phases, including eclipses, new moons and full moons, can all affect your mood. All of these events are explained and listed in the diary, enabling you to plan ahead with the full knowledge you're moving in synchronicity with the sun and the moon. On the following pages are the moon's phases for 2024 for both the southern and northern hemispheres.

JANUARY

S	M	T	W	T	F	S
	1	2	3	4	5	6
7	8	9	10	11	12	13
14	15	16	17	18	19	20
21	22	23	24	25	26	27
28	29	30	31			

FEBRUARY

S	M	T	W	T	F	S
				1	2	3
4	5	6	7	8	9	10
11	12	13	14	15	16	17
18	19	20	21	22	23	24
25	26	27	28	29		

MARCH

S	M	T	W	T	F	S
31					1	2
3	4	5	6	7	8	9
10	11	12	13	14	15	16
17	18	19	20	21	22	23
24	25	26	27	28	29	30

APRIL

S	M	T	W	T	F	S
	1	2	3	4	5	6
7	8	9	10	11	12	13
14	15	16	17	18	19	20
21	22	23	24	25	26	27
28	29	30				

MAY

S	M	T	W	T	F	S
			1	2	3	4
5	6	7	8	9	10	11
12	13	14	15	16	17	18
19	20	21	22	23	24	25
26	27	28	29	30	31	

JUNE

S	M	T	W	T	F	S
30						1
2	3	4	5	6	7	8
9	10	11	12	13	14	15
16	17	18	19	20	21	22
23	24	25	26	27	28	29

2024 SOUTHERN HEMISPHERE MOON PHASES

JULY

S	M	T	W	T	F	S
	1	2	3	4	5	6
7	8	9	10	11	12	13
14	15	16	17	18	19	20
21	22	23	24	25	26	27
28	29	30	31			

AUGUST

S	M	T	W	T	F	S
				1	2	3
4	5	6	7	8	9	10
11	12	13	14	15	16	17
18	19	20	21	22	23	24
25	26	27	28	29	30	31

SEPTEMBER

S	M	T	W	T	F	S
1	2	3	4	5	6	7
8	9	10	11	12	13	14
15	16	17	18	19	20	21
22	23	24	25	26	27	28
29	30					

OCTOBER

S	M	T	W	T	F	S
		1	2	3	4	5
6	7	8	9	10	11	12
13	14	15	16	17	18	19
20	21	22	23	24	25	26
27	28	29	30	31		

NOVEMBER

S	M	T	W	T	F	S
					1	2
3	4	5	6	7	8	9
10	11	12	13	14	15	16
17	18	19	20	21	22	23
24	25	26	27	28	29	30

DECEMBER

S	M	T	W	T	F	S
1	2	3	4	5	6	7
8	9	10	11	12	13	14
15	16	17	18	19	20	21
22	23	24	25	26	27	28
29	30	31				

◯ New moon ● Full moon

2024 NORTHERN HEMISPHERE MOON PHASES

JANUARY

S	M	T	W	T	F	S
	1	2	3	4	5	6
7	8	9	10	11	12	13
14	15	16	17	18	19	20
21	22	23	24	25	26	27
28	29	30	31			

FEBRUARY

S	M	T	W	T	F	S
				1	2	3
4	5	6	7	8	9	10
11	12	13	14	15	16	17
18	19	20	21	22	23	24
25	26	27	28	29		

MARCH

S	M	T	W	T	F	S
31					1	2
3	4	5	6	7	8	9
10	11	12	13	14	15	16
17	18	19	20	21	22	23
24	25	26	27	28	29	30

APRIL

S	M	T	W	T	F	S
	1	2	3	4	5	6
7	8	9	10	11	12	13
14	15	16	17	18	19	20
21	22	23	24	25	26	27
28	29	30				

MAY

S	M	T	W	T	F	S
			1	2	3	4
5	6	7	8	9	10	11
12	13	14	15	16	17	18
19	20	21	22	23	24	25
26	27	28	29	30	31	

JUNE

S	M	T	W	T	F	S
30						1
2	3	4	5	6	7	8
9	10	11	12	13	14	15
16	17	18	19	20	21	22
23	24	25	26	27	28	29

iv • *2024* **HOROSCOPES**

2024 NORTHERN HEMISPHERE MOON PHASES

JULY

S	M	T	W	T	F	S
	1	2	3	4	5	6
7	8	9	10	11	12	13
14	15	16	17	18	19	20
21	22	23	24	25	26	27
28	29	30	31			

AUGUST

S	M	T	W	T	F	S
				1	2	3
4	5	6	7	8	9	10
11	12	13	14	15	16	17
18	19	20	21	22	23	24
25	26	27	28	29	30	31

SEPTEMBER

S	M	T	W	T	F	S
1	2	3	4	5	6	7
8	9	10	11	12	13	14
15	16	17	18	19	20	21
22	23	24	25	26	27	28
29	30					

OCTOBER

S	M	T	W	T	F	S
		1	2	3	4	5
6	7	8	9	10	11	12
13	14	15	16	17	18	19
20	21	22	23	24	25	26
27	28	29	30	31		

NOVEMBER

S	M	T	W	T	F	S
					1	2
3	4	5	6	7	8	9
10	11	12	13	14	15	16
17	18	19	20	21	22	23
24	25	26	27	28	29	30

DECEMBER

S	M	T	W	T	F	S
1	2	3	4	5	6	7
8	9	10	11	12	13	14
15	16	17	18	19	20	21
22	23	24	25	26	27	28
29	30	31				

○ New moon   ● Full moon

Patsy Bennett, a rare combination of astrologer and psychic medium, contributes horoscopes to magazines internationally and in Australia and has appeared on several live daytime TV and radio shows. She is also a speaker and provides astrology and psychic consultations, and she holds astrology and psychic development workshops in Byron Bay, Australia, where she lives.

Patsy runs www.astrocast.com.au, www.patsybennett.com, facebook@patsybennettpsychicastrology and instagram @patsybennettastrology.

FURTHER INFORMATION

For an in-depth personal astrology chart reading contact Patsy Bennett at patsybennettastrology@gmail.com.

Further astronomical data can be obtained from the following:

- Michelsen, Neil F. and Pottenger, Rique, *The American Ephemeris for the 21st Century 2000–2050 at Midnight*, ACS Publications, 1997.
- The computer program Solar Fire from Esoteric Technologies Pty Ltd.

A Rockpool book
PO Box 252
Summer Hill
NSW 2130
Australia

rockpoolpublishing.com
Follow us! **f** ⓘ rockpoolpublishing
Tag your images with #rockpoolpublishing

Published in 2023 by Rockpool Publishing
Copyright text © Patsy Bennett 2023
Copyright design © Rockpool Publishing 2023

ISBN 9781922785190

Design by Sara Lindberg, Rockpool Publishing
Edited by Lisa Macken
Illustrations from Shutterstock

Printed and bound in China
10 9 8 7 6 5 4 3 2 1

All dates in the diary pages are set to Greenwich Mean Time (GMT). Astrological interpretations take into account all aspects and the sign the sun and planets are in on each day and are not taken out of context.

CONTENTS

INTRODUCTION

Make 2024 your best year yet! Start the year with clarity, seeing your amazing year ahead for love, luck, loot and lifestyle. We all consult our horoscopes, but what we really want to know is how best to plan ahead for ourselves personally. Astrology is the study of the movement of celestial objects and their impact on us on Earth, but we need to know what that means on an individual level.

This guide doesn't just show you when good things will happen to you; it also shows you how to view positive astrological days as opportunities to initiate new ideas, organise wonderful events in your life and see challenging days as days to excel, draw on your inner reserves and find success by overcoming obstacles. Your greatest achievements will often occur when you overcome hurdles and allow your inner hero to rise to the challenge.

In *2024 Horoscopes* you'll find insight into your own strengths and weaknesses and into your particular way to move ahead throughout the year. Success is all in the timing and in knowing what to do with your own strengths in mind, and there's no better time than the present to consult your individual guide to success in 2024. This is the time to embrace your star power, starting now!

Astrology is not a phenomenon that happens to you – you need to take action, and it all depends on who you are. For example, if you're a Leo, when the sun passes through your sign from 22 July to 22 August you will tend to feel energised and motivated, so this is the time to get things rolling. For Scorpios this phase may not be the same; there will be more focus on career, direction and hard work as opposed to simply feeling energised.

2024 Horoscopes will provide invaluable direction to help you find your best-case scenario during various phases of the year and know the pitfalls to avoid.

MERCURY, VENUS AND MARS RETROGRADE PERIODS IN 2024

The dates listed in this section indicate when Mercury, Venus and Mars will be retrograde in 2024. A planet is termed 'retrograde' when it appears to be going backwards from our point of view on Earth. No planet actually goes backwards – it's an optical illusion – but these phases do exhibit certain characteristics. During the Mercury retrograde phase communications can tend to be a little more difficult than during the direct phase, when the planet does not appear to be going backwards. Travel may be delayed or cancelled; for example, computers may lose information. However, the Mercury retrograde phase can be an excellent time for reviewing your circumstances and for reorganising your various duties. Plan to take a slightly slower line in life such as a holiday, and don't expect communications to be perfect and for computers to run without a hitch.

During the Venus retrograde phase you might find that relationships are less likely to forge ahead in a straightforward manner, and that sometimes when a Venus retrograde phase coincides with a Mercury retrograde phase communications may be complex or predisposed to arguments. The plus side is that Venus retrograde phases provide an ideal time to take things a little more slowly, to be less demanding of yourself and others within your relationships and be kind. Patience is truly a virtue during the Mercury and Venus retrograde periods.

A Mars retrograde period can indicate a time when you feel less enthusiastic about your ventures, especially if Mars is retrograde in your zodiac sign. It's generally not a good time to initiate a project, as you may find other people do not welcome your ideas as much as they might at other times. On the plus side, it's is a good idea to look after your health and review your fitness schedule with a view to putting a gentler pace in practice.

Mercury retrograde phases in 2024:
1 to 25 April; 5 to 27 August;
26 November to 15 December

Venus retrograde phases in 2024: none
Mars retrograde phase in 2024:
6 December 2024 to 24 February 2025

ARIES

20 March – 19 April

FINANCES

The re-entry of Pluto into Aquarius signals key changes in your career and general direction in 2024, which will invariably mean financial change. You will be reviewing the ideas you contemplated earlier in 2023 and implementing them this year. Uranus continues to transit your second house of finances, bringing considerable changes to your investments. Luckily, Jupiter in your money zone from the start of the year until the end of May will protect your finances from adverse impacts. Nevertheless, risk-taking is not advised, especially in the first half of the year and at the end of August and December. As significant expenses are likely in 2024 it would be best to put in place a foolproof budget or set aside money to cover all eventualities, particularly regarding household expenses.

HEALTH

You will be carrying more responsibilities in 2024, even if in the process you do gain an opportunity to pursue a life that suits you and provides an increased sense of fulfilment. The eclipse seasons from March to April and from September to October will fall across both your sign and the sign of Libra, suggesting you must find a balance in life between being on the one hand overly active and productive and on the other finding time for peace and harmony. You will be drawn to accessing your deeper resolve and a sense of purpose, and you may even be surprised by how resilient and efficient you are.

LOVE LIFE

Be prepared to turn a corner in your love life in 2024, especially if you were born at the end of March or in early April. The lunar eclipse on 25 March, the solar eclipse on 8 April and the solar eclipse on 2 October will all be significant, as a new beginning in your love life will dawn. If you're single, this is the year to make a change in your status if you wish. Couples will find the need to establish more balance, peace and harmony in your love life, with September and October being excellent months to do so.

CAREER

The re-entry of Pluto into the sign of Aquarius will bring with it the chance to alter your direction career-wise and also your status, particularly if you had projects and ideas you floated in 2023 you are now ready to put into gear. Look out for wonderful opportunities, especially in the first quarter, and be inspired by new avenues. During the year be prepared to tweak and make changes within your career, especially around the dates of the 20th to the 23rd of every month. With Jupiter in your money zone until May you can be optimistic about your career changes; however, you must avoid being idealistic. It is far better to do your research than to act hastily.

HOME LIFE

Much of your focus will be on your status and career in the first six months of the year, with a view to investing more fully in yourself and your abilities. As your focus changes from your work to your home life and family towards July and August, you'll find so much of what you wish to enjoy and have been working towards rests in the domestic aspect of your life. An adventurous approach to investing in your home life and enjoying more time with those you love – and on yourself – will increasingly appeal and become the focus. The beautification of your home and possibly even a renovation or DIY project will appeal in the final quarter of the year, when Mars in Cancer will provide you with enough energy to put into your home-based projects.

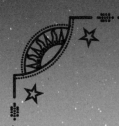

January

1 JANUARY

The year begins with a question mark: how hard or easy is it going to be to fulfil your goals? Who has your back and who doesn't? Be bold, work hard and be optimistic and you will attain goals.

2 JANUARY

This is a good day to get things on track work-wise and in your usual daily routine. Just avoid forgetfulness.

3 JANUARY

You have high expectations of yourself and especially in a relationship and financially. If differences arise, look for common ground and a solution.

4 JANUARY

This is a good day to consider how to make your plans and projects more realisable and realistic so you can attain your goals more easily.

5 JANUARY

Someone close may be feeling more emotional than usual, so be sure to tread carefully to avoid arguments and fallout.

6 JANUARY

You can make progress with a work and personal matter but must be prepared to extend yourself and even put yourself out on a limb. You may be asked for help, and if you need it it's available.

7 JANUARY

There's an adventurous and outgoing atmosphere to the day, and you may be drawn to travelling and upbeat activities that take you outside your comfort zone. Just avoid forgetfulness.

8 JANUARY

This is a good day to take the initiative with work and personal plans. You may be surprised by events over the next two days.

9 JANUARY

Be sure to double-check details, avoiding mix-ups and travel delays by planning ahead. You may be prone to daydreaming, so focus extra hard at work for the best results.

10 JANUARY

You will enjoy a change of routine and a surprise or spontaneous situation may arise. It's a good day to take the initiative at work and in your personal life.

11 JANUARY

The Capricorn new moon will kick-start a fresh phase in your status, career or direction. Be prepared to let bygones be bygones. It's a good day for a health treat and get-together.

12 JANUARY

This is another good day to take the initiative with your plans and projects as you're likely to succeed, so be bold. A trip will be exciting.

13 JANUARY

Meetings and get-togethers could be transformational and enjoyable. A trip will bring out your adventurousness.

14 JANUARY

The next few weeks will be ideal for putting your plans and projects into workable format and for making concrete arrangements to do with study, travel and even legal matters.

15 JANUARY

You'll feel inspired and even nostalgic at the moment, so take a moment to get your feet on the ground to put inspiration in motion.

16 JANUARY

Once the moon is in your sign you'll feel more motivated, so be prepared to take action and put your dreams into gear. You may enjoy an uplifting event or news.

17 JANUARY

This is a good time for a reunion and also to touch base with an expert or adviser who can help you with a health or work matter if necessary.

18 JANUARY

This is a good day to be serious about your work and projects and reach out to those who can help further your interests. You'll enjoy news or a get-together.

19 JANUARY

A trip, meeting or news is likely to be pleasant yet it's also likely you'll experience a mystery, delay, confusion or mix-up. Take the rough with the smooth and avoid forgetfulness.

20 JANUARY

Key developments at work or, if you don't work, regarding your general direction and projects are likely. You could make long-term changes. Keep things light-hearted for the best results.

21 JANUARY

A change in your circumstances will be exciting on the one hand yet slightly disorienting for some. Be prepared to think outside the box.

22 JANUARY

Be guided by your intuition and avoid feeling overly sensitive, especially in connection with the past. Avoid misunderstandings by being super clear.

23 JANUARY

You'll enjoy cocooning and relaxing at the end of the day. You may feel a little emotional or tired, so take things slowly and you can build a sense of fulfilment.

24 JANUARY

You or someone close may be feeling sensitive once again, so be prepared to go the extra mile to be tactful and supportive. If you need a little help it will be available.

25 JANUARY

The Leo full moon will spotlight a personal, family or domestic matter. You may be inclined to rush things, so take things carefully to avoid minor bumps and scrapes and making mistakes.

26 JANUARY

A vulnerable situation will be in the spotlight and you'll be needed to say just the right thing at the right time to the right person. It's a good day for a health appointment.

27 JANUARY

Key news or a meeting will take your focus. Avoid arguments, as these may simply arise due to different values. Try to find common ground and progress from there.

28 JANUARY

You'll enjoy getting together with like-minded people. A reunion or return to an old haunt will be enjoyable.

29 JANUARY

This is a lovely day for progress, especially at work and in your personal life. If you have key financial matters to discuss this is the time to do it!

30 JANUARY

You'll be looking for ways to find peace and relaxation at the end of the day. You'll gain a great deal of ground with your activities, so take the initiative.

31 JANUARY

This is also a good day for work and improving your health. You may enjoy a meeting with someone uplifting at the end of the day.

February

1 FEBRUARY

The next two days are ideal for getting on top of your projects and plans, especially at work and concerning your health and beauty. You'll enjoy the arts.

2 FEBRUARY

You have a natural empathy with someone important such as a colleague or work boss, so you have charisma on your side! You'll be drawn to creativity, film and music.

3 FEBRUARY

Someone close may seem a little more intense than usual, so be sure to avoid arguments that flare up from nowhere. Romance could blossom.

4 FEBRUARY

You'll feel more inclined to be positive about collaborations, both at home and at work. Someone close will be motivational and help you get things done.

5 FEBRUARY

This is likely to be a busy or even intense day, especially at work. It's a good time to boost your health and well-being, so ensure you take adequate breaks.

6 FEBRUARY

You'll enjoy being your usual upbeat and dynamic self, taking the time to arrange get-togethers and fun events. However, you must also keep your mind on practicalities.

7 FEBRUARY

You'll enjoy getting together with like-minded people both at work and in your personal life, so take the initiative. You may receive unexpected news or enjoy an impromptu event.

8 FEBRUARY

Be prepared to think on your toes as you may receive surprise news or discover a spanner in the works.

9 FEBRUARY

The Aquarian new moon supermoon is ideal for being innovative and setting in motion clever and imaginative projects and plans. It's a good day for meetings and financial decisions.

10 FEBRUARY

You'll appreciate the opportunity to relax and let your mind unwind. You'll be inspired by music, the arts and upbeat fun people.

11 FEBRUARY

This is a lovely day to focus on your health and well-being and to find the time for a beauty or health treat. Romance could blossom.

12 FEBRUARY

You'll feel increasingly energetic and upbeat once the moon enters your sign, so be positive. Trust your intuition as it is spot on.

13 FEBRUARY

You'll be drawn to being spontaneous and finding time for someone you admire or love. The arts, film and creativity will appeal. Romance could blossom.

14 FEBRUARY

Happy St Valentine's Day! This may be an intense day and a friend or work situation may test your patience, so ensure you pace yourself.

15 FEBRUARY

You'll be drawn to being practical about your projects and ideas, as the alternative would be feeling a little overwhelmed. Take things one step at a time.

16 FEBRUARY

You'll appreciate the opportunity to meet new people, either socially or at work. You may find that your projects and interests take you into new territory.

17 FEBRUARY

This is a lovely day for romance, the arts and generally finding ways to transform your circumstances. A meeting may be intense.

18 FEBRUARY

You may hear from an old friend or will receive news from the past. If health has been a concern, take time out to adequately rest. Someone may ask for your help.

19 FEBRUARY

You may be required to go over old ground at work. It's a good day for a health or beauty appointment. You may enjoy a reunion or receive the news you've waited for.

20 FEBRUARY

Over the next few days you may feel people are more intense or argumentative, so give them a wide berth if possible to avoid conflict.

21 FEBRUARY

You'll feel motivated to get things shipshape at home. Just avoid becoming so organised you inadvertently appear to control the freedom of movement of the people you live with.

22 FEBRUARY

This is a lovely day for social occasions and romance. Be sure to organise a get-together or a visit somewhere beautiful.

23 FEBRUARY

The next few weeks will be inspiring as you find more time to devote to your health and well-being, spiritual interests and to looking after someone special.

24 FEBRUARY

The full moon in Virgo will shine a light on your health and daily routines. You may ask how you could improve these so they suit you better.

25 FEBRUARY

This is a good day for chores and housework, gardening and generally getting paperwork shipshape – and then to relax!

26 FEBRUARY

You'll enjoy a productive day as you get to go over outstanding chores and clear up loose ends.

27 FEBRUARY

You like to be independent and entrepreneurial, and sometimes your independence can seem threatening to others. Focus on collaborating and co-operating for the best results.

28 FEBRUARY

This is another good day to focus on good relationship and communication skills as you could make great headway both socially and at work.

29 FEBRUARY

You'll enjoy a reunion at work and socially. This is a good day for meetings and for financial planning.

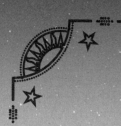
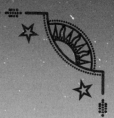

March

1 MARCH

This is a beneficial time to make work commitments. If you're considering a new health routine, it's a good day to begin this.

2 MARCH

You'll experience a surprise this weekend that may put a spanner in the works. However, if you can be creative with developments you'll appreciate get-togethers.

3 MARCH

It's a good day to have a long look at your finances: could you minimise your outlay? If you're shopping, be sure to avoid overspending. Avoid arguments, as they may be unexpected.

4 MARCH

An outgoing and upbeat attitude to work projects will work well. Avoid taking other people's vagueness or unreliability personally.

5 MARCH

This is a good day for meetings, both at work and in your personal life. You may meet someone who is more significant than meets the eye.

6 MARCH

This is a good day for a health or beauty appointment. Just avoid minor bumps and scrapes and impulsiveness. Your help or advice may be needed.

7 MARCH

You'll enjoy a reunion or catching up by phone with someone you like. If you need advice or expert guidance, reach out.

8 MARCH

This is a lovely day for a reunion and for indulging in the arts and all that you enjoy in life. The arts, music and romance will appeal.

9 MARCH

You'll enjoy an impromptu get-together or an activity that takes you outside your usual routine. Avoid rushing and making rash decisions.

10 MARCH

The Pisces new moon supermoon will bring a nostalgic feel to the day. It is, however, a good time to let go of aspects of the past you have idealised or romanticised. A meeting could be transformative.

11 MARCH

You'll begin the week on a dreamy note, perhaps even idealising some aspects of your life. Avoid having to undergo a reality check by keeping your feet on the ground.

12 MARCH

The moon in your sign adds a spritz of energy to your day, but you must avoid appearing a little bossy. A beauty or health treat may appeal.

13 MARCH

This is a good day to make changes in your work life and for meetings. Romance could blossom.

14 MARCH

Be practical with abrupt changes of schedule or a little upheaval. You must also avoid being stubborn if you are taken outside your comfort zone.

15 MARCH

The Gemini moon encourages good communications, so this is an ideal time to take the initiative with delicate conversations.

16 MARCH

Financial and personal matters could move forward. If you're shopping, you may find an ideal buy. You'll enjoy a get-together.

17 MARCH

This is a lovely day for romance, the arts, music and dance and for nostalgia and reminiscing. You may revisit an old haunt.

18 MARCH

You may tend to have your head in the clouds over the next few days, so be prepared to focus a little more and especially at work.

19 MARCH

You'll enjoy taking the initiative with talks and communications, and may even appreciate an ideal outcome to a work project. Just avoid making assumptions.

20 MARCH

As the sun enters your sign you'll appreciate regaining energy over the coming weeks. A health appointment may assist. News from an adviser or a helpful moment will arise.

21 MARCH

This is a good day to make concrete agreements, especially at work and financially and particularly arrangements that will create change.

22 MARCH

The next five weeks will be truly creative and inspiring. You may be drawn to the past and to bringing old projects to life.

23 MARCH

A strong connection with the past or significant relationship will catch your attention. You may be drawn to making a key investment. Be prepared to learn something new.

24 MARCH

This is a good day to get on top of household chores and tidy up outstanding bills and debts.

25 MARCH

The lunar eclipse will bring work matters to a head for most Aries, and a relationship will be a focus for some March Aries. You'll find a reunion or meeting productive even if intense.

26 MARCH

Someone close or whom you work with will have news for you. It's a good day to schedule a beauty or health treat.

27 MARCH

You may experience stronger emotions than usual. Someone close may seem more expressive or intense, so take things one step at a time.

28 MARCH

You'll experience a surprise or unexpected development. Someone may pay you a compliment. A financial or personal matter could progress.

29 MARCH

Your intuition is spot on and you'll feel more in tune with people as a result. Just avoid feeling a little sensitive by keeping your feet on the ground.

30 MARCH

You have natural empathy with people today, making this an excellent time for socialising and activities such as sport and favourite interests.

31 MARCH

You're adventurous and outgoing, putting the focus on upbeat activities. Just avoid rocking the boat with someone you have already clashed with.

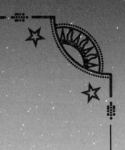

April

1 APRIL

Mercury, the planet associated with communications and travel, will turn retrograde tomorrow, so try to get the loose ends of key plans tied up to avoid potential delays.

2 APRIL

You may receive key news that will deserve careful attention. It's a good time over the coming weeks to focus on health and well-being.

3 APRIL

It's an excellent day for a reunion and for improving health and beauty. You may need to unravel, and spiritual matters will appeal.

4 APRIL

You'll enjoy a talk or meeting with someone special or could receive key news that may be more significant than meets the eye.

5 APRIL

As Venus, the planet associated with love, art, beauty and money, enters your sign, expect your focus to go to these important aspects over the coming three weeks.

6 APRIL

The Pisces moon will bring out your romantic qualities. You may be inclined to act on a hunch but must avoid forgetfulness over the next two days.

7 APRIL

You'll enjoy indulging in the luxuries of life and may also be inclined to overindulge, so spare a thought for tomorrow's headache!

8 APRIL

The total solar eclipse in Aries signifies that a completely fresh start is waiting in the wings, especially if it's your birthday. A focus on health and well-being will be appealing.

9 APRIL

If you need the advice of an expert it will be available. Someone may ask you for help. It's a good day for a health appointment.

10 APRIL

An important work or health meeting will bring you up to date. You may be pleasantly surprised by an impromptu meeting or news.

11 APRIL

You'll enjoy catching up with an old friend or receiving the news you've been waiting for. For some there will be a strong focus on finances.

12 APRIL

You're likely to feel more talkative now that the moon is in Gemini, but you must be careful with conversations to do with work.

13 APRIL

This is a healing weekend that is ideal for relaxing and getting back on top of your health schedule.

14 APRIL

This is a good day to cocoon and enjoy the quiet of your home life. Tact and diplomacy may be necessary with someone who can be feisty.

15 APRIL

You and your advice are likely to be in demand and you may need to review or even revise some work or health matters. An expert will be invaluable.

16 APRIL

You'll be inclined to be a little impatient, yet some things simply take time. You'll gain positive results from being unruffled yet motivated and diligent.

17 APRIL

Your playful side will seek expression and you'll enjoy being with like-minded people. Theatre, the arts, fun activities and socialising will appeal.

18 APRIL

The next few days will be ideal for reunions and generally catching up with work and getting on top of chores.

19 APRIL

As the sun leaves your sign you'll appreciate the sense you are more grounded and can be practical about enjoying life, finances and love. You may get some surprise news.

20 APRIL

This is a good time to work towards a more stable financial situation. However, you may also be inclined to overspend, so be careful at the shops! You'll enjoy a reunion.

21 APRIL

Tensions may be prevalent, especially if someone's behaviour seems erratic or an unpredictable element enters proceedings. Be prepared to seek balance.

22 APRIL

You may enjoy an impromptu call or get-together, surprise compliment, ego boost or even financial improvement.

23 APRIL

This is a good time to look for balance in a relationship, especially if you have argued recently.

24 APRIL

The Scorpio full moon will spotlight a particular business or personal relationship. This is an excellent day for communications, especially if you must review paperwork or agreements.

25 APRIL

It's a good day to talk as the Mercury retrograde phase ends. You may receive key news.

26 APRIL

This is a good time to get together with like-minded people, and you may enjoy a reunion or news from the past. It's a good time for a return to an old haunt.

27 APRIL

The Sagittarian moon will encourage you to be outgoing. It's a good weekend for sports, other hobbies and interests and being in nature.

28 APRIL

This is a lovely day for romance, the arts and relaxation. Enjoy! Just avoid overspending as you'll regret it.

29 APRIL

As Venus leaves your sign you'll begin to focus a little more on how to build wealth and a more stable love life. This is a super-romantic and creative day, so take the initiative!

30 APRIL

Proactive and upbeat Mars enters your sign, and you'll appreciate the boost in energy levels and motivation. Just avoid conflict until early June as Mars in Aries could bring your feisty side out.

May

1 MAY

Mars recently arrived in your sign and may bring out your feisty side. Today's tense stand-off between Venus and Pluto may further create tension, so tread carefully.

2 MAY

You'll enjoy a reunion or the chance to connect with someone special. Romance could blossom. You may receive key news from a friend or organisation.

3 MAY

This is a good day to get on top of outstanding chores, especially at work. You'll feel motivated to get things done.

4 MAY

You'll appreciate the opportunity to rest and recover from an up-tempo time. If on the other hand you have a busy weekend planned, you'll certainly enjoy being upbeat.

5 MAY

A get-together is likely to go well. You'll enjoy a reunion or return to an old haunt.

6 MAY

You may feel a little more emotional in your communications, so take a moment to get your feet on the ground and your efforts will succeed.

7 MAY

This is a good day to be practical and organise your schedule, projects and chores. It's also a good day for a health or beauty appointment.

8 MAY

The new moon in Taurus is an ideal time to start something fresh, especially financially or in your personal life. You may experience a surprise.

9 MAY

You'll find communications flow a little better, and if you have key financial matters to organise this is a good time to do so.

10 MAY

This is another improved day for communications, although you may experience a little tension with someone in authority so pace yourself.

11 MAY

You'll experience an improvement: for some this will be financially and for others health-wise. You may simply experience an ego boost and will enjoy a get-together.

12 MAY

This is a lovely day to self-nurture and focus on your home and those you love.

13 MAY

You may experience a surprise. It's a good day to take the initiative and try something new. Finances may improve.

14 MAY

You or someone close will be feeling a little more outgoing and dynamic. This is a playful and fun day, so organise something enjoyable!

15 MAY

As Mercury enters Taurus you'll find being practical about your ventures will appeal increasingly over the coming weeks. Avoid making rash statements.

16 MAY

An earthy, grounded approach at work and to your health and well-being will pay off.

17 MAY

Leave extra time for travel and be careful to avoid mix-ups in communications and financial transactions.

18 MAY

You'll enjoy expressing your lust for life but risk overspending and overindulging, which you'll regret. You may bump into someone or hear unexpected news.

19 MAY

This is a lovely day for the arts, a treat and reconnecting with someone special.

20 MAY

You'll enjoy a sociable day and will be in touch with someone who has a key role to play in your life at the moment. Meetings or discussions may be super significant.

21 MAY

This is a good day for talks, a short trip and making long-term changes. You may receive good news.

22 MAY

The lead-up to a full moon can be intense, so ensure you pace yourself. An adventurous outlook needn't cause mistakes if you're careful.

23 MAY

The full moon in Sagittarius spotlights a fresh chapter in circumstances such as shared finances or a relationship. Romance could blossom. For some a favourite activity such as sports, travel, a legal matter or study may culminate.

24 MAY

You'll enjoy being sociable and reaching out to others. A key financial agreement may be made.

25 MAY

The Venus–Pluto aspect this weekend is ideal for making positive changes. The arts, romance and financial investments could all flourish.

26 MAY

You may find that travel and exploration will both appeal over the coming days and weeks. You're likely to be busy with communications and get-togethers.

27 MAY

This is a good day to get organised; just avoid being at loggerheads with someone you must rely on. Aim to collaborate where possible.

28 MAY

This is a good day to make an agreement, especially at work and regarding a health regime. A financial matter may be decided upon and a debt may be repaid.

29 MAY

You'll appreciate the help of an expert and your expertise may be in demand. Avoid rushing as mistakes could be made.

30 MAY

This is a good day to discuss matters that need a little clarity. Just avoid being impulsive and rushing into decisions.

31 MAY

You're inspired and creative when the moon is in Pisces. Just avoid being forgetful, idealistic and absent-minded.

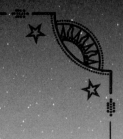

June

1 JUNE

You'll enjoy being a little more outgoing this weekend and will appreciate the chance to do something different. You may even be surprised!

2 JUNE

An impromptu or unusual trip or get-together will encourage you to spend time with people you admire and like.

3 JUNE

This is a good day to plan ahead for an upbeat week. Ask yourself how you could move ahead most productively and then take steps to do so.

4 JUNE

Whether you're travelling or meeting personal or work friends this is likely to be a busy day, so be prepared! Romance could blossom.

5 JUNE

This is an excellent day for talks, chats and getting together with like-minded people. If you have a new project to begin the next few days will be ideal.

6 JUNE

Venus will align with the new moon in Gemini, bringing your focus on love, money and the arts. Be prepared to advance in one or all of these areas! It's a good time to talk.

7 JUNE

This is a good time to plan travel and make changes at home to allow for your plans.

8 JUNE

As Mars prepares to leave your sign you may feel impatient to get things done. Avoid clashes, especially over chores and with someone you love.

9 JUNE

You may feel a little idealistic about your plans, so ensure you are practical. Be realistic and prepared to listen to someone else's ideas.

10 JUNE

You'll appreciate the chance to indulge a little in a luxury or treat. Trust your intuition, as it is spot on!

11 JUNE

There is a healing quality in today's stars, so take the initiative with plans and talks to come to mutually agreeable outcomes. It's a good day for a health treat.

12 JUNE

Avoid being at loggerheads with someone who can be stubborn, as you could exacerbate your differences. Plan extra time for travel and finances to avoid delays and making mistakes.

13 JUNE

You'll enjoy being spontaneous and doing something different or going somewhere new. You may be surprised by news.

14 JUNE

This is a good day for talks, and you may be drawn to travel or welcoming a visitor.

15 JUNE

This is another day when being spontaneous will be enjoyable as you may hear from a friend about a get-together or enjoy a change of environment.

16 JUNE

You'll enjoy socialising, travel and getting out into the world. However, you may also be prone to overindulging so be careful!

17 JUNE

You may experience a case of Mondayitis. Keep an eye on forgetfulness. A key meeting may feel a little emotional and misunderstandings and delays are likely.

18 JUNE

You may feel more convinced of your ideas yet encounter some opposition, so be sure to back up your ideas with facts for the best results.

19 JUNE

Certain matters may come to light, and as they do you'll feel differently about circumstances. Be proactive but avoid making rash decisions.

20 JUNE

The solstice is always a lovely time to consider how far you've come this year. There may be a little nostalgia or forgetfulness, so be realistic.

21 JUNE

You won't always agree with everyone, so take a moment to plan ahead. Find common ground rather than accentuating differences. You'll enjoy a get-together or making changes at home.

22 JUNE

The full moon in Capricorn will spotlight your career, general direction and status. You may be ready to turn a corner.

23 JUNE

The delicate art of negotiation and communication is in demand. Find ways to indicate tactfully how you feel about long-term plans for the best effect.

24 JUNE

Be innovative with your various plans and projects, as you will succeed all the better as a result. A quirky friend or organisation may be super helpful.

25 JUNE

Reach out to someone who you know has your back, as they are likely to be super helpful.

26 JUNE

This is a good day to discuss important matters, especially with someone who shares responsibilities with you and at home.

27 JUNE

If you're arguing with someone important at the moment check that your values are the same. You may simply have different priorities and common ground must be re-established.

28 JUNE

A delicate matter deserves careful attention. It's a good day to focus on health and well-being, especially in the home and your personal life.

29 JUNE

You'll enjoy a more upbeat tempo and the chance to enjoy your home life and the company of favourite people. Romance could blossom.

30 JUNE

You'll enjoy an impromptu visit or get-together and may even be surprised by news you receive. Be open to something different!

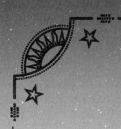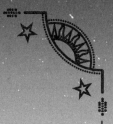

July

1 JULY

If you feel a little head in the clouds you'll need to focus extra hard, especially at work. You'll be increasingly motivated as the day goes by.

2 JULY

A change of routine or the chance to reconnect with someone from your past will arise. You may be drawn to making changes at home or doing something different with family.

3 JULY

You may need to undergo fairly intense conversations. If you're making changes at home or at work these are likely to go well if you plan adequately.

4 JULY

It's a good time to initiate fresh ideas in the lead-up to the new moon, so take a moment to decide how you'd like some of your projects to progress.

5 JULY

The Cancerian new moon is a good time to begin fresh projects at home or with family. You may be drawn to making changes at work, especially if you work from home.

6 JULY

You may feel ready to discuss sensitive topics with someone in your family. Someone close may need some help. If you need support it is be available, so reach out.

7 JULY

This is a lovely day to catch up with an old friend or family member. You may be surprised by an impromptu visit, news or guest.

8 JULY

Someone close will prove to be supportive. You'll enjoy spending time with a favourite character. You may be surprised by news or a financial situation.

9 JULY

You may find someone demands your attention so you'll need to choose your priorities carefully.

10 JULY

When the moon is in Virgo work and chores are generally easier to complete. However, you must avoid taking on an overly heavy workload to avoid fatigue.

11 JULY

You'll be feeling more playful over the coming weeks, beginning now! You can achieve a great deal, so take the initiative. You'll enjoy a reunion and romance could thrive.

12 JULY

Emotions may run high and romance and passion could flourish, so why not organise a date? Avoid contentious topics.

13 JULY

This is a good weekend to look for balance in your life, especially if you feel you overindulged or overspent yesterday.

14 JULY

You'll appreciate the opportunity to relax and enjoy creature comforts. However, you may need to be tactful with someone who can be stubborn.

15 JULY

You may be surprised by developments. Avoid rushing as you may be a little accident prone, especially around the house. It's a good day for a health appointment.

16 JULY

The moon in Scorpio can bring out people's emotions and you may be surprised by someone's mood swings. Avoid contributing to tense circumstances.

17 JULY

You'll appreciate a more adventurous and upbeat feel to the day. You may be drawn to connecting with fun people for a midweek catch-up.

18 JULY

You may be surprised by developments at home concerning family or property. An unpredictable person will behave true to form.

19 JULY

There are healing aspects to the day. Your help may be in demand. It's a lovely day for meetings and a reunion with someone special.

20 JULY

This is the start of a busy and sociable time. You may enjoy a visit somewhere beautiful or a family catch-up.

21 JULY

The full moon in Capricorn will shine a light on your personal life, family and friendship circle. If you experience a disappointment or intense conversations, look for common ground.

22 JULY

You'll appreciate enjoying a light-hearted approach to the week but must nevertheless keep an eye on clear communications and avoid delays. You could make great progress.

23 JULY

You are a powerful force to be reckoned with, but then so is someone else – making this a good time to avoid conflict and work towards your goals. Sidestep power struggles.

24 JULY

Trust your intuition as it will be spot on, but you must avoid daydreaming and forgetfulness.

25 JULY

You'll need to pay close attention to details, and if you work in an area where minor mistakes have big consequences you'll need to focus extra hard to avoid errors.

26 JULY

This will be a busy and productive day. However, you may feel sensitive or under the weather, so take mini breaks when you can.

27 JULY

There is a little tension in the air, so take things one step at a time. Be careful if you are making financial decisions and ensure you do your research.

28 JULY

This is an excellent day to relax – luckily it's Sunday! Take a moment to spoil yourself and those you love. Just avoid minor disagreements if possible.

29 JULY

You'll be drawn to improving your personal life, such as friendships and family dynamics, over the coming two days. A healing approach will work wonders.

30 JULY

This is a lovely day for a health or beauty treat and to take the time to beautify your surroundings such as your home or office.

31 JULY

You'll appreciate the opportunity to meet someone influential. A reunion will be enjoyable. You may return to an old haunt or hear from an old friend.

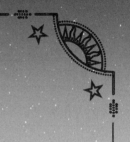

August

1 AUGUST

This is another good day for get-togethers, so why not plan something special? Consider taking the stress out of making your home perfect and go out.

2 AUGUST

You may be surprised by developments, so stay on your toes. Avoid taking the reactions of other people personally and work on finding solutions to issues.

3 AUGUST

The lead-up to a new moon is a good time to initiate fresh intentions, so take a moment to ground yourself and be practical as well as inspired about your goals.

4 AUGUST

The Leo new moon shines a light on your creativity, family and projects. You may need to find clever ways to untangle a mystery but must avoid making assumptions.

5 AUGUST

Try to get key paperwork and negotiations agreed upon by today. You may hear key news to do with work or someone close. Avoid power struggles.

6 AUGUST

This is a good day to get organised, especially with paperwork and finances. You may need to review a circumstance.

7 AUGUST

You'll enjoy meeting with someone you love or admire. A financial matter may be decided upon but you must avoid gambling.

8 AUGUST

This is a lovely day for a reunion. Romance, the arts and love could flourish. You may need to review or revise a personal decision and a return to an old haunt may appeal.

9 AUGUST

You'll be looking for balance and harmony at work and may need to labour extra hard to find it – but you will!

10 AUGUST

This is a passionate weekend in which you'll enjoy indulging in your favourite activities, from sports to romance and meeting favourite people.

11 AUGUST

This is a good day for planning. You'll appreciate the opportunity to discuss your long-term plans and daily schedule with someone you can rely on.

12 AUGUST

You'll appreciate the chance to get ahead at work through careful planning and industriousness.

13 AUGUST

You'll enjoy feeling more adventurous and outgoing as you get into your week, feeling the need also to connect with like-minded people.

14 AUGUST

Be prepared to think on your feet as developments are likely to come thick and fast, especially in connection with communications.

15 AUGUST

If mistakes were made yesterday, this is an excellent day to mend bridges. You may find that your expertise is in demand. If you need advice it will be available. Avoid forgetfulness.

16 AUGUST

Think before you leap as you may be liable to making rash decisions. This may be largely out of frustration due to delays or work issues.

17 AUGUST

You'll be drawn to doing something different. Think laterally, as you'll find answers to conundrums.

18 AUGUST

A reunion and the chance to go over old ground regarding a previous decision or personal matter may reveal some surprises. Avoid misunderstandings for the best results.

19 AUGUST

The full moon in Aquarius will shine a light on your link with a friend, group or organisation. Key news, a meeting or trip will mean you must reach a new agreement that may involve money.

20 AUGUST

Take things one step at a time as the full moon may still reveal a surprise or two. Be prepared, nevertheless, to take optimistic action.

21 AUGUST

Keep on top of changes, as you may be inclined to see the present through the eyes of the past as opposed to a freshly evolving circumstance.

22 AUGUST

The sun will be in your work and health zones for the next four weeks, bringing your attention to these important aspects. Work hard and avoid misunderstandings for the best results.

23 AUGUST

Be tactful and diplomatic to avoid clashes with colleagues and important people in your life. It's a lovely day for a reunion or romance.

24 AUGUST

You'll appreciate the opportunity to boost health and well-being. A favourite activity may require more application than usual, but the effort will be worthwhile.

25 AUGUST

This is a good day to clear chores such as household and gardening work. You'll also appreciate a change of environment or get-together. Be productive.

26 AUGUST

The moon in Gemini will bring out your chatty side, which is excellent for work meetings, but you must avoid being easily distracted.

27 AUGUST

Expect a surprise. You may enjoy a pleasant change of routine and the chance to show off just what you're made of.

28 AUGUST

You may receive key news or make a valid decision in connection with work, health or family. It's a good day for romance and creativity, but you must avoid being forgetful.

29 AUGUST

Venus in your partnership zone for the next three weeks will bring attention to personal and business relationships and how to improve them. This is a lovely day for a get-together and romance.

30 AUGUST

You're likely to get a second wind later in the day, making this a good evening for going out or, if you're at home, for getting on top of chores. Romance could blossom.

31 AUGUST

You'll enjoy a change of pace and the chance to visit somewhere different and bring new experiences and activities into your life. You may even surprise yourself.

September

1 SEPTEMBER

You may need to review a work or health situation. Keep communications on an even keel to avoid arguments and over-idealising your circumstances.

2 SEPTEMBER

This is a good day to discuss sensitive topics as you're likely to be understood. It's also a good day to review health and work practices.

3 SEPTEMBER

The new moon in Virgo will highlight your work, health and daily schedules. Ask yourself how you could organise these better so they suit you.

4 SEPTEMBER

You may hear important news at work or regarding your health and well-being. You'll feel more instinctive than usual, so trust your gut.

5 SEPTEMBER

The moon in Libra tends to put your mind on other people. You could gain insight into a business or personal partnership, so be open to new ideas.

6 SEPTEMBER

This is a good time to seek collaborations rather than looking for the differences between yourself and others.

7 SEPTEMBER

You'll appreciate the opportunity to invest in the people closest to you and in your home life and relationships.

8 SEPTEMBER

This is a good day to make a commitment to a person or a project. However, you must be certain you have done adequate research, especially if you are making financial changes.

9 SEPTEMBER

You'll be communicating well over the coming weeks, making this a progressive time at work. However, you must avoid power struggles today with someone in power.

10 SEPTEMBER

You'll enjoy being outgoing and upbeat, and outdoors activities such as walking, sports and visits somewhere beautiful will appeal.

11 SEPTEMBER

You may need to work a little harder to get the same results as before. Avoid raking over old coals and focus on a good outcome.

12 SEPTEMBER

Some communications and travel may be delayed or a little more complex than usual, so be patient. However, this is still a good time to get ahead with projects and work.

13 SEPTEMBER

The moon in Capricorn brings out your industriousness and you could get a great deal done. Just avoid overtiring yourself.

14 SEPTEMBER

This is an excellent day for a health or beauty treat, as you'll welcome a change of pace and a little time spent on yourself. Someone may need your help.

15 SEPTEMBER

You'll appreciate some quirky company or decide to alter your usual Sunday routine. A sociable day will please you.

16 SEPTEMBER

You may be feeling a little more sensitive or even forgetful than usual, so focus extra hard at work. Avoid speaking without forethought as you may regret it.

17 SEPTEMBER

This is another day to focus a little more on your chores and projects as you're liable to have your head somewhat in the clouds. You may also feel more vulnerable, so take things easy.

18 SEPTEMBER

The partial lunar eclipse supermoon in Pisces brings focus on key decisions that can no longer be put off, for many concerning work and health matters. Avoid impulsiveness.

19 SEPTEMBER

You'll appreciate a sense that some of the confusion or stress of the past two days dispels today as a lovely synchronicity arises. You may enjoy a surprise development.

20 SEPTEMBER

You may be made a quirky offer or will need to accommodate or at least understand someone's quirky behaviour. Be practical and realistic above all else.

21 SEPTEMBER

You'll enjoy relaxing, romance, the arts and generally losing track of time for a change. However, the risk is that you forget important commitments and have mix-ups.

22 SEPTEMBER

The sun in your seventh house of partnerships for the next four weeks will place your focus on good relationships. There is no time like the present to improve communications skills. Romance could blossom but may be intense.

23 SEPTEMBER

Your communications skills will be in demand and you'll find you may be particularly good at getting your point across, so take the initiative.

24 SEPTEMBER

The moon in Cancer this evening may bring out your emotions, so avoid difficult interactions if possible.

25 SEPTEMBER

Sensitive topics or mysterious conundrums that require additional focus will arise, so be prepared to concentrate at work. Check details if you are making work decisions.

26 SEPTEMBER

You'll feel drawn to looking for peace and common ground in conversations and relationships over the coming weeks. This is a good day to initiate a transformative work or relationship cycle.

27 SEPTEMBER

Your usual sparkly and energetic personality will come to the fore. Many people will respond well but some may feel overshadowed, so watch out for delicate egos to avoid offence being taken.

28 SEPTEMBER

You'll enjoy being outgoing and upbeat, meeting friends, taking a trip somewhere beautiful and generally appreciating life, so plan something fun!

29 SEPTEMBER

A lovely reunion will warm your heart. You'll enjoy a get-together or chat or the chance to catch up with housework and paperwork.

30 SEPTEMBER

This is another lovely day for meetings and get-togethers. You may receive key news to do with your work or home lives or from someone special.

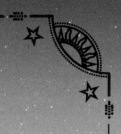

October

1 OCTOBER

You'll enjoy the structure of being at work and getting chores done. However, you must be a little careful with conversations to avoid power struggles.

2 OCTOBER

The solar eclipse in Libra is a good time to turn a corner in a business or personal partnership if you were born at the end of March and for April Aries to begin a fresh, more balanced chapter at work.

3 OCTOBER

You'll enjoy romance, meetings at work and the chance to generally collaborate.

4 OCTOBER

Someone you share duties or space with at home or at work may be more passionate or feisty than usual. This is a lovely time for romance, a reunion and for getting things shipshape at home.

5 OCTOBER

Over the next two days it's in your interest to be super clear with communications and to avoid making hasty decisions, as you may be impulsive.

6 OCTOBER

Be prepared to think twice about some decisions. You may tend to be rushed off your feet or, alternatively, impatient due to delays. Plan talks and travel ahead of time to avoid hold-ups.

7 OCTOBER

You're an outgoing, upbeat character and will enjoy putting the wind in your sails this week. Just keep an eye on your energy levels and avoid overdoing things.

8 OCTOBER

You may be liable to grab the wrong end of the stick or someone else may be a little vulnerable despite a lovely day that includes travel and romance.

9 OCTOBER

You may be drawn to slowing things down as you gain the chance to recharge your energy levels.

10 OCTOBER

You have a go-ahead attitude, but you may need to first review or rethink projects and ideas.

11 OCTOBER

You may receive mixed messages that will merit a little careful analysis. Someone may behave out of character. Your hard work will pay off.

12 OCTOBER

Some conversations and developments will require more focus to ensure you have grabbed the right end of the stick. A reunion may be a mixture of happiness and nostalgia.

13 OCTOBER

Choose your words carefully as someone close may be feeling sensitive; you'll avoid conflict as a result. You may need to help someone. If you need advice it will be available.

14 OCTOBER

Tread carefully, as you may be stamping on someone's ego. You may feel a little sensitive or under the weather yourself; nevertheless, you will be productive. Avoid making rash decisions.

15 OCTOBER

If you're working, keep your professional hat on as you may be easily distracted. A health or well-being matter is best attended to earlier rather than later. Avoid making rash decisions.

16 OCTOBER

This is a lovely day and evening for romance, the arts and generally reconnecting with people you have found difficult to get on with recently.

17 OCTOBER

The full moon supermoon in Aries signals a fresh chapter ahead. For most this will regard an agreement or relationship and for some in your daily work or health routine.

18 OCTOBER

Be practical when making decisions as you may tend to be led by emotions and anxiety rather than by rationality.

19 OCTOBER

Trust your instincts as news or developments may draw on your inner reserves. You'll rise to any challenges in a change of routine.

20 OCTOBER

You'll enjoy the opportunity to relax but may need to accomplish various tasks and fulfil commitments first, so be patient.

21 OCTOBER

You may have a case of Mondayitis at work, so focus extra hard to get on top of chores.
If you're on holiday you'll enjoy the chance to relax.

22 OCTOBER

As the sun enters Scorpio it is the start of a passionate and potentially feisty four weeks. It will,
however, be productive. Avoid ego battles.

23 OCTOBER

This is a good day to make agreements with someone special. Romance could flourish,
so make a date.

24 OCTOBER

You'll feel motivated to get things done and could make some lovely arrangements and
agreements in your personal life.

25 OCTOBER

You'll enjoy being spontaneous and upbeat about your projects at work and in your personal
life. A change in your usual routine will appeal.

26 OCTOBER

You may be surprised or delighted by developments and the chance to enjoy a little freedom of
movement.

27 OCTOBER

This is a lovely day to rest up and pamper yourself and someone close. You or someone close
may be feeling a little sensitive, so take things carefully.

28 OCTOBER

You may discover a past mistake or realise you've been labouring under a misapprehension.
Find time to carefully evaluate the best way ahead. Your intuition is spot on.

29 OCTOBER

Be prepared to think on your feet over the next two days. You may receive unexpected news
or bump into an old friend.

30 OCTOBER

Financial matters could benefit from a close look to ensure you're on the right track.
Avoid gambling and be prepared to think laterally.

31 OCTOBER

You'll enjoy the flavour of the evening as Hallowe'en is certainly a Scorpio moon–type evening.
A little mystery or trick or treating will add spice to your life!

November

1 NOVEMBER

The current Scorpio new moon is a particularly potent time to make a wish, such as that your life could truly improve. Take action, as a path will become clearer for you.

2 NOVEMBER

It's an ideal day for taking time out and treating yourself to a breath of fresh air, such as a trip somewhere beautiful or a health retreat. It's a good day to improve relationships.

3 NOVEMBER

This is a healing day that is ideal for building strong relationships. A trip or meeting could be fun. It's a romantic time, but you must avoid conflict as it could fire up unexpectedly.

4 NOVEMBER

You can truly build solid bonds with people at work and those you would like to make a commitment to. You may also feel energy levels improve over the coming weeks.

5 NOVEMBER

Avoid taking someone's unpredictable or unusual behaviour personally. Someone may need your help or you may need to ask for help.

6 NOVEMBER

This is a good day for boosting your work circumstances and health, so take the initiative. You'll feel emotionally invested in your activities, which will help you succeed.

7 NOVEMBER

This is a lovely day for a reunion, improving communications and deepening close relationships, so take the initiative!

8 NOVEMBER

You may experience unexpected obstacles or conundrums but rest assured: if you look for an innovative solution you'll reach your goals.

9 NOVEMBER

You'll welcome the chance to relax but must be wary of forgetfulness and the tendency to overindulge.

10 NOVEMBER

This is another good day to take things one step at a time, as you'll appreciate the chance to relax. If you're missing someone or feel lost yourself, take time to regain direction.

11 NOVEMBER

This is a good day to begin the week optimistically but to avoid making assumptions about someone close.

12 NOVEMBER

The more you can be precise with your communications the better your day will proceed, especially if you're working. Avoid mix-ups.

13 NOVEMBER

The Aries moon will motivate you to get chores done. However, you may appear bossy unless you're careful and may feel more sensitive about random comments, so retain perspective.

14 NOVEMBER

You'll appreciate feeling more grounded. Being practical will certainly help you get things done, as otherwise you may feel overwhelmed by developments in the lead-up to the full moon.

15 NOVEMBER

The full moon in Taurus puts a spotlight on your finances, values and principles. You may experience a surprise or will enjoy being more spontaneous.

16 NOVEMBER

You'll enjoy doing something a little different and may even surprise someone close. Be prepared to factor in someone else's wishes to avoid arguments.

17 NOVEMBER

The Gemini moon brings out your inner socialite and you'll enjoy chatting, meeting people and generally being outgoing.

18 NOVEMBER

Key meetings, a trip or news may be more significant than meets the eye. If you experience a difference of opinion it may come down to contrasting values.

19 NOVEMBER

A matter to do with your past is likely to come to your attention; you may simply enjoy a reunion. It's a good day for a health or beauty treat.

20 NOVEMBER

As Pluto re-enters Aquarius you may experience a change in your social circles and who you spend time with. Be prepared to enter fresh territory.

21 NOVEMBER

Over the next four weeks you'll feel motivated to enjoy life, spending more time with people and activities you enjoy. You may experience a pleasant change today.

22 NOVEMBER

This is a good day for making progress at work. It's also a good time to improve your appearance and health and for making a commitment to someone you love.

23 NOVEMBER

This is a lovely day for get-togethers and romance; just avoid putting pressure on someone you love. Singles may meet someone attractive.

24 NOVEMBER

The moon in Virgo will help you to be productive, especially with improving your domestic environment and interpersonal dynamics.

25 NOVEMBER

This is a go-ahead time for you and you'll feel motivated to get your work done. It's a good time to remind yourself that high self-esteem often helps achieve goals.

26 NOVEMBER

Try to tie up loose ends with paperwork and important talks before the end of the day. You may receive key news or be drawn to travelling. A get-together is likely to go well.

27 NOVEMBER

You'll feel eager and energetic, which will help you fulfil goals. You may be drawn to socialising or spending time with someone who needs your help. If you need support it will be available.

28 NOVEMBER

You may experience a lack of self-confidence or a minor setback, so be careful to remain positive and be measured in your responses if you feel you have been criticised.

29 NOVEMBER

This is a good day for talks and to review your circumstances. You may enjoy a return to an old haunt or a reunion.

30 NOVEMBER

You'll welcome the chance to relax and be yourself this weekend, enjoying upbeat and energetic activities such as sports.

December

1 DECEMBER

The new moon in Sagittarius will open fresh options in connection with exciting activities such as creative projects or travel and the chance to be more adventurous in your love life.

2 DECEMBER

You'll enjoy an upbeat start to the week, with the opportunity to improve relationships, health and your status at work.

3 DECEMBER

The moon in Capricorn helps you to be more practical, especially at work and with your long-term plans, so think ahead!

4 DECEMBER

You won't always agree with everyone, and today is one such day when choosing your words carefully will determine the outcome of some key conversations and collaborations.

5 DECEMBER

Think outside the square for the best results, especially in connection with collaborations, friendships and extracurricular activities.

6 DECEMBER

Your sign's ruler, Mars, is turning retrograde today so you may experience a change of tempo or of circumstance in your personal life. It will be important to get a financial matter or meeting right.

7 DECEMBER

Think laterally and enjoy something different and exciting such as a trip. Be prepared to commit to a plan of action to avoid confusion or intense feelings.

8 DECEMBER

You'll feel inspired and perhaps even nostalgic. You risk daydreaming your day away, so be prepared to motivate yourself.

9 DECEMBER

Meetings and communications will deserve extra focus to avoid making mistakes. Be inspired but also avoid absent-mindedness.

10 DECEMBER

There are therapeutic aspects to the day, so why not organise an activity that has healing effects on you? It's a good day for a health treat. You may be asked to help someone.

11 DECEMBER

You're an energetic and charismatic person but risk appearing bossy or stubborn, so be prepared to be adaptable and amenable.

12 DECEMBER

A significant meeting or news will ask that you review some of your preconceptions of someone close. Avoid making rash decisions as you'll regret them.

13 DECEMBER

A key financial or personal matter may deserve a mini review. You'll enjoy a reunion and romance could flourish, so plan a date!

14 DECEMBER

You communicate well when the moon is in Gemini, so be sure to take the initiative with talks and planning ahead. You may be drawn to travelling but will need to first attend to duties.

15 DECEMBER

The full moon in Gemini shines a light on the need to be clearer in your communications, especially where confusion has arisen. You may need to upgrade or repair a communication device or even a vehicle.

16 DECEMBER

The moon in Cancer brings a strong need to cocoon and spend time with family or someone special. Trust your intuition, as it is strong. It's a good time for minor DIY projects.

17 DECEMBER

You may be prone to resuming a power struggle from earlier in the year with someone in a position of power. Avoid raking over the coals as it could bring conflict.

18 DECEMBER

You are known as a proactive character but you can also be sentimental. This time of year brings up nostalgia, so avoid being super idealistic to avoid making mistakes.

19 DECEMBER

This is a good day for financial matters. You may also experience an ego boost or compliment. You'll enjoy a get-together or work meeting.

20 DECEMBER

This is a lovely day for a trip and for getting together with like-minded people.

21 DECEMBER

This is the solstice. You'll appreciate the sense that some aspects of your life will slow down a little for now.

22 DECEMBER

A favourite activity such as travel or sports will appeal and you'll enjoy a change of scenery. If you'd like to make long-term changes this is a good day to do so.

23 DECEMBER

You may need to contend with a clash of schedules or expectations. Luckily, you'll find a solution through careful reasoning and planning.

24 DECEMBER

You'll appreciate the healing aspects of the day but may also be prone to experience setbacks such as travel delays, so be patient and schedule in extra time for travel and communications.

25 DECEMBER

Merry Christmas! This is a beautiful day but it can be intense, so choose your words carefully to avoid offence being taken. You'll accomplish a lot by channelling energy into optimistic outcomes.

26 DECEMBER

A trip, get-together or news will be significant. However, delays are possible, so be prepared to plan well ahead and be patient.

27 DECEMBER

Your links with the past or work will require you to be upbeat and talkative. However, you may again experience delays, disagreements or conundrums so patience will be necessary.

28 DECEMBER

You may be surprised by developments in your personal life or financially. Be prepared to work constructively towards a positive outcome.

29 DECEMBER

This is a lovely day to be physically active and enjoy the outdoors and being optimistic and upbeat.

30 DECEMBER

The new moon in Capricorn will be at the zenith of your chart, suggesting you're ready for something new in your career, status and general direction. Plan carefully and you could make great progress.

31 DECEMBER

Happy New Year! Your focus will be on relationships, those you love and health and well-being. Just avoid overindulging, as a healthy start to 2025 will suit you more than a long recovery on 1 January!

TAURUS

19 April – 20 May

FINANCES

Abundant Jupiter in your finance sector from the end of May will mean two things: an opportunity to build wealth and also an opportunity to spend big! If you action these two options in the order listed you'll enjoy an abundant year, but if you spend big before you have grown wealth then this year you risk beginning a debt-laden cycle. This is all the more reason to plan carefully. Mid-year will be an excellent time to reappraise your finances and put a clever budget in place to ensure you grow wealth rather than squander it, after which signs of a wealthy future will take root, especially from August onwards.

HEALTH

The year 2024 is a wonderful one to look for new and vibrant ways to stay healthy, as the eclipses in March, April and October will provide opportunities to open doors to refreshing daily schedules. You'll find out earlier in the year rather than later if you have to focus a little more on your health than in previous years. It's in your interest to avoid overtiring your body in 2024 and to avoid overwork, as these will be hindrances to your physical movements and overall health – especially at the end of January, in mid-September and during the last quarter of the year.

LOVE LIFE

This is likely to be a smoother year in your love life than last year. January will include a lovely opportunity to start the year on a more optimistic note, especially if you wish to take your love life into more adventurous territory. You may, for example, consider a trip somewhere new with someone special. The first six months of the year will be sociable, which will be ideal for singles to meet people, while August and early October will be ideal for rekindling fun and creativity in your love life.

CAREER

Are you ready for something new and to action thoughts and plans you formulated in 2023 and take them to the next level? Then 2024 is your year! Be brave. The secret to success lies in careful planning. The fortunate Saturn–Jupiter aspect at the end of January could bring positive developments in your career during the entire first quarter of the year, so this is the year to think innovatively about your next career step. The eclipses in March, April and October will invariably bring changes to your career, status or direction, so be prepared to take advantage of developments and initiate a positive cycle.

HOME LIFE

A focus on improving family dynamics and your home life in 2024 will be a drawcard, and some DIY projects or even home renovation will appeal. You'll find that making your home a priority will truly pay off. Mercury will be in your fourth house of home life from June until early October, bringing your focus on your domestic realm during these months. You may be drawn to reviewing your home life during the Mercury retrograde phase in August or decide to visit an old haunt such as a family home.

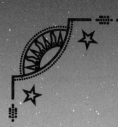
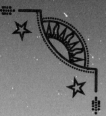

January

1 JANUARY

Being a grounded person means you'll wish to invest in someone special, yourself, and your house and get things shipshape for the year. Avoid a Mexican stand-off with someone if possible.

2 JANUARY

It's a good day to choose your words carefully to avoid a misunderstanding with someone special. It's always a tense time at the start of the year, so if possible take things slowly.

3 JANUARY

Find the time to pace yourself. If differences arise, look for common ground and a solution.

4 JANUARY

You're adept at maintaining the peace and always finding the most practical and reasonable way ahead, and today is no exception.

5 JANUARY

A busy or up-tempo day will engage you and may even bring out strong feelings, so be prepared to regain perspective if necessary.

6 JANUARY

You or someone close may be a little vulnerable, sensitive or even accident-prone, so tread carefully. You may be asked for help, and if you need help it will be available.

7 JANUARY

This is a good day to relax and get to the bottom of differences in a productive, caring and nurturing way, especially if you've argued recently. Just avoid misunderstandings.

8 JANUARY

You'll appreciate feeling a little more outgoing, upbeat and optimistic. It's a good day for taking the initiative with shared project and duties.

9 JANUARY

Keep an eye on communications and meetings to avoid making mistakes. Be sure to double-check details and avoid travel delays by planning ahead. You may be prone to day dreaming and forgetfulness.

10 JANUARY

Be prepared for a new opportunity, as it's likely to improve your career or personal situation. Be spontaneous and ready for change.

11 JANUARY

The Capricorn new moon will kick-start a fresh phase in your status, career or direction. Some Taureans will welcome a fresh interest or project such as study or travel. It's a good day to focus on your health.

12 JANUARY

This is a good day to take the initiative with your plans and projects. A trip or change at work or in your personal life will be exciting.

13 JANUARY

This is a good day for get-togethers, both professionally and in your personal life. You'll find ways to share and discuss duties. Romance could flourish.

14 JANUARY

The next few weeks will be ideal for communicating and actioning your projects and making concrete plans, especially with someone you may need to persuade about your ideas.

15 JANUARY

An inspired and intuitive start to the week will help you to move ahead in practical ways.

16 JANUARY

You'll be interested by the arts, romance and creativity and will feel fulfilled if you can weave these inspiring qualities into your work and activities. Avoid forgetfulness. Romance could flourish.

17 JANUARY

The next two days are good for professional and social meetings. Take the initiative. It's a good time to make financial plans.

18 JANUARY

This is a good day to discuss work plans and make financial decisions. You'll enjoy a get-together or news.

19 JANUARY

You'll appreciate the opportunity to discuss important financial matters or will enjoy a financial or ego boost. However, you must avoid spending as quickly as you earn, along with forgetfulness and making assumptions.

20 JANUARY

You may receive key news to do with your work, status, direction or projects. This may be an intense day, so pace yourself.

21 JANUARY

Be prepared to enter fresh territory. For some this will be due to a change at work and for others due to a change in your general status and direction. Think laterally.

22 JANUARY

You may be prepared to set in motion ideas and plans you floated in 2023. Research your options for the best results.

23 JANUARY

The stars are aligning to help you to take things one step at a time, especially with your projects, activities, study, travel and, for some, with legal matters.

24 JANUARY

Your vulnerabilities may come out in the lead-up to the full moon, so ensure you retain perspective. Trust your instincts. It's a good time for a health appointment.

25 JANUARY

The Leo full moon will spotlight a domestic or personal matter. It may be time for something new. Avoid minor bumps and scrapes and unintentionally shooting yourself in the foot.

26 JANUARY

By taking rash actions you may disadvantage yourself or someone close. Take a moment to choose your words to avoid causing offence. It's a good day for a health appointment.

27 JANUARY

Key news or a meeting will take your focus. You may need to be on your toes but must avoid arguments. Try to find common ground and progress from there.

28 JANUARY

This is a lovely day to indulge in your favourite activities and socialise. You could make a valid financial plan.

29 JANUARY

A change of place or of pace and the chance to enjoy someone's company will bring a smile to your face.

30 JANUARY

Be prepared to think outside the square, especially regarding work. Your imagination is fertile now and ideal for creative work.

31 JANUARY

You may be called to be a mediator in a situation that has become stuck. If you need advice or a mediator yourself, an expert or loyal friend will help.

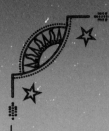

February

1 FEBRUARY

The next two days are ideal for getting on top of your work and for improving your looks and health. You'll enjoy the arts.

2 FEBRUARY

This is a lovely day for socialising and networking. Your charisma is shining, so be sure to use it! You may enjoy a favourite activity or meeting.

3 FEBRUARY

You'll need to feel motivated to do anything, so think for a moment what would truly get your foot tapping and take action.

4 FEBRUARY

A partner or someone close will be motivational, helping you to gain more enthusiasm about life and chores that need to be completed around the house.

5 FEBRUARY

A meeting will be therapeutic even if it feels a little intense. A trip or activity will ask that you draw on your inner resources. It's a good day for a health appointment.

6 FEBRUARY

Be prepared to look outside the box at your various options, especially to do with long-term plans. Be practical above all else.

7 FEBRUARY

It's a lovely day for socialising, networking and enjoying favourite activities. You may receive unexpected news or enjoy an impromptu event.

8 FEBRUARY

You like life to move forward steadily and can mistrust sudden changes, but today you may experience a surprise development so you must be on your toes.

9 FEBRUARY

The Aquarian new moon supermoon will shine a light on quirky or unexpected developments. It's a good day for meetings and financial decisions.

10 FEBRUARY

Life has a habit of bringing unusual developments your way at the moment. You'll appreciate the opportunity to digest recent developments.

11 FEBRUARY

It's a lovely day to relax and take some time for a little rest and recuperation. Romance could blossom.

12 FEBRUARY

It's a good day to find a little stability and security in your life, so if possible make tracks to steady things.

13 FEBRUARY

A work or social connection will prove helpful and enjoyable, so be sure to connect with like-minded people. Romance could blossom.

14 FEBRUARY

Happy St Valentine's Day! This may be an intense day, so ensure you pace yourself. A work situation may test your patience, so be prepared to put your best foot forward.

15 FEBRUARY

When the moon is in your sign you tend to find life more manageable, so be sure to take the initiative with your ideas and projects.

16 FEBRUARY

Be prepared to step into new territory with your projects and adjust your approach to your ventures and progress. Be innovative.

17 FEBRUARY

This is another potentially intense day, as you are up for a change in direction in your status or beliefs. Romance could blossom.

18 FEBRUARY

Meetings will be significant and romance could flourish, but you must be wary of sensitive topics with a fiery character. Think outside the box with a change of circumstance.

19 FEBRUARY

You may be required to go over old ground at work or review a health matter. A reunion or return to an old haunt may be significant.

20 FEBRUARY

The Cancerian moon may bring your sensitivities to the surface, so take things one step at a time and take reasonable action.

21 FEBRUARY

Discussions and get-togethers may still be a little intense, so be sure to take time out if necessary. Trust your intuition.

22 FEBRUARY

Key meetings, news or a change at work will take your focus. Your best approach is to welcome the new rather than hang on to the past.

23 FEBRUARY

In the lead-up to the full moon you may feel more vulnerable than usual, so maintain perspective. A particular group or friend will prove inspiring.

24 FEBRUARY

The full moon in Virgo will shine a light on your personal, family and creative life. It's a good time to be inspired but also practical.

25 FEBRUARY

You can accomplish a great deal, especially around the house or garden. You'll enjoy being inspired by music and art.

26 FEBRUARY

You'll enjoy a productive day as you get to complete outstanding chores and clear up loose ends.

27 FEBRUARY

You can attain a great deal, but if you encounter an obstacle to your plans be prepared to work collaboratively with those who see things differently by establishing common ground.

28 FEBRUARY

You'll see eye to eye with someone you must get on with, so look for ways to work together. A meeting may be more significant than meets the eye. It's a good day to socialise.

29 FEBRUARY

You'll enjoy a reunion at work and socially. This is a good day for meetings and for financial planning.

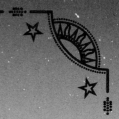

March

1 MARCH

This is a lovely day for get-togethers and mending bridges if you have argued. It's also a good day for making financial plans and agreements if you've done your research.

2 MARCH

You're likely to feel active and passionate about what you do, so you'll appreciate the chance to get things done and socialise but may be prone to arguments.

3 MARCH

You may be surprised by developments or must make an unexpected change to your plans. Be prepared to look after yourself and relax.

4 MARCH

The next two days are ideal for developing a more stable and productive health and daily schedule. Take the initiative with meetings as your ideas are likely to be well received.

5 MARCH

Be proactive at work and with projects, but avoid appearing bossy or controlling. You'll enjoy getting together with someone whom you love or admire.

6 MARCH

This is a good day for a health or beauty appointment and to seek expert advice. If you need support or information it will be available.

7 MARCH

This is another good day for get-togethers, socialising and making agreements, especially at work, and for working on a solid financial plan.

8 MARCH

This is a lovely day for indulging in the arts, romance and well-being. You will enjoy a reunion. It's a good day for spiritual and self-development.

9 MARCH

You'll enjoy being spontaneous, and a sense of freedom and adventure could even take you somewhere new. Just avoid rushing and making rash decisions.

10 MARCH

The Pisces new moon supermoon is excellent for self-reflection and self-development. You'll appreciate the chance to clear clutter from your environment and put your hopes for the future in place.

11 MARCH

You'll begin the week on a hopeful note, but you may tend to have your head in the clouds. You'll enjoy socialising and networking and will also look for inspiration to keep you motivated.

12 MARCH

The moon in Aries will promote a strong work ethic. However, it may also highlight a health matter or underlying worry, so take time out to boost your well-being if necessary.

13 MARCH

Changes at work or in your social circle will turn out to be for the best, even if some matters are intense.

14 MARCH

You'll feel more practical and grounded about your activities and be able to get things done in your own time. Just avoid stubbornness.

15 MARCH

The Gemini moon will spotlight your communication skills, enabling you to be more outgoing. However, you must think before you speak to avoid rash words.

16 MARCH

You'll enjoy getting together with an old friend or family member. If you're shopping, you could find something ideal. It's a good day to focus on a budget.

17 MARCH

This is an excellent time for self-development and spiritual work. You'll enjoy a reunion and romance but must avoid being absent-minded or super idealistic, as you'll feel disappointed.

18 MARCH

Trust your instincts, especially at home or regarding family. You'll enjoy cocooning.

19 MARCH

You'll enjoy moving certain projects and incentives forward. Just avoid appearing impatient or bossy, as this will be counterproductive. You may have a spiritual epiphany.

20 MARCH

This is a good time to focus on finances and how to build a better budget. It's a good day for a health appointment and review with an expert.

21 MARCH

This is a good day to make progress at work and in your status. A change in either area will be transformative in the long term. You may consider making a new financial or personal agreement.

22 MARCH

Mars will be in your social and networking zone for the next five weeks, bringing your attention to these important aspects. Just avoid forgetfulness and idealism during this phase.

23 MARCH

Be prepared to learn something new. You may have overdramatised a circumstance. A strong connection with someone will be on your mind and a key investment may appeal, but you must research it first.

24 MARCH

While you'll feel motivated or anxious to move your ideas and projects along, just ensure you have checked the facts to avoid making mistakes.

25 MARCH

The lunar eclipse signals a fresh approach will be effective for April Bulls regarding your well-being and daily schedule and for May Bulls regarding your personal life.

26 MARCH

This is a good day for a health or beauty appointment. A relationship may prove to be therapeutic or helpful.

27 MARCH

You'll be drawn to looking for balance and a steady pace at work and in your personal life to avoid overloading yourself.

28 MARCH

You may experience a surprise change in your routine or a chance encounter. Someone may behave unexpectedly or you may need to alter arrangements.

29 MARCH

You'll find out something invaluable about a business or personal partner. They may seem more passionate or persuasive than usual, so maintain a steady view of your own goals.

30 MARCH

You'll enjoy being outgoing and adventurous this weekend, and a friend or partner will be motivational. You'll enjoy a trip or return to an old haunt.

31 MARCH

This is a good day to get up to date with your paperwork and finances so that things are shipshape when Mercury goes retrograde on Tuesday.

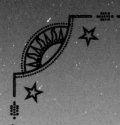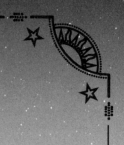

April

1 APRIL

This is a good day to get the loose ends of key plans tied up to avoid potential delays over the coming weeks.

2 APRIL

You may receive key news at work or concerning your health that will deserve attention. It's a good time over the coming weeks to focus on a healthy schedule.

3 APRIL

This is a lovely day for a romantic get-together. You may be drawn to reuniting with an ex but you must ensure you're not being idealistic. The arts and creativity will thrive.

4 APRIL

You'll enjoy a reunion or may receive key news that may be more significant than meets the eye. It's a good day to gain advice, especially from a health or beauty expert.

5 APRIL

As Venus, the planet associated with love, art, beauty and money, enters Aries it's a good time to prepare and arrange for more of these elements to enter your life.

6 APRIL

The Pisces moon will bring out your romantic qualities. You may discover over the next two days whether you have underestimated someone and, if so, will have a reality hit.

7 APRIL

You'll enjoy indulging in the luxuries or life but may be inclined to overindulge, which you'll regret. Avoid over-romanticising a situation but, nevertheless, you'll enjoy daydreaming!

8 APRIL

The total solar eclipse in Aries signifies a completely fresh start, especially regarding work and, for some, health and well-being.

9 APRIL

Be prepared to shine, and if you need the advice of an expert it will be available. Someone may ask you for help.

10 APRIL

An important get-together will present the chance to make a fresh agreement. Just avoid impulsiveness but be prepared to be spontaneous – a fine line!

11 APRIL

You'll enjoy a reunion or will receive news regarding work or a financial matter. A debt may be repaid or you will repay one.

12 APRIL

The Gemini moon will bring out your and everyone else's chattiness and you may find communication easier as a result. Just avoid stubbornness and look for common ground.

13 APRIL

This is an excellent weekend to slow down and find a healing moment as it's ideal for relaxing and formulating a strong health schedule. You may overcome a past hurt.

14 APRIL

You'll appreciate the opportunity to connect with someone you admire or love. However, some topics may be sensitive, so be tactful to avoid offence being taken.

15 APRIL

You will be in demand at work. If a health matter has been bubbling in the background it's a good day to review it and take action to overcome it. An expert will be invaluable.

16 APRIL

You'll feel motivated to get things done at home but must avoid appearing bossy. It's a good day to attend to your health and well-being, but you must avoid impulsiveness.

17 APRIL

You'll enjoy hearing from or catching up with someone from your past. You'll appreciate the opportunity to indulge in a favourite pastime.

18 APRIL

As an earth sign you tend to prefer taking things one step at a time, yet a more spontaneous aspect of your personality will come out and you'll enjoy impromptu get-togethers.

19 APRIL

As the sun enters your sign you'll appreciate the sense that your mojo is rising. You may enjoy surprise news or a spontaneous get-together. There will be changes at work, health-wise or financially.

20 APRIL

You'll appreciate the opportunity to get your feet back on the ground after a busy week. A social or work commitment will command your attention.

21 APRIL

If you're working, aim to organise priorities so that other commitments don't clash. Bear in mind it can't all be done. You may need to make impromptu decisions.

22 APRIL

You may be surprised by an impromptu call or get-together or surprise development at work or in your personal life. Be prepared to think on your feet.

23 APRIL

This is a good time to look for balance in your daily routine and avoid being caught up in the busyness of your everyday life. Find time to pace yourself.

24 APRIL

The Scorpio full moon will spotlight a particular business or work situation. This is an excellent day for communications, especially if you must review paperwork or agreements.

25 APRIL

You may receive key news from someone special. It's a good day to talk as the Mercury retrograde phase ends.

26 APRIL

You'll appreciate the sense of freedom the weekend presents to you. A friend or partner will be motivational and you'll enjoy being proactive with your favourite activities.

27 APRIL

The Sagittarian moon will encourage you to be outgoing. It's a good weekend for a reunion, reviewing some of your recent decisions and a trip to an old haunt.

28 APRIL

Your interest in the arts, film, romance and beauty will all blossom. You'll also appreciate the chance to relax.

29 APRIL

As Venus enters your sign your attention will be on romance and how to create more beauty and love in your life, so take the initiative!

30 APRIL

Proactive and upbeat Mars will encourage you to be more socially outgoing over the coming weeks. You'll also enjoy feeling more spirited in groups and organisations.

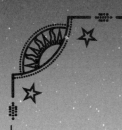
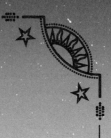

May

1 MAY

Today's strained stand-off between Venus and Pluto may produce tension so tread carefully, especially at work and with a close friend or colleague.

2 MAY

You may receive key news at work or from a friend. Take a moment to decide whether you'd like to act on information you receive; you will have time to decide.

3 MAY

You are productive and will attain a great deal, but you must be wary of impulsiveness.

4 MAY

You'll enjoy resting and relaxing and allowing your mind to unwind. The arts, romance and a reunion will appeal.

5 MAY

You'll enjoy a get-together or return to an old haunt. You'll also appreciate the chance to get on top of chores.

6 MAY

You will not automatically agree with everyone, and today is a case in point. You may need to tread carefully with an authority figure such as an employer.

7 MAY

You'll appreciate the opportunity to clear a big workload. If you need advice it will be available. It's a good day for a health or beauty appointment.

8 MAY

The Taurus new moon will kick-start a fresh personal circumstance. If you were born later in May this is a good time to refresh your daily routine or work or health schedule.

9 MAY

You'll find communications flow a little better over the next two days, and if you have key financial or personal matters to organise consider doing so now.

10 MAY

Be prepared to collaborate with someone in authority as opposed to feeling in opposition if possible. You'll enjoy a reunion and the chance to boost your mood.

11 MAY

You'll enjoy a get-together with someone who has deep significance to you. Romance, the arts, good food and company will all appeal, so reach out!

12 MAY

The moon in Cancer will draw your attention to your home life, health and finding the time for yourself and those you love. Avoid overindulging as you'll regret it tomorrow!

13 MAY

Be prepared to vary your usual schedule and make spontaneous decisions. If you are making financial and work commitments, rest assured you'll fulfil your duties.

14 MAY

You'll enjoy being playful and dynamic about your work and daily choices. Just be sure to keep focus at work.

15 MAY

As Mercury enters your sign you'll feel more in your element, especially with communications, health decisions and work commitments. Take the initiative.

16 MAY

When the moon is in Virgo your work ethic takes a turn for the better. Just be wary of overloading your work schedule if you are making fresh commitments.

17 MAY

While you'll feel a little more secure in how you approach people you may experience tension with someone in power, so be tactful. Avoid making rash decisions.

18 MAY

You'll enjoy doing something different; you may feel like celebrating life and all it has to offer. Just avoid overspending and overindulging, which you'll regret.

19 MAY

This is a romantic and also nostalgic time. Be sure not to resume a project or relationship through sentimentality.

20 MAY

You may hear unexpected news or bump into an old friend. Be prepared to think on your feet at work, as opportunity may knock!

21 MAY

You'll enjoy feeling motivated at work. This is a good time to collaborate with colleagues and employers and approach prospective employers, as you have charm on your side.

22 MAY

This is an excellent time to make changes in your career, at work and in your general direction. Be proactive and positive!

23 MAY

The full moon in Sagittarius spotlights a fresh chapter in a business or personal relationship. Romance could blossom, so ensure you organise a treat.

24 MAY

This is an excellent time to be adventurous with people whose company you admire and at work. Be prepared to try something new.

25 MAY

The Venus–Pluto aspect this weekend is ideal for making positive changes in your life. The arts, romance, socialising and financial investments could all flourish. Just avoid overspending.

26 MAY

The adventurous and inquisitive aspects of your nature will seek expression over the coming weeks and months, beginning now. Travel will appeal, so it's a good time to plan a holiday or new vehicle.

27 MAY

Your organisational skills will be in demand, so look for ways to innovate. Just avoid rushing as minor errors could be made over the next few days.

28 MAY

This is a good day for talks and meetings in association with work, finances and health. A debt may be repaid.

29 MAY

Your expertise will be in demand and you may be unexpectedly asked for help. You'll appreciate the help of an expert.

30 MAY

This is another good day to discuss matters at work, regarding finances and/or health. Just avoid being impulsive and think things through.

31 MAY

Your dreamy and nostalgic sides come out when the moon is in Pisces. You'll feel inspired but must avoid absent-mindedness.

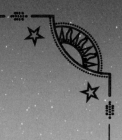

June

1 JUNE

You may be surprised to bump into an old friend or hear from someone from the past. A fresh opportunity may arise spontaneously, so be prepared to think on your feet.

2 JUNE

There are opportunities around you that will improve your life, status and direction. Be sure to consider broadening your horizons.

3 JUNE

You may receive unexpected or good news to do with your finances, work, career or status. It's a good time to make changes in these areas with the right advice.

4 JUNE

You'll enjoy meetings and get-togethers and could make valid commitments and decisions. Romance could blossom.

5 JUNE

The moon in Gemini brings out your more adaptable qualities, and you'll appreciate seeing the new options on offer due to current developments.

6 JUNE

The new moon in Gemini brings the focus on love, money, romance and the arts, so be prepared to advance in one or all of these areas. It's a good time to talk.

7 JUNE

You will not always agree with everyone, but the subtle art of persuasion is not lost on you. Trust your instincts.

8 JUNE

Choose your activities carefully this weekend to avoid making rash decisions. If you're investing in a large financial or personal commitment, ensure you do your research for the best measure.

9 JUNE

Consider whether a difference of opinion stems from divergent values as opposed to contrasting plans or expectations. Be prepared to take action but avoid making snap decisions.

10 JUNE

The Leo moon brings your restlessness into focus. Be sure to channel excess energy into sports and constructive activities and avoid impulsiveness.

11 JUNE

If you have recently argued with someone this is a good day to make amends. It's also a good time for a health appointment.

12 JUNE

A financial or personal matter will deserve careful focus. Avoid making assumptions and ensure you check your facts, especially at work.

13 JUNE

You may be surprised by news, an impromptu get-together or financial circumstance but will take things in your stride.

14 JUNE

Some talks and meetings may require more work than you'd hoped, but others will be therapeutic in nature. A healing day brings the chance to boost your well-being and self-esteem.

15 JUNE

You'll enjoy being spontaneous and a get-together. However, if you're shopping you must avoid impulse buys you may come to regret.

16 JUNE

This is the perfect day to rediscover peace and balance in your life. Try to avoid sensitive topics, overindulgence and overspending, which you'll regret.

17 JUNE

You may have your head in the clouds and be prone to forgetfulness. A key meeting and travel may be delayed. Be clear, as misunderstandings are likely.

18 JUNE

People you work and collaborate with may seem more feisty, moody or intense than usual, so if possible give them a wide berth. Focus on your own success.

19 JUNE

Someone close is likely to feel more outspoken and upbeat than yesterday, so find time to enjoy something different if you can.

20 JUNE

The solstice is always a lovely time to consider how far you've come this year. You must again avoid absent-mindedness. Find the time to research a mystery if necessary.

21 JUNE

This is a good time to take things in your stride and avoid intense talks if possible. A financial or ego boost is on the way. Avoid overspending.

22 JUNE

The full moon in Capricorn will highlight a special venture and a financial or shared personal matter such as a collaboration or relationship. It's time to plan ahead.

23 JUNE

Take a moment to decide how you feel about a relationship or trip. The delicate art of negotiation will be a skill set to embrace.

24 JUNE

The moon at the zenith of your chart brings out your innovative qualities, and you'll enjoy being outgoing and resourceful. A change at work or in your personal life may be surprising.

25 JUNE

News from the past or a reunion is likely to boost your feel-good factor. Be prepared to take positive action.

26 JUNE

This is a good day to discuss important matters, especially concerning work and with a group, friend or organisation. Put your values and goals on the table.

27 JUNE

You'll be drawn to being optimistic about your projects but must look at the worst-case scenario to avoid making mistakes.

28 JUNE

Certain topics may be off limits, so avoid opening Pandora's box. It's a good day to focus on health and well-being and research your options moving forward.

29 JUNE

A lovely meeting, reunion or return to an old haunt will be enjoyable. Romance could blossom, so take the initiative.

30 JUNE

You'll enjoy an impromptu trip or get-together and may be surprised by news you receive. Be open to something different!

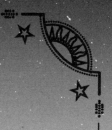

July

1 JULY

The moon in your sign will help you to feel grounded and avoid making mistakes. You may nevertheless be prone to daydreaming.

2 JULY

A change of routine or the chance to reconnect with someone from your past will arise. You may be drawn to making changes at home or doing something different with your family.

3 JULY

It's a good day for talks both at home and at work, but you must avoid entering intense conversations as these are likely to escalate. Find time for financial planning.

4 JULY

The lead-up to the new moon is a good time to consider fresh ideas and plans, so take a moment to decide how you'd like some of your projects to progress.

5 JULY

The Cancerian new moon is a good time to begin fresh ways to bring more nurturance into your relationships at home and at work. You may be drawn to planning travel or a holiday.

6 JULY

You'll enjoy being proactive about long-range plans and also with a view to finding more peace and nurturance at home. If you need expert advice it will be available, so reach out.

7 JULY

You'll enjoy a sense of togetherness with a family member or close friend. You may be surprised by an impromptu visit.

8 JULY

A situation you had anticipated is likely to come about, albeit in a surprising way. Luckily, you're likely to be pleasantly surprised so take the initiative.

9 JULY

The next few days are ideal for finding more purpose and meaning in your daily routine. Consider adding an activity you love to your schedule.

10 JULY

This is a good day for planning and getting things shipshape; however, you must avoid obsessing over details or you risk being controlling.

11 JULY

You'll appreciate creating a more light-hearted atmosphere at home. A little beauty or luxury in your surroundings will raise your spirits. Avoid rushing at work.

12 JULY

You're likely to feel things more deeply than usual, which will cause passions to soar and arguments to spring up. Avoid contentious topics.

13 JULY

You'll appreciate an opportunity to regain a sense of relaxation and unwind this weekend. You may need to turn off your phone or ignore the doorbell to make it happen.

14 JULY

A prior commitment may cut into your weekend of relaxation, so to avoid offence being taken a degree of flexibility on your part will be necessary. Find the time to self-nurture.

15 JULY

You may be surprised by developments and will need to be flexible. However, someone is likely to need your help. A domestic or personal matter may need extra focus.

16 JULY

This may be another disrupted day, so be adaptable if possible. The Scorpio moon can bring out people's emotions, so you may be surprised by someone's mood swings.

17 JULY

As an earth sign you prefer life on an even keel, so current developments may be disruptive. Find time to regain perspective and peace of mind.

18 JULY

A little spontaneity is called for during times of change, so find the time to enjoy the company of different circles of people as you'll appreciate the diversity.

19 JULY

There are therapeutic aspects to the day. It's a good time for a health appointment and to build bridges with someone you've fallen out with, or at least to offer an olive branch.

20 JULY

As Mars leaves your sign you may feel a little restless or impatient. Take a moment to regain a sense of balance.

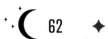

21 JULY

The full moon in Capricorn will shine a light on your status, career and general direction. It's a good time to plan ahead and marginalise disruptions. Romance could flourish.

22 JULY

This week will be motivational and you could make a great deal of progress at work and with your projects. Be inspired.

23 JULY

You'll feel motivated to get things done, both at home and at work. Just avoid power struggles by being assertive as opposed to aggressive.

24 JULY

The Pisces moon will bring your idealistic qualities to the surface, so bear in mind the realities of your circumstances but don't lose track of your goals.

25 JULY

You may be inclined to look at the details to the detriment of the bigger picture, so take time out if you feel you need to regain perspective.

26 JULY

This will be a busy and productive day and you'll accomplish a great deal, especially at home and with personal matters. Be proactive and positive.

27 JULY

You have personal goals, and sometimes these do not match up with those of other people or the community or big picture. Rest assured you'll find a way to overcome this.

28 JULY

The moon in your sign will encourage you to rest up and enjoy some creature comforts and a touch of luxury. Just avoid misunderstandings.

29 JULY

The next two days are ideal for focusing on your health and well-being. If started now, a beauty or fitness program could be successful.

30 JULY

This is a good day to improve your domestic circumstances. If you're travelling you may visit somewhere beautiful and therapeutic. Someone may prove helpful.

31 JULY

You'll enjoy a reunion and the chance to improve a family or other close relationship. A domestic improvement will be beneficial.

August

1 AUGUST

You may enjoy being a little more spontaneous in your working and social lives and are likely to enjoy the outcome.

2 AUGUST

You are feeling a little more outgoing and even feisty than usual and may surprise someone or yourself. Just avoid unintentionally disrupting people's lives.

3 AUGUST

The lead-up to a new moon is a good time to make a wish. Consider tactfully broaching sensitive topics.

4 AUGUST

The Leo new moon will kick-start a fresh chapter in your personal and domestic lives. You may be more outspoken than usual, so take a moment to avoid misunderstandings.

5 AUGUST

Try to get key paperwork and finances agreed upon by today to avoid having to review ideas at a later date. You may hear key news from someone close.

6 AUGUST

This is still a sensitive time when power struggles may bubble up, so be sure to avoid contentious topics if you wish to maintain a sense of peace.

7 AUGUST

This is a proactive and more upbeat day. You'll be drawn to connecting well with others, so it's a good day for talks.

8 AUGUST

You'll enjoy a reunion or trip somewhere you love. Romance, the arts and love could flourish. You may need to review or revise a personal decision.

9 AUGUST

You'll manage to find a peaceful way forward even if things at work or with an organisation seem more stressful than they need to be. Be diligent and you'll succeed.

10 AUGUST

The moon in Scorpio will bring out your passionate and earthy sides and you'll be drawn to investing in yourself and those you love. A little retail therapy may appeal but you must avoid overspending as you'll regret it.

11 AUGUST

You'll enjoy your favourite activities, and if you love competitive sports you'll enjoy planning strategy. It's a good time to get things shipshape at home.

12 AUGUST

You may be drawn to deepening your understanding of a colleague or someone who is close. They may seem erratic, so a steady approach will smooth the way.

13 AUGUST

You'll appreciate the camaraderie of those close to you, be this at home or at work. If someone is dragging their feet a motivational approach will work.

14 AUGUST

Certain conversations and interactions may be tense, so find a way to overcome nerves and look for a solution. Avoid impulsiveness and overspending as you'll regret it.

15 AUGUST

A little more research will help you get ahead with your projects. Avoid making assumptions. It's a good day to overcome hurdles, so be resourceful.

16 AUGUST

Think before you leap as you may be liable to making rash decisions. Ensure you carefully research facts if you're considering a large investment.

17 AUGUST

You'll be drawn to projects and activities that are interesting and different. If you feel a little stretched, trust that your efforts will pay off.

18 AUGUST

You may need to go over old ground with an existing agreement in your personal life. Avoid misunderstandings and gambling for the best results.

19 AUGUST

The full moon in Aquarius will shine a light on your social life. You may be drawn to a new friend or argue with an old one. Differences will encompass principles and values.

20 AUGUST

The full moon may spotlight certain relationships you have outgrown. For some these may be at work and in your career. Be prepared, nevertheless, to take action optimistically.

21 AUGUST

You may discover you have over- or underestimated someone or a situation. If so, you'll gain the opportunity to get back on track.

22 AUGUST

The sun will spotlight your personal life for the next four weeks, bringing your attention to difficulties as opposed to good aspects. Avoid misunderstandings for the best results.

23 AUGUST

This is a good day for talks, especially if you have disagreements to iron out. Just ensure you avoid arguments and instead look for common ground.

24 AUGUST

You'll appreciate the opportunity to improve your fitness, beauty and general well-being. You'll enjoy a get-together. Avoid taking the random comments of other people personally unless criticism is merited.

25 AUGUST

This is a good day to get back to basics and clear a backlog of chores, and also to earth your plans and projects with friends and family. Be productive.

26 AUGUST

The moon in Gemini will bring out your chatty side, which is excellent for work meetings, but you must avoid gossip and being easily distracted.

27 AUGUST

If you'd like to bring positive and exciting change into your life this is the day to do it! Expect a surprise. You may enjoy the chance to demonstrate just what you're made of.

28 AUGUST

This is a lovely day for romance, so ensure you plan a date. You may receive key news to do with home or family.

29 AUGUST

Venus in your work zone for the next three weeks will help you improve your daily existence and schedule. This is a lovely day to look for improved conditions at work and for a beauty boost.

30 AUGUST

You'll feel motivated to get things shipshape at home and with family. Romance could blossom, so organise a treat.

31 AUGUST

You'll enjoy an unexpected change of pace and doing something different. You may even surprise yourself.

September

1 SEPTEMBER

It's a good time for a mini review of your status and career. If you're happy with the track you're on then all well and good, but if not it's time to make changes.

2 SEPTEMBER

Consider ways to bring more stability into your life. A clean bill of health will support you moving forward, making this a good time for a health check.

3 SEPTEMBER

The new moon in Virgo is a good time to kick-start a personal project such as home improvements or creative activities. You may be ready to consider altering family dynamics.

4 SEPTEMBER

Some things are simply impossible to know right down to the details, but you can trust your gut instincts to help you to make decisions. You'll enjoy a meeting and romance.

5 SEPTEMBER

The moon in Libra will help you formulate your ideas and plans, especially at work and financially. Trust that you have the reasoning power you need to succeed.

6 SEPTEMBER

You'll be required to be diplomatic and tactful or act as mediator in conversations and arrangements both at work and in your personal life.

7 SEPTEMBER

You'll appreciate the opportunity to invest in yourself via your favourite activities. However, if shopping counts as a favourite activity you'll be inclined to overspend, so be careful.

8 SEPTEMBER

This is a good time to make a commitment to a plan of action or person. However, it's important you do adequate research before acting.

9 SEPTEMBER

You'll be communicating well over the coming weeks, making this a progressive time for you. However, today you must avoid power struggles with someone in power.

10 SEPTEMBER

You'll enjoy being outgoing but may be liable to appear larger than life to someone whose opinion you value. Avoid dimming your light, but equally avoid overshadowing someone else.

11 SEPTEMBER

You may need to work a little harder to get your usual results. Rest assured that your efforts will be worthwhile.

12 SEPTEMBER

You have every reason to believe in positive outcomes; however, you may discover a minor obstacle that will require careful handling and rectification.

13 SEPTEMBER

The moon at the zenith of your chart will encourage you to be practical but may also put your heart on your sleeve. Avoid taking other people's vulnerabilities as your own.

14 SEPTEMBER

You'll welcome a change of pace and a little time spent on yourself. Someone may need your help or encouragement. Avoid taking the random comments of other people personally.

15 SEPTEMBER

You may be feeling super sensitive yet you have every reason to be optimistic. A shopping spree may raise morale, and the chance to boost your health certainly will.

16 SEPTEMBER

This is a good day to consider how to boost your appearance. A beauty treat or fresh hair style may appeal. You may need to tread carefully with someone's ego.

17 SEPTEMBER

In the lead-up to the full moon you may find certain issues come to a head. You may be easily influenced by others, so ensure you're clear about your options.

18 SEPTEMBER

The partial lunar eclipse supermoon in Pisces spotlights a key work or health decision. You may receive news that clarifies your best path forward. Be open to change but avoid impulsiveness.

19 SEPTEMBER

You'll welcome a positive development that may come as a surprise. For some Taureans events will be ideal, but if not you must find ways to move ahead in the most practical way.

20 SEPTEMBER

Important matters will deserve clear focus yet you may be unclear of the true circumstances of your situation. Consider researching things further and be diligent, as your efforts will be rewarded.

21 SEPTEMBER

This is an excellent time to relax, take your mind off work if possible and treat yourself well. However, you may also feel escapist but must look at a viable way forward. Avoid gambling and misunderstandings.

22 SEPTEMBER

Your daily life deserves to be calm, but if it isn't it's a good time to set things right. However, you must be diplomatic and avoid arguments.

23 SEPTEMBER

It's important to be optimistic but also realistic. If you're in a tricky situation find ways to defuse anger, and if life is rosy find ways to enjoy this to the max!

24 SEPTEMBER

You'll enjoy being spontaneous and may also find ways to establish a little more peace and calm in your life. The arts, music and romance will appeal.

25 SEPTEMBER

You'll feel drawn to developing your intuition and may find you pick up all kinds of information. It's a good time for self-development.

26 SEPTEMBER

This is a good day for work meetings and boosting your status and direction in life. This is a good day to initiate a transformative work or relationship cycle.

27 SEPTEMBER

You'll enjoy indulging in your fun, playful side and a meeting with like-minded people later today will be enjoyable.

28 SEPTEMBER

A lovely reunion or return to an old haunt will appeal. If you're stuck at work, rest assured your efforts will be productive and worthwhile.

29 SEPTEMBER

A key trip or news will add a fresh aspect to your usual Sunday routine. You may bond better with someone close, so this is a good day for romance.

30 SEPTEMBER

This is a lovely day for meetings and get-togethers, especially at work. You may receive key news to do with health. Be inspired, as you could make solid plans.

October

1 OCTOBER

This will be a productive day at work, so be prepared to get things done there and at home. You may surprise yourself with how productive you are!

2 OCTOBER

The solar eclipse in Libra will help you turn a corner in your daily health or work routine, so be sure to seek a more balanced chapter at work as it is possible. Just avoid making snap decisions.

3 OCTOBER

This is a lovely day for meetings, both in your personal life and at work. It's also a good day to treat yourself to a new look or outfit.

4 OCTOBER

You'll appreciate the opportunity to spend relaxing time with someone you love, so organise something special. A work meeting will be productive.

5 OCTOBER

You'll appreciate the chance to indulge in your favourite activities such as sports and personal development with like-minded people.

6 OCTOBER

This is another good day to indulge in favourite projects and spend time with loved ones. However, you must avoid misunderstandings. Plan travel ahead of time to avoid delays.

7 OCTOBER

This will be an upbeat start to the week, and someone close such as a partner, friend or colleague will prove motivational. Just beware of mix-ups and travel delays.

8 OCTOBER

This is an excellent day for get-togethers, both at work and socially. A trip will be productive. A health matter could see progress, and it's a good day to find support at work if necessary.

9 OCTOBER

You will be in demand at work. Look for ways to get ahead with the support of colleagues, and be prepared to delegate and share workloads. It's a good day to focus on your health.

10 OCTOBER

The moon at the zenith of your chart will put your mind to work on your duties. Look for ways to get ahead that support your well-being to avoid overtiring yourself.

11 OCTOBER

You are generally a good communicator, but not everyone will be on the same page as you so find new ways to get your message across if necessary, especially at work.

12 OCTOBER

Once again, some conversations will require more focus to ensure you're all on the same page. Some travel and communications may be delayed, so be patient.

13 OCTOBER

This is an excellent day for housework and gardening as you'll be productive, especially this afternoon. Choose your words carefully, as someone close may be feeling sensitive.

14 OCTOBER

This is a good day for a health appointment. You or someone close may feel a little sensitive but, nevertheless, you will be productive. Avoid making rash decisions as someone may surprise you.

15 OCTOBER

You'll appreciate finding a little time to yourself to gain your bearings. Again, avoid making snap decisions, especially if you feel a little restless.

16 OCTOBER

Romance, the arts and reconnecting with people you've found it difficult to get on with recently will appeal. It's a good day for self-development.

17 OCTOBER

The full moon supermoon in Aries signals a fresh chapter in your daily work or health routine. You'll appreciate finding the time to focus a little more on your well-being.

18 OCTOBER

This is a perfect day to get things shipshape at work, especially if you feel you've lagged behind. It's also a good day to clear up outstanding financial matters.

19 OCTOBER

You'll enjoy a change of routine even if some developments will be unexpected. Work hard at your goals and you'll succeed.

20 OCTOBER

This is a lovely day to relax and focus on de-stressing. A get-together or visit somewhere beautiful may involve logistics but you will appreciate the outcome.

21 OCTOBER

You are communicating well but must avoid being forgetful and vague. Perhaps you'll be dealing with someone who is vague, so be patient!

22 OCTOBER

As the sun enters Scorpio, the next four weeks will be busy. Someone close may be a little feisty, and if it's you it's important to avoid ego battles as they could quickly escalate.

23 OCTOBER

This is an excellent day for get-togethers, both socially and at work. You may hear spontaneously from an old friend.

24 OCTOBER

The moon in your domestic realm will encourage you to feel like cocooning this evening. Keep conversations with someone in power on an even keel to avoid arguments.

25 OCTOBER

You'll enjoy a spontaneous get-together or visit somewhere different. You may receive an unexpected guest or news.

26 OCTOBER

You'll enjoy spending time on yourself and your home. Just avoid being a perfectionist and preventing yourself from relaxing.

27 OCTOBER

This is a lovely day to focus on your health and well-being and those of someone close. Just avoid taking random comments personally unless criticism is merited.

28 OCTOBER

If you've been overly idealistic you may experience a reality hit. Disagreements may come down to a difference in expectations or values. You'll enjoy relaxing, the arts and music this evening.

29 OCTOBER

You'll be looking for a peaceful day yet you'll also need to collaborate well with someone important, either at work or at home.

30 OCTOBER

Someone will surprise you, either through their news or behaviour. Be prepared to think laterally.

31 OCTOBER

Embrace a degree of give and take to appreciate today's events. A little mystery or trick or treating will add spice to your life!

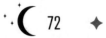

November

1 NOVEMBER

The Scorpio new moon is a particularly potent time to make a wish, for April Taureans in your personal life and for May Taureans at work. You could turn an important corner.

2 NOVEMBER

It's a good day to improve relationships, both at work and at home. You may receive key health news or have a debt repaid.

3 NOVEMBER

There are therapeutic aspects to the day and you may receive a financial or ego boost. Romance could blossom. Avoid conflict as it could fire up unexpectedly, especially at work and home.

4 NOVEMBER

This is a good day to build a solid foundation for yourself, so reach out to people who could help you do so. You may feel more energised over the coming weeks.

5 NOVEMBER

This is another day to avoid conflict, as it could escalate quickly and unexpectedly. Nevertheless, you could complete a great deal of chores.

6 NOVEMBER

Be prepared to research circumstances that don't add up, for example, financial or personal situations. An expert may be helpful in this regard.

7 NOVEMBER

You'll enjoy a get-together and deepening close relationships, so take the initiative.

8 NOVEMBER

Certain relationships and circumstances may present an unexpected hurdle, so find time to navigate around these and you could excel as a result.

9 NOVEMBER

This weekend is ideal for reviewing where you stand. You may experience an unexpected development or uncover a mystery. Romance may appeal, but avoid making assumptions.

10 NOVEMBER

Take a moment to relax and reflect, and if you've experienced a setback then plan a more stable path ahead.

11 NOVEMBER

You're good at planning, so you'll understand that you needn't be pressured or rushed into decision-making, especially in relation to money and love.

12 NOVEMBER

It's likely that you will at some point be talking at cross purposes with someone. Avoid mix-ups and delays by planning ahead and being patient.

13 NOVEMBER

You may discover your own vulnerability or that of someone close. It's a good day to talk.

14 NOVEMBER

The lead-up to the full moon in your sign can be intense. It's time to turn a corner and look ahead at ways to create stability and security, especially in your personal life.

15 NOVEMBER

The full moon in Taurus puts a spotlight on your personal life, and on work if you were born in mid-May. You may be surprised by developments.

16 NOVEMBER

You'll enjoy doing something a little different and a change of routine may even be a surprise. You may need to make a compromise with someone to avoid arguments.

17 NOVEMBER

This is a good weekend for talks and to consider how you might work on a better budget, especially if you discover you've recently overspent.

18 NOVEMBER

Key meetings, a trip or news will be important, especially in relation to finances, self-esteem, health and well-being. Be prepared to discuss your options.

19 NOVEMBER

You'll enjoy a reunion and romance could flourish, so why not organise a get-together? Work meetings will be busy but you must keep your expectations realistic.

20 NOVEMBER

As Pluto re-enters Aquarius you may experience a surge at work or a fresh opportunity in your career. Be prepared to enter new territory and be spontaneous.

21 NOVEMBER

Over the next four weeks you'll enjoy spending more time with people and activities you love. A partner may be more outgoing and motivational. You may already experience a pleasant change today.

22 NOVEMBER

This is a good day for enjoying the activities you love. You may be drawn to socialising, and if study is a drawcard a meeting could go well.

23 NOVEMBER

This is a lovely day for get-togethers and romance. You will also enjoy investing more in your home and family.

24 NOVEMBER

The moon in Virgo will motivate you to improve your home environment and the interpersonal dynamics there, and you may be drawn to gardening.

25 NOVEMBER

You're thinking clearly, a prerequisite for a happy working day, and you'll enjoy planning ahead for projects you'll enjoy. Try to tie up loose ends with paperwork and important talks before the end of the day.

26 NOVEMBER

You may receive key news from a business or personal partner. A meeting or news will be productive. Just avoid having overly high expectations.

27 NOVEMBER

Your domestic and family-related projects are likely to advance. You'll enjoy some DIY projects or investing more time in your home and environment.

28 NOVEMBER

You may receive news from the past that will require more focus so you can move forward. If advice is needed it will be available.

29 NOVEMBER

You'll enjoy the chance to discuss some of your plans with those they concern. It's a good day for a mini financial review.

30 NOVEMBER

This is likely to be an active, outgoing weekend even if you spend it at home! It's a good time to reinvest in your closest relationships as your efforts will pay off.

December

1 DECEMBER

The new moon in Sagittarius will kick-start a fresh chapter in a shared circumstance such as a business or personal partnership. It's a good time for a mini financial review.

2 DECEMBER

This is a good time to review some of your agreements and arrangements such as your daily health schedule. You may be pleasantly surprised by news at work or in your personal life.

3 DECEMBER

When the moon is in fellow earth signs Capricorn and Virgo you tend to feel more capable of getting things done, so be productive!

4 DECEMBER

A financial matter will benefit from a little focus; you may need to reconsider an arrangement or agreement. Work hard and you'll overcome any obstacles.

5 DECEMBER

It's a lovely time to devote a little extra attention to family and domestic matters. You may be ready to turn a corner there.

6 DECEMBER

Mars is turning retrograde today so you may experience a change of tempo or circumstance at home or in your personal life. It's a good day for meetings and to discuss finances.

7 DECEMBER

You're known as an earthy, practical person yet you also like to be spontaneous and outgoing on occasion. You'll enjoy a get-together, and romance and the arts will thrive.

8 DECEMBER

You'll feel inspired by a friend, group or organisation. It's a good time for self-development and improving self-esteem. Just avoid arguments that are basically a battle of egos.

9 DECEMBER

While some communications and get-togethers may be tense you have every chance to build bridges, so take the initiative.

10 DECEMBER

It's a good time for a health treat for yourself or someone close. You may be asked to help someone, and if you need advice it will be available. A romantic get-together will be enjoyable.

11 DECEMBER

A restless feel to the day needn't cause you to act irrationally. Stay centred and you'll manage to enjoy meetings and talks.

12 DECEMBER

A key meeting, either at work or in your personal life, will merit careful attention. You'll gain the results you want by not making rash decisions.

13 DECEMBER

Despite this being Friday the 13th it's a good day for a reunion and talks at work. Romance could flourish, so plan a date!

14 DECEMBER

It's a chatty day ideal for sorting out paperwork and financial issues. If you're Christmas shopping you must avoid overspending if you're already in debt.

15 DECEMBER

The full moon in Gemini shines a light on joint matters such as shared finances and space at home. Be prepared to voice your opinion and find common ground.

16 DECEMBER

The moon in Cancer brings out your more sensitive side, so trust your intuition and avoid taking things personally.

17 DECEMBER

As the excitement builds towards Christmas you'll appreciate the atmosphere. A reunion or the prospect of a change at home will merit an open mind.

18 DECEMBER

You're known for your trustworthiness but even you can be forgetful, so you must avoid having your head in the clouds. A mystery may arise.

19 DECEMBER

You'll manage to unravel misunderstandings or mysteries as you get your feet on the ground. This is a good day for financial matters. You'll enjoy a get-together or work meeting.

20 DECEMBER

A lovely social or group event will be enjoyable and could also boost morale. You may be in line for a financial improvement.

21 DECEMBER

This is the solstice. You'll appreciate the sense over the coming weeks that plans have been made and you know where you stand. If you're Christmas shopping, avoid overspending if you're in debt.

22 DECEMBER

If you'd like to discuss or make long-term changes this is a good day to do so. A shared activity or boost to your status will be pleasing.

23 DECEMBER

You will not always agree with everyone, so a little tact and diplomacy will work wonders.

24 DECEMBER

When you feel under pressure your worst characteristics emerge; try to give yourself and someone close leeway in this regard. A therapeutic get-together is on the way.

25 DECEMBER

Merry Christmas! You'll appreciate the wonderful greetings and/or sense of togetherness but you must choose your words carefully to avoid offence being taken.

26 DECEMBER

A trip or get-together will be significant. A business or personal partner will have news. If you're back at work it will be busy. However, delays are possible, so be patient.

27 DECEMBER

A get-together may be delayed. It's important to be discerning with communications to avoid disagreements or conundrums, so patience will again be necessary.

28 DECEMBER

You may be surprised by developments in your personal life or socially. A meeting may need to be rescheduled. Be prepared to work constructively towards a positive outcome.

29 DECEMBER

You'll enjoy a breath of fresh air and the chance to reconnect with someone special.

30 DECEMBER

The new moon in Capricorn points to something new for you in your activities. You're set to broaden your horizons, so plan ahead for an exciting 2025!

31 DECEMBER

Happy New Year! A strong link with your past may be therapeutic. You may decide to focus on a healthy start to 2025, which will suit you more than a long recovery on 1 January.

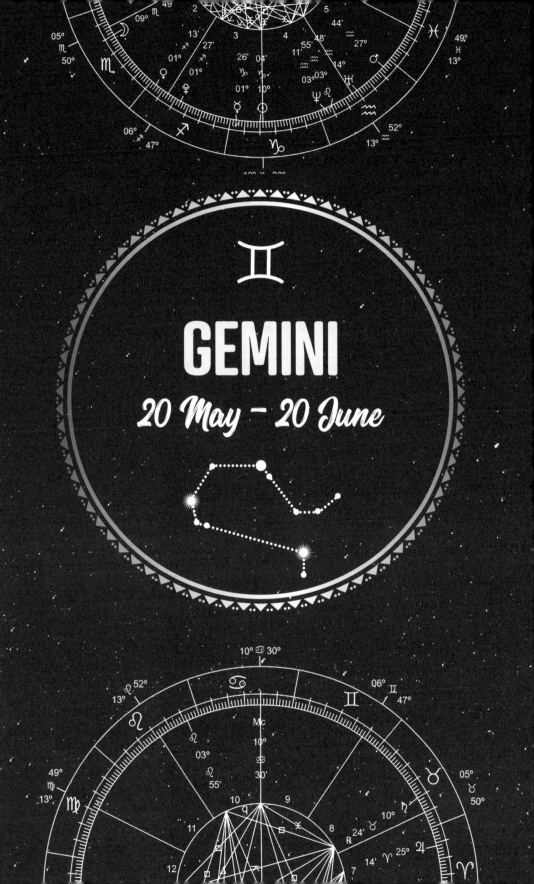

GEMINI

20 May – 20 June

FINANCES

The year 2024 is an excellent one to build wealth, although you must be wary of gambling and get-rich-quick schemes. Hard work and research into wealth creation will pay off. The first four months of the year offer the opportunity to improve your career and status, so take the initiative early as you could set yourself up for the entire year through careful planning and by being open to new opportunities. The measure of a successfully navigated financial year will come down to whether you enjoy what you do to make money. If not, this is the year to change that.

HEALTH

You'll improve your health in 2024 by being careful to schedule strength and fitness routines that suit your circumstances. If you're sedentary during work hours ensure you plan to engage in physical movement before or after your main working hours, as this invariably buoys your mood while at the same time keeping you physically fit. Otherwise, the first few months of 2024 could see you becoming idle health-wise and missing good options to stay fit. Luckily, Jupiter in your sign from the end of May onwards will add a spritz of energy and dynamism but Jupiter can also lead to overindulging, so you must avoid too much rich food or you'll discover the hard way that too much of a good thing is not so great after all!

LOVE LIFE

This will be a sociable year ideal for single Geminis to meet a varied and dynamic group of people. Couples will enjoy being more outgoing and joining new clubs. Once Jupiter enters your sign at the end of May you'll appreciate a sense of joy and abundance and, with it, increased self-confidence and the chance to broaden your horizons. The eclipses in March, April and October will be key turning points in your personal life, such as with family, and these changes will have an impact on your love life. Above all you must avoid making rash decisions in these months as you do not want to come to regret them.

CAREER

Saturn in your career sector can provide you with the stability you need. Early in the year will be ideal for establishing yourself as a force to be noticed in your field, although hard work will be necessary to do so. Luckily, January will feature every opportunity to gain attention and traction in your career, so seize the day when opportunity knocks. A word of warning: in the process of establishing and stabilising your career during the year you must avoid hemming yourself in and restricting your growth potential too much, especially later in the year in August and September. Just ensure you avoid taking on too much at once. The key to success in 2024 lies in maintaining a healthy balance.

HOME LIFE

Travel, broadening your horizons through study for example and self-development will capture much of your attention in 2024. Your home life may come a poor second to these enticing activities – that is, unless you make it your priority to find time to ground yourself and your projects so you don't lose touch with your domestic life. From mid-July through to mid-August and then November will be ideal times to invest more time and energy in your home life and family, as your efforts are likely to succeed.

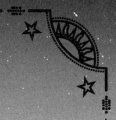

January

1 JANUARY

You'll wish to get things shipshape for the year ahead, so be patient if today's obstacles slow you down. Avoid arguments if possible.

2 JANUARY

Success does come down to good planning for you in 2024 and the first quarter is ideal for investing in yourself and those you love, so plan away today!

3 JANUARY

If your heart is not in what you're doing, take a break and work out how to get back on track. You may be surprised by how relatively easy this can be.

4 JANUARY

Financial and shared concerns will take much of your focus over the coming weeks, and today's development will give you an idea of how best to navigate these areas of your life.

5 JANUARY

You like to be passionate about what you do and you'll gain the motivation to excel. Just avoid a slight potential for arguments this morning.

6 JANUARY

No one is an island so collaboration is the key to success, even if you feel someone is not pulling their weight. A little diplomacy will work wonders.

7 JANUARY

You'll appreciate the chance to feel the wind in your sails and enjoy a little freedom of movement. Just be careful to avoid misunderstandings.

8 JANUARY

It's a good day for taking the initiative with a shared project and duties. A disagreement over a project or with an employer needn't get in your way unless you allow it to.

9 JANUARY

Keep an eye on communications and meetings to avoid making mistakes, as you or someone close may be prone to daydreaming and absent-mindedness.

10 JANUARY

You'll enjoy being spontaneous, and a work or sociable get-together will add some excitement to your day. You may hear good news from the past or a partner.

11 JANUARY

The Capricorn new moon will kick-start a fresh phase in a shared project or duty. You may need to discuss finances and long-term goals to ensure you're on track.

12 JANUARY

This is a good day to take the initiative in your business and personal relationships. Be prepared to make solid agreements and plans as they are likely to take shape.

13 JANUARY

You'll enjoy a change of pace or of place. A relationship could improve if you discuss how you see your future together in a light-hearted, positive way.

14 JANUARY

A degree of restlessness and the need for individual freedom needn't get in the way of forming solid, stable friendships and enjoying time spent with someone special.

15 JANUARY

You'll appreciate being able to develop your ideas and being inspired. It's a good time for self-development.

16 JANUARY

An inspiring group, friend or organisation will lead you to wonder if circumstances could take you somewhere ideal. Avoid forgetfulness. Romance could flourish.

17 JANUARY

The next two days are good for taking the initiative with your plans and projects, especially with the help of a friend or organisation. It's also a good time to make progress at work.

18 JANUARY

This is a good day to discuss work plans and for improving relationships with experts and people in a position of authority. You'll enjoy a get-together or news.

19 JANUARY

Meetings at work and in your personal life will thrive. You'll enjoy a reunion or return to an old haunt. However, you must avoid forgetfulness and making assumptions.

20 JANUARY

You'll enjoy the next four weeks as the sun in Aquarius will open your mind to new ideas and projects such as travel, study, collaborations and investments. However, this may be an intense day so pace yourself.

21 JANUARY

Be prepared to enter fresh territory. You may literally travel somewhere different or receive news that will take you somewhere else. Think laterally.

22 JANUARY

You may be prepared to set in motion ideas and plans you floated in 2023. If you're unsure about your decision, consider where your values lie and follow these.

23 JANUARY

Take things one step at a time, especially with your financial investments, collaborations and, for some Geminis, financially. Be practical above all with romantic decisions.

24 JANUARY

As an analytical person you tend to discount your intuition yet it is strong, so be sure to trust your hunches. Avoid making snap decisions.

25 JANUARY

The Leo full moon will spotlight your general direction in life and important decisions that must be made to do with your career or status. Avoid making snap decisions you'll regret.

26 JANUARY

This is a good time to seek the advice of an expert, and your support and advice may be needed. Show tact with a group, friend or organisation for the best results.

27 JANUARY

Key news or a meeting will take your focus. For some Geminis this will be in connection with finance and for others a personal matter. Try to find common ground and progress from there.

28 JANUARY

This is a good day for discussions with someone close and to overcome past differences. You could make a valid financial or career plan. It's a good day to make a romantic commitment.

29 JANUARY

You'll enjoy being with like-minded people. You may be drawn to spontaneous travel or organising a meeting you know you'll love.

30 JANUARY

The peace and harmony you're looking for in your personal life is possible. If you need someone's collaboration it's a good day to take the initiative to find common ground.

31 JANUARY

Be realistic about the kinds of agreements you can make. You may feel particularly sensitive or emotional, so take breaks if you feel overwhelmed.

February

1 FEBRUARY

The next two days are ideal for finding ways to collaborate and co-operate with someone you must get on with. You'll enjoy the arts and socialising.

2 FEBRUARY

You'll appreciate the opportunity to relax and a favourite activity or meeting. Romance could flourish.

3 FEBRUARY

You'll be drawn to being busy and will enjoy time out with friends and doing your favourite activities. A change of pace will feel refreshing and re-energising.

4 FEBRUARY

If you're feeling a little restless, find ways to channel excess energy into favourite activities such as sport. It's a good day to get on top of outstanding chores.

5 FEBRUARY

You tend to live on your nerves so you must avoid overworking. Aim to multitask to get on top of a busy schedule. If some news is intense, look for ways to de-escalate stress.

6 FEBRUARY

You or someone close may be stubborn without realising it, so look for room to move if you feel you're at a stalemate. You'll uncover an original solution.

7 FEBRUARY

You may be surprised by news from the past or a reunion. Look for inspiring activities that will help you get out of a rut if necessary.

8 FEBRUARY

You may experience an unexpected change of schedule or surprise at work. Find a path to getting on top of changes in a down-to-earth way.

9 FEBRUARY

The Aquarian new moon supermoon will shine a light on your status, career and general direction. It's a good time for meetings and financial commitments but you must be prepared to think laterally.

10 FEBRUARY

You'll enjoy a different weekend from your usual one, even if it's because your routine is disrupted or due to a chore. It is said that a change is as good as a holiday!

11 FEBRUARY

You'll appreciate the chance to relax and gather your thoughts, so ensure you find space for yourself. You may be surprised by relationship developments.

12 FEBRUARY

You'll enjoy socialising, networking and spending time with like-minded people. Be prepared to adapt to new circumstances or a fresh project.

13 FEBRUARY

You'll be entering fresh territory and it may at first seem a challenge, but rest assured you will find a way to connect with people. Romance could blossom.

14 FEBRUARY

Happy St Valentine's Day! This may be an intense day, so ensure you pace yourself. A project or favourite activity will absorb your focus but you must avoid arguments.

15 FEBRUARY

When the moon is in Taurus you'll look for peace and calmness and the chance to review your circumstances. Romance could flourish this evening, so organise a date.

16 FEBRUARY

Your life and activities are taking you into fresh territory, which you'll enjoy even if it is slightly disorienting at first. Be innovative.

17 FEBRUARY

You'll enjoy visiting somewhere beautiful and bringing more romance, creativity and enjoyment into your life. Avoid adding to an intense circumstance if you feel stress is bubbling up.

18 FEBRUARY

You'll enjoy being upbeat, chatty and sociable, but you'll also appreciate time out to collect your thoughts.

19 FEBRUARY

A circumstance is going to bring out your sensitivity or that of someone close, so be prepared to step lightly. Your expertise may be in demand.

20 FEBRUARY

The Cancerian moon may bring out your indecision, making hard and fast decisions about long-term choices difficult. Trust your gut feelings.

21 FEBRUARY

You'll be feeling adventurous and ready to embrace new ideas, but your emotions may hold you back. Be sure to be courageous, as you can succeed with your projects.

22 FEBRUARY

A trip, visit, study or the chance to embrace fresh activities will be appealing. Ensure you have done your research, then take a step into something new!

23 FEBRUARY

You're better known as an analytical thinker than an intuitive character, but now that Mercury is in Pisces you may find your instincts are much clearer for a few weeks.

24 FEBRUARY

The full moon in Virgo will shine a light on your personal, family, domestic and creative lives. It's a good time to be inspired but to also be practical concerning matters close to home.

25 FEBRUARY

Be practical and think of the most reasonable way to clear chores, because when you do you'll also be able to formulate plans based on inspiration and abstract ideas.

26 FEBRUARY

You present as an upbeat, innovative person at the moment even if you don't feel that way! Trust that your plans and ideas can be effective and take the initiative.

27 FEBRUARY

Wouldn't it be lovely to click your fingers and have all your work done? Unfortunately, that can't be, so it's a case of hard work and patience being virtues.

28 FEBRUARY

You're in a much stronger position than you realise, so be prepared to shine. Avoid hiding your light simply because someone else believes you or they are worth less than you are.

29 FEBRUARY

You'll enjoy a friendly get-together. Work and projects could advance and romance could flourish. Singles may meet someone who seems familiar even if you've never met before.

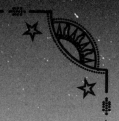

March

1 MARCH

This is a lovely day for both work and personal get-togethers. You may make a valid agreement or commitment. There are therapeutic aspects to the day.

2 MARCH

You'll enjoy an upbeat and productive day with a focus on enjoying life. However, if you've been fatigued it's important you find time to rest.

3 MARCH

You may experience a sudden change of plan or will need to reschedule a planned activity. You may receive unexpected news.

4 MARCH

You have your ideals, and they will not automatically match everyone else's. Be amenable, as you are more likely to be accepted even if your ideas are different.

5 MARCH

If you're looking for work or a promotion this is a good time to reach out to employers, organisations and groups as your efforts will be successful. You'll enjoy a meeting.

6 MARCH

You're likely to receive good news from a friend or organisation, especially if you didn't get it yesterday. It's a good day for a health or well-being appointment.

7 MARCH

Your ideas and work are likely to be well received, and it's a good day to be making headway with your plans and projects. You'll enjoy a trip somewhere beautiful.

8 MARCH

You'll enjoy socialising and networking. It's a good day for the arts and spiritual and self-development.

9 MARCH

You'll be busy, especially if you're working. It's a good day to get chores done and for indulging in the arts, romance and creativity. Avoid forgetfulness.

10 MARCH

The Pisces new moon supermoon will be inspiring. It's a good time to begin a shared project or collaboration and transform the way you share joint duties or space.

11 MARCH

Be prepared to take your ideas and projects from the drawing board and put them into action.

12 MARCH

You'll be feeling proactive and prepared to take the bull by the horns. Be ready also to collaborate or you may tend to appear bossy.

13 MARCH

This is a good day to make changes in your work calendar or activities. You'll enjoy going somewhere new with someone special.

14 MARCH

A grounded, earthy approach to work and your chores will produce excellent results. Be practical; just avoid stubbornness.

15 MARCH

You feel in your element when the moon is in your sign, as your communication skills are usually on top form. You'll enjoy a reunion or catch-up by phone with someone special.

16 MARCH

Working Twins will be busy. You'll appreciate the chance to catch up on chores. It's a good day to focus on devising a budget if you've overspent.

17 MARCH

This is a super sociable and potentially also a romantic day, so why not organise a treat? If you're single you may meet someone attractive. It's a good day for spiritual and self-development.

18 MARCH

You'll instinctively know if something doesn't sound right, so trust your intuition. A reunion or the need to review a project will engage your mind.

19 MARCH

It's a good day to take the helm at work and motivate both yourself and others to do your/their best. Just avoid cutting corners and rushing.

20 MARCH

You'll feel more outgoing socially over the coming few weeks, even if today you feel sensitive or unsure of yourself. Be brave and stride ahead even if you feel vulnerable.

21 MARCH

This is a good day to make a commitment to a work project or a long-term change in your career or direction.

22 MARCH

You'll feel increasingly inspired by your activities and ventures over the next five weeks, so if you've been considering a new idea take the initiative.

23 MARCH

News from your past or the chance to reconnect with an old haunt will appeal. You may learn something at work or via a friend or organisation.

24 MARCH

It's a good day to choose your activities wisely, as you may otherwise go with the flow and feel as a result that the day hasn't been yours to enjoy.

25 MARCH

The lunar eclipse will spotlight long-term plans, which are best supported by research. You'll feel more able to follow through with your ideas once you know where you stand.

26 MARCH

A friend or colleague may need your help. If you're looking for expert advice it will be available, so reach out.

27 MARCH

You'll feel increasingly motivated at work and by your activities as the day goes by, so be prepared to work hard. Just avoid exhausting yourself.

28 MARCH

You'll enjoy an impromptu get-together or the chance to do something different. You may receive unexpected news.

29 MARCH

There will be inspiring aspects to the day. Just ensure you collaborate and co-operate with others as well as you can to avoid difficulties.

30 MARCH

An outgoing and adventurous approach to your weekend will be productive. Activities with a friend, group or organisation will keep you motivated.

31 MARCH

This is a good day to get up to date with your paperwork and put in place a solid health and fitness routine so you feel shipshape when Mercury goes retrograde on Tuesday.

April

1 APRIL

This is a good day for research and to ensure you have your taxes, finances and general paperwork and agreements in place. Try to get any new arrangements on the table before tomorrow.

2 APRIL

You may receive key news at work or concerning health. It's a good time over the coming weeks to focus on building a healthy daily work and fitness schedule.

3 APRIL

You'll feel inspired by a friend or organisation. The arts, film and music will appeal. This is a lovely day for a romantic get-together.

4 APRIL

A reunion or return to an old haunt may be more significant than meets the eye. It's a good day for a get-together, as you may make a deep impression.

5 APRIL

As Venus enters Aries it's a good time to schedule more socialising and networking, as you'll feel more upbeat and outgoing over the coming weeks.

6 APRIL

The Pisces moon will bring out your romantic or even nostalgic qualities. You have a strong connection with the past and a certain group or organisation right now.

7 APRIL

You'll enjoy socialising and networking but may be prone to over-romanticise a situation. Nevertheless, you'll enjoy daydreaming!

8 APRIL

The total solar eclipse signifies a fresh start involving someone special such as a work colleague, friend or organisation. You may feel vulnerable even if your circumstances are promising. Look for the positives in health news.

9 APRIL

Be prepared to move forward and let your vulnerabilities fall away. You may be asked to help someone, and if you need support it is available.

10 APRIL

You may be surprised by news and must avoid a knee-jerk or uninformed reaction to events. Be inspired and do your research for the best results.

11 APRIL

You'll enjoy reconnecting with someone and finding out a little more about your options moving forward. You may simply enjoy socialising. It's a good day to talk.

12 APRIL

The Gemini moon will bring out your feelings and you may even surprise yourself with some of your thoughts. You'll appreciate a lovely get-together. Romance could flourish.

13 APRIL

A sociable weekend will appeal, as you'll enjoy discussing your ideas and meeting like-minded people or groups or visiting galleries, cinemas or clubs. You may manage to heal a relationship.

14 APRIL

You'll enjoy connecting with someone special but you won't suffer fools gladly this weekend, so choose your company carefully!

15 APRIL

You'll need to review a situation or get-together that may put you in a vulnerable frame of mind. Be strong and trust your luck and gut instincts.

16 APRIL

It's a good day to take the initiative with talks and meetings to ensure your ideas are heard.

17 APRIL

You'll enjoy hearing from or catching up with someone from your past. You'll appreciate the opportunity to indulge in a favourite pastime. An expert may be super helpful.

18 APRIL

As an air sign you like to think things through, yet you'll enjoy impromptu get-togethers today. Just avoid making snap decisions about long-term matters.

19 APRIL

As the sun enters Taurus you'll appreciate the sense that a little more stability will be attainable in your life, yet you'll also enjoy being socially spontaneous.

20 APRIL

This is a good day to be inspired by what you do, so choose your activities carefully. The arts, music and enjoying good company will appeal.

21 APRIL

You may experience an unexpected change of plan and activities may be delayed. It's a good time to look after your health and well-being. You'll enjoy an impromptu get-together.

22 APRIL

As an adaptable person you'll find ways to alter your usual routine so it suits you well. You may receive unexpected news.

23 APRIL

You'll be drawn to looking for balance in your daily routine, at work and health-wise. Just avoid exhausting yourself with overwork or trying to establish a fresh health routine. Pace yourself.

24 APRIL

The Scorpio full moon will spotlight a fresh daily routine that could mean less chaos and more security. But if it means the opposite, it's important to discuss your concerns with those they involve.

25 APRIL

A group, friend or organisation will have important news for you. It's a good day to talk as the Mercury retrograde phase ends.

26 APRIL

You'll appreciate being proactive at work and meeting your deadlines. A fun event in the evening will appeal as a way to unwind.

27 APRIL

Being with like-minded people will keep you active. It's a good weekend for socialising and networking.

28 APRIL

This is a lovely day for romance and to relax. Music, the arts, meeting favourite people and unwinding will be enjoyable.

29 APRIL

As Venus enters Taurus you'll be drawn to creature comforts and sensual delights, so romance could be prevalent over the coming weeks.

30 APRIL

Proactive and upbeat Mars will encourage you to be more outgoing in all areas of your life over the coming weeks. You'll feel re-energised but must avoid fatigue and appearing bossy.

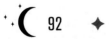

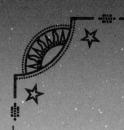
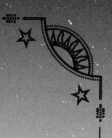

May

1 MAY

Today's tense stand-off between Venus and Pluto will motivate you to be productive although arguments are also likely, so be prepared if possible to find common ground.

2 MAY

This may be another intense day, especially in relation to work or a favourite project. Avoid feeling under pressure and find ways to de-stress.

3 MAY

It's a good day to press ahead with your ventures. You'll enjoy socialising and networking.

4 MAY

A friend, colleague or family member will inspire you to engage in activities you love. The arts, romance and relaxing will appeal.

5 MAY

You'll enjoy a reunion or return to an old haunt. You may hear from an old friend.

6 MAY

It's a good day to schedule in favourite activities for later in the week and to plan productive breaks and meetings. A little planning will go a long way.

7 MAY

You'll be productive even if you have a lot on your plate. It's a good day to mend bridges with people you've argued with recently. A group or friend will prove helpful.

8 MAY

The Taurus new moon will kick-start a fresh work or health cycle. Be prepared to schedule a productive daily routine that includes time for fitness and self-nurture.

9 MAY

You'll appreciate feeling more in your element over the next two days, especially with communications and relationships.

10 MAY

Be prepared to collaborate with someone in authority as opposed to feeling you're an adversary, or arguments could arise. You'll enjoy socialising later in the day.

11 MAY

You'll enjoy a little self-nurture, pampering or looking for a new outfit. You'll appreciate the chance to reconnect with someone special.

12 MAY

The moon in Cancer will draw your attention to your values, principles and money. You'll find ways to overcome a difference of opinion. It's a good day for a mini financial review.

13 MAY

A surprise development needn't be a spanner in the works. You'll find a way to work productively with circumstances outside your control.

14 MAY

An outgoing, upbeat approach to people in your social group or at work will be productive. You'll enjoy taking the lead if need be.

15 MAY

Be sure to trust your intuition over the coming few weeks, as you'll be picking up hidden or underlying information more readily. Work discussions will merit focus.

16 MAY

This is a good day to turn your mind to your home life, relationships and agreements. You may be liable to misunderstand someone, so be super discerning and clear.

17 MAY

Factor in a little more time for your usual trip and be sure to avoid misunderstandings and ego battles, as they may be prevalent. Avoid making rash decisions.

18 MAY

You'll enjoy a reunion or return to a familiar place. It's a good day for a mini health or financial review. If you're shopping avoid overspending, especially if you're already in debt.

19 MAY

This is a romantic time and you'll enjoy socialising, music, film and the arts. Prepare to relax at the end of the day!

20 MAY

Prepare to feel more energised over the coming weeks, and if you feel you've lost your mojo you'll find it again. A meeting or chat may be sudden or motivational.

21 MAY

You'll enjoy feeling motivated to get things done and possibly passionate about a project. Keep things in perspective for the best results.

22 MAY

This is an excellent time to make changes at work or your general direction and in your status and favourite activities. Be proactive and positive!

23 MAY

The full moon in Sagittarius spotlights a fresh chapter in your daily health or work routine. You may receive key news that could be ideal. A debt may be repaid.

24 MAY

Be adventurous at work and with your favourite activities as you could be super productive and effective.

25 MAY

The Venus–Pluto aspect this weekend is ideal for making positive changes in your life. You'll appreciate the chance to touch base with like-minded people. Romance could flourish.

26 MAY

As Jupiter enters your sign it's time to be optimistic, especially in connection with the past, your work, productivity and relationships. Romance could flourish, so plan a date!

27 MAY

You're thinking outside the box, which will be useful at work and with new arrangements you'd like to make. Just avoid rushing as you may make minor errors.

28 MAY

This is a good day for talks and meetings in association with work, finances and health. A debt may be repaid.

29 MAY

You may be called on for help or be under pressure. If you need support at work, ensure you ask for it or delegate chores. It's a good day for a health appointment.

30 MAY

You'll get the information you're looking for, so be prepared to do some research. You can progress and improve your health and well-being, so take the initiative.

31 MAY

You'll be feeling inspired, which will motivate you to succeed with your endeavours. Music, the arts and spiritual development will appeal.

June

1 JUNE

You'll enjoy being spontaneous and may take to the road to meet someone whose company you enjoy. You may bump into someone unexpectedly.

2 JUNE

You'll enjoy being outgoing, socialising and being with like-minded people, so take the initiative!

3 JUNE

It's a good time to make changes, especially in your personal life via travel, education or legal matters. You may be drawn to expanding your self-knowledge.

4 JUNE

It's a lovely day to meet new people and for discussions and developing a deeper interest in your hobbies and pastimes. Romance could also blossom.

5 JUNE

The lead-up to the new moon in your sign is an excellent time to make a wish, as it will come true – so be careful what you wish for!

6 JUNE

The new moon brings your focus on love, money, romance and the arts. If you were born later in June it's a good time to begin a fresh work or health routine. Avoid power struggles.

7 JUNE

You'll feel motivated to succeed with your projects. You'll also enjoy socialising and networking. Just avoid being at loggerheads with someone in authority and trust your instincts.

8 JUNE

While this is a time of transformation, it's important to find the right experts and advisers. Avoid a battle of egos and be prepared to carefully consider a financial investment.

9 JUNE

Consider whether a difference of opinion stems from contrasting values, not alternate plans or expectations. Avoid a Mexican stand-off and conflict as it could turn into a stalemate.

10 JUNE

You're communicating clearly although others may not be, so be sure to establish common goals. Channel excess energy into sports and constructive activities and avoid impulsiveness.

11 JUNE

There are therapeutic aspects to the day. Take the initiative to smooth over disagreements. You may be drawn to a beauty or health treat.

12 JUNE

Tread carefully with a personal or work matter. Choose your words carefully. Avoid making assumptions and ensure you check your facts, especially financially.

13 JUNE

It's a good day for an impromptu get-together. You may hear unexpected news. You may be surprised by a financial or personal improvement.

14 JUNE

It's a good day for talks and meetings but you must be prepared to work hard to get the results you want. You'll gain clarity about a health situation.

15 JUNE

You'll enjoy being spontaneous and organising a reunion. Someone's news will surprise you. A matter from your past may be unexpected.

16 JUNE

You'll find out whether you've overestimated someone. Avoid absent-mindedness, overindulgence and overspending, which you'll regret. Someone will be helpful, so reach out for advice.

17 JUNE

You may need to be super clear about where you stand, especially with someone you miss or who has revealed new information. A key meeting and travel may be delayed.

18 JUNE

You may tend to be a little idealistic or have your head in the clouds, so take time out to focus on your goals.

19 JUNE

A proactive approach to your daily chores and general goals will be productive. Avoid romanticising or glamorising a person or organisation, as you may be easily misled.

20 JUNE

The solstice is a lovely time to consider how far you've come this year. Be sure to put some goals into the month ahead. Find the time to research a mystery if necessary.

21 JUNE

This is a good time to talk and for financial improvements. However, you mustn't underestimate your romantic and financial worth.

22 JUNE

The full moon in Capricorn suggests you're ready to turn a page in a business or personal partnership. Be prepared to work toward your goals. It's a good day to talk and pay off a debt.

23 JUNE

The delicate art of negotiation will be a skill set to embrace as you won't always get on with everyone. Work hard to overcome differences and you will.

24 JUNE

Be innovative and resourceful, as you could make great progress with a project.

25 JUNE

This is a good day to collaborate and think creatively with colleagues, friends and family so you can work together to create the results you want.

26 JUNE

You can break the pattern of tense communications with a friend or organisation and may be surprised by the outcome. Just avoid pushing your values onto others.

27 JUNE

You'll be drawn to socialising and networking and may feel more empathetic towards others. Trust your instincts, as they are spot on.

28 JUNE

Certain topics may be off limits, so avoid opening Pandora's box and especially if your principles or values differ from those of someone close. Be prepared to focus on health and well-being.

29 JUNE

You'll enjoy a lovely meeting, reunion or return to an old haunt. Romance could blossom, so take the initiative.

30 JUNE

You'll enjoy an impromptu trip or get-together and may be surprised by news you receive. Be open to experiencing something different!

July

1 JULY

While you're known to be a quick thinker and can be fidgety, you'll prefer taking things one step at a time today. You'll avoid tricky conversations as a result.

2 JULY

You're likely to feel more outspoken over the coming weeks. Just be careful not to inadvertently cause offence.

3 JULY

This is a good day for talks with a friend, group or organisation, but you must avoid entering intense conversations as these are likely to escalate.

4 JULY

The lead-up to the Cancerian new moon is an ideal time to take stock of your finances and feelings. Could you invest your time and energy better? If so, now's the time to make changes.

5 JULY

The Cancerian new moon is a good time to begin fresh ways of bringing more nurturance into your life via good relationships and financial planning. You may be drawn to making a different agreement.

6 JULY

You'll enjoy being proactive about long-term plans with a view to creating a more nurturing health routine. If you need expert advice it is available, so reach out.

7 JULY

You'll enjoy socialising and will appreciate the company of someone who understands you. If you need a day off this is an ideal day for a rest.

8 JULY

You may receive positive news and will enjoy a get-together with someone you feel close to.

9 JULY

The next few days are ideal for deepening your relationship with someone at home or at work. It's a good time for decluttering and a tidy up.

10 JULY

You're communicating well so you can achieve the goals you have that involve collaboration and co-operation.

11 JULY

You'll be drawn to being more outgoing and travel and adventure will appeal. Just plan ahead well to avoid making hasty decisions.

12 JULY

Communications and travel may be intense, so take things one step at a time and plan well ahead to avoid travel delays. Romance could ignite but so too could conflict.

13 JULY

You'll appreciate the chance to get things shipshape at home. You'll manage to digest recent developments and establish a positive frame of mind moving forward.

14 JULY

You'll enjoy finding time for a favourite activity but may need to alter your usual routine to accommodate it. Find the time to self-nurture.

15 JULY

You may need to adapt to someone else's demands as a sudden change of plan arises. If you need help it is available. Your expertise is also likely to be in demand.

16 JULY

You'll feel motivated to get on with your chores. You may once again need to adapt to the demands of the day but will be well equipped to do so.

17 JULY

As an air sign you can tend to analyse events so they make sense, and you are well placed to adapt to disruptions. Just avoid living off your nerves.

18 JULY

You may experience a surprise at work or in your personal life. A debt may be repaid. It's a good time to be spontaneous and adventurous.

19 JULY

There are therapeutic aspects to the day. You may be drawn to DIY projects or improving domestic dynamics. It's a good time to build bridges with someone you have fallen out with.

20 JULY

As Mars enters your sign you'll gain a sense of vitality over the coming weeks but may be prone to fiery or rash behaviour.

21 JULY

The full moon in Capricorn will spotlight the shared areas of your life such as joint finances and duties. It's a good time for planning and limiting disruptions. Romance could flourish.

22 JULY

This is likely to be a busy day, so you'll be on your toes. You'll feel more energised, which will help you get things done.

23 JULY

It's a good time for collaborations. Avoid power struggles and taking someone's intense personality personally. A financial matter may be rectified.

24 JULY

The Pisces moon will be inspiring but you may also be a perfectionist, so bear in mind the realities of your circumstances and don't lose track of your goals.

25 JULY

You may be inclined to look at the details to the detriment of the bigger picture either at home or in your social life, so be sure to maintain perspective.

26 JULY

This is a good day for talks and meetings, both at work and socially. Be proactive and positive.

27 JULY

You'll manage to attain your goals but must be careful with communications, especially at home or with family. Work together as a team with someone close.

28 JULY

The moon in your 12th house will encourage you to rest and recuperate and take time out for yourself. If you're working, you'll enjoy cocooning later today.

29 JULY

This is a productive time for you that is ideal for work and projects, but you must avoid overstretching yourself.

30 JULY

You'll appreciate the opportunity to focus a little more on your home life and family. A trip or visit could be therapeutic.

31 JULY

A friend or organisation may prove to be particularly influential or helpful, so if you need help around the house or at work reach out.

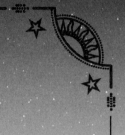

August

1 AUGUST

A change in your usual routine may be unexpected but rest assured: someone will step in to help if necessary.

2 AUGUST

You may need to choose between work and domestic duties, as time spent doing one or the other could take more time than you'd hoped. A friend or organisation will prove supportive.

3 AUGUST

The lead-up to a new moon is a good time to make a wish. It's important to choose your words carefully to avoid causing offence.

4 AUGUST

The Leo new moon spotlights your communications and travel options. You may be ready to upgrade a device or vehicle. Take a moment to get paperwork shipshape.

5 AUGUST

You may hear key news regarding property or someone close. Try to get key paperwork and agreements on the table to avoid having to review it at a later date.

6 AUGUST

This is still a sensitive time when power struggles may bubble up, so be sure to avoid contentious topics.

7 AUGUST

This is a more upbeat day and you may receive good news at work or financially. A trip will be enjoyable.

8 AUGUST

You'll enjoy a reunion or positive development at home or with family. You'll appreciate romance, the arts and music. You may review or revise a domestic decision.

9 AUGUST

You're a good thinker, and this is a beneficial time to uncover a solution to a problem and find peace and harmony, both for yourself and others.

10 AUGUST

The moon in Scorpio will bring out your passionate and sensual sides and you'll be drawn to enjoying creativity, the arts and music.

11 AUGUST

You may find that chores or work get in the way of your restful Sunday, so if they're unavoidable get them done early so you can enjoy the day!

12 AUGUST

A proactive interest in your work will bring good results your way, even if you begin the day feeling more like having a holiday.

13 AUGUST

This is a lovely day to invest in your well-being and that of those close to you. You may need to focus a little harder on your goals, but your efforts will be worthwhile.

14 AUGUST

This is a good day to take the initiative both at home and at work, but if some talks and interactions are tense then look for common ground.

15 AUGUST

You'll find ways to remedy circumstances, especially at home. Avoid making assumptions. It's a good day to overcome hurdles, so be resourceful.

16 AUGUST

You're a powerhouse at the moment but others may not be moving at your speed, so be patient. Ensure you research facts carefully if you're considering a large investment.

17 AUGUST

Slowly and carefully wins the day, so be prepared to plan your weekend and find ways to bring a little innovation into it.

18 AUGUST

You may be surprised by someone's news that alters an agreement or routine. A snap change of plan may arise, so look for ways to build another plan.

19 AUGUST

The Aquarian full moon will spotlight your direction in your life, career and status. You may enjoy a change at home or a reunion. Just avoid arguments; build security instead.

20 AUGUST

The full moon may spotlight certain relationships you have outgrown. For some these may be at work and in your career, so be prepared to take optimistic action.

21 AUGUST

You'll find out whether you've been super idealistic about a work or personal matter. A course correction will get you back on track.

22 AUGUST

The sun will spotlight your domestic life and communications for the next four weeks. Consider bringing more order into your life and be prepared to work towards this end.

23 AUGUST

This is a good day for a reunion or return to an old haunt. It's also a good time to choose your company and activities carefully. Avoid arguments.

24 AUGUST

You'll appreciate being proactive about domestic improvements. You may be drawn to travelling. You'll enjoy creating a time of healing and calm in your environment.

25 AUGUST

You'll be drawn to creature comforts and to boosting your sense of stability. This could also be a sensual and romantic time, so consider organising a treat.

26 AUGUST

The moon in Gemini puts you in your element and communications will flow. Just be wary of assuming everyone else is on the same page as you.

27 AUGUST

You'll enjoy a surprise from the past such as good news you've been waiting for. You may bump into an old friend or experience a boost in self-esteem.

28 AUGUST

News at home concerning someone close will be relevant, and you'll gain the chance to further explore a relationship. Romance could blossom, so organise a date.

29 AUGUST

You'll be looking for peace and are likely to find it. You may experience a positive development in your personal life, but if not look for ways to calm the waters.

30 AUGUST

The moon in Leo brings out your playful, light-hearted side. This will encourage you to socialise and network, which you'll enjoy.

31 AUGUST

You may have a surprise if you're working or will bump into an old friend. An unexpected or impromptu change of pace will be enjoyable. Just avoid making rash decisions.

September

1 SEPTEMBER

It's a good time to review your general direction, status and career and whether these support your family and personal lives. If not it's time for a fresh appraisal.

2 SEPTEMBER

You'll appreciate the chance to bring a little healing into your domestic or work life. Consider how you could make your daily routine healthier.

3 SEPTEMBER

This new moon in Virgo is a good time to consider improving family dynamics or a personal involvement. Consider whether practicalities need to be sorted out before expectations can be met.

4 SEPTEMBER

A key meeting or news will be significant and will provide insight into your best way forward financially or in your personal life.

5 SEPTEMBER

The moon in Libra will encourage you to find more balance in your daily life and look for peace of mind.

6 SEPTEMBER

You'll enjoy the company of like-minded people, although you may feel that you must go out on a limb to help someone or to be heard. Your efforts will be worthwhile.

7 SEPTEMBER

You'll feel drawn to favourite places, people and activities. A little effort will be required to gain the results you want but you will succeed.

8 SEPTEMBER

A social event or meeting may require more effort than you'd hoped, although this is a good time to make a commitment to a plan of action or to a person, so be optimistic.

9 SEPTEMBER

A detailed approach to your ventures and projects will pay off, so be prepared to go the extra mile.

10 SEPTEMBER

You'll enjoy being outgoing and will be productive but would be wise to avoid arguments with someone in a position of authority.

11 SEPTEMBER

A creative, social or personal project can go well, and if you encounter a minor hiccup you will overcome it. Avoid emotional and financial gambling.

12 SEPTEMBER

You have a larger-than-life personality right now, which adds to an optimistic outlook, but you must avoid arguments. Focus instead on good communication skills.

13 SEPTEMBER

This is a good day to be practical and realistic with projects to get them done in good time. You'll enjoy touching base with someone you admire.

14 SEPTEMBER

A change of pace or of place is as good as a holiday, and you'll appreciate the opportunity to spend an uplifting time in good company.

15 SEPTEMBER

A change in your usual activities and the chance to do something different will breathe fresh air into interpersonal dynamics.

16 SEPTEMBER

Take a moment to consider your long-term plans and then make tracks to fulfil goals. Just be careful to put the health and well-being of yourself and those close to you first.

17 SEPTEMBER

You'll appreciate the opportunity to dream a little and enjoy lovely company. The arts, music and socialising will appeal. Just avoid being absent-minded.

18 SEPTEMBER

The partial lunar eclipse supermoon in Pisces spotlights your hopes: will you follow your dreams or choose a down-to-earth path? Choose carefully, although both paths may converge.

19 SEPTEMBER

You'll enjoy news from your past or a reunion with family or a friend.

20 SEPTEMBER

Important matters will deserve clear focus yet you may lack clarity about your circumstances, so be prepared to undertake research.

21 SEPTEMBER

You'll enjoy music, the arts and romance, so organise a special treat. You may be prone to misunderstandings, so be prepared to dig deep to avoid mix-ups.

22 SEPTEMBER

You'll appreciate the sense that your projects and personal relationships can gain a more even keel. It's a good time to bring extra peace and harmony into your life.

23 SEPTEMBER

The moon in your sign will bring out your chatty side, but you must be careful to focus on work as you may be easily distracted.

24 SEPTEMBER

This is a good time to make strong connections both with colleagues and at home. An interest such as a hobby could flourish.

25 SEPTEMBER

You're thinking laterally and creatively, which is ideal for artistic work. Romance will appeal; just avoid misunderstandings.

26 SEPTEMBER

This is a good day for meetings and to engage in activities you love. A hobby or favourite activity can flourish, so take the initiative. A trip may be transformative.

27 SEPTEMBER

You'll enjoy being outgoing and upbeat and will appreciate the chance to reconnect with someone special.

28 SEPTEMBER

This is an excellent weekend for a lovely reunion and family time. You may reconnect with someone special.

29 SEPTEMBER

Take the initiative with your plans and projects as you're likely to succeed. A shopping trip will be enjoyable, but you must avoid overspending. A reunion will be memorable.

30 SEPTEMBER

You'll enjoy catching up with paperwork and feeling that you can have a positive effect on your environment, at work and with the people you love.

October

1 OCTOBER

The lead-up to this new moon is a good time to set your intentions for the future, especially regarding your family, personal life and creativity.

2 OCTOBER

The solar eclipse in Libra will help you turn a corner in your personal life and creativity, so be sure to look for ways to allow your love life and family relationships to flourish.

3 OCTOBER

This is a lovely day for meetings, both in your personal life and at work. It's also a good day to treat yourself to a new look or outfit.

4 OCTOBER

This is an excellent time to get ahead at work, so be sure to take the initiative and be prepared to socialise and network. A work meeting will be productive.

5 OCTOBER

You'll feel motivated to enjoy your weekend to the max. Agreements and commitments made now could be transformative.

6 OCTOBER

There may be some tension in your interactions, so be prepared to look for common ground and avoid arguments. This aside, it's another good day to enjoy life.

7 OCTOBER

An upbeat start to the week will be motivational and you can certainly get a lot done. Just avoid misunderstandings and delays by planning ahead.

8 OCTOBER

You'll enjoy get-togethers. It's a good day for a health appointment. Someone may need your help, and if you need advice it will be available. A financial situation will merit attention.

9 OCTOBER

You can truly steam ahead at work and make your mark. Just be sure to be super clear to avoid mix-ups and making mistakes.

10 OCTOBER

The Capricorn moon helps you to keep your feet on the ground, which will be useful as hard work and application will certainly pay off. A beauty or health matter will deserve focus.

11 OCTOBER

Be prepared to think on your feet, as your ability to multitask will be in demand. Your efforts will be worthwhile.

12 OCTOBER

Keep an eye on details as you may tend to over-romanticise some circumstances. If you're shopping avoid overspending, as you'll regret it.

13 OCTOBER

You're likely to feel passionately about a principle or person. Choose your words carefully, as someone close may be feeling sensitive or will take exception.

14 OCTOBER

Embrace tact and diplomacy for the best results, otherwise a hastily spoken work taken out of context could land you in hot water. You'll enjoy a change of pace or of place.

15 OCTOBER

You'll feel in your element with a group or organisation and could impress. You have charm on your side, so why not dress up to match your mood?

16 OCTOBER

This is a good day to be optimistic about your abilities, especially if you must work with a group or organisation you're unfamiliar with. Romance and the arts will appeal.

17 OCTOBER

The full moon supermoon in Aries spells a busy time for you in your personal and/or social lives. You'll enjoy meeting new people and being more adventurous at work.

18 OCTOBER

You'll appreciate being able to slow things down slightly and, at the least, getting your work and chores on a more even keel.

19 OCTOBER

Be prepared to alter your course or expectations to work with other people's timetables. You may be surprised by news or a change of circumstance.

20 OCTOBER

You'll enjoy indulging in your favourite pastimes but may again need to factor other people's needs into your day. Nevertheless, you will appreciate the outcome.

21 OCTOBER

Trust your instincts and take action if it feels right. If not, you may wish to do a little more research into your choices and circumstances before making a commitment.

22 OCTOBER

As the sun enters Scorpio, the next four weeks will feel more passionate. Someone close may have intense news. Avoid arguments, as they will escalate.

23 OCTOBER

You'll enjoy meetings and socialising. If you're single you may meet someone who seems compatible. It's a good day to reach out for help from an expert if needed.

24 OCTOBER

An upbeat and optimistic approach to your chores and communications will be rewarding.

25 OCTOBER

You'll enjoy being spontaneous and will find the time to adapt to a different schedule. You may also enjoy an impromptu get-together.

26 OCTOBER

You'll appreciate the opportunity to make changes at home. A trip somewhere different or a visit to someone's home will temporarily satisfy your wanderlust.

27 OCTOBER

You'll appreciate the chance to spend time on yourself and someone special. There are therapeutic aspects to the day, but you may need to overcome a hurdle first.

28 OCTOBER

You'll be inspired by your work or someone special but must avoid making assumptions, especially in connection with work and finances.

29 OCTOBER

Be prepared to be on your toes as your schedule may change abruptly or you may receive unexpected news. Look for balance to enjoy a peaceful evening.

30 OCTOBER

You'll be surprised by a change of circumstance. Avoid making rash decisions as a result but be prepared to adapt, especially at work.

31 OCTOBER

This will be a fun-filled Hallowe'en but it may also be intense, so if you prefer a quiet time it would be better to turn the lights out and cocoon!

November

1 NOVEMBER

The Scorpio new moon is a particularly potent time to make a wish, and your hopes for progress at work can be realised if you're practical about what you want and take steps to achieve goals.

2 NOVEMBER

You'll appreciate the chance to boost your well-being, health and appearance. A reunion could be therapeutic.

3 NOVEMBER

Romance and meetings with people you admire and love will raise spirits. You may be drawn to travelling and are motivated to express yourself. Avoid conflict, as it could flare up unexpectedly.

4 NOVEMBER

This is a good day to build a solid foundation for yourself, especially at work, so be prepared to make connections with people in a position to help you.

5 NOVEMBER

You're likely to feel more fired up about your ideas and plans over the coming weeks, which will be motivational, but you must avoid arguments, which will be rife, and making rash decisions.

6 NOVEMBER

Keep your feet on the ground without being stubborn, as this will help you to navigate circumstances.

7 NOVEMBER

This is a lovely day for get-togethers and improving social and work relationships, so take the initiative!

8 NOVEMBER

A friend, partner or colleague may have unexpected news or will need to alter arrangements with you. It could work out for the better for you.

9 NOVEMBER

You may be drawn to unravelling a mystery or doing more research on a project or activity. Someone close may give mixed messages, in which case you could ask for clarity.

10 NOVEMBER

You'll be drawn to inspiring people and activities such as listening to music, dance and spiritual development. It's a lovely day to relax and reflect.

11 NOVEMBER

You may be put on the spot at work and must complete tasks despite being under pressure. Rest assured: you will accomplish your goals. Plan carefully and delegate chores if possible.

12 NOVEMBER

You're one of the zodiac's best communicators yet even you could get the wrong end of the stick, so be vigilant. There may be travel and communication delays.

13 NOVEMBER

You're sensitive to other people's feelings, which will give you the edge in communications. Be prepared to work hard. It's a good day to talk.

14 NOVEMBER

The lead-up to the full moon can be intense. This is a good time to consider how your daily life, including work and health schedules, could improve.

15 NOVEMBER

The full moon in Taurus puts a spotlight on your everyday life, work and health. It's time to take action to improve these areas and/or be more spontaneous. A surprise may crop up.

16 NOVEMBER

You'll enjoy a change of schedule or an impromptu get-together may be a surprise. You may need to compromise with someone to avoid arguments.

17 NOVEMBER

It's a good day to mull over and discuss your well-being and how your work life fits into a healthy picture – or not. You'll enjoy a get-together.

18 NOVEMBER

This is a good day for meetings regarding work and health. A talk with a business or personal partner will be important. A financial negotiation may be necessary.

19 NOVEMBER

You'll enjoy a reunion and romance, so why not organise a get-together? Work will be busy, but if you keep your expectations realistic you could make steady progress.

20 NOVEMBER

As Pluto re-enters Aquarius an increasingly adventurous outlook will appeal over the coming weeks and months. Just keep those your actions affect in the loop.

21 NOVEMBER

Over the next four weeks you'll enjoy being more proactive in your daily life, enjoying your interests and a healthier approach to life. You may already experience a pleasant change today.

22 NOVEMBER

This is a good day to make a commitment, either in your personal life or at work or both. Romance could blossom, so take the initiative.

23 NOVEMBER

You'll enjoy a sense of connection with someone special. This is a lovely day for get-togethers and romance and also for self-development.

24 NOVEMBER

It's a great day to catch up on chores at home and in the garden while also enjoying your own space and music, the arts and romance.

25 NOVEMBER

Your feelings about someone are likely to become stronger. Just double-check you're not seeing the world through rose-coloured glasses. If you aren't you'll enjoy this inspiring time.

26 NOVEMBER

You may receive key news from someone close. Try to get paperwork and discussions on the table by the end of the day to avoid delays further down the line.

27 NOVEMBER

You'll enjoy the proactive tone of the day, as you'll be productive at work and with your chores. You may hear good news from a friend or organisation.

28 NOVEMBER

Be prepared to see another person's point of view, or you may feel disappointed by developments. You may be asked for help, and if advice is needed it will be available.

29 NOVEMBER

You'll enjoy the chance to discuss some of your plans with those they concern. Talks are likely to go well. It's a good day for a mini financial review and for romance.

30 NOVEMBER

This is likely to be an active, outgoing weekend with time spent doing what you love. It's a good time to reinvest in your favourite activities.

December

1 DECEMBER

The new moon in Sagittarius will kick-start a fresh chapter in your daily routine. If you're about to go on holiday you'll enjoy the change of pace. New doors will open at work and health-wise.

2 DECEMBER

This is a good time to review some arrangements such as your health schedule and agreements with a friend or organisation. You may enjoy a surprise or change of routine.

3 DECEMBER

When the moon is in earth signs Taurus, Capricorn and Virgo you tend to feel more organised and practical, so be productive. It's an ideal day to plan ahead.

4 DECEMBER

Developments will deserve careful appraisal to avoid a Mexican stand-off. You may need to review a trip or discussion. Be inspired, but avoid idealism. Romance could blossom.

5 DECEMBER

Your ability to look outside the box will be a useful quality, enabling you to be optimistic about your options as opposed to feeling stuck or vulnerable.

6 DECEMBER

You may experience a change of tempo or circumstance. Travel, discussions and negotiations are best approached carefully. Avoid making rash decisions.

7 DECEMBER

New horizons will beckon and you'll enjoy being upbeat and outgoing. Travel, get-togethers and romance will all appeal but this could also be an intense day, so pace yourself.

8 DECEMBER

It's a good day to discuss your ideas and plans with those you know have your back; they will inspire you. It's a good time for self-development and improving self-esteem.

9 DECEMBER

You'll feel increasingly upbeat, so if some communications and get-togethers are tense initially you'll find developments more productive as the day goes by.

10 DECEMBER

You may receive good news from a friend or organisation. It's a good time for a health treat for yourself or someone close, and you'll enjoy a favourite pastime or romance.

11 DECEMBER

A quiet internal debate about the merits of various choices you can make will take you into an introspective time. Be prepared to review where you stand.

12 DECEMBER

A reunion may be fun but could also open new doors, so be careful when making decisions. If you enter into an argument, avoid long-term conflict as this will be detrimental.

13 DECEMBER

Despite this being Friday the 13th it's a good day for get-togethers and also for clearing up a backlog of chores and paperwork. A reunion could be exciting.

14 DECEMBER

In the lead-up to the full moon in your sign consider this: how would you like your personal life to progress? It's a good time to step towards your goals.

15 DECEMBER

The full moon shines a light on your relationships and, for mid-June Twins, on your work and daily chores. Key news or a get-together will put a new slant on matters.

16 DECEMBER

You'll feel determined and motivated to make waves and turn some of your plans into something more tangible. Just be sure you have done your research first.

17 DECEMBER

You or someone close may feel vulnerable and appear intense or moody. Give them some space and find the time for short breaks if you're under pressure.

18 DECEMBER

Be prepared to look carefully at information and transactions as mistakes can be made. A mystery may arise.

19 DECEMBER

It's a good day for talks and meetings, both at work and socially. You'll enjoy a favourite activity. It's also a beneficial day for making a commitment to a solid budget.

20 DECEMBER

A lovely development will boost morale, while study, travel and romance could also lift spirits. You may be in line for a work or financial improvement.

21 DECEMBER

This is the solstice. You'll enjoy the Christmas spirit and a sense over the coming weeks that plans have been made and you can establish more stability in your life.

22 DECEMBER

It's a good day to discuss or make long-term changes with a business or personal partner or friend. You'll enjoy a get-together.

23 DECEMBER

A little tact will work wonders, as you may find yourself at odds with someone else. Consider whether their goals are so very different from yours.

24 DECEMBER

This is a good day to build bridges with someone you have argued with. A trip or get-together will be therapeutic. However, you may need to keep your expectations real.

25 DECEMBER

Merry Christmas! You'll appreciate the wonderful greetings and/or sense of togetherness, but a little diplomacy will go a long way towards creating a happy day.

26 DECEMBER

A reunion or news from the past will be significant. Some travel or communication delays may be expected, so be patient.

27 DECEMBER

Transactions and travel may be delayed, so be patient about your expectations. If you're back at work it will be a busy day, but you will manage to get things done.

28 DECEMBER

Be prepared for a surprise. If developments don't play into your hands, be adaptable and flexible and you'll find ways to get ahead.

29 DECEMBER

An optimistic and outgoing attitude to a change in your routine will reap rewards. Be prepared to reach out to others, as talks will be enjoyable.

30 DECEMBER

The new moon in Capricorn points to something new for you in your business or personal partnerships. You're prepared to find more stability and security or make a commitment.

31 DECEMBER

Happy New Year! There is a healing quality to get-togethers that you'll enjoy. You may decide to focus on a healthy start to 2025.

CANCER

20 June – 22 July

FINANCES

The eclipses in March, April, September and October will bring changes to your career and/or home lives that will have an impact on your finances. Luckily the outlook is positive: you have every opportunity to rejig your finances so your arrangements suit you better, especially in July when the positive impacts of the sun, Mercury and Venus traversing your money box will help refill them. Finding the right balance between super optimism and pessimism will be crucial, so be careful not to overcommit financially on the one hand and, on the other, not to underestimate your investment potential.

HEALTH

Your sense of emotional well-being will improve in 2024 as you'll gain the opportunity to nourish both your business and personal relationships. As emotional happiness is the foundation stone of overall happiness, this year stands to be a healthy one. However, physically it's vital that you don't overtire or over-exert yourself as you will be inclined to bite off more than you can chew at work and take on too many responsibilities. Be sure to pace yourself to avoid exhaustion and niggling health issues, especially in August, September and December.

LOVE LIFE

The new moon on 11 January and developments mid-year will kick-start a fresh phase in your love life that could bring more security and stability. For couples, 2024 is ideal for building a strong base from which to nurture your relationship. For singles, this year is ideal for broadening your social circle and potentially meeting someone you click with. This is a good year for all Cancerians to socialise, be this via an online forum or in person. The months of January and February are particularly conducive to romance, so be sure to organise special events then. If that's not practical, other romance hotspots will occur in March and October.

CAREER

If you'd like to make considerable changes in your career this year is a good time to do so. Equally, if you're looking for stability and the chance to create a strong platform for yourself in your career then 2024 will deliver. The best phase for you to take steps to transform your career will be during the first quarter of the year. You may find it's tougher than usual to maintain the status quo in August, September and December, so it's best to make your choices earlier in the year rather than later and to set the ball rolling in January.

HOME LIFE

Your home life is important to you, perhaps more so than for other zodiac signs, so it's important to give it as much attention as you can. In 2024 you will be drawn to looking for peace, calmness and balance in your life and at home, perhaps to the detriment of your self-development. When peace at all costs becomes a priority you may inadvertently miss out on personal growth, so be prepared to seize opportunities to grow in 2024 rather than feel the need to bunker down at home. This will be especially relevant during the eclipses in March, April, September and October, as they are likely to bring unexpected surprises your way that will impact considerably on your home life and consequently on your peace of mind.

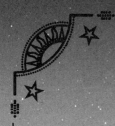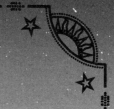

January

1 JANUARY

You'll be drawn to getting things shipshape, starting the year the way you mean to carry on. A delay will require patience. Avoid arguments if possible.

2 JANUARY

It's an excellent day to resume planning and tidying up at home, especially if you were delayed or distracted yesterday.

3 JANUARY

A strong work ethic will see you completing chores. If you're on holiday, take a little extra time and slow down as you'll enjoy relaxing.

4 JANUARY

You'll appreciate the sense that some relationships and people will become more supportive and proactive, which you'll enjoy.

5 JANUARY

Being with like-minded people is motivational, and you'll enjoy finding the time for someone special.

6 JANUARY

Collaboration is the key to success, even if you feel someone is not pulling their weight or they need to abruptly change arrangements. Avoid taking other people's remarks personally.

7 JANUARY

You'll appreciate the chance to feel the wind in your sails and enjoy a little freedom of movement. Just be careful to avoid misunderstandings.

8 JANUARY

While you'll be keen to get ahead with your work and projects, it's in your interest to be careful with communications and travel as there may be delays.

9 JANUARY

Be prepared to keep an eye on the details at work, as absent-mindedness and general mistake making could arise. You or someone close may be delayed or a mystery may crop up.

10 JANUARY

You'll enjoy an impromptu get-together and may receive unexpected news, so be spontaneous.

11 JANUARY

The Capricorn new moon will kick-start a fresh phase in a relationship and, for some, in a shared project or duty. You'll enjoy improving your appearance and may find this an eventful day.

12 JANUARY

You'll enjoy being proactive with your plans and socialising. Negotiations could go well.

13 JANUARY

You'll enjoy making changes in your usual daily routine. It's a good day to talk. Someone close may wish to discuss changes they'd like to implement.

14 JANUARY

This is a good day to work towards finding more stability in your daily routine and relationships. A little give and take will be worthwhile.

15 JANUARY

Take a little time out to find inspiration in your day, as you'll feel all the more motivated as a result. It's a good time for self-development.

16 JANUARY

You'll enjoy being with like-minded people. Someone may inspire you to be more proactive, but you must avoid being easily influenced. Romance could flourish.

17 JANUARY

You'll enjoy the company of upbeat and proactive people. It's a good time to be imaginative and take practical steps to attain your goals.

18 JANUARY

This is a good day to discuss work plans and for improving relationships with people in a position of authority. If you're looking for work, take the initiative.

19 JANUARY

You'll enjoy being upbeat at work and a change in your usual duties or schedule will be enjoyable. However, you must avoid forgetfulness and making assumptions.

20 JANUARY

Be prepared to review shared space and duties. You may like to alter an arrangement. This may be a strained day, so if possible avoid tense topics in discussions.

21 JANUARY

Be prepared to enter fresh territory, especially in a relationship or shared circumstance. Think laterally.

22 JANUARY

You may be prepared to set in motion ideas and plans you floated in 2023, especially where they concern others.

23 JANUARY

You'll appreciate the sense that your daily schedule will calm down after a period of growth or high activity. Be practical above all with work decisions.

24 JANUARY

When the moon is in your sign you can tend to be more intuitive but today you may be super sensitive to others, so maintain perspective. Avoid making snap decisions.

25 JANUARY

The Leo full moon will spotlight finances and especially those you share with others, such as expenses and investments. Avoid making snap decisions you'll regret.

26 JANUARY

This is a good time to be careful with your communications to avoid mistakes. It's a good time to seek the advice of an expert. Your help may also be in need.

27 JANUARY

You or someone close may be feeling fiery, and while this will be energising for sports and for chores you must avoid arguments. Try to find common ground where possible.

28 JANUARY

This is a productive day and you'll appreciate seeing positive results for your hard work, especially if you manage to avoid arguments and being easily influenced.

29 JANUARY

You'll enjoy socialising, networking and meeting interesting people. You may be drawn to altering your usual routine so you can meet someone fun.

30 JANUARY

It's a good time to look for harmony at home. If you need someone's collaboration, it's a good day to ask for it and to try to find common ground.

31 JANUARY

Take things one step at a time to avoid tiring yourself, as you may need to work hard.

February

1 FEBRUARY

Consider organising something enjoyable or romantic for tomorrow evening or the weekend, especially if you feel tired today.

2 FEBRUARY

The arts, romance, music and dance will all appeal. You'll appreciate the chance to meet someone you admire or love.

3 FEBRUARY

A change of pace will feel refreshing and re-energising. You'll feel more passionate about someone or a hobby, so this is the best time to indulge!

4 FEBRUARY

An upbeat, fun approach to Sunday will pay off. You may be drawn to sports, music, dance and spending time with family, which you'll enjoy.

5 FEBRUARY

Key news and developments will add a fresh focus on a work or personal relationship. You may be needed at a moment's notice and must avoid cutting corners and rushing.

6 FEBRUARY

A practical approach to your day will be successful. Find time to get your feet on the ground. Avoid taking people's random comments personally.

7 FEBRUARY

You may be surprised by news from a business or personal partner. You'll enjoy socialising, networking and romance.

8 FEBRUARY

You may receive unexpected news or must make a swift change of plans for the day. A friend, group or organisation may surprise you.

9 FEBRUARY

The Aquarian new moon supermoon will shine a light on the shared areas of your life, such as duties and agreements. It's a good time to make financial and personal commitments.

10 FEBRUARY

This is a lovely weekend to indulge in your favourite pastimes and for self-development.

11 FEBRUARY

You may be wearing your heart on your sleeve, so take time out to unwind. You could be surprised by relationship developments.

12 FEBRUARY

An upbeat, optimistic approach to your various chores and work will be rewarding. You'll be inspired to be creative over the next two days and the arts will appeal.

13 FEBRUARY

A business or personal partner may have news for you, and having an open mind will help you be resourceful. Romance could blossom, so take the initiative.

14 FEBRUARY

Happy St Valentine's Day! This is an intense day and you or your partner may feel under pressure, so pace yourself. Romance could flourish but you must avoid arguments.

15 FEBRUARY

A practical approach to your various chores, socialising and networking will be effective. You may be prepared to enter new territory, so be bold!

16 FEBRUARY

A business or personal partnership will be taking you somewhere different, and as long as you're happy with the direction this will be a fulfilling time.

17 FEBRUARY

Romance, love and passion will flourish and singles may meet someone passionate. Don't let disagreements get the better of you as they will mar an otherwise enjoyable time.

18 FEBRUARY

You'll appreciate the chance to catch up with someone from your past. You will enjoy cocooning, relaxing and being with someone special.

19 FEBRUARY

You may have your head slightly in the clouds so be prepared to focus on facts. You may be put on the spot at work or will be asked for help. If you need advice it is available.

20 FEBRUARY

The Cancerian moon will bring your feelings to the surface and someone may surprise you. Trust your gut feelings.

21 FEBRUARY

You may receive mixed messages but must avoid second-guessing someone. If you want to know where you stand ask, and be prepared for the answer.

22 FEBRUARY

This is another lovely day for romance but you must avoid putting someone under pressure. If you feel under pressure, consider finding ways to cool things down.

23 FEBRUARY

You're better known as an intuitive character and Mercury in Pisces for the next few weeks will sharpen your instincts, so be sure to trust them.

24 FEBRUARY

The full moon in Virgo will spotlight a relationship. You may need to attend to details that will improve communications and travel such as updating a device or vehicle.

25 FEBRUARY

Be prepared to think outside the box, especially in relation to a partnership or collaboration. Be practical too, and avoid seeing things through rose-coloured glasses.

26 FEBRUARY

You'll be productive during the first half of the day and in the second half you may be more drawn to daydreaming, so be prepared to focus if you're at work.

27 FEBRUARY

It's impossible to get on with everyone all the time. A friend, group or organisation may grate on your nerves, so be sure to maintain perspective and avoid making snap decisions.

28 FEBRUARY

You'll appreciate the opportunity to invest in your home and family. However, work chores may demand your time, so reorganise your priorities or schedule if necessary.

29 FEBRUARY

A work meeting may be more significant than meets the eye. It's a good day to circulate your résumé and for a job interview. Romance could also thrive.

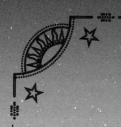 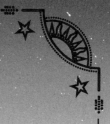

March

1 MARCH

This is a lovely day for work and socialising. You may make a valid agreement or commitment. There are therapeutic aspects to the day.

2 MARCH

An adventurous approach at work will be rewarding. Just ensure you have all the details if you are making important long-term decisions.

3 MARCH

You may be surprised by the news you receive. Think laterally if you're put on the spot.

4 MARCH

While you like to be inspired, you already know the merits of being realistic and practical. Combine your hopes and wishes with a methodical approach in order to succeed.

5 MARCH

This is a good day to reach out to like-minded people and build bridges with social and networking circles, as your efforts are likely to succeed.

6 MARCH

You may receive good news from a group, friend or organisation. It's a good day for self-development and to deepen your understanding of self-nurture.

7 MARCH

Your interests and activities will be fulfilling, so be sure to organise events you enjoy. Work meetings and career decisions point to success.

8 MARCH

You're communicating well at the moment and will feel inspired to discuss your feelings. It's a creative day that is ideal for the arts, self-development and spirituality.

9 MARCH

You may receive unexpected news or will enjoy an impromptu get-together. Activities will be inspiring. Be spontaneous but avoid feeling rushed into making decisions.

10 MARCH

The Pisces new moon supermoon could kick-start a fresh chapter in your career or general direction. Be inspired and prepared to discuss changes with someone close.

11 MARCH

You'll appreciate the chance to enter fresh territory with your ventures and interests. You may even find the time for self-nurturance, self-development and the arts.

12 MARCH

You'll enjoy socialising and networking. Your advice may be sought, and if you need expert help it will be available.

13 MARCH

A lovely get-together will encourage you to be more outgoing. Partners may be prepared to take your relationship into new territory and make changes.

14 MARCH

A grounded, earthy approach to your interactions with people you know and socially will prove effective. Be practical; just avoid stubbornness.

15 MARCH

You'll feel a little chattier and relaxed and will appreciate it being the end of the week. Talks at work or regarding a commitment will be productive.

16 MARCH

This is a good day for serious discussions about your future and also, if you're ready, to make a commitment to a plan or project. You'll enjoy a favourite hobby or get-together.

17 MARCH

There will be ideal aspects to your day whether you're working or relaxing. A truly romantic, artistic and musical atmosphere will inspire. It's a good day for self-development.

18 MARCH

The moon in your sign will add to your intuitive insight, so trust your gut. You may also feel sensitive so you must avoid taking random comments personally.

19 MARCH

You'll feel motivated to get things done but may hit speed humps. Be patient and find clever ways to catch up.

20 MARCH

A friend or organisation may prove to be particularly helpful to you, so be sure to reach out. You'll appreciate being proactive and striding ahead even if you feel vulnerable.

21 MARCH

This is a good day to make changes within an agreement such as a work contract or personal arrangement, so be prepared to discuss ideas.

22 MARCH

You'll feel increasingly inspired by travel, spirituality, your favourite hobbies and people. If you're studying, be prepared to explore new ideas but avoid distractions.

23 MARCH

A lovely get-together or meaningful interaction will raise spirits. You'll enjoy deepening your understanding of yourself and others. A group or friend will be good company.

24 MARCH

A lovely domestic day will fill your heart with peace and a sense of belonging, so be sure to organise some me time as friends or family may want your attention.

25 MARCH

The lunar eclipse will spotlight your domestic life, property or family. Be proactive with your long-term plans. You may enjoy a trip, fun activity or study. It's a good day to talk.

26 MARCH

You could excel at your work and chores and someone may look up to you as result, so be proud of your efforts. You may need to help someone.

27 MARCH

This is a good time to build a positive impression of yourself to others. You may enjoy setting a good example or improving your appearance or health.

28 MARCH

You'll enjoy being spontaneous and may experience a surprise, either at work or socially.

29 MARCH

There will be upbeat and fulfilling aspects to the day and you may experience a sense of progress in your projects even if you must work hard.

30 MARCH

Being active and outgoing will appeal. Sports, a trip and engaging in new activities will be fulfilling. Try to get key discussions on the table if possible to avoid them lingering.

31 MARCH

You'll enjoy socialising and may take a trip to an old haunt. Just avoid misunderstandings. Plan ahead to avoid travel delays.

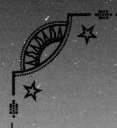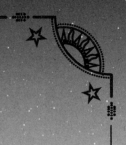

April

1 APRIL

You may feel a little idealistic about various plans and projects, so be practical and you'll find this a productive day.

2 APRIL

You may receive key news from a friend, group or organisation. Avoid knee-jerk reactions and find time to consider your best path forward.

3 APRIL

You'll feel inspired by someone you admire. The arts, film and music will appeal. This is a good day for romance but you must avoid being super idealistic at work.

4 APRIL

Key talks with a group, friend or organisation will be significant. You'll find the time to review paperwork, so avoid feeling under pressure.

5 APRIL

As Venus enters Aries you'll feel more energetic about making changes at work and with your general direction and status. Just avoid making snap decisions.

6 APRIL

The Pisces moon will inspire you to discuss your big-picture plans with those they concern. The more you can research and plan your path ahead the better for you.

7 APRIL

With so much going on it's important you find time for yourself and take stock. Fortunately, this is an excellent day to do so.

8 APRIL

The total solar eclipse signifies a fresh start in your relationship with a friend, group or organisation. Someone may need your help, and if you need some support then rest assured it is available.

9 APRIL

If you've been super sociable prepare for a quieter time, and if you've been a hermit be prepared to be more outgoing. You'll enjoy it!

10 APRIL

You may be surprised by an impromptu get-together or news from a friend. You may be drawn to investing in a project or entering a new agreement.

11 APRIL

You'll enjoy a reunion or news from an old friend. It's a good time to review your loyalties to a group, friend or organisation. Paperwork may also deserve a review.

12 APRIL

The Gemini moon will provoke your curiosity and you may be inclined to reveal more than you should about confidential information, so be discerning! Avoid malicious gossip.

13 APRIL

You'll enjoy socialising and being spontaneous with your activities. The Cancer moon will help you create a calm and peaceful atmosphere at home and away.

14 APRIL

You can't always agree with everyone but will enjoy time with like-minded people. This is a good weekend for self-care and looking after those you love.

15 APRIL

A personal or health situation may require a review. A meeting may put you on the spot, but you will find a positive way forward.

16 APRIL

It's a good day to take the initiative with talks and meetings to ensure your ideas are heard, but you must avoid taking people's random comments personally unless criticism is merited.

17 APRIL

This is a good day for get-togethers, both at work and socially. If singles meet someone new they may seem familiar or will be significant or influential in some way.

18 APRIL

As a water sign you like to be intuitive, yet sometimes action needs to be taken swiftly. Just avoid making snap decisions about long-term matters.

19 APRIL

As the sun enters Taurus you'll appreciate gaining a little more direction in life. You'll enjoy being spontaneous socially and may receive good news at work.

20 APRIL

This is a good day to be inspired by your home and family and what you're creating in your personal life. The arts, music and enjoying good company will appeal.

21 APRIL

Unexpected news, an impromptu get-together or unusual event will arise. It's a good day to undergo a healing treat.

22 APRIL

An unusual development will see you on your toes at work or in connection with a friend or organisation. Be prepared to be flexible for the best results.

23 APRIL

You may feel developments are particularly emotional, so it's in your interest to maintain the status quo. Pace yourself.

24 APRIL

The Scorpio full moon will spotlight your personal life, family or a creative project. You have every chance to shine so believe in yourself, even if you feel emotional.

25 APRIL

Key news or a get-together could be transformative as you gain the chance to turn a corner in your status or career. It's a good day to talk as the Mercury retrograde phase ends.

26 APRIL

This weekend is a lovely time to plan upbeat and active events with someone you admire. You may begin the weekend early with a trip or activity you love.

27 APRIL

You'll enjoy activities such as sport and self-development, anything that stretches your mind and body.

28 APRIL

This is a lovely day to relax and enjoy the company of someone you love. You'll be inspired by music, the arts, film and dance. Romance could flourish.

29 APRIL

As Venus enters Taurus you'll enjoy being practical both at work and in your personal life. You will not suffer fools gladly; just be sure you have the full facts.

30 APRIL

Proactive Mars will encourage you to be more outgoing over the coming weeks. You'll enjoy exploration through travel and your favourite activities.

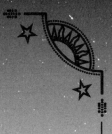

May

1 MAY

You'll be productive but arguments are possible, so be prepared to find common ground to avoid escalating differences of opinion.

2 MAY

This may be another intense day. If you don't manage to mend bridges with someone then rest assured you will eventually do so, although it may take time.

3 MAY

You'll feel outspoken and upbeat but must avoid appearing aggressive, especially at work. It's a good day to press ahead with ventures. A relationship may blossom.

4 MAY

The moon will put your heart on your sleeve and you may be more sensitive or emotional than usual. You'll gain the chance to deepen your understanding of someone close.

5 MAY

You'll enjoy a reunion or return to an old haunt. Socialising and networking will appeal.

6 MAY

A little planning will go a long way, especially if you find some business or personal relationships tense. Avoid a Mexican stand-off.

7 MAY

A group or friend will prove helpful, so be prepared to ask for information or support if needed. A health or personal matter may impact on work decisions.

8 MAY

The Taurus new moon will kick-start a fresh chapter in your social life or with a friend and organisation. If you've been sociable prepare for a quieter time, and vice versa.

9 MAY

The Gemini moon brings out your communicative, chatty side and you'll enjoy spending time with like-minded people. Just avoid oversharing.

10 MAY

A friendly get-together will be enjoyable. You may experience a meeting or news that is therapeutic.

11 MAY

There are therapeutic aspects to the weekend, so it's a good time for self-nurture and self-development. You'll enjoy socialising, and singles may meet someone alluring.

12 MAY

You'll feel drawn to connecting with friends and like-minded people. However, anyone who rocks the boat will annoy so choose your company carefully!

13 MAY

You'll enjoy a vibrant day and may make several new friends or colleagues you know will be supportive. It's a good day for a financial review.

14 MAY

You'll feel proactive and can certainly get a great deal done at work. However, some developments or a friend or organisation may slow you down, so be patient.

15 MAY

You'll appreciate the sense that you can create more stability in your work and status. Be prepared to approach communications methodically.

16 MAY

Be prepared to work hard towards your goals. Someone close may have different viewpoints to you but you're better to avoid arguments, as they could escalate.

17 MAY

Someone close has a unique approach to life, and while this is enlightening it can be impractical on occasion. Look for common ground and solutions.

18 MAY

You'll enjoy broadening your horizons through travel, an organisation or being with a different social circle.

19 MAY

This is a romantic day and you'll appreciate the chance to relax, indulge in favourite activities and enjoy the arts and good company.

20 MAY

Over the next four weeks your instincts will be stronger and you may even wonder where some of your impressions come from. Be prepared to consider new ideas.

21 MAY

Your creative and lively sides will emerge and you'll appreciate the company of someone fun. However, you may be feeling more emotional, so be prepared.

22 MAY

A romantic or work-related meeting is likely to be enjoyable or productive. Be proactive and positive!

23 MAY

The full moon in Sagittarius spotlights a fresh chapter in your personal life. If you've been considering a new venture, developments will point you towards the right group or organisation.

24 MAY

Romance could flourish, so be sure to organise a date. You'll enjoy socialising and networking.

25 MAY

This weekend is ideal for making positive changes in personal and professional relationships. You'll appreciate the chance to touch base with like-minded people. Romance could flourish.

26 MAY

As Jupiter enters Gemini it's time to deepen your connection with someone – perhaps even yourself! It's a good time to talk but you must avoid divulging someone's secret.

27 MAY

A diligent and practical approach to your chores will pay off, but you must be adaptable or you risk getting stuck by a one-track mind.

28 MAY

This is a good day for talks and meetings associated with work, finances and a group or organisation. You could make a valid agreement. Reach out; you'll be glad you did.

29 MAY

Take the initiative both at work and at home and offer help or support to those who need it. If you need support ask for it, as it is available. It's a good day for a health appointment.

30 MAY

It's a good day to talk, especially regarding delicate topics, as you're likely to be more understood than usual. Be prepared to be tactful for the best results.

31 MAY

You'll appreciate the chance to dream a little and indulge in your favourite activities. Just avoid allowing your mind to wander at work as you will appear distracted.

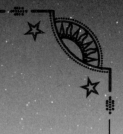

June

1 JUNE

You'll enjoy being spontaneous and an impromptu get-together will be enjoyable. Just avoid rushing so you don't make mistakes.

2 JUNE

You'll enjoy being physically active and improving your health and well-being. You'll feel motivated but others may prefer to relax, so find common ground.

3 JUNE

It's a good time to implement changes through your relationships. You may meet a new circle or friends or organisation, and this could be transformative.

4 JUNE

You'll enjoy a reunion or return to an old haunt. A trip will broaden horizons and romance could blossom. Someone in a position of authority may prove helpful.

5 JUNE

Consider spending a little time reviewing your progress so far this year, as tomorrow's new moon will be ideal to implement fresh strategies at work or health-wise.

6 JUNE

The new moon brings your focus on work and health and offers the chance to boost your circumstances. You may also be drawn to improving your appearance. Avoid power struggles.

7 JUNE

You'll feel inspired to succeed with your projects at work and boost your feel-good factor. Just avoid being at loggerheads with someone in authority. Trust your instincts.

8 JUNE

Be prepared to see someone else's point of view – within reason. This is a good time to alter your usual weekend routine one step at a time if you feel it's become stale.

9 JUNE

You can't always agree with everyone but you must avoid conflict and a Mexican stand-off, as it could turn into a stalemate. Be prepared to find common ground.

10 JUNE

The Leo moon will bring out your proactive, positive sides. Just be sure to avoid arguments.

11 JUNE

There are therapeutic aspects to the day. You'll appreciate the chance to boost your appearance and profile. Someone may need your help, and you will receive help if you need it.

12 JUNE

You're communicating well but you may be at loggerheads with someone important, so tread carefully. Travel may be delayed, so put plenty of time aside.

13 JUNE

Someone may surprise you. A sudden change of routine could be enjoyable if you're flexible with arrangements. It's a good day for an impromptu get-together.

14 JUNE

It's a good day for talks and meetings but you must be prepared to work hard to gain the results you want. You'll get clarity about a venture.

15 JUNE

You'll enjoy doing something different and spending time with an interesting group of people. Someone's news may surprise you and a matter from your past may be unexpected.

16 JUNE

This is an excellent day to find some peace and balance in your life. You may simply feel like cocooning with someone special at home.

17 JUNE

You'll increasingly feel like expressing your feelings and deeper thoughts; just ensure you have the right end of the stick if you are making long-term decisions. A key meeting and travel may be delayed.

18 JUNE

You'll feel motivated by who and what pleases you but this could take you into murky waters if you dislike your job, so be prepared to be tactful.

19 JUNE

A proactive approach to your work will be productive. Avoid romanticising or glamorising a person or organisation as you may be easily misled or disappointed.

20 JUNE

The solstice is a lovely time to consider how far you've come this year. If you find today's events mystifying, take this as motivation to change things that don't add up.

21 JUNE

The more effort you put into today's events the more you'll enjoy them, even if some developments present hurdles. Be proactive and you'll enjoy the outcome.

22 JUNE

The full moon in Capricorn suggests you're ready to turn a page in work, health or daily scheduling circumstances. It's a good day to talk, so tee up meetings and calls.

23 JUNE

Be prepared to meet someone halfway: the delicate art of negotiation will be a skill set to embrace now.

24 JUNE

An innovative approach to the start of the working week will be rewarding. You may be prepared to make changes in a key agreement.

25 JUNE

Reach out to like-minded people as you'll enjoy being with a supportive group. Just avoid making rash decisions, especially at work.

26 JUNE

You know who you get on with and who you don't. Find the time to work a little harder on relationships that need more effort, especially at work.

27 JUNE

An inspired approach to someone who can be lacklustre or tends to throw their weight around will work.

28 JUNE

Be prepared to oil the wheels of professional relationships with tact. Avoid taking someone's off-the-cuff comments personally. Your help may be sought.

29 JUNE

This is a lovely weekend for socialising and networking. If you're single love could flourish, so be sure to organise a date.

30 JUNE

Be open to experiencing something different! You'll enjoy an impromptu trip or get-together and may be surprised by news.

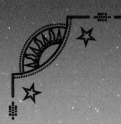

July

1 JULY

The Taurus moon will encourage you to be practical with groups and work. Certain discussions could be productive, but you must avoid tricky conversations.

2 JULY

As Mercury leaves your sign it will spotlight your finances and self-esteem. Consider whether you could boost both and, if so, take steps to make it happen!

3 JULY

A friend, business or personal partner has news, but you must avoid intense talks as these are likely to escalate. You could make a valid work or financial agreement.

4 JULY

The lead-up to the Cancerian new moon is an ideal time to take stock of your personal life. If you wish to make changes this is the day to consider how.

5 JULY

The Cancerian new moon is a good time to turn a corner in your personal life. Some mid-July Cancerians may be drawn to making a fresh work agreement or devising a different health regime.

6 JULY

It's a good day to self-nurture as you may feel sensitive. It's a good day to boost health. Someone may need your help, and if you need advice it will be available so reach out.

7 JULY

The Leo moon brings a more upbeat feel to the day. You'll enjoy your favourite activities.

8 JULY

You may receive unexpectedly positive news and will enjoy an impromptu get-together.

9 JULY

The next few days are ideal for focusing on the details at work but you must avoid being a perfectionist. It's a good time for a tidy up in the garden, office or neighbourhood.

10 JULY

You'll appreciate finding a little peace at home and gaining some direction in your personal life. Avoid perfectionism: be prepared to accept no one is perfect.

11 JULY

You'll appreciate making progress with your ventures. Your focus will switch to finances and self-esteem and you may receive a financial or ego boost. Romance could flourish.

12 JULY

This could be an intense day, so take things one step at a time. Avoid conversations that could turn toxic and be tactful. Romance could ignite but so too could conflict.

13 JULY

You'll appreciate the chance to relax and find a little balance in your life. A friend or family member will prove supportive. You'll enjoy a reunion.

14 JULY

You'll enjoy finding time for a favourite activity and socialising but must avoid taking other people's agendas personally. Find the time to self-nurture.

15 JULY

You may be surprised by news or someone else's demands. If you need help it is available. Your expertise is likely to be in demand.

16 JULY

Your passionate but also excitable sides will emerge and you may seem erratic to others unless you're careful to channel energy into productive activities.

17 JULY

As a water sign you are intuitive and your instincts are on form, so be sure to trust them. Seek expert advice if needed. Your help may be required.

18 JULY

You'll enjoy a pleasant get-together, either socially or at work. You may be surprised by news. It's a good time to be spontaneous and adventurous.

19 JULY

There are healing aspects to the day. You may experience a compliment, promotion at work or financial improvement. It's a good time to build bridges with someone you have fallen out with.

20 JULY

As Mars enters Gemini you'll enjoy mixing with a new and diverse group of people.

21 JULY

The full moon in Capricorn will spotlight changes in key personal or business relationships. It's a good time for planning. Romance could flourish but you must avoid mix-ups.

22 JULY

This is an excellent time to get things done. A new business or personal relationship is likely to be eventful and successful and also potentially transformative.

23 JULY

It's a good time for collaborations, but you must avoid taking someone's passion personally and avoid power struggles. A relationship begun now will be transformative but also intense.

24 JULY

The Pisces moon will bring out your philosophical side, and you'll manage to organise your day well despite disruptions. Just keep communications clear.

25 JULY

You prefer to be instinctive but a more analytical approach may be necessary to avoid misunderstandings and making mistakes.

26 JULY

This is a good day for socialising and networking. Be proactive and positive.

27 JULY

You'll enjoy deepening friendships and other relationships but extra attention to details, especially financially, may be necessary. Avoid power struggles.

28 JULY

The Taurus moon helps you relax and enjoy the sumptuousness of life and a little luxury. If you're working it's a productive time.

29 JULY

As the day progresses you'll feel increasingly in your element, and communications will feel easier as a result.

30 JULY

There are therapeutic aspects to the day. You could build bridges with colleagues and employers. You may experience a financial or ego boost.

31 JULY

This is an excellent day to boost your status, career or general profile, so be sure to take the initiative. A meeting or talk may be particularly significant.

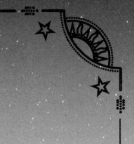

August

1 AUGUST

You may experience a surprise that will lead to re-evaluation of some of your principles or ideas. If you're shopping avoid overspending, as you'll regret it.

2 AUGUST

Expect a surprise if you didn't already have one yesterday. You'll get around logistics. A friend or organisation will prove supportive.

3 AUGUST

The lead-up to the new moon is a good time to choose your words carefully to avoid making mistakes. Finances will merit careful attention to avoid overspending.

4 AUGUST

The Leo new moon spotlights your finances and work options. Be prepared to make bold decisions and take a moment to get paperwork shipshape.

5 AUGUST

You may hear key news regarding travel. Consider updating your communications systems such as a device. Try to get key agreements on the table to avoid having to review them at a later date.

6 AUGUST

Be prepared to schedule extra time for travel and avoid being frustrated by delayed communications. Keep conversations clear for the best results.

7 AUGUST

This is an active, busy day and you may receive good news at work or financially. You'll enjoy a trip or get-together.

8 AUGUST

You'll enjoy a reunion or good news and may review or revise a personal decision. You may hear from an old flame.

9 AUGUST

You'll appreciate the opportunity to find peace and harmony, both for yourself and others. A domestic or work development may bring out emotions.

10 AUGUST

The moon in Scorpio will bring out your passionate and sensual sides and you'll be drawn to enjoy creativity, the arts and music. DIY projects may appeal.

11 AUGUST

You may find that work gets in the way of your favourite activities. Avoid arguments over chores; consider setting a schedule in place.

12 AUGUST

A strong work ethic will prove to be effective, but you must avoid idealising certain people or circumstances so you don't feel disappointed.

13 AUGUST

Consider how doing something different in your schedule will free up time to boost your well-being. You'll feel motivated to be more active.

14 AUGUST

Key news from the past or concerning work or health will require focus. You may be inclined to misunderstand someone, so be sure to focus on the facts.

15 AUGUST

You'll find ways to achieve the results you want at work, financially and in your personal life. You may need expert advice. Just avoid making assumptions.

16 AUGUST

If you encountered arguments in recent days then look out, as they may resurface and especially at work or with someone in authority. That aside, hard work will pay off.

17 AUGUST

Slowly and surely you will manage to get on top of chores and may even appreciate getting your environment, home and garden shipshape. Then you'll enjoy relaxing.

18 AUGUST

You may be surprised by someone's news or by developments and a change of plan. A friend or partner will prove resourceful.

19 AUGUST

The Aquarian full moon will spotlight your activities, projects and ideas. You may be prepared to do something new or different. Talks will be productive.

20 AUGUST

The full moon may spotlight certain agreements or activities you have outgrown. Be prepared to take optimistic action.

21 AUGUST

Be inspired by your plans and ideas although ultimately you must also be practical. You'll find out whether you've overestimated your circumstances and will be able to make amends.

22 AUGUST

The sun will spotlight how to take practical action and the need to engage in constructive talks over the next four weeks. Be proactive and positive.

23 AUGUST

This is a good day to discuss finances but you must avoid making snap decisions. You'll enjoy a reunion but won't suffer fools gladly, so be patient.

24 AUGUST

It's a great weekend to catch up on chores around the house. You may be tempted to slow things down and look after your health or that of someone else. A reunion will be enjoyable.

25 AUGUST

You'll be drawn to creature comforts and boosting your sense of security and personal happiness. This could be a sensual and romantic time.

26 AUGUST

The moon in Gemini will help communications flow at work. Just be wary of assuming everyone else is on the same page as you.

27 AUGUST

You'll enjoy being spontaneous and an impromptu get-together will delight. You will also enjoy visiting somewhere beautiful and meeting new people.

28 AUGUST

Financial and personal developments will put you on the right track and may be therapeutic. It's a good day for romance, the arts and love.

29 AUGUST

You'll be looking for love and harmony and are likely to find them through compromise and collaboration. If someone lets you down you'll find other people to spend time with.

30 AUGUST

You are highly intuitive, so be prepared to listen to your instincts. Creative Cancerians are likely to be inspired.

31 AUGUST

You may be pleasantly surprised by developments. An unexpected or impromptu change of pace will be enjoyable. Just avoid making rash decisions.

September

1 SEPTEMBER

You'll gain the chance to reconnect with someone special. Consider whether you could improve relationships by being more spontaneous and proactive.

2 SEPTEMBER

Your intuitive approach to a friend or group will work wonders. You may enjoy reconnecting with someone special in new circumstances.

3 SEPTEMBER

The new moon in Virgo is a good time to consider improving family dynamics or a domestic situation. You may also be ready to update some communication devices or a vehicle.

4 SEPTEMBER

A key meeting or news will be significant and will provide insight into your best way forward at home or work or in your personal life.

5 SEPTEMBER

The moon in Libra will encourage you to find more balance at home and look for peace of mind.

6 SEPTEMBER

Your home, family and nurturance are important aspects of your life and the moon in Libra will provide an opportunity to focus on these key areas.

7 SEPTEMBER

You'll enjoy being with the people you hold dear. You'll also be drawn to music, the arts and creativity.

8 SEPTEMBER

This is a good time to make a commitment to a plan or person, so be positive. A change at home may lead to a better sense of stability. Avoid mix-ups for the best results.

9 SEPTEMBER

More attention to detail won't go amiss. Be prepared to plan travel and communications ahead of time to avoid delays.

10 SEPTEMBER

You'll enjoy being motivated and engaged in your activities and will be productive at work. If you're not working be sure to schedule something fun.

11 SEPTEMBER

You may need to prioritise family over work or will need to sacrifice important time spent with those you love. Choose your duties carefully. Avoid emotional and financial gambling.

12 SEPTEMBER

Focus on good communication skills at home and at work to avoid feeling taken for granted in either area. Delegate chores if necessary.

13 SEPTEMBER

It's another productive day and you'll appreciate your achievements. Just avoid overtiring yourself; schedule some downtime.

14 SEPTEMBER

It's a good day for a health or beauty treat. A domestic matter may require some work, but rest assured your efforts will be worthwhile.

15 SEPTEMBER

Some interpersonal dynamics will merit a little more attention and patience than usual to grease the wheels of your relationships. Just avoid putting yourself second.

16 SEPTEMBER

Consider what you're sacrificing either at home or work. Avoid making snap decisions that could disadvantage you in the long term. Your expertise will be in demand.

17 SEPTEMBER

You may experience stronger feelings than usual. You will also be more intuitive, so be sure to trust your gut and be inspired by people and activities you love.

18 SEPTEMBER

The partial lunar eclipse supermoon in Pisces spotlights your career, direction and status. It's a good time to make a commitment to a plan or person as long as you have the facts.

19 SEPTEMBER

You'll enjoy a fun or spontaneous event. A group, friend or organisation may prove helpful at home.

20 SEPTEMBER

Keep an eye on your priorities or you may tend to be easily influenced and create unforeseen problems. If you encounter an obstacle, rest assured you'll overcome it.

21 SEPTEMBER

You'll enjoy improving your domestic circumstances via DIY projects or improved interpersonal dynamics or through a trip or receiving guests. Just avoid travel delays and misunderstandings.

22 SEPTEMBER

You'll appreciate seeing your domestic life, family circumstances or spirituality developing over the coming weeks. It's a good time to bring more peace and harmony into your life.

23 SEPTEMBER

The moon in Gemini will encourage you to review some of your projects and get things shipshape at work for the week.

24 SEPTEMBER

You'll enjoy socialising and networking. If you need help or support it will be available from someone you trust or admire. It's a good time to make progress at work.

25 SEPTEMBER

This is a good day to talk, but you must be clear about facts or misunderstandings will arise. The arts and romance will appeal.

26 SEPTEMBER

This is a good day for talks with a business or personal partner as you could make positive agreements. A get-together may be transformative.

27 SEPTEMBER

It's another good day for get-togethers and talks. You'll be feeling more positive and inspired.

28 SEPTEMBER

This is an excellent weekend for focusing on your family and home and love lives. You'll enjoy a lovely reunion and family time. You may reconnect with someone special.

29 SEPTEMBER

A visit or development at home will create a deeper sense of purpose, providing increased direction moving forward.

30 SEPTEMBER

It's a good day to talk. You'll enjoy catching up with paperwork and feeling you can have a positive effect at work and with the people you love. A reunion may be significant.

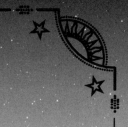

October

1 OCTOBER

During the dark of the moon is a good time to set your intentions for the future, especially regarding key relationships, travel and long-term projects.

2 OCTOBER

The solar eclipse in Libra will help you turn a corner in your personal life and creative projects, so be sure to look for ways to allow your love life and family relationships to flourish.

3 OCTOBER

This is a lovely day for meetings, both in your personal life and at work. Romance and a fun event will raise morale.

4 OCTOBER

This is an excellent time to get ahead at work, so be sure to take the initiative. A commitment made now in your personal life will be well placed to succeed.

5 OCTOBER

You'll feel the need to connect with like-minded people and enjoy favourite activities. Agreements and commitments made now could be transformative.

6 OCTOBER

You won't always agree with everyone, so be prepared for some give and take to avoid arguments. Also avoid making snap decisions.

7 OCTOBER

Make the most of a proactive feel to the start of the week. Just avoid needless disagreements.

8 OCTOBER

Some talks may bring out your vulnerabilities or those of someone else. Find common ground and work towards a positive outcome, which you can reach.

9 OCTOBER

It's a good day to be practical and take things one step at a time, as you'll make vast progress at home and work. Be methodical with a strong fitness routine.

10 OCTOBER

The Capricorn moon helps you to plan ahead and make rational decisions, so this is a good time to contemplate long-term strategies to attain your goals.

11 OCTOBER

It's a good day to talk but be prepared to listen to the ideas of others and find common ground, especially at home.

12 OCTOBER

Keep an eye on details as you may tend to over-romanticise some circumstances.

13 OCTOBER

You're likely to feel increasingly passionate about your plans, especially at home; bear in mind that others may not agree. Choose your words carefully to avoid arguments.

14 OCTOBER

The more tactful and helpful you are the better will be the outcome. Avoid angry outbursts and making snap decisions. Be prepared to be spontaneous or meet someone halfway.

15 OCTOBER

Trust your instincts as they are spot on. You may prefer to daydream, but you will need to focus hard on your projects and avoid distractions.

16 OCTOBER

This is a good day for creativity, romance and the arts. Just avoid absent-mindedness and focus on your goals.

17 OCTOBER

The full moon supermoon in Aries spells a busy time for you as your career, status or general direction undergo change. Be adventurous about new opportunities.

18 OCTOBER

You'll appreciate the support and help of like-minded people, so be sure to reach out at work and socially.

19 OCTOBER

You may be surprised by news or a change of circumstance. You'll appreciate the chance to be adventurous but will not appreciate disruption. Choose your activities carefully.

20 OCTOBER

You'll enjoy indulging in your favourite pastimes but may need to factor other people's needs into your day. Avoid losing track of your own goals.

21 OCTOBER

Your communication skills are in top form, so if you feel you're not connecting with others they may be being difficult. Find ways to understand them to avoid mix-ups.

22 OCTOBER

As the sun enters Scorpio the next four weeks will feel busier or more intense in your personal life. Tread carefully with someone who may otherwise cause conflict.

23 OCTOBER

You'll appreciate the chance to meet or talk with someone you love or admire. Be sure to find time for your favourite interest as you'll be glad you did.

24 OCTOBER

You'll be admired for your positive and upbeat approach. An optimistic attitude will be rewarding.

25 OCTOBER

You'll receive unexpected news or will be pleased by a debt that is repaid. Be prepared to be spontaneous as you'll enjoy a change of routine or a fun event.

26 OCTOBER

You'll appreciate the opportunity to touch base with your favourite people. If someone close seems intense they may need extra breathing space.

27 OCTOBER

Some communications will be easier than others. If you find yourself digging a hole, find ways to resurface and you will!

28 OCTOBER

A steady and careful approach will work wonders, as some people may be in a bad mood. If it's you, avoid seeing only the negatives. Romance and the arts could thrive.

29 OCTOBER

You'll find balance and a peaceful time at home, so be prepared to work hard for your goals. When you do you'll attain them.

30 OCTOBER

Unexpected news needn't put the cat among the pigeons. Be prepared to innovate. If you experience a disappointment it will open a door to something new.

31 OCTOBER

Be on your toes this Hallowe'en because it may be intense, as someone close will provide the tricks or the treats!

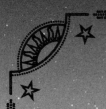

November

1 NOVEMBER

The Scorpio new moon will kick-start a fresh phase in your personal life. Make a wish but be careful, as it will come true. Developments will assume their own momentum.

2 NOVEMBER

There is a therapeutic aspect to the weekend. You may enjoy a beauty or health treat. Someone's attention will be uplifting.

3 NOVEMBER

You'll enjoy showing yourself in the best light and boosting your appearance. This will be a passionate day, so avoid conflict as it could fire up unexpectedly.

4 NOVEMBER

You may feel adamant about your principles and ideas and must avoid arguments. This is a good day to build a solid foundation for yourself but you may be prone to overspending.

5 NOVEMBER

You'll feel motivated to get things done and seek co-operation to make your dreams come true, and could slowly build a plan. Just avoid arguments and making rash decisions.

6 NOVEMBER

Keep your feet on the ground as this will help you to navigate circumstances. Someone may be stubborn; if it's you, consider whether you could find room for new ideas.

7 NOVEMBER

This is a good day for work meetings and talks. It's also a good time to meet or reach out to people who inspire you.

8 NOVEMBER

An unexpected change of plan may seem to upset the applecart, but if you focus on your goals you'll succeed despite any disruptions.

9 NOVEMBER

You may be drawn to unravelling a mystery or doing more research on a project or activity. Avoid daydreaming and absent-mindedness; keep an eye on your house keys!

10 NOVEMBER

The moon at the zenith of your chart will put your heart on your sleeve. You'll feel soothed by music, the arts and spirituality.

11 NOVEMBER

Your creativity and ability to read the room will be invaluable as you may be put on the spot at work and must complete tasks despite being under pressure.

12 NOVEMBER

While you'll feel more grounded at work, beware of misunderstandings by being super focused. There may be travel and communication delays.

13 NOVEMBER

You're sensitive to people's feelings, which will give you the edge in communications, but you must avoid taking the random comments of other people personally.

14 NOVEMBER

The lead-up to the Taurus full moon can be intense. This is a good time to consider how to improve your personal life, family and creativity.

15 NOVEMBER

The full moon in Taurus puts a spotlight on intense or unpredictable aspects of your personal life. It's time to improve these areas and/or be more spontaneous. A surprise may arise.

16 NOVEMBER

You'll enjoy being sociable and an impromptu event will appeal. You may need to be super tactful or discreet about a personal or work matter.

17 NOVEMBER

You'll appreciate the opportunity to boost your health and well-being and catch up with a good friend. A backlog of chores is best approached one step at a time.

18 NOVEMBER

You may need to renegotiate an agreement. This is a good day for meetings regarding work and health.

19 NOVEMBER

You'll enjoy the arts, romance, being inspired and spirituality. Work will flow but may be demanding and require you to show your understanding of someone.

20 NOVEMBER

As Pluto re-enters Aquarius a close personal or business relationship will step into new territory. Be prepared to handle the unexpected with your usual aplomb.

21 NOVEMBER

Over the next four weeks you'll enjoy giving time to your interests and furthering relationships. It's a lovely day for romance and creatively improving relationships.

22 NOVEMBER

This is a good day to make a change in your everyday routine to include more beauty, love and romance. It's also a good day to make a new agreement, so take the initiative.

23 NOVEMBER

If you're working you'll be busy and will enjoy a sense of purpose and fulfilment. You'll be drawn to spending time with favourite people, deepening your relationships.

24 NOVEMBER

You'll appreciate the chance to clear the air with someone who may have given you mixed messages in the past. Just avoid pushing for answers.

25 NOVEMBER

You are strong and able to excel with your projects, so take the initiative! Try to get paperwork and loose ends tied up before the start of tomorrow's Mercury retrograde phase.

26 NOVEMBER

You may receive key news at work or regarding health and well-being. It's a good day for meetings with like-minded people who will be helpful.

27 NOVEMBER

This is an excellent day to be proactive, as you'll complete a great deal at work and in your personal life. Romance and family ties could flourish.

28 NOVEMBER

You have every opportunity to succeed with your projects but you may find someone will need your attention or create waves. Be prepared to help out and also to help yourself.

29 NOVEMBER

You'll enjoy the chance to review some of your agreements at work and home. Talks are likely to go well. You'll enjoy a reunion and romance.

30 NOVEMBER

You'll appreciate the opportunity to discuss personal ventures and ideas with someone special. It's an active, outgoing weekend, so plan favourite activities.

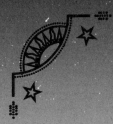

December

1 DECEMBER

The Sagittarian new moon will kick-start a fresh chapter in your personal life. You'll enjoy the chance to plan ahead. For some, new doors will open at work and health-wise.

2 DECEMBER

This is a good time for a health or beauty appointment and a review at work. You'll get the chance to discuss new ideas and will enjoy an impromptu get-together.

3 DECEMBER

It's an ideal day to plan ahead but you must factor into your plans the possibility that someone has different ideas from you. Be prepared to negotiate to avoid arguments.

4 DECEMBER

You'll enjoy a reunion or the chance to cover old ground. Be inspired but avoid idealism with negotiations or you'll hit an impasse. Romance could blossom.

5 DECEMBER

Someone close may surprise you with their unpredictable ideas or behaviour. Consider how you might find a strong foundation for progress in the relationship.

6 DECEMBER

A key meeting or news will provide food for thought concerning work and, for some, your general direction and plans with family or someone special. Avoid making rash decisions.

7 DECEMBER

New horizons will beckon in a close personal or work relationship so it's a good time to think laterally. However, feelings will be intense so pace yourself.

8 DECEMBER

You'll appreciate the chance to consider your situation in conversation with those you know have your back. It's a good time for relaxation, inspiration and self-development.

9 DECEMBER

Consider whether you're seeing your position emotionally rather than factually. Be prepared to research the best outcome and work towards that.

10 DECEMBER

This is a good day to build bridges with someone you have disagreed with. It's a therapeutic day. Your help may be required more so than usual at work and an expert will help you.

11 DECEMBER

You have a lot of energy at your disposal, so be prepared to channel it into positive activities as opposed to anger or frustration. Someone close will prove helpful.

12 DECEMBER

This is a fiery day that is ideal for romance and a reunion, but anger and outbursts could ignite unless you're careful to avoid arguments.

13 DECEMBER

Despite this being Friday the 13th it's a good day for get-togethers and romance. A reunion could be inspiring.

14 DECEMBER

Feelings will bubble up. It's a good time to work towards your goals in subtle ways, but the best way would be via talks with those people your goals concern.

15 DECEMBER

The full moon promises a fresh chapter in your work and health. A spanner in the works needn't deter you from your goals. News from someone close will be uplifting.

16 DECEMBER

The moon in your sign will encourage you to be strong and proactively chase your goals. Just be sure to have first done your research.

17 DECEMBER

You are seen as being someone with a sympathetic approach to your work and the people you love, so make the most of this productive time.

18 DECEMBER

Be prepared to look carefully at information and transactions as mistakes can be made. A mystery may arise at work or concerning someone close.

19 DECEMBER

It's a good day for talks, especially with a partner or family member. It's also a good time to discuss financial matters. An expert will prove helpful.

20 DECEMBER

You'll enjoy the seasonal spirit and a lovely social event will be enjoyable. Romance could blossom, so take the initiative!

21 DECEMBER

This is the solstice. You'll enjoy a change of pace over the coming weeks and the sense that plans you have made will bring more stability into your daily life.

22 DECEMBER

It's a good day to make changes in your daily routine and with a business or personal partner. You'll enjoy a get-together and work meetings will be productive.

23 DECEMBER

A change of routine or your work schedule may take a little diplomacy. Be prepared to be adaptable and patient to avoid frustration.

24 DECEMBER

There are therapeutic aspects to the day, as a meeting proves to be healing. You may need to keep your expectations real to avoid arguments with someone tricky.

25 DECEMBER

Merry Christmas! A little tact will go a long way towards a happy day, as some people you will click with and others not at all.

26 DECEMBER

A reunion or news from the past will be significant. Some travel or communication delays may be expected, so be patient. Avoid tough arguments you know no one can win.

27 DECEMBER

Conversations with someone in a position of authority or power may be tough. Transactions and travel may be delayed, so be patient. Working Cancerians will be productive.

28 DECEMBER

Expect something out of the ordinary unless you already experienced a surprise yesterday. If you are adaptable and flexible you'll find ways to get ahead.

29 DECEMBER

You'll enjoy an exciting change of pace and, at the least, the chance to focus on your health and well-being. Be prepared to reach out to others as talks will be enjoyable.

30 DECEMBER

The new moon in Capricorn points to something new for June Cancerians in your business or personal partnerships. July Cancerians should be prepared to find more stability in your daily life.

31 DECEMBER

Happy New Year! This is a therapeutic time, so whether you love your work or prefer holidays you'll enjoy a healing day. Just avoid overindulging as you'll regret it tomorrow!

LEO

22 July – 22 August

FINANCES

The year 2024 will bring ideal opportunities to seek new ways to manage finances in order to make your money work for you rather than you working constantly for it without seeming to gain ground. A pitfall, however, would be to be overly idealistic about what you can and can't do financially in 2024. Pay attention to developments at work in January and February as these will be indicators of the financial circumstances for the year ahead. If you feel you can count on a steady income throughout the year, this is the year to consider new ways to invest. If you run your own business this is an ideal year to grow it.

HEALTH

You'll relish the chance to broaden your understanding of your ability to improve your physical, mental and emotional health and also that of others. You'll be drawn to adventure, travelling and entertaining new projects as a way to sustain mental and emotional health. The conjunction of Chiron and the moon's north node in February may bring out an underlying health issue, making this an excellent time to focus intently on boosting health and well-being – your own and/or that of someone close.

LOVE LIFE

A lovely aspect between Saturn and Jupiter in the first quarter of the year provides a fantastic opportunity to carefully nurture growth in your primary relationships and create stability while also growing as an individual. This Saturn–Jupiter aspect will help you channel the restlessness and sense of adventure you'd love to embrace this year into activities you'll enjoy. This in turn will help you to work in practical terms towards building the circumstances you want in your love life. Just avoid feeling you must control every aspect of your love life, especially at the end of August and in December. Be spontaneous to keep romance alive!

CAREER

The re-entry of Pluto into Aquarius in your work zone will shake things up in this important area of your life. You'll be ready to take your various ideas and plans from 2023 forward into the future. Be prepared to innovate and think laterally, as clever plans, ideas and innovation are where your success lies. You'll notice already in January that a sense of restlessness and your need to renew your work practices will arise. As a result you'll potentially change how you go about what you do from day to day.

HOME LIFE

You're seeking adventure and change in 2024 and will be drawn to setting long-term, fun and upbeat projects in motion. As your focus will be on adventure and innovation your enterprises could put your home life on the backburner for now, but a real pitfall would be ignoring the importance of your home life. A truly functional approach to your home as a strong base from which to take exciting adventures will support your need for freedom and adventure as opposed to holding you back, so be innovative about ways your home could support you more.

January

1 JANUARY

Happy New Year! Did you get your New Year's Eve wish? If not, it's time for a fresh one. Factor into your plans a realistic step-by-step process and avoid arguments if possible.

2 JANUARY

You'll appreciate the chance to talk to those your projects and plans concern to ensure you're on the same page. Avoid perfectionism and allow spontaneity to bloom.

3 JANUARY

A strong work ethic will see you completing chores, but a little give and take will also put everyone in a better mood. Set the pace and enjoy some fun!

4 JANUARY

Now that the new year has definitely begun you'll benefit from strategising and planning, especially work and health schedules. Holidaying Leos will enjoy the break.

5 JANUARY

Investing in yourself is productive, and investing in your family, home or property brings a sense of fulfilment.

6 JANUARY

Be prepared to look after yourself or someone close as you or they may be feeling a little under the weather. Take time out for a health or beauty treat.

7 JANUARY

You'll enjoy investing in your favourite activities such as sports, music and dance. The arts will appeal but you must be careful to avoid misunderstandings.

8 JANUARY

A proactive approach to all areas of your life will bring a sense of accomplishment, but be careful with communications and travel as there may be delays.

9 JANUARY

You'll discover whether you misjudged a circumstance. Travel may be delayed and misunderstandings prevalent. A mystery may arise.

10 JANUARY

A change of pace will be uplifting. If you're back at work you'll enjoy the atmosphere. Opportunity could knock, so be prepared to be spontaneous.

11 JANUARY

The Capricorn new moon will kick-start a fresh phase at work or in your usual daily routine. You may receive uplifting personal or work news. An expert will be helpful.

12 JANUARY

This is a good day to reach out to people who could help you such as employers or investors. Be prepared to take the initiative. Negotiations could go well.

13 JANUARY

This is another good day to talk. You'll enjoy making changes in your usual daily routine. Someone close may wish to discuss changes they'd like to implement.

14 JANUARY

You'll gain the chance to discuss ways to establish more stability in your daily routine and relationships. Be prepared to look outside the box.

15 JANUARY

A little inspiration will motivate you to succeed. You may discover whether you've been idealistic about someone and will gain the chance to overcome issues.

16 JANUARY

You'll enjoy being inspired by your activities. Music, dance and romance could all flourish, so be sure to make time to be inspired.

17 JANUARY

You'll appreciate feeling you can get a lot done but must avoid imagining everyone is on the same page. Take practical steps to attain your goals.

18 JANUARY

This is a good day to discuss collaborative ventures and activities such as family events. You can make solid plans and an agreement may be reached.

19 JANUARY

This is another good day for discussions and to progress with your projects, but you must avoid forgetfulness and making assumptions.

20 JANUARY

A change of pace will take you into fresh territory this weekend and may be intense. It's a good day to transform your appearance, so take the initiative.

21 JANUARY

Think laterally to add a little variety to your usual Sunday. You may be prepared to resume ideas or projects you floated in 2023.

22 JANUARY

You're communicating well but must avoid assuming others are on the same page as you. Be prepared to research your ideas and be innovative.

23 JANUARY

You'll appreciate the sense that your personal life and work schedule will calm down after a period of growth or high activity. Be practical above all with your decisions.

24 JANUARY

When the moon is in Cancer you can tend to be more intuitive but also more sensitive to others, so maintain perspective and focus on your goals.

25 JANUARY

The Leo full moon will spotlight a culmination of events in July Leos' personal lives and at work or health-wise for August Leos. Be ready to make a tough call but avoid making snap decisions.

26 JANUARY

This is a good time for a reunion that is a little different. Be ready to help someone and to ask for help if you need it. Avoid minor bumps and scrapes.

27 JANUARY

You will not always agree with everyone and must avoid arguments, especially at work as someone may be erratic or angry. If it's you, ensure you take time to relax.

28 JANUARY

This is a good day to make a solid commitment to someone such as a family member or employer, but you must be sure you have the same goals.

29 JANUARY

You'll enjoy an upbeat or varied day and will appreciate the chance to try something new. You may even surprise yourself with your abilities. Romance could flourish.

30 JANUARY

This is still a productive time for you so be sure to take the initiative, especially if you're looking for change at work or in your general direction.

31 JANUARY

Be prepared to meet someone halfway, especially if they tend to get under your skin. You can find a fresh arrangement or way to relate.

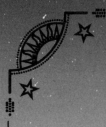

February

1 FEBRUARY

It's a beneficial day to build bridges and focus on good communication skills.

2 FEBRUARY

This is another good day for talks and meetings and to find ways to communicate your thoughts, hopes and aspirations with someone important.

3 FEBRUARY

You'll enjoy doing something different at home or via a trip and romance could blossom this evening, so plan something special!

4 FEBRUARY

You'll enjoy an upbeat and fun approach and activities such as sports will appeal. Just avoid minor bumps and scrapes. Your help may be needed.

5 FEBRUARY

There are therapeutic aspects to the day and you may be drawn to improving your appearance. A meeting or news could be transformative at work or health-wise.

6 FEBRUARY

New opportunities are on the way. Meanwhile, if some relationships are difficult try to be tactful, and if the relationship is irreparable try to find a way forward.

7 FEBRUARY

You may be surprised by news that will mean a change of plan. It's a good day to collaborate and research your circumstances, especially financial ones.

8 FEBRUARY

Your schedule may change at a moment's notice, so be adaptable.

9 FEBRUARY

The Aquarian new moon supermoon will refresh a professional or personal relationship and, if you were born in mid-August, a daily routine. It's a good time to make a commitment.

10 FEBRUARY

You'll enjoy taking time out and dreaming a little. Some activities may be delayed, so be patient. Romance could flourish.

11 FEBRUARY

The Pisces moon will bring out your idealistic and dreamy sides and romance could truly flourish. Just avoid absent-mindedness and daydreaming if you're working.

12 FEBRUARY

This is a creative and inspiring time but you will need to focus that little bit more at work to avoid making mistakes.

13 FEBRUARY

Be positive and creative, but you must avoid being super idealistic or you could be heading for a disappointment. Romance could blossom, so take the initiative.

14 FEBRUARY

Happy St Valentine's Day! This is an intense day and you may feel under pressure at work, so be sure to take breaks. Romance could flourish but you must avoid arguments.

15 FEBRUARY

Be practical at work as your efforts will be effective. Just avoid being stubborn if you disagree with someone as differences are likely to blow over.

16 FEBRUARY

You work or daily schedule is likely to be different, but as long as you're happy with the new direction this will be a fulfilling and upbeat time.

17 FEBRUARY

Meetings and news will lead to a fresh understanding of a situation. You may enjoy a different look or health treat. Romance will go off the dial for Leos born around 24 to 25 July.

18 FEBRUARY

You'll enjoy entering new territory and socialising and networking. Just avoid going too far outside your comfort zone as this could be an intense time.

19 FEBRUARY

You may discover the thorn on the rose or must make a tough call. You may be put on the spot or will be asked for help. If you need advice it is available.

20 FEBRUARY

The Cancerian moon will sharpen your intuition, so pay attention to your instincts. Be prepared to look under the veneer of a circumstance.

21 FEBRUARY

You may receive mixed messages but must avoid second-guessing someone. If you want to know where you stand ask, and be prepared for the answer.

22 FEBRUARY

This could be another intense day: for July Leos in your personal life and for August Leos at work or due to a change in your routine or health. Find ways to cool things down.

23 FEBRUARY

Mercury in Pisces for the next few weeks will sharpen your instincts about someone you work with or someone close. Be prepared to trust them.

24 FEBRUARY

The full moon in Virgo will spotlight a relationship or finances. If things are not as they seem, it's time to look into the details.

25 FEBRUARY

This is a good time to formulate a fresh arrangement with someone but you must do adequate research. Discuss ideas and avoid making rash decisions. Romance could flourish.

26 FEBRUARY

A detailed approach to your work will work wonders as you may otherwise be drawn to daydreaming, so be prepared to focus if you're at work.

27 FEBRUARY

You'll find out whether you've misjudged a circumstance, and the good news is this will enable you to set things straight. Just avoid pressuring someone.

28 FEBRUARY

It's a good day for communications and to find a happy medium, especially if you've argued recently.

29 FEBRUARY

You'll appreciate the support or guidance of someone you know has your back. Romance could thrive.

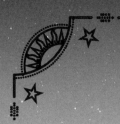

March

1 MARCH

There are therapeutic aspects to the day and it's a lovely one for discussing common ground and collaborations. You may reach a valid agreement or commitment.

2 MARCH

You'll enjoy being proactive about domestic matters. Just ensure you have all the details if you're making important long-term decisions.

3 MARCH

A change of plan or direction merits a careful as opposed to knee-jerk reaction. Think laterally if you're put on the spot.

4 MARCH

The key to a successful day lies in being prepared to collaborate and co-operate. Avoid a Mexican stand-off with someone important; look for common ground.

5 MARCH

This is a good day to reach out to like-minded people and build bridges with co-workers and employers and those you collaborate with in your daily life.

6 MARCH

There is a therapeutic aspect to the day. It's a good time to look for ways to boost your health, vitality and mental and emotional well-being. Relationships can be improved; just avoid impulsiveness.

7 MARCH

You'll feel fulfilled by your activities, so be sure to organise events you enjoy. If you need to repair any relationships this is the day to do so! Romance could flourish.

8 MARCH

This is a creative day that is ideal for the arts, romance, self-development and spirituality. You may gain a deeper understanding of someone close; just avoid idealism and forgetfulness.

9 MARCH

You'll enjoy doing something different and an impromptu get-together. Romance will thrive, so organise a date!

10 MARCH

The Pisces new moon supermoon will kick-start a fresh chapter in a relationship that will be inspiring and potentially transformative.

11 MARCH

You'll appreciate the chance to enter fresh territory at work and in your daily schedule. You may also wish to find more time for the arts, music, dance and romance.

12 MARCH

The key to progress at work is being proactive and upbeat and taking the initiative to prove how well you can lead and collaborate at the same time.

13 MARCH

This is another good day to take the initiative with important talks, at work and with someone special, as you're likely to make progress.

14 MARCH

The Taurean moon brings your earthy, sensual aspects to the surface and you'll be drawn to spending time with people who appreciate your quirky yet down-to-earth nature.

15 MARCH

You'll enjoy socialising and networking, although some duties or even finances may curtail what you do. Talks at work or regarding a commitment will be productive.

16 MARCH

This is a good day to dive deeply into your favourite activities and for organising finances. A commitment could be made.

17 MARCH

This is an ideal day for romantic, artistic and musical endeavours and for self-development. Just avoid being super idealistic if you're making solid commitments.

18 MARCH

The moon in Cancer will bring your instincts to the surface but also potentially your vulnerability, so take things one step at a time.

19 MARCH

This is a great day for discussions and meetings, especially in connection with a favourite project or interest and with someone close.

20 MARCH

You'll find constructive ways to navigate key news. You may be asked to help someone, and if you require more information or expert advice it is available.

21 MARCH

This is a good day to discuss your various chores and arrangements so they suit you and those close to you better. It's a good time to make financial decisions.

22 MARCH

You'll feel increasingly inspired to look for peaceful ways to collaborate and get on with people. You may be drawn to new philosophies, spirituality and the arts.

23 MARCH

You'll enjoy favourite activities such as sports. A group, influential person or friend will be good company. You may find a way to gain an increased sense of purpose.

24 MARCH

The lead-up to a full moon eclipse can be intense, so be sure to pace yourself and take time to look out for your own interests. Avoid forgetfulness.

25 MARCH

This lunar eclipse in Libra is a good time to look for balance in relationships and communications and to discuss changing some arrangements in the name of fair play.

26 MARCH

Your expertise will be in demand and you may need to help someone. There are therapeutic aspects to the day so it's a good time for a health or beauty treat.

27 MARCH

You'll enjoy putting your attention on your home life, property or family. During the day, the more tactful you can be the better for you.

28 MARCH

You'll enjoy a surprise or impromptu get-together. You may receive an unexpected financial or ego boost.

29 MARCH

It's a good day to be original and try something new. You may be drawn to leaving your comfort zone.

30 MARCH

You'll appreciate the chance to be active and outgoing, although you may need to compromise with people you must collaborate with.

31 MARCH

A trip, visit or the chance to be proactive will appeal. Sports, health, fitness and spending time with like-minded people will also appeal.

April

1 APRIL

Try to get key paperwork and ideas on the table for discussion and tie up loose ends before Mercury turns retrograde tomorrow to avoid having to redo some arrangements.

2 APRIL

You'll hear news to do with work and your general projects. A trip will benefit from a little focus to avoid delays.

3 APRIL

You'll feel inspired by your favourite projects and hobbies. The arts, film and music will appeal. This is a good day for romance, but you must avoid being a perfectionist.

4 APRIL

You'll appreciate a get-together with someone who is helpful and potentially dear to you. A reunion will appeal.

5 APRIL

Over the coming weeks you'll feel more proactive about what truly motivates you in life. A trip, the chance to enjoy fun events and being physically active and fit will appeal.

6 APRIL

This is a romantic and changeable weekend, one you'll enjoy especially if you like variety in life.

7 APRIL

The lead-up to the new moon is an ideal time to make a wish. You'll be considering a fresh career phase or direction in life, so be careful what you wish for.

8 APRIL

The total solar eclipse signifies a change in status, direction or career. You may need to better look after your health or that of someone else. There are therapeutic aspects to the day.

9 APRIL

You'll appreciate the sense that life can regain a more even keel and will find the time to unwind.

10 APRIL

You'll receive unexpected news and, for some, this will be financial in nature. You'll appreciate the chance to progress with an interest or project. Avoid overspending.

11 APRIL

You'll enjoy a reunion and may receive news to do with your career, status or direction. Paperwork or a conversation will require a review.

12 APRIL

You'll enjoy socialising and networking. However, some talks may be a little tense so be tactful to avoid fallout.

13 APRIL

A light-hearted feel to the day will raise morale. You'll appreciate the chance to nurture your mind, body and soul.

14 APRIL

You'll gain insight into the feelings of someone close. It's a good day to find time to unwind after a busy few days.

15 APRIL

You may need to revisit a delicate issue and being diplomatic will work in your favour. It's a good day for a health or beauty appointment.

16 APRIL

It's a proactive day ideal for getting things done, especially where you must review or go over old ground. You must avoid rushing and cutting corners.

17 APRIL

You'll enjoy a get-together or a favourite activity. If singles meet someone new they may seem familiar or will be significant in some way.

18 APRIL

As a fire sign you like to be proactive, yet sometimes considering your actions first will be more effective and especially about long-term matters.

19 APRIL

As the sun enters Taurus you'll appreciate gaining a little more security in your life. You'll enjoy a reunion. Someone close may have surprising news.

20 APRIL

You'll enjoy devoting at least some time to healthy and uplifting activities. You may be surprised by developments this weekend that could open new doors.

21 APRIL

Be prepared to factor in the need to get chores done first and look after your health and well-being. An impromptu get-together or unusual event will take your focus.

22 APRIL

You'll appreciate the chance to improve your status, interests and projects. Be prepared to be flexible for the best results.

23 APRIL

People around you may be a little emotional or intense. You'll appreciate the chance to unwind at the end of the day.

24 APRIL

The Scorpio full moon will spotlight a turning point in your domestic life and status. Take things one step at a time to avoid feeling overwhelmed. It's a good day to make a commitment.

25 APRIL

A key get-together, trip or news will set you on a clearer path moving forward. It's a good day to talk as the Mercury retrograde phase ends.

26 APRIL

You'll appreciate the opportunity to invest time in yourself and your home and those you love. Upbeat, sporty and favourite interests will gain traction, so be active!

27 APRIL

It's another excellent day to focus on what and who makes you happy. Just avoid arguments, as not everyone will be as willing to embrace an active weekend.

28 APRIL

Romance, the arts and spending time with a like-minded person will appeal. If you're creatively or spiritually minded your activities will flourish.

29 APRIL

As Venus enters Taurus you'll enjoy being practical about establishing more peace and calmness in your life. You may tend to be a little idealistic, so be realistic.

30 APRIL

Proactive Mars will encourage you to be more outgoing in your relationships, communications and favourite activities over the coming weeks, so plan ahead!

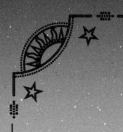

May

1 MAY

You'll manage to accomplish a great deal but some circumstances will be intense, so be prepared to work harder than usual. Your efforts will pay off. Avoid conflict.

2 MAY

A change in your usual routine will lead to a chance to transform how you go about your usual schedule. You may be drawn to looking for a fresh health routine or look.

3 MAY

You'll enjoy the company of a like-minded character. A relationship may blossom. This is a good day to set the ball in motion for a new look or health schedule.

4 MAY

You'll be inspired by someone you share common ground with such as a housemate, family member, business or personal partner. The arts and romance will appeal.

5 MAY

You'll enjoy a reunion or return to an old haunt. You may welcome the chance to retrace your steps with a project or relationship.

6 MAY

It's a case of cranking up your tact, patience and diplomacy to ensure the week gets off to a good start!

7 MAY

Ask for help and collaborate and compromise, as you will attain your goals all the better. A health or learning opportunity will arise. A trip may need to be rethought.

8 MAY

The Taurus new moon will kick-start a fresh chapter in your general direction, career or status, and the more practical you are with your decisions the better it will be.

9 MAY

The Gemini moon brings out your playful side and you'll appreciate the opportunity to get down to brass tacks at work. Be prepared to study or research your plans.

10 MAY

There's a lovely sociable vibe to the day, and work may entail an end-of-the-week celebration or the chance to enjoy fun chats.

11 MAY

This will be a busy time, and you'll appreciate the chance to indulge in someone close and your favourite activities. It's a good time for a health or beauty treat.

12 MAY

You're known for your lion-like courage and big character yet you can be a kitten. You may prefer to take things easy.

13 MAY

You may be surprised by developments and these could work well. It's a good day to make changes in your career status or direction and for a financial review.

14 MAY

The moon in your sign will help you be upbeat and dynamic. However, some people, especially at work, will require a subtle approach to avoid crossing swords.

15 MAY

A slow and steady approach to communications, projects and developments will reap rewards. Avoid feeling pressured or rushed if possible.

16 MAY

Remember the tortoise and the hare? Once again, a measured approach will work wonders. Avoid mix-ups and misunderstandings.

17 MAY

There is always merit in being timely but rarely merit in rushing, especially now. Avoid needless arguments; look for solutions. Plan ahead to avoid delays.

18 MAY

You may receive welcome news from out of the blue. An opportunity will be hard to miss; just ensure it aligns with your big-picture values and aims and then enjoy!

19 MAY

This is a romantic day and an excellent time to make a romantic commitment.

20 MAY

Over the next four weeks you'll be communicating well and your company will be enjoyed. A project or development could be all it seems and more.

21 MAY

You're thinking laterally and analytically yet your heart is as equally motivated to be heard. A clever mix of brains, heart, intuition and wisdom will lead to success.

22 MAY

This is a good time to positively transform your career, status, work or health. A new look may appeal.

23 MAY

The full moon in Sagittarius spotlights a fresh chapter at home or with family or property. A change at work or in your status will have a bearing. Romance could blossom.

24 MAY

The moon in a fellow fire sign will encourage you to be active and enjoy seeing results for your hard work. A fun musical, friends-based or creative evening will appeal.

25 MAY

This is a super-sociable and active weekend that you'll enjoy. If you're trying to change your usual routine then today will deliver.

26 MAY

As Jupiter enters Gemini you'll increasingly enjoy expressing your outgoing, upbeat and sociable sides. You may be drawn to spending more time with a friend or organisation.

27 MAY

Attention to detail and the willingness to work hard will reap rewards. Avoid seeing only obstacles at work; be positive!

28 MAY

Talks and meetings are likely to go well. If you have shared matters to discuss you could make a valid agreement, especially financially.

29 MAY

Be prepared to go out on a limb – within reason! You may feel vulnerable, so look for expert advice and provide good advice yourself. Take regular breaks to avoid making mistakes.

30 MAY

It's a good day to talk, especially regarding delicate topics, as you're likely to come to mutually agreeable outcomes. A health matter can progress.

31 MAY

Artistic and creative Leos will truly feel inspired, and if you have a logical mindset take time to think things through as you may be slightly idealistic.

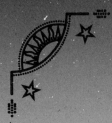
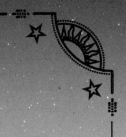

June

1 JUNE

You'll love taking the initiative and making things happen. Just avoid making rash decisions, especially if you're working.

2 JUNE

The Aries moon will add an upbeat, proactive quality to your day. You'll feel motivated to be active, and focusing on health and well-being will appeal.

3 JUNE

There's change in the air, and you may experience it the most in your daily routine. For some this is due to developments at work and for others due to health and well-being.

4 JUNE

You'll enjoy socialising and networking. It's a good day for any kind of meeting, information gathering and get-together.

5 JUNE

This is an excellent day to get paperwork, discussions and financial matters shipshape.

6 JUNE

The new moon will help you turn a page at work, with a personal matter and financially, so be sure to initiate important talks and plans.

7 JUNE

You'll feel inspired to spend time with a friend, group or organisation and will enjoy talks and meetings. Just avoid being at loggerheads with someone whose ideas differ from yours.

8 JUNE

A shared circumstance such as space at home, the office or joint finances will merit a patient approach. Be sure to have all the details to hand to avoid conflict.

9 JUNE

Be prepared to find common ground, especially financially and with shared duties. You must avoid a Mexican stand-off as it could become long term.

10 JUNE

The Leo moon will bring out your demonstrative, happy but showy sides. Just avoid a power struggle.

11 JUNE

An expert or adviser will prove their weight in gold, so if you need advice it will be available. Your help may be in demand.

12 JUNE

You are independent and like to lead; just avoid putting someone offside as it could be the wrong person to have as a rival.

13 JUNE

You'll appreciate the opportunity to be spontaneous and shine. It's a good day for an impromptu get-together and someone's news may surprise you.

14 JUNE

You'll enjoy socialising and your favourite activities. Work and financial transactions will require a little more focus to avoid making mistakes.

15 JUNE

You'll enjoy doing something different and spending time with a like-minded group of people.

16 JUNE

You'll be drawn to experiencing something light-hearted and will avoid intense topics for that reason. You'll find a way to encourage others to see the light side of life.

17 JUNE

You'll feel inspired by people you mingle with but may need to set or adhere to a clear boundary regarding your own role. Avoid misunderstandings for the best results.

18 JUNE

A Scorpio moon tends to bring emotions to the surface and it's in your interest to maintain the status quo, especially at home.

19 JUNE

Developments beyond your control will add to a mixed day on which focusing on your abilities and skill sets will lead to success.

20 JUNE

The solstice is a lovely time to review the year so far. You may need to unravel a mystery.

21 JUNE

Reach out to friends and family as they may help you overcome an obstacle. A social or networking event will be fun.

22 JUNE

The full moon in Capricorn suggests you're ready to turn a page in your everyday routine. Put yourself first so you can better look after your duties. A meeting will be motivational.

23 JUNE

A meeting may be delayed or rescheduled. Spend a little time considering your true priorities and following them more rigorously if need be.

24 JUNE

Begin the week the way you mean to carry on; a little light-heartedness and inspiration will take you a long way.

25 JUNE

You'll gain a sense of direction and purpose by wholeheartedly diving into your projects and plans. Just avoid rushing.

26 JUNE

This is a great day to be practical and reach out to experts and those you know have your back. You could build a strong foundation for yourself; just avoid being put off by naysayers.

27 JUNE

An inspired approach to a work or financial project will pay off. You may contemplate a commitment.

28 JUNE

A personal, health or work matter will be worth looking into in more detail if you feel uneasy. Your help may be sought.

29 JUNE

You have the wind beneath your wings and your efforts will pay off. If you're single love could thrive, so be sure to organise a date.

30 JUNE

A reunion or return to an old haunt may include a surprise. Be prepared to look outside the box at your options.

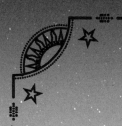

July

1 JULY

The Taurus moon will encourage you to get things done at work. There's something inspiring about today's events and you'll feel ready to commit to a venture.

2 JULY

As Mercury enters Leo discussions will merit focus, especially in connection with a trip, project, study or legal matter. It's a good day to get on track with your plans.

3 JULY

It's a busy, productive day ideal for work projects, but you must avoid power struggles. You could make a valid work or financial agreement.

4 JULY

The lead-up to the Cancerian new moon is an ideal time to take stock of your collaborations, especially at work and financially.

5 JULY

The Cancerian new moon is a good time to revitalise your work and health and put in place a supportive daily routine. You may be drawn to a fresh financial agreement.

6 JULY

It's a good day to boost your health, especially if you're feeling a little sensitive. Someone may ask for your help or will alter plans abruptly. If you need advice it will be available, so reach out.

7 JULY

The Leo moon brings a more upbeat feel to the day. You'll enjoy being in touch with like-minded people and a change of pace.

8 JULY

This is a lovely day for an impromptu get-together both at work and in your personal life. Your connection with someone who can help you progress with your projects could blossom.

9 JULY

An upbeat, outgoing attitude will certainly get things done, but you must avoid putting off-kilter someone who prefers things on an even keel.

10 JULY

You'll be getting the help you need to ensure your projects and plans can succeed, so be sure to reach out.

11 JULY

As Venus enters Leo you'll notice your attention go to love and money over the coming weeks; this is a great time to improve these areas. Romance could flourish.

12 JULY

You'll feel motivated to succeed at work and remedy past matters, but you must avoid allowing emotions to get the upper hand. Romance could ignite but so too could conflict.

13 JULY

When you put your focus on creating peace and calm in your life that is exactly what you will create, starting today! Just avoid being pressed to enter into activities.

14 JULY

You may need to be assertive in order to be heard, so be sure to find a way to communicate your feelings without creating upset. A trip or event will be enjoyable.

15 JULY

Developments may be unexpected or out of the ordinary and put you in a stressful situation, so be sure to take short breaks whenever you can. Think laterally.

16 JULY

You like to feel truly passionate about what you do and currently you have the opportunity to invest deeply in a plan or project, which you'll enjoy.

17 JULY

As a fire sign you like to be proactive so you'll enjoy the upbeat feel to the day, which will encourage you to make optimistic progress.

18 JULY

You'll enjoy a pleasant reunion or news from the past that will enable you to make solid progress in your chosen field.

19 JULY

There are therapeutic aspects to the day. You'll enjoy reconnecting with activities and friends who truly make your heart soar.

20 JULY

As Mars enters Gemini it is the start of a sociable phase. Just avoid spreading yourself too thinly.

21 JULY

The full moon in Capricorn will spotlight changes in key personal or business relationships for some Leos and, for many, in your daily or work routine. Avoid misunderstandings.

22 JULY

The sun in your sign for the next four weeks will be truly motivational. This is an excellent time to make changes that are long overdue.

23 JULY

It's a good time to transform your daily, health and work schedules but you must avoid overwork and overdoing things, as otherwise circumstances will feel intense.

24 JULY

This is an excellent time to be tactful with those you must collaborate with and, ultimately, rely upon.

25 JULY

A close and detailed perspective, especially towards finances, will certainly put you in a strong position.

26 JULY

This is a lovely day to be spontaneous and enjoy spending time with fun and inspiring people. Be proactive and positive but avoid being pressured into undertaking activities.

27 JULY

This is an excellent time for a mini review of your finances; you'll find ways to put a strong personal budget in place. Avoid power struggles.

28 JULY

The Taurus moon helps you focus on being practical and getting chores done but also to enjoy the sumptuousness of life and a little luxury.

29 JULY

A slower or even frustrating aspect to the day will soon shift as the day progresses, and communications will feel easier as a result.

30 JULY

There are healing aspects to the day. You could build bridges with colleagues and employers and may experience a financial or ego boost.

31 JULY

This is an excellent day to be in touch with those who inspire you such as teachers and role models. A meeting or talk may be particularly significant.

August

1 AUGUST

Your feelings are bubbling under the surface, so if you're unsure of a decision allow your thoughts to bubble up over the coming days. Avoid making rash decisions.

2 AUGUST

You may need to adjust to someone's expectations of you and could come up against a roadblock. Rest assured someone loyal will be supportive.

3 AUGUST

The lead-up to the new moon in Leo will be a good time to consider how best to revitalise your daily life, work – mostly for July Leos – and personal life.

4 AUGUST

The Leo new moon spotlights your everyday routine: how could you feel more supported by your activities and those you love, and how could you better support them?

5 AUGUST

A group, friend or organisation will prove particularly supportive. Avoid a battle of egos, especially at work.

6 AUGUST

Now that Mercury is retrograde you'll gain the chance to review your finances and career. Keep conversations clear for the best results.

7 AUGUST

You'll appreciate the chance to connect with someone who can help you and/or whose company you enjoy.

8 AUGUST

This is an excellent time to review your budget. You may experience a financial or ego boost and a debt may be repaid.

9 AUGUST

While the views of certain groups, colleagues or friends may seem at counterpoint to yours, there is a way to find common ground.

10 AUGUST

A determined approach to enjoying your weekend will certainly pay off. You'll appreciate a gathering of friends or a family get-together. A favourite activity will prove healing.

11 AUGUST

Consider whether your feelings are overriding practicalities, especially if you find yourself in hot water. You'll appreciate the chance to invest in your home.

12 AUGUST

Strong emotions could get the upper hand while the moon is in Scorpio, so be sure to maintain a professional approach at work and look for solutions at home.

13 AUGUST

Trust your instincts as they are spot on. You'll find the chance to alter your usual routine but will need to persuade someone to back up your ideas.

14 AUGUST

A friend, colleague or organisation will prove supportive if you can get them on your side. Be optimistic, but also be sure to be precise and avoid cutting corners.

15 AUGUST

There are therapeutic aspects to the day; for example, you may receive good news at work or gain the chance to relax. Just avoid making assumptions.

16 AUGUST

You are dynamic and don't like delays so you'll need to be patient, especially with someone who can be a thorn in your side. Your hard work will pay off.

17 AUGUST

You'll enjoy a change of pace and doing something different but you must plan ahead well to avoid delays.

18 AUGUST

Be prepared to be flexible as a change of plan, delay or surprise news will merit a patient approach.

19 AUGUST

The Aquarian full moon will spotlight a relationship. Talks will be productive even if you feel you're going over old ground or people are being difficult. A contract may be agreed upon.

20 AUGUST

You may be seeing life through rose-coloured glasses, so be sure to obtain the facts so you don't make rash decisions.

21 AUGUST

Negotiations will take you a long way towards your desired outcome. Be prepared to reconfigure your finances and/or personal arrangements.

22 AUGUST

The sun in Virgo over the next four weeks will spotlight how to take practical action regarding your aspirations and finances moving forward. Be proactive and positive.

23 AUGUST

This is a good day to review your finances and personal matters, but you must avoid arguments as these will result in a stalemate.

24 AUGUST

It's a great weekend to catch up with friends and like-minded people, as you'll feel motivated and anchored by them. You may receive an impromptu invitation.

25 AUGUST

This is a good day for a mini financial review, especially if you're in debt. A self-nurturing evening will appeal, especially if you're drawn to sports during the day.

26 AUGUST

Be prepared to look outside the box at your various options at work and in the long term. It's a good day for research.

27 AUGUST

You'll enjoy an impromptu or surprise development, for some at work and for others in your personal life. You'll enjoy an ego or financial boost.

28 AUGUST

Be prepared to focus in more detail on an arrangement or agreement, especially if you feel it's one-sided. It's time to talk.

29 AUGUST

Look for peace and happiness in your work and financial life. It's a good day to discuss your long-term plans with those they concern. A job interview will be transformative.

30 AUGUST

You'll appreciate the chance to reconnect with someone close to your heart. It's a good day to take time out if possible for a health or beauty treat.

31 AUGUST

You may be pleasantly surprised by developments. An impromptu get-together will be enjoyable; just avoid making rash decisions.

September

1 SEPTEMBER

You'll enjoy a chatty, sociable day, although you'll be choosy about who you spend your time with as you're not suffering fools gladly.

2 SEPTEMBER

You may need to go over old ground at work or with a health routine to ensure it still suits your schedule and needs.

3 SEPTEMBER

This new moon in Virgo is a good time to revitalise your finances and personal commitments. Consider your true priorities.

4 SEPTEMBER

Mars in your 12th house of work and health will encourage you to put your energy where it is needed in both these areas. A get-together will provide clarity.

5 SEPTEMBER

The moon in Libra will encourage you to be more outspoken and proactive about your choices and activities.

6 SEPTEMBER

A little extra focus on your communication and negotiation skills will work wonders, especially if you feel you're at loggerheads with someone important.

7 SEPTEMBER

Choose your words carefully as they will be hard to take back. Shoppers will be inclined to overspend, so keep an eye on your budget.

8 SEPTEMBER

While you can sometimes be generous you can be seen as the opposite, so be careful to balance finances and deflect arguments over money. Avoid forgetfulness.

9 SEPTEMBER

As Mercury leaves Leo key talks and transactions could be intense, so be prepared to focus on details but avoid obsessing over them.

10 SEPTEMBER

You'll enjoy being motivated and engaged in your activities, especially at home. A fun get-together will raise morale.

11 SEPTEMBER

Certain talks or financial transactions may be tense, but rest assured that your hard work and tact will pay off.

12 SEPTEMBER

This is a good time to steam ahead with your plans and projects but you must avoid biting off more than you can chew. Keep your expectations real.

13 SEPTEMBER

The more practical you are the better, especially at work and regarding logistics and planning.

14 SEPTEMBER

You'll appreciate the chance to unwind but may find a need to sort out work or financial matters. Take time out to focus on your health.

15 SEPTEMBER

You'll enjoy making the most of your Sunday, even if someone needs your focus. Special attention to your health will be rewarding.

16 SEPTEMBER

You'll enjoy the chance to reconnect with someone important such as a family member. However, some of your interactions will require patience, especially at work.

17 SEPTEMBER

The lead-up to a full moon can be intense and the lead-up to a lunar eclipse even more so. Be patient with communications and interactions.

18 SEPTEMBER

The partial lunar eclipse supermoon in Pisces spotlights your extracurricular activities and pastimes. You may make a commitment or financial agreement.

19 SEPTEMBER

A trip or visit will open your eyes to new ways of doing things and you'll enjoy meeting an upbeat, if different, group of people.

20 SEPTEMBER

A tactful approach to others will work well for you. Think laterally for the best results.

21 SEPTEMBER

A trip or guests will take some of your focus and you'll enjoy preparing for a get-together. Romance or a favourite activity will thrive. Just avoid travel delays and misunderstandings.

22 SEPTEMBER

You'll appreciate seeing your relationships and daily life thrive over the coming weeks, but to do so you must aim to bring more harmony into your life.

23 SEPTEMBER

The moon in Gemini is ideal for networking and socialising, so be prepared to enjoy both personal and work get-togethers. You're communicating well.

24 SEPTEMBER

You may be pleasantly surprised by news or a trip. It's a good time to make progress at work.

25 SEPTEMBER

You may be easily influenced, so be careful with investments. This is a good day to talk, but you must avoid misunderstandings. The arts and romance will appeal.

26 SEPTEMBER

You'll look for a fair go and may experience a situation in which you feel justice could be better served. A trip, change at work or get-together may be transformative.

27 SEPTEMBER

The moon in Leo over the next two days will bring out your proactive side. However, some may find you a little overbearing so be prepared to step back.

28 SEPTEMBER

This is an excellent weekend for building strength in a key relationship. You may reconnect with someone special or return to an old haunt.

29 SEPTEMBER

A trip or reunion will appeal. Just avoid making rash decisions if you're travelling.

30 SEPTEMBER

It's another good day for getting together with old friends or family. You'll be well prepared to work hard. If you're on holiday you'll relish the change of pace.

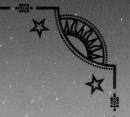

October

1 OCTOBER

During the dark of the moon is a good time to set your intentions for the future, especially regarding finances, long-term plans, key relationships and travel.

2 OCTOBER

The solar eclipse in Libra will help you turn a corner in your personal life and creative projects. It's a good time to set sail on a fresh venture, trip, study and legal matter.

3 OCTOBER

You'll enjoy getting together with someone at home, either yours or theirs, and if you've been considering a little home decoration or DIY project it's likely to go well.

4 OCTOBER

This is an excellent time to get ahead with domestic matters. A commitment made now will place you well to succeed at work and in your personal life.

5 OCTOBER

You'll feel drawn to investing in people who mean the most to you, especially at home or with family. A move undertaken now augurs well for the future.

6 OCTOBER

You won't always agree with everyone, so be prepared for some give and take to avoid arguments. If you're travelling, organise extra time to avoid delays.

7 OCTOBER

A positive and proactive approach to the start of the week will be beneficial, especially at home. Just avoid misunderstandings and traffic delays by planning ahead.

8 OCTOBER

You'll enjoy a trip or specific news that is positive. Some talks may bring out your vulnerabilities or those of someone else, so be pragmatic.

9 OCTOBER

Your communication skills may be put to the test over the next two days, so be sure to express yourself clearly and double-check you have the facts.

10 OCTOBER

The Capricorn moon helps you to plan ahead and make rational decisions, but you may be inclined to be stubborn. Be prepared to see someone else's point of view.

11 OCTOBER

Think outside the box for the best results, as you may experience surprise news or will need to be adaptable.

12 OCTOBER

A mystery may be in the making, and rather than second-guessing someone ask them where you stand – but be prepared for the answer.

13 OCTOBER

You'll feel increasingly passionate about your ideas, thoughts and plans. Bear in mind that others may not and choose your words carefully to avoid arguments. A trip may be delayed.

14 OCTOBER

Be prepared to be spontaneous and adaptable or to meet someone halfway, as you may be surprised by developments that will merit careful attention.

15 OCTOBER

You can make headway with domestic and personal matters. Seek information from an organisation and undertake constructive talks. Avoid distractions.

16 OCTOBER

This is one of the best days for romance this year, so be prepared to organise a treat! It's also a good time for improving domestic décor and dynamics.

17 OCTOBER

The full moon supermoon in Aries will bring a particular relationship or venture to a head. There are therapeutic aspects to developments. Look for adventure and be positive.

18 OCTOBER

You'll enjoy creature comforts and finding the time to relax at home. In the meantime, be practical with projects for the best results.

19 OCTOBER

A surprise development or unusual event will require you to be well organised, but you will rise to the challenge.

20 OCTOBER

You may tend to be easily distracted and will need to focus a little harder on tasks, but when you do you'll gain good results at home and with your ventures.

21 OCTOBER

The fun factor is hard to miss. You'll enjoy sports, upbeat activities at home and generally celebrating life.

22 OCTOBER

As the sun enters Scorpio, the next four weeks will revolve around attaining more joy and contentment. You may need to reorganise some chores and work so you can. Avoid conflict as it will escalate.

23 OCTOBER

You'll enjoy a favourite interest and spending time with someone you love, so organise a date if you haven't already!

24 OCTOBER

The Leo moon brings out your optimism and you'll feel creative and inclined to be positive, which makes for a productive day.

25 OCTOBER

You'll enjoy a reunion or the chance to do something different. You may hear news you've been waiting for. Be spontaneous but avoid rushing.

26 OCTOBER

This is an excellent weekend for getting things shipshape – anything from financial budgets to housework and paperwork.

27 OCTOBER

You'll enjoy being active and upbeat but some communications and activities will be easier than others. Your efforts will be worthwhile.

28 OCTOBER

You may need to do remedial work with a work or domestic project. Avoid being a perfectionist, as this could stall your efforts. Be realistic and practical instead.

29 OCTOBER

You'll be looking for fair play and a fair go, and communications will reflect this. Just avoid being idealistic, as it could backfire.

30 OCTOBER

Unexpected news will require you to innovate. If you experience a disappointment it will open the doors to something new.

31 OCTOBER

Happy Hallowe'en! Trick or treat: you decide. Avoid taking things too literally and find time to unwind after a busy day.

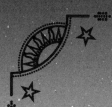

November

1 NOVEMBER

The Scorpio new moon will kick-start a promising fresh phase in your domestic life and, for some, in your neighbourhood. Be prepared for change.

2 NOVEMBER

There is a therapeutic aspect to the weekend. You may enjoy a favourite activity, spiritual development opportunity or trip somewhere beautiful.

3 NOVEMBER

You'll enjoy romance, the arts and being with like-minded, upbeat people. However, a change of routine may be intense. Avoid conflict if possible.

4 NOVEMBER

This is a good day to make a commitment to a person or project. Mars in your sign for the next few weeks will add to a proactive and dynamic phase.

5 NOVEMBER

Combine your outgoing and charismatic approach with practicalities and you could move mountains!

6 NOVEMBER

Keep your feet on the ground as this will help you to navigate circumstances, especially at work and in your daily life. A health matter will benefit from a methodical approach.

7 NOVEMBER

You'll appreciate the opportunity to enjoy some time at home and with someone you love and admire. A get-together will be enjoyable.

8 NOVEMBER

If you handle an obstacle or an unexpected development well you may discover a positive way forward. Be diligent.

9 NOVEMBER

You'll discover whether you've had unrealistic expectations. The good news is you'll be able to reset your compass. Avoid overindulgence and absent-mindedness.

10 NOVEMBER

You'll enjoy relaxing with someone special, but if you've got important topics to discuss ensure you're practical and realistic and stick with the facts.

11 NOVEMBER

You have the ability to get on well with others although you may feel under pressure, so take short breaks if necessary during the day.

12 NOVEMBER

It's quite likely that communications and financial decisions will be tense, so it's in your interest to take things one step at a time.

13 NOVEMBER

The Aries moon over the next two days will be motivational and you'll certainly feel more inclined to make inroads into your various projects.

14 NOVEMBER

The lead-up to the Taurus full moon can be intense. This is a good time to consider how to improve your status, career and general direction.

15 NOVEMBER

The full moon in Taurus puts a spotlight on intense or unpredictable aspects of your work life, status or general direction. You may need to think on your feet due to surprise news.

16 NOVEMBER

An adaptable and spontaneous approach to developments will help you make the most of the day. However, you're unlikely to get on with everyone so be prepared to be tactful.

17 NOVEMBER

You'll enjoy being sociable and meeting a diverse crowd. If you enjoy writing, reading and travel you'll enjoy your day all the more!

18 NOVEMBER

This is an excellent day for meetings, a trip to an old haunt and reconnecting with old friends and acquaintances.

19 NOVEMBER

You'll enjoy a romantic time and the arts and finding time to bring a little comfort and luxury into your home, all of which will feel therapeutic.

20 NOVEMBER

As Pluto re-enters Aquarius your usual daily routine will become more varied and you may resume a schedule. Be prepared to think laterally for the best results.

21 NOVEMBER

Over the next four weeks you'll enjoy being more outgoing with friends and family, and a change of schedule will be beneficial.

22 NOVEMBER

If you've been looking for a commitment from somebody you're likely to obtain it. It's a good day to make a new agreement and for romance.

23 NOVEMBER

If you're working you'll be busy and will appreciate a sense of purpose and fulfilment. You'll enjoy a reunion or the chance to revisit an aspect of your home life or family.

24 NOVEMBER

This is a good day to review your finances and personal obligations and tie up loose ends with paperwork, especially to do with home or family.

25 NOVEMBER

You have a pragmatic approach to friends and colleagues and your fair-mindedness will put you in a strong position at work.

26 NOVEMBER

You may receive key news from someone close. This is a good time to review how much time you spend on your favourite projects versus how much time you spend working and to find a balance.

27 NOVEMBER

You'll find your relationships will thrive under the current stars and it's certainly a good time to take the initiative with relationships. Romance and family ties could flourish.

28 NOVEMBER

A personal or health matter is best approached pragmatically. You may be asked for help, and if you need help it will be available so reach out.

29 NOVEMBER

Meetings and talks are likely to go well, especially at work and regarding health and beauty. Be prepared to review a situation and turn it around.

30 NOVEMBER

The lead up to the new moon is perfect for placing an intention to be more active and involved with those you love.

December

1 DECEMBER

The Sagittarian new moon will kick-start a fresh chapter in your personal or family life. You'll enjoy being active and outgoing and may also enjoy a reunion.

2 DECEMBER

You may be surprised by developments. It's a good time to work on a constructive, fresh daily routine that supports your health. You'll enjoy an impromptu get-together.

3 DECEMBER

This is a good time to discuss what's on your mind, as you'll avoid a Mexican stand-off. Be diplomatic for the best results.

4 DECEMBER

A trip, visit or meeting will shed light on your best path forward. You may enjoy a lovely reunion. Be prepared to be adaptable and open-minded to avoid conflict.

5 DECEMBER

Think outside the box for the best results and maintain perspective, especially if you must focus on serious or intense issues. A change of pace or of place will be constructive.

6 DECEMBER

You may be more outspoken or drawn to fire up quickly, so you must avoid impulsiveness. A meeting or the chance to discuss finances and long-term plans will arise.

7 DECEMBER

You'll appreciate the chance to alter your appearance and boost your health and vitality. A meeting may be intense, albeit enjoyable, so pace yourself.

8 DECEMBER

It's time to dream a little and relax. If you can't do so, it's important to avoid seeing only the negatives in life. A change of perception will boost your mood.

9 DECEMBER

A more upbeat tone to the day will lead you to make progress with your ventures. An expert, teacher or mentor will prove invaluable.

10 DECEMBER

You'll appreciate the help of someone who knows more than you, so be prepared to open your mind to new ideas. A meeting will be constructive.

11 DECEMBER

Be practical with your various decisions, as your happiness will depend on being realistic. Just avoid being stubborn and unwilling to adapt.

12 DECEMBER

Meetings and discussions to do with work, your personal life and health will be constructive, even if you feel you're going over old ground.

13 DECEMBER

Despite this being Friday the 13th it's a good day for get-togethers, both at home and at work. Be prepared to review your circumstances and adjust accordingly.

14 DECEMBER

Your chatty, sociable side will seek expression. It's best to choose your company wisely, as someone in particular may rankle. It's your weekend!

15 DECEMBER

The full moon promises a fresh chapter in your social life and loyalties. You may be surprised by news. Be prepared to focus on your goals and avoid being easily led.

16 DECEMBER

The moon in Cancer will encourage you to maintain a strong stance vis-à-vis a tough circumstance. When you do you'll work wonders.

17 DECEMBER

Trust your intuition and you'll gain insight into a person or situation that is up in the air. Be prepared to work constructively towards a positive outcome.

18 DECEMBER

Consider the facts carefully as you may otherwise tend to idealise a situation or be easily misled, especially regarding an emotional or financial investment.

19 DECEMBER

It's a good day for talks, especially regarding shared financial matters and work. An expert will prove helpful.

20 DECEMBER

You'll appreciate the sense that your star is rising despite the odds. Be prepared to think laterally and see the big picture. It's a positive day, so be proactive.

21 DECEMBER

This is the solstice. You'll appreciate the sense that you can bring more stability into your personal life, but you must be prepared to see the points of view of other people.

22 DECEMBER

A change of pace or of place will transform your day. It's a good day for get-togethers and for romance and also for a beauty or health treat.

23 DECEMBER

You won't always get on with everyone. You may prefer your own company or will need to minimise time with someone in particular. Tact will be very useful.

24 DECEMBER

There are healing aspects to the day. A change of pace will be relaxing but some activities or talks will be intense, so be prepared to minimise stress.

25 DECEMBER

Merry Christmas! A little tact will go a long way towards a happy day as you're in the process of relaxing. A change of routine will require you to adapt.

26 DECEMBER

Key family, domestic and, for some, work meetings will be a focus. A change of environment will involve travel, and you must factor delays into the trip to avoid frustration.

27 DECEMBER

While working Leos will be productive, some conversations are best postponed if possible. If not, you must avoid a Mexican stand-off by looking for common ground.

28 DECEMBER

An unexpected change of plan or unusual news will impact your day. Be prepared to adjust and avoid knee-jerk reactions for the best results.

29 DECEMBER

An optimistic, outgoing approach to your day will reap rewards. You'll be in a strong position to build bridges with someone if need be. It's a good day for sports and a health or beauty treat.

30 DECEMBER

The new moon in Capricorn points to something different in your personal life. Be prepared to adapt and find more stability. A creative project could thrive.

31 DECEMBER

Happy New Year! This is a therapeutic time for you. Be prepared to let bygones be in the past and focus on a healing 2025. Just avoid overindulging as you'll regret it tomorrow!

FINANCES

Be prepared to embrace a fresh approach to your finances in 2024. Luckily, you'll be able to update traditional and ingrained perceptions about how to save and manage your finances and where to invest. The first quarter is likely to be a lucrative time as long as you avoid gambling, as this would be a true pitfall this year. Digital platforms may encourage you to view your finances in a different light, but you must be careful with shared financial commitments and who you trust with your financial investments. Do your research first and foremost.

HEALTH

A practical and organised approach to your daily health routine will pay off in 2024, otherwise you risk leaving this important aspect of your life to the end of the day as more pressing duties take your focus. As a result, you could miss out on the benefits of a scheduled health routine. Be prepared to include exercise and a nutritious diet in your everyday schedule so that your health routine becomes as important as your work routine. The first quarter will be best for putting a new schedule in place. Be creative about fitness: consider joining groups of like-minded people in a fresh and healthy context, such as nature rambles or dune care.

LOVE LIFE

You'll be drawn to fresh experiences in 2024. For example, couples will enjoy the opportunity to experience your relationship in new ways and there may be changes within family circumstances, which will alter your love life. Singles will be drawn to meeting a fresh social group and will also contemplate a partnership, as you experiment with feelings, sensuality and also potentially different types of relationships. The first quarter will be the most proactive romantically, so aim to find the time for your love life then so that you establish a rhythm for the year. Mid- to late February and early April will be particularly romantic, so take the initiative then!

CAREER

Workhorse Saturn will encourage you to take on work as if it were nothing at all, so you risk overcommitting to projects you cannot physically find the time to complete. Ensure you avoid overwork in 2024, otherwise fatigue will arise as if from out of the blue. The first quarter will be ideal for getting things done and focusing on how collaborations may help you better achieve your goals. Be careful to choose collaborators wisely and be sure to delegate work if you do take on more than you can manage yourself.

HOME LIFE

This is an optimistic year domestically as there's a sense of opportunity and the chance to repair relationships and the terms and conditions or circumstances of your domestic life. The year begins with concentrated focus on your home life; this may simply be because you alter your home or environment in some way via gardening or a trip away. Changes in your personal life may shake things up a little, especially at the end of January and at the end of the year. You love to achieve a sense of stability in your life, so be sure to aim to find more of this elusive quality and you will.

January

1 JANUARY

Happy New Year! A practical approach to organising your day will pay off, especially for workers. Just avoid being controlling of others as they will react in kind.

2 JANUARY

You will discover whether you've been a little idealistic, especially financially and in your personal life, providing the opportunity to reset your goals.

3 JANUARY

Your aims and goals are likely to differ from those of someone else, but if you maintain a strong stance you'll gain ground. Just avoid being sidetracked.

4 JANUARY

You'll benefit from strategising and planning, especially concerning your home life and, if you work in property, at work. Holidaying Virgos will enjoy feeling more grounded.

5 JANUARY

Investing in your work, relationships and communication skills will bring a sense of fulfilment.

6 JANUARY

Someone close may require additional care and attention, so keep an eye out for them. A shared situation will benefit from an open mind and dedication to fairness.

7 JANUARY

You'll enjoy investing in your home, family and creativity. If you're away you'll love exploring your environment.

8 JANUARY

This is a good day to discuss shared concerns such as domestic and financial matters. Stick with the facts to avoid confusion.

9 JANUARY

Be careful with communications, especially if someone is giving you mixed messages. Be prepared to find out what the mystery is and clear the air.

10 JANUARY

You'll enjoy a fun activity or change of pace. A friend, colleague or family member may be in touch from out of the blue.

11 JANUARY

The Capricorn new moon will kick-start a fresh phase in your personal life, with family or a creative project. Be prepared to take the reins at home as this will be a therapeutic time.

12 JANUARY

Your efforts will be successful, especially in connection with your home, family and favourite activities. A trip will be fulfilling.

13 JANUARY

This is a good day to talk and make changes at home and with family and friends. If you're moving or undertaking a DIY project it's likely to succeed. Just be clear about what you want.

14 JANUARY

A clear, productive approach to making your home your castle will succeed; just avoid being distracted and interrupted. Be prepared to think laterally if problems arise.

15 JANUARY

You're thinking creatively and abstractly yet some of your chores will merit a more hands-on approach, so be sure to be practical as well.

16 JANUARY

This is a lovely day for romance, the arts and being creative. A family get-together or personal news will be inspiring.

17 JANUARY

A proactive and dynamic approach to shared concerns such as collaborations at work and at home will pay off. Take practical steps to attain your goals.

18 JANUARY

This is a good day to make progress at work and at home, and if you need to discuss finances today's the day to do it. Just focus on facts and avoid distractions.

19 JANUARY

This is another good day for discussions and to progress with your projects, especially at home, but you must avoid making assumptions, forgetfulness and being easily led.

20 JANUARY

A key get-together or project could be transformational. Romance could blossom, so if you're single it's a positive day for socialising.

21 JANUARY

You may be drawn to resurrecting a past relationship or idea, but if tension is in the air avoid conflict as it will escalate.

22 JANUARY

The moon will put your heart on your sleeve. However, you will be communicating well and must be prepared to consider or even float new ideas.

23 JANUARY

You'll appreciate the sense that developments in your domestic or home life and a property can begin to settle down over the coming weeks. Be practical above all with your decisions.

24 JANUARY

Be prepared to look at your circumstances from an objective point of view or you may tend to be reactive to someone else's circumstances.

25 JANUARY

The Leo full moon will spotlight your personal and social life, bringing matters to a head. Ensure you avoid making snap decisions and do not take the random comments of others personally.

26 JANUARY

A personal, family or shared experience may bring out vulnerabilities. Be ready to help someone and to ask for help if you need it. Avoid minor bumps and scrapes.

27 JANUARY

A personal matter deserves to be discussed but you must avoid arguments, as they could spiral with someone who may be erratic or angry. If it's you, ensure you take time out.

28 JANUARY

This is a good day to discuss matters that affect your home, work and shared duties. Just keep things on an even keel for the best results and avoid anger, as it'll spark conflict.

29 JANUARY

This is a better day for discussions and getting things done. You'll enjoy fresh interests and activities. It's a good time for improving your home. Romance could flourish.

30 JANUARY

You're looking for a peaceful and constructive day, and this is possible if you focus on tact and diplomacy.

31 JANUARY

Be prepared to see someone else's point of view or meet them halfway. If you feel vulnerable, find an expert who can offer advice. Your expertise may be in demand.

February

1 FEBRUARY

It's a good day to gain a sense of direction with your projects and priorities. Consider for a second who and what your priorities are and make tracks!

2 FEBRUARY

You'll appreciate the opportunity to connect more deeply with someone important. Romance, the arts, film and dance will all thrive.

3 FEBRUARY

Upbeat, proactive and fun activities will appeal to you. However, you may need to focus a little more than usual to get the results you want, but your efforts will be worthwhile.

4 FEBRUARY

It's a good day to contemplate whether you could reshuffle some of your usual schedule so it suits you better. Be adventurous and discuss your ideas with someone close.

5 FEBRUARY

There are therapeutic aspects to the day. A discussion or meeting with someone you admire will work wonders. Just avoid taking random comments personally.

6 FEBRUARY

New opportunities are on the way. To make the most of them it's a good time to establish common ground with those you share space with, such as at home.

7 FEBRUARY

You'll appreciate breathing fresh air into a close relationship and at home. You could bring more comfort and sumptuousness into your home to feel more relaxed.

8 FEBRUARY

You may be surprised by someone's news. Avoid feeling you must alter your entire mindset; take things one step at a time with an open mind.

9 FEBRUARY

The Aquarian new moon supermoon will encourage you to turn a new leaf in your personal or family life; you may be surprised where developments take you. It's a good time to talk.

10 FEBRUARY

You'll enjoy relaxing and taking that all-important me time. However, some interactions may be more stressful than you'd prefer, so choose your company carefully. Avoid gambling.

11 FEBRUARY

The Pisces moon will bring your idealistic, dreamy side out. You may be frustrated by delays and mix-ups if you have places to go and people to see. Be patient.

12 FEBRUARY

If you work artistically and creatively you'll find the current stars inspiring, but if you need to be precise and logical the current stars may be frustrating. Again, be patient.

13 FEBRUARY

This is one of the best days this year for romance, so be sure to organise a date! Take the initiative with family and creative projects.

14 FEBRUARY

Happy St Valentine's Day! Be prepared to take romance into new realms. You may experience a super-fun time, so take the initiative. Just avoid arguments with someone special.

15 FEBRUARY

You will be drawn to anchoring your projects, plans and ideas in practical terms so they can take root and flourish all the better.

16 FEBRUARY

Once again your love life and, more broadly, personal life are likely to take you into fresh terrain. Be prepared to go the hard yards as it will be worthwhile.

17 FEBRUARY

This is another romantic day so make the most of these stars. You must be sure to avoid intense or sensitive topics as passion abounds and so, too, does potential conflict.

18 FEBRUARY

You'll enjoy entering a chatty, sociable time, but if you're working you'll need to delay romance and socialising in favour of a busy day.

19 FEBRUARY

You may uncover a sensitive topic or someone close will need a shoulder to lean on. Your help will be in demand, and if you need advice it will be available.

20 FEBRUARY

Trust your instincts as you gain insight into your best way forward, especially regarding a shared situation or personal matter.

21 FEBRUARY

You're willing to try new things, meet different people and broaden your horizons. All of these can meet with resistance, but if you remain inspired you'll succeed.

22 FEBRUARY

The Leo moon brings out your feisty side and you may surprise someone with your upbeat outlook. A meeting, news or get-together will be significant.

23 FEBRUARY

Mercury is in Pisces for the next few weeks and will add to a sense of potential and exploration within your daily schedules and, as the days go by, in your relationships.

24 FEBRUARY

The full moon in Virgo spotlights the end of a key cycle, for some August Virgos in your personal life and for many Virgos at work and health-wise. It is time for something new!

25 FEBRUARY

This is a good time to discuss work and your ideas and plans for your personal life. You could make a valid commitment but must base your decisions on facts, not expectations.

26 FEBRUARY

A detailed approach to your communications and interactions will work wonders, but you must be practical and realistic.

27 FEBRUARY

You have every reason to be optimistic about your potential and projects, but also to accept that sometimes events take their own sweet time.

28 FEBRUARY

It's a good day to focus on good relationships and factor in time to enjoy something special. You may make a solid commitment.

29 FEBRUARY

You'll enjoy a get-together with someone who is on the same wavelength as you, either at work or in your personal life.

March

1 MARCH

This is a lovely day for collaborations and making binding commitments. Take the initiative. There are therapeutic aspects to the day.

2 MARCH

You'll enjoy being proactive and outgoing, and romance and spending time with like-minded people and someone special will thrive.

3 MARCH

You may be surprised by a change of pace or of place. Someone's news may be unexpected. Think laterally for the best results.

4 MARCH

You'll appreciate the opportunity to ground your efforts and be adventurous at the same time with personal matters. Just avoid expecting everything to go your way. Be diplomatic.

5 MARCH

If you need to know where you stand this is a good day to find out, both at work and in your personal life. If not, you'll enjoy a lovely get-together.

6 MARCH

This is a lovely day to focus on bringing like-minded people together, such as family and friends. There is a therapeutic aspect to the day.

7 MARCH

If you need to make a change to your usual schedule you'll manage to accommodate your activities. Someone close will prove to have a positive influence.

8 MARCH

Someone close may seem forgetful and absent-minded; at worst, they may let you down. This aside, it's a good time for romance and spirituality.

9 MARCH

This is an excellent weekend to try something new. You'll enjoy a change of pace or of place. Romance will thrive for some, but for others a disruption could get in the way.

10 MARCH

The Pisces new moon supermoon will kick-start a transformative chapter in a relationship and, for mid-September Virgos, in a work or health routine.

11 MARCH

Be prepared to think big, to dream a little and put your best foot forward over the coming weeks, especially at work and regarding your usual health routine.

12 MARCH

The key to progress at work is adopting an amenable approach to your colleagues and work schedule. It's a good day to consider a fresh look or outfit.

13 MARCH

This is another good day to adopt a constructive yet friendly approach at work as you could make positive changes within your usual routine.

14 MARCH

The Taurean moon will encourage you to find logical ways to work towards your goals while also adopting an innovative approach.

15 MARCH

A chatty day will contribute to a sense of progress with your favourite projects and people. However, you must tread carefully with some work projects or colleagues.

16 MARCH

You'll find the time to discuss your plans with those they concern, making this an excellent day to plan ahead. A little retail therapy will appeal.

17 MARCH

This is an ideal day for romantic, artistic and musical endeavours and self-development. Just avoid being super idealistic if you are making a romantic commitment.

18 MARCH

The moon in Cancer will bring your sensitivities to the surface and also potentially your vulnerability at work, so be prepared to focus on your goals.

19 MARCH

This is a great day for discussions and meetings, especially at work, regarding health and well-being and in your personal life, as your efforts are likely to succeed.

20 MARCH

The sun will shine on your collaborations and partnerships, providing the opportunity to discuss any areas or issues you need to remedy. Health or well-being news will arrive.

21 MARCH

This is another good day for talks, especially about shared responsibilities and duties, as you could make the changes you're hoping for. A commitment may be made.

22 MARCH

You'll feel increasingly inspired to look for projects and work that lead to a sense of fulfilment. You may be drawn to a fresh daily or health routine.

23 MARCH

You'll enjoy activities such as sports and developing a favourite project. An expert such as a mentor or manager will be particularly inspiring.

24 MARCH

The lead-up to a full moon eclipse can be intense, so be sure to pace yourself and take time out to look for fair play and balance. Avoid feeling everything can be sorted out in one day.

25 MARCH

This lunar eclipse in Libra is a good time to look for balance, especially fair play and harmony in relationships. Take time to relish a sense of progress at work.

26 MARCH

This is a good day to build bridges with someone you may have argued with in the past. There are healing aspects to the day, so be sure to make the most of these.

27 MARCH

You'll enjoy putting your energy into good interpersonal skills to reap the rewards of pleasant interactions and relationships.

28 MARCH

A business or personal friend or partner may surprise you, and you'll appreciate being more spontaneous and enjoying something different.

29 MARCH

It's time to focus on you and your own happiness, especially at home and with someone special.

30 MARCH

An outgoing and upbeat approach to shared space and duties will reap rewards. Avoid looking at the glass as being half empty as you may get stuck on negative feelings.

31 MARCH

A DIY project or the chance to tidy up your home and enjoy time spent with someone special will appeal. Avoid feeling you can make everything perfect in one day.

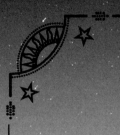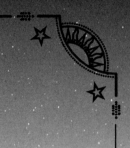

April

1 APRIL

It's a good day to formulate travel plans and any paperwork that needs tying up before Mercury turns retrograde tomorrow to avoid having to redo some arrangements.

2 APRIL

Key news to do with a project or plan may arrive. A colleague or collaborator may wish to discuss some shared initiatives. A trip will benefit from a little focus to avoid delays.

3 APRIL

This is a perfect day to organise a romantic event. The arts, film and music will appeal. Singles may find someone dreamy. Just avoid forgetfulness.

4 APRIL

A reunion or meeting may be more significant than meets the eye. It's a good day to get on top of shared ventures and plan ahead for upbeat escapades.

5 APRIL

Over the coming weeks you'll feel more proactive about shared ventures, including romance. You may surprise yourself with how bold you can be!

6 APRIL

This is a romantic weekend and an ideal time to float new ideas with friends or family.

7 APRIL

The lead-up to the new moon is an ideal time to make a wish. A fresh project or venture such as a trip, new study course or spiritual development will appeal.

8 APRIL

The total solar eclipse signifies a change in a special venture, and you could boost your status. For some there will be a fresh start in a relationship. A health matter will deserve attention.

9 APRIL

Keep your feet on the ground, especially if you feel some aspects of life are too intense.

10 APRIL

Take the initiative with a work or personal relationship. You'll be glad you did, as you'll discover unexpected benefits.

11 APRIL

You'll enjoy a reunion or return to an old haunt. You may need to go over paperwork or an agreement.

12 APRIL

The Gemini moon brings out your chatty side, especially at work. However, some talks may be a little tense so be tactful to avoid fallout.

13 APRIL

You may wish to float this weekend and forget about timetables, so you may need to reschedule an appointment. That said, you'll enjoy doing something different.

14 APRIL

You'll enjoy socialising with someone special but will need to choose your company carefully.

15 APRIL

You may revisit a delicate issue, and using tact will work well. It's a good day for a return to an old haunt and a health or beauty appointment.

16 APRIL

It's a good day to review a sensitive topic, as you're likely to find common ground. You may receive news to do with health. You must avoid rushing and cutting corners.

17 APRIL

You'll enjoy a reunion and romance could thrive. If you're single and you meet someone new, they may seem familiar or will be significant in some way.

18 APRIL

As an earth sign you like to be practical and methodical, yet sometimes you know you can trust your intuition and you certainly can today!

19 APRIL

As the sun enters Taurus your plans can start to take shape, especially concerning broadening your horizons. You'll enjoy a reunion. Someone close may have surprise news.

20 APRIL

The moon in your sign adds to your ability to take action carefully and considerately, but not everyone will be in form. A change of routine, trip or meeting may surprise you.

21 APRIL

Be prepared to understand a situation that is outside your control; you may need to empathise with someone you don't understand. Expect important news or a surprise.

22 APRIL

You'll gain insight into the best way forward with unpredictable circumstances. An expert or adviser will prove helpful.

23 APRIL

An intense situation is best handled carefully, as people may be a little emotional. You'll appreciate the chance to unwind this evening.

24 APRIL

The Scorpio full moon will highlight how you see someone close and, potentially, the relationship. It's a good time to consider a fresh communication device, trip or project.

25 APRIL

Key news or an agreement or discussion will set you on a clearer path moving forward. It's a good day to talk as the Mercury retrograde phase ends.

26 APRIL

You'll appreciate the opportunity to invest time in yourself, your home and those you love. You'll appreciate a change of tempo at home.

27 APRIL

Collaborations, both in the home and outside, will thrive this weekend. Be prepared to meet someone halfway if possible.

28 APRIL

Creativity, the arts and self-development will thrive. Romance and spending time with like-minded people will appeal.

29 APRIL

As Venus enters Taurus you'll appreciate seeing more stability in your projects and plans. You may enjoy a truly ideal development in the right direction.

30 APRIL

Someone close such as a business or personal partner will have news; you may even be surprised by their ideas. You, too, will be ready to act on fresh information.

May

1 MAY

You will succeed by focusing on your goals, but you must be wary of driving yourself and others too hard as an intense interaction could result. Avoid conflict.

2 MAY

This is a good time to state your case carefully and assertively, but be prepared to negotiate and compromise otherwise you may enter a stalemate.

3 MAY

A relationship could blossom, so this is an ideal day to repair relationships if need be. Romance will also thrive but so will fiery exchanges, so if possible avoid sensitive topics.

4 MAY

You'll be inspired by someone close and will enjoy investing time in romance and favourite activities. You'll gain a second wind after a little relaxation.

5 MAY

Teamwork such as sports and group meetings will be enjoyable. You may meet someone you feel a strong connection with.

6 MAY

Consider other people's feelings, especially family and work colleagues, as you may otherwise experience pushback against some of your ideas or actions.

7 MAY

This is an excellent day to get things done and you could remedy an outstanding issue, either financially, in a shared situation or concerning health.

8 MAY

The Taurus new moon will kick-start a fresh chapter in your favourite activities, interests and hobbies. You may be ready to anchor a project or reveal it.

9 MAY

The Gemini moon at the zenith of your chart may contribute to a restless or indecisive feeling to the day, so it's best to avoid making big decisions unless you have the full facts.

10 MAY

A busy or chatty day will bring your communication skills but not everyone else's centre stage, so you may need to tread carefully with someone.

11 MAY

There is a therapeutic quality to the day's events. A lovely chat or get-together with someone special will be motivational. Romance could thrive.

12 MAY

The Cancerian moon is conducive to relaxation, self-care and nurturance of those close to you, so you have the green light to unwind!

13 MAY

A change of scenery or surprise news and developments will encourage you to be more outspoken. You'll gain the chance to establish a good outcome to the day.

14 MAY

You'll enjoy socialising with like-minded people. Just avoid entering a battle of wills with someone whose ideas are different from yours.

15 MAY

A grounded approach to shared responsibilities and communications will be productive. Be careful with communications over the next two days for the best results.

16 MAY

The moon in your sign helps you take action in measured ways, which means you're in top form! Just avoid allowing intense talks to escalate.

17 MAY

It's likely that some communications and financial matters will merit more care and attention than usual, so be prepared to be diplomatic. Plan ahead to avoid travel delays.

18 MAY

You'll enjoy doing something different and sports, your favourite activities and hobbies will appeal.

19 MAY

This is a romantic day, so plan a date! You'll also enjoy filling your day with favourite activities and people, the arts and travel.

20 MAY

Over the next four weeks your career, status, favourite projects and general direction will take much of your focus. Be prepared to dream big. You'll meet someone special.

21 MAY

You'll feel more motivated to get your projects and plans up and running, giving you the impetus to reach out and discuss your ideas.

22 MAY

This is a good time to positively transform both your professional and personal lives. Consider which area would benefit from the most attention and make changes!

23 MAY

The full moon in Sagittarius will spotlight plans such as those for travel, study, self-development or a legal matter. You may be ready to alter the course of a relationship.

24 MAY

An outgoing and upbeat approach to your collaborations will be productive. However, tact will still be a useful skill set.

25 MAY

You'll appreciate the opportunity to do what you love. A favourite activity or person will make your spirit soar and a trip or visit will be refreshing.

26 MAY

As Jupiter enters Gemini you'll increasingly enjoy expanding your horizons over the next 12 months through travel, study, self-development and spirituality.

27 MAY

You'll achieve a great deal even if you feel things are developing slowly or are a little stuck. Be methodical for the best results.

28 MAY

This is a good day to discuss long-term plans, both at work and in your personal life. You may make an agreement or key financial decision.

29 MAY

Someone you collaborate or share space or duties with may require support. If you need advice it will be available from an expert, so reach out.

30 MAY

Your help or expertise will be in demand, and if you need advice or expert help it will be available. A trip or meeting may be particularly therapeutic.

31 MAY

The moon in Pisces brings out your creative, dreamy, artistic sides. You'll enjoy relaxing, romance and being with like-minded people. Just avoid forgetfulness and idealism.

June

1 JUNE

You'll love doing something different and will enjoy being spontaneous. An impromptu meeting will be revitalising. Just avoid making rash decisions.

2 JUNE

The Aries moon will add an upbeat quality to your day. You'll feel motivated by someone who is active and positive; just avoid being bossed around!

3 JUNE

This is a lovely day to be creative and make changes in your life where you see they are necessary. A visit or appointment is likely to be transformational.

4 JUNE

A trip or meeting will bring out your chatty side. You will be drawn to broadening your horizons, and travelling or booking a holiday will appeal.

5 JUNE

The lead-up to a new moon is a good time to consider what you'd like to improve in your life, especially regarding relationships, travel, study and communications.

6 JUNE

The new moon will help you initiate talks and plans. Consider how you'd best like to progress and make tracks to do so through communications, emails and phone calls.

7 JUNE

A caring and nurturing approach to those around you will be appreciated. You may need to focus a little harder at work as there will be distractions.

8 JUNE

The key to happiness today is good communication and relationship skills, as someone's ideas will differ from yours. Romance could thrive but you must avoid being easily influenced.

9 JUNE

Certain activities may seem stuck and someone may decide to be stubborn, so be prepared to negotiate to avoid a Mexican stand-off.

10 JUNE

The Leo moon will bring out your sociable side, encouraging you to get on well with colleagues, friends and family.

11 JUNE

There are therapeutic aspects to the day that will encourage you to reach out to people you have perhaps argued with in the past, but you must avoid being super sensitive to criticism.

12 JUNE

You're a good communicator but not everyone else is, so if you encounter tough talks find a way to be tactful to de-escalate a potential argument.

13 JUNE

You'll enjoy the chance to be spontaneous and do something different. It's a good day for an impromptu get-together, and someone's news may surprise you.

14 JUNE

You may receive key news at work or regarding your general direction or career. If you've been waiting for news it's likely to arrive. A trip could be therapeutic.

15 JUNE

You'll enjoy being spontaneous and spending time with like-minded people. A trip somewhere on the spur of the moment will be fun. You may receive surprising news.

16 JUNE

You'll be looking for peace and calmness, although you may be needed at work or to clear chores at home. Why not get the work done first so you can relax later in the day?

17 JUNE

You'll appreciate that there are changes afoot either at work or in your general direction. Key news will arrive or a meeting occur. Be clear with communications for the best results.

18 JUNE

It's a good day to focus on the results you want, especially at work, but also to be flexible and sensitive to the ideas and needs of others.

19 JUNE

Being passionate about your beliefs and what you do will motivate you to succeed but you must avoid appearing dogmatic, and especially at work.

20 JUNE

The solstice is a lovely time to review how far you've come this year. A conundrum or mystery may arise, so be prepared to look for answers.

21 JUNE

You'll enjoy a trip or favourite activity with like-minded people. However, you may inadvertently enter an ego battle, so look for ways to de-escalate tension.

22 JUNE

The full moon in Capricorn will spotlight your domestic and personal lives. Spiritually minded Virgos may experience an epiphany. It's a good day for get-togethers and meetings.

23 JUNE

Communications and travel will deserve extra focus to avoid mix-ups. A meeting may need to be delayed or rescheduled.

24 JUNE

A bright, innovative approach to your projects and interactions will reap rewards. Be prepared to think laterally for the best results.

25 JUNE

You'll enjoy being in touch with someone special. Just avoid feeling under pressure from someone or pressuring someone whose collaboration is necessary.

26 JUNE

This is a good day to make progress at work and with your projects. A trip will be successful. You could make a long-term agreement as long as your principles match.

27 JUNE

An inspired approach to communications and collaborations will pay off. You'll enjoy socialising and networking.

28 JUNE

You are communicating well, but someone you interact with may well get the wrong end of the stick so be prepared to be super clear.

29 JUNE

You'll enjoy being with a team or group of people whose company you love. It's a great day for socialising and love could also thrive!

30 JUNE

You'll enjoy being spontaneous, and a get-together will open your eye to a new social circle or activities.

July

1 JULY

As you work slowly towards meeting new people and having new experiences your connections will thrive. Choose your company carefully, though.

2 JULY

Someone close such as a colleague or partner has news for you. It may be ideal, but you must check both your plans align if you are making long-term decisions.

3 JULY

It's a good time to make a valid work, personal or financial agreement. You may receive important news from someone close or a group.

4 JULY

The lead-up to the Cancerian new moon is an ideal time to take stock of your career aims and consider how you wish to proceed over the coming weeks and months.

5 JULY

The Cancerian new moon is a good time to kick-start a new career cycle. You may be ready to turn a corner in your general direction or status and make a commitment.

6 JULY

Be prepared to see someone else's point of view, as you may both tend to get the wrong end of the stick. Avoid taking criticism to heart unless it's warranted.

7 JULY

The Leo moon brings a more upbeat feel to the day. You'll enjoy socialising and being active in favourite activities such as sports and being in nature.

8 JULY

This is a lovely day for an impromptu get-together. Your connection with someone will flourish, perhaps in unexpected ways or circumstances.

9 JULY

You'll appreciate the chance to get on with your projects but must avoid expecting everyone to be as positive as you. An upbeat, outgoing attitude will certainly get things done.

10 JULY

You're a practical person but not everyone else is, and you may need to contend with someone who expects things to be done quickly rather than methodically.

11 JULY

You'll notice your attention go to work and your daily routine, health and well-being. This is a great time to improve your career and social life. Romance could flourish.

12 JULY

You'll feel motivated to be creative and indulge in your favourite pastimes. Romance could ignite but so too could conflict.

13 JULY

The Libran moon will put your focus on creating abundance in your life, so if you feel frustrated by events find time to take breaks and focus on what you want, which is peace.

14 JULY

You'll enjoy a fun event and significant get-together. Some practicalities may be frustrating but rest assured: you will find a solution to conundrums.

15 JULY

Be prepared to be adaptable, as a surprise or change of circumstance will arise. Avoid taking circumstances and comments personally unless you must accept responsibility.

16 JULY

Trust your intuition as it's strong and will help you find a way to look outside the box at solutions should issues arise.

17 JULY

As an earth sign you like to take things one step at a time, yet the upbeat feel to the day will encourage you to be more outgoing and adventurous.

18 JULY

You'll enjoy being spontaneous, and a new opportunity may arise. You'll appreciate the thrill of something different.

19 JULY

There are therapeutic aspects to the day, so it's a good time for a health appointment. It's also a good day to build bridges with anyone you have argued with.

20 JULY

You'll appreciate the sense of connection you have with a group of like-minded people. You may be drawn to booking a holiday or to travelling, study and broadening your horizons.

21 JULY

The full moon in Capricorn will spotlight changes in key personal and work relationships for some Virgos and, for others, at home. Avoid misunderstandings.

22 JULY

A change of routine or circumstance could be the start of something truly transformational. Be positive, and avoid misunderstandings and delays by planning ahead.

23 JULY

It's a good time to transform your personal life or social circle. An intense or romantic get-together may be ideal, but if conflict or frustration is brewing avoid arguments.

24 JULY

A group, friend or organisation may prove particularly helpful, so be sure to reach out. Just avoid disagreements, as some people will take these as prompts to fire up.

25 JULY

As chatty Mercury enters your sign you'll feel more in tune with communications over the coming weeks, although today you must double-check facts to avoid making mistakes.

26 JULY

This is a lovely day to dig right into your chores and work projects as your efforts will be productive. You may enjoy an impromptu get-together.

27 JULY

This weekend is an excellent time for a mini review of your work and priorities. Avoid power struggles and misunderstandings. Romance could thrive.

28 JULY

The Taurus moon will encourage you to take a moment to self-nurture and enjoy a favourite place or the company of someone you love.

29 JULY

Step by step you will attain your goals, and as the day goes by you're likely to complete your chores and projects.

30 JULY

There are therapeutic aspects to the day. It's a good time for a health or beauty treat and to look after yourself and someone you love. An expert will prove helpful.

31 JULY

This is an excellent day to get together with someone special. If you're single you may meet someone who seems strangely familiar even if you've never met before.

August

1 AUGUST

You may feel more sensitive, so be sure to keep a professional stance at work and avoid taking things personally. Trust your instincts.

2 AUGUST

An unexpected development will require you to be flexible. You'll appreciate the collaboration and support of someone who gets you.

3 AUGUST

The lead-up to the new moon in Leo will be a good time to consider how best to revitalise your social life and be discerning about who you align yourself with professionally.

4 AUGUST

The Leo new moon spotlights your social circle: is it time to meet new people, or will you find fresh ways to interact with your existing network? Trust your intuition if a mystery surfaces.

5 AUGUST

This is a good time to get your paperwork and decisions shipshape to avoid having to retrace your steps over the coming weeks.

6 AUGUST

Now that Mercury is retrograde you'll gain the chance to review recent personal decisions. Keep conversations clear for the best results and avoid power struggles.

7 AUGUST

You'll appreciate the chance to be heard at work and in your general decisions moving forward. A fun colleague or friend will prove supportive.

8 AUGUST

You'll enjoy a reunion or the chance to review certain matters in your personal life or at work. This is a good day for a health or beauty appointment.

9 AUGUST

You'll be striving towards an upbeat, productive day, and the more you focus on your good communication skills the better will be the outcome.

10 AUGUST

Be prepared to focus on the chores at hand and go the extra mile to clear a backlog of work, then you'll enjoy the time to relax properly.

11 AUGUST

The Scorpio moon will put passion into your ventures, and you'll enjoy feeling your efforts are paying off once you get motivated to take action.

12 AUGUST

You'll gain ground at work and with your chores but you must be careful to avoid a battle of egos.

13 AUGUST

Trust your instincts, as they are spot on. You'll get on top of important communications by being diligent. Avoid mix-ups and travel delays by planning ahead.

14 AUGUST

Be optimistic but also prepared to be precise and avoid cutting corners, especially with someone special. Avoid rushing a project through and pressuring someone.

15 AUGUST

There are therapeutic aspects to the day. It's a good day to organise a healing treat, and if you've had difficult topics to discuss it's likely to go better if you stick with the facts.

16 AUGUST

You'll feel drawn to moving quickly and getting chores expedited. However, some of your plans may be delayed or will need to be changed, so be adaptable.

17 AUGUST

You'll enjoy a change of pace and doing something different but must avoid misunderstandings and distractions for the best results.

18 AUGUST

You may receive unexpected news from a friend or group. Be prepared to be flexible, as a change of plan or surprise will merit a patient approach.

19 AUGUST

The Aquarian full moon will spotlight a change in your usual schedule, either at work or health-wise. Talks will be productive albeit intense or challenging.

20 AUGUST

You'll gain a sense of direction by being patient with your various plans and meticulous with facts.

21 AUGUST

A friend, partner or colleague's ideas will prove to be inspiring, although you may need to work out a way for your ideas to mesh with theirs.

22 AUGUST

The sun in your sign over the next four weeks will spotlight your personal life and well-being. Be practical and you could transform this aspect of your life.

23 AUGUST

This is a good day for a health or beauty treat and for a reunion, but you must avoid arguments at work or with someone special.

24 AUGUST

It's a great weekend to catch up with chores. You'll enjoy a get-together but must be sensitive to someone else's feelings. Be careful to avoid overspending if your budget is tight.

25 AUGUST

You'll enjoy indulging in a little luxury or treat and will find time for someone special or a favourite pastime.

26 AUGUST

The moon in Gemini at the zenith of your chart will bring out your inner chatterbox. You'll enjoy being proactive at work and with a change of location or schedule.

27 AUGUST

You'll enjoy being spontaneous or a change of pace or place. You may receive unexpected news.

28 AUGUST

You may receive news concerning health or work. A personal matter could be ideal and romance, the arts and music will thrive, but you must avoid being super idealistic.

29 AUGUST

As Venus leaves your sign your focus will go gradually on money and how to maintain a steady budget. A close relationship may enter fresh territory. Romance can thrive.

30 AUGUST

You'll enjoy being upbeat, and your proactive stance will put you in a strong position to enjoy romance, fun events and a change of pace.

31 AUGUST

Immersing yourself in favourite pastimes will appeal. Be prepared for a change of pace.

September

1 SEPTEMBER

You'll enjoy a chatty, outgoing and upbeat day although you'll be choosy about the company you keep, as you won't suffer fools gladly.

2 SEPTEMBER

You may need to go over old ground with a personal matter. Changes you make are likely to work well in the long term. It's a good day to build bridges with someone close.

3 SEPTEMBER

The new moon in Virgo is a good time to turn a corner in your personal life and, if you were born later in September, to embrace a fresh daily or work routine. Consider your true priorities.

4 SEPTEMBER

You'll appreciate being more discerning about the groups and organisations you spend time with, trusting your intuition. A get-together will boost self-worth. Love will thrive.

5 SEPTEMBER

The moon in Libra will encourage you to be more outspoken and proactive about your principles and morals. A little tact will go a long way at work.

6 SEPTEMBER

Extra focus on your finances will work wonders, especially if you're in debt. Take time to discuss long-term plans with someone special.

7 SEPTEMBER

The Scorpio moon will bring your passions to the surface and you'll enjoy favourite pastimes. However, you must avoid a clash of wills. A commitment can be made.

8 SEPTEMBER

A business or personal partner may wish to make an agreement or commitment. Consider all the variables and research the facts. Avoid mix-ups.

9 SEPTEMBER

As Mercury enters your sign key talks and transactions could be intense, so be prepared to focus on details but avoid obsessing over them.

10 SEPTEMBER

Your adventurous side will seek expression and you may tend to speak before you think, so be careful. A fun get-together will raise morale.

11 SEPTEMBER

Certain talks or financial transactions will be beneficial, but they may involve a hurdle to cross.

12 SEPTEMBER

Your opinions are likely to differ from those of someone you work or spend time with, so if possible be prepared to meet them halfway. Talks will be productive.

13 SEPTEMBER

A constructive and methodical approach to your home and personal life will work well. It's a good time to consider logistics and financial planning.

14 SEPTEMBER

You may be sensitive to the moods of others, so be prepared to seek your own counsel where possible. You may need to help someone, and if you need help it will be available.

15 SEPTEMBER

An original approach to interpersonal dynamics will revitalise relationships.

16 SEPTEMBER

Some of your interactions will require patience, especially at work, so be prepared to take things one step at a time.

17 SEPTEMBER

Be patient with communications and interactions as a new chapter unfolds in a relationship. Be prepared to discuss a fresh arrangement or agreement.

18 SEPTEMBER

The partial lunar eclipse supermoon in Pisces spotlights your relationships. You may make or break a commitment or financial agreement.

19 SEPTEMBER

You'll enjoy being spontaneous and a trip, visit or occasion will be enjoyable. You may experience a surprise.

20 SEPTEMBER

Be prepared to be flexible with some of your arrangements, as you may find benefit in doing so. Avoid overspending if you're already in debt.

21 SEPTEMBER

This is a romantic day on which you'll enjoy time spent engaged in the arts, music and creativity. However, some communications or travel will be complex or delayed.

22 SEPTEMBER

This is another lovely day for romance, but you must avoid both emotional and financial gambling.

23 SEPTEMBER

The moon in Gemini will bring out your chatty, communicative side, which is ideal for work and networking and getting paperwork done.

24 SEPTEMBER

You may be pleasantly surprised by news or developments. It's a good time to make progress with plans to travel or study and for self-development.

25 SEPTEMBER

You may be easily influenced, so be careful if you're investing or making a commitment. This is a good day to talk but you must avoid misunderstandings. Romance could thrive.

26 SEPTEMBER

You'll appreciate the opportunity to deepen a relationship with someone special. Creative and personal projects can thrive; just avoid forgetfulness.

27 SEPTEMBER

The moon in Leo over the next two days will bring out your sociable side, and you'll enjoy deepening close relationships.

28 SEPTEMBER

This is an excellent weekend for discussing important plans and ideas with someone close, as talks will be constructive.

29 SEPTEMBER

You'll hear from someone special and may consider a reunion. A trip will appeal.

30 SEPTEMBER

News may require you to review your plans and ideas. You may be drawn to returning to an old haunt. It's a good day to go full steam ahead with work and health initiatives.

October

1 OCTOBER

The dark of the moon is a good time to set your intentions for the future, especially regarding work and your personal life and long-term financial goals.

2 OCTOBER

The solar eclipse in Libra will help you turn a corner in your personal life and financially. It's a good time to put in place aims that will provide you with more stability and balance.

3 OCTOBER

This is a good day for financial decisions. You'll enjoy getting together with someone you admire. Talks and transactions are likely to go well.

4 OCTOBER

This is an excellent time to get ahead with work and financial matters, so take the initiative to build a strong foundation.

5 OCTOBER

You'll feel drawn to investing in your projects at work and your financial well-being.

6 OCTOBER

You're a good communicator but you won't always agree with everyone, so be prepared for some give and take to avoid arguments. Be patient, especially if you're working.

7 OCTOBER

The Sagittarian moon will prompt you to be outgoing and upbeat, but you must be sure to avoid appearing bossy as this will be counterproductive.

8 OCTOBER

You'll enjoy a trip and positive news at work or financially. Be sure to avoid taking random comments personally. You may be asked for help, and an expert will prove supportive of you.

9 OCTOBER

Your communication skills are a key asset, and they will help you to overcome any minor hurdles.

10 OCTOBER

The Capricorn moon helps you take things one step at a time and avoid making rash decisions. Be prepared to see someone else's point of view.

11 OCTOBER

Someone's unpredictable or erratic behaviour may test your mettle, but rest assured that if you are approachable and positive you will triumph over any minor hurdles.

12 OCTOBER

A conundrum, delay or frustrating developments will test your resilience. However, someone close such as a partner or colleague will prove supportive.

13 OCTOBER

You'll feel increasingly expressive and passionate about your ideas and plans. You must choose your words carefully to avoid arguments. A trip or plan may be delayed.

14 OCTOBER

This is a good day to be careful with communications to avoid offence being taken, by you or someone else. You'll be surprised by developments, a trip or news.

15 OCTOBER

Trust your instincts, as they are spot on. It's another good day to be careful with interactions. Financial transactions such as tax matters will require some focus.

16 OCTOBER

This is a lovely day for romance, the arts and inspiration; however, you may be inclined to be forgetful. It's a good day for self-development.

17 OCTOBER

The full moon supermoon in Aries will spotlight an investment. For some this will be financial in nature and for others emotional. Be prepared to step into new territory.

18 OCTOBER

This is a delightful day to make practical plans with those you love. Some people are not on your wavelength, and you may decide to keep them at arm's length.

19 OCTOBER

A surprise development or change of plan may rattle your cage, but you will gain the chance to enjoy your day regardless. You will rise to any challenges by being well organised.

20 OCTOBER

You may tend to easily be distracted and will need to focus a little harder on tasks, but when you do you'll gain good results at home and with your ventures.

21 OCTOBER

You'll enjoy romance, the arts and celebrating life, but if you're shopping avoid overspending and especially if you're already in debt.

22 OCTOBER

As the sun enters Scorpio the next month will prompt you to gain a sense of accomplishment and purpose in life. Communications may be tense. Avoid conflict as it will escalate.

23 OCTOBER

This is a lovely day for a get-together with someone you love or admire, so take the initiative!

24 OCTOBER

You may feel particularly passionate about an issue, principle or moral. Take the time to organise your thoughts.

25 OCTOBER

Your plans and ideas can come together; engage the skills of experts if necessary. Be spontaneous, as you may enjoy a surprise or impromptu event. Avoid rushing.

26 OCTOBER

This is an excellent weekend for allowing recent developments to sink in, as you may otherwise overload yourself. That aside, it's a good day for socialising!

27 OCTOBER

This is a good day to take stock, slow down and spend time with someone special. A healing, therapeutic atmosphere will be restorative.

28 OCTOBER

A difference of opinion or a tough task will merit a patient approach. When you do you can make great progress and achieve great goals. It's a good day to socialise and network.

29 OCTOBER

Once again, look for common ground in discussions and potential disagreements as you will otherwise encounter resistance. Be sure the facts support your views.

30 OCTOBER

Be prepared for a sudden change of plan or surprise news. You may need to factor in more time for travel or communications due to disruptions.

31 OCTOBER

Happy Hallowe'en! You'll be looking for peace and quiet but are prepared to put on a show this ghoulish night. Just reserve time for your happiness where possible.

November

1 NOVEMBER

The Scorpio new moon will kick-start a fresh phase in your relationships and may prompt you to upgrade a device or vehicle. For some Virgos this is a good time to begin a fresh project.

2 NOVEMBER

You'll enjoy a favourite activity or even a health treat. A get-together may be healing. You may be asked for help, and if you need advice it is available.

3 NOVEMBER

You'll enjoy romance, the arts and being with like-minded, upbeat people. However, some interactions may be intense, so if possible avoid conflict.

4 NOVEMBER

This is a good day to make solid tracks towards creating a strong foundation, either at work or financially. It's a good day for a work interview or gaining financial advice.

5 NOVEMBER

Combine your outgoing and dynamic approach with practicalities and you could move mountains, especially in your personal life and concerning collaborations.

6 NOVEMBER

Be practical at home and with family. You may need to find common ground with someone to avoid arguments.

7 NOVEMBER

You'll appreciate the opportunity to get together with someone special. A trip or talk will be revitalising.

8 NOVEMBER

An unexpected or unusual development or project will merit a diligent approach. Be prepared to look for solutions to sudden developments.

9 NOVEMBER

Someone close may be forgetful or unreliable and you may accordingly need to alter your plans. Avoid absent-mindedness.

10 NOVEMBER

The moon in Pisces will encourage you to relax and dream a little. If you're working, ensure you are practical and realistic and stick with the facts.

11 NOVEMBER

A pragmatic and rational approach to someone who can be forgetful will work wonders. Your communication skills and tact will be in demand.

12 NOVEMBER

It's likely that communications and travel will be delayed or tense, so be sure to be patient. Plan ahead to avoid travel delays.

13 NOVEMBER

The Aries moon over the next two days means people will appear to be a little more outgoing or feistier than usual, and you may need to adjust your responses accordingly.

14 NOVEMBER

The lead-up to the Taurus full moon can be intense. This is a proactive and restless time, so be sure to anchor your projects to avoid losing sight of your goals.

15 NOVEMBER

The full moon in Taurus spotlights a favourite activity or relationship and you may be surprised by developments.

16 NOVEMBER

A trip or get-together will take you into new territory. You will need to be tactful, as changes at home or with someone special may stretch your patience.

17 NOVEMBER

A key meeting or news will be significant. You may prefer to take a little time out to assimilate the busy phase you're in.

18 NOVEMBER

Developments will merit a measured perspective to avoid going over the top with responses that are out of proportion with events. Be prepared to review circumstances.

19 NOVEMBER

This is a good day for talks and meetings. You may experience a healing or therapeutic event. It's a lovely day to invest in your domestic décor or dynamics.

20 NOVEMBER

As Pluto re-enters Aquarius you're ready to turn a corner in a personal matter. Be prepared to think laterally for the best results.

21 NOVEMBER

Over the next four weeks you'll enjoy being more outgoing with communications and travel will appeal. You'll enjoy a get-together or short trip.

22 NOVEMBER

It's a good day to make a domestic or work commitment and plan ahead for family events, and also to make positive changes to your daily routine.

23 NOVEMBER

You'll appreciate the help and support of someone who understands you well. A friend or group may be significant. You'll enjoy socialising and romance could blossom.

24 NOVEMBER

It's a good day to relax, but if restlessness prevails you'll feel happier if you channel your energy into clearing chores so you can then relax.

25 NOVEMBER

This is a good day to get on top of paperwork, especially to do with your home or family such as bills. You'll enjoy a reunion. Be super clear at work to avoid mix-ups.

26 NOVEMBER

You may receive key news concerning work or your home. Be prepared to push towards a positive outcome with someone special.

27 NOVEMBER

You'll enjoy socialising and networking, and a trip or news will be motivational.

28 NOVEMBER

Approach a personal or collaborative project realistically for the best results. Avoid taking other people's weaknesses or problems personally.

29 NOVEMBER

You can navigate difficult talks at home and someone you love will prove helpful. A change of pace or of place will be pleasant.

30 NOVEMBER

The lead up to the new moon is perfect for setting an intention to be more adventurous, especially in relationships. You may consider updating a device or vehicle.

December

1 DECEMBER

The Sagittarian new moon will kick-start a fresh chapter in a relationship. You may consider a trip or will welcome a guest.

2 DECEMBER

You may be surprised by developments. There are healing aspects to communications, even if they are difficult. Be prepared to be the bigger person.

3 DECEMBER

Take things one step at a time to avoid overloading yourself with commitments. Be diplomatic for the best results.

4 DECEMBER

Some conversations and trips are likely to be more intense than you'd hope, so be prepared to look at practicalities. You'll enjoy a treat and romance will thrive.

5 DECEMBER

Be prepared to think laterally and consider new ways to go about your usual routine. Life is busy right now but it will slow down. Expect news or a visit at home.

6 DECEMBER

You'll appreciate the chance to review some of your recent decisions and invest in time at home or at someone else's home. A reunion will be enjoyable.

7 DECEMBER

Be prepared to see another person's point of view, otherwise interactions could be intense. Romance will thrive, so make a date.

8 DECEMBER

It's time to dream a little and relax. Someone close may appear a little vague, but you will find a way to connect.

9 DECEMBER

Consider the parameters of your situation and find ways to gain ground. You may need to set in place boundaries so everyone is clear about their position.

10 DECEMBER

This is a good day to invest in yourself and your home and family. It's also a good day for romance and meetings with people you admire, so take the initiative!

11 DECEMBER

A busy or restless day will merit a little care and attention to avoid tiring yourself out. Pace yourself.

12 DECEMBER

This is potentially another romantic day, so be prepared to initiate a meeting and especially if you're single. However, conflict may be brewing, so avoid crossing swords.

13 DECEMBER

Despite this being Friday the 13th it's a good day for get-togethers and a short trip. Be prepared to review your circumstances and adjust accordingly.

14 DECEMBER

You'll enjoy being upbeat and outgoing and, in the lead-up to the full moon, to consider the year so far and what you'd still like to accomplish.

15 DECEMBER

The full moon promises a fresh chapter in your career, general direction or status. You may receive key news at home or a surprise. Travel will appeal.

16 DECEMBER

The moon in Cancer brings out your caring side, and someone may ask for your advice or help. A group or friend will prove supportive to you.

17 DECEMBER

Over the next two days be prepared to be super clear with your communications to avoid misunderstandings and making mistakes. You will be productive.

18 DECEMBER

Someone's behaviour may confuse you, so be prepared to ask them to clarify things.

19 DECEMBER

It's a good day for talks, especially regarding personal matters and work. You'll enjoy a get-together and could make a valid commitment.

20 DECEMBER

You'll appreciate the sense that you are productive and effective. You will enjoy the festive mood, and romance and a fun gathering will appeal.

21 DECEMBER

This is the solstice. You'll appreciate the sense that you can bring more stability into your domestic life, but you must be prepared to see other people's points of view.

22 DECEMBER

This is a good time to set an intention to get on well with those at home and in your environment to transform dynamics for the better.

23 DECEMBER

A little tension in the air with someone needn't get in the way of a lovely day. Focus on creating a positive, healing atmosphere at home or at work. Tact will be very useful.

24 DECEMBER

An upbeat and relaxed approach to the day will nurture a therapeutic atmosphere. Avoid allowing complex or frustrating logistics to detract from your mindset.

25 DECEMBER

Merry Christmas! A change at home and general logistics will merit careful focus, but rest assured that dedication to enjoying your day means you will enjoy it.

26 DECEMBER

A trip, meeting or talk may bring about a strong reaction. You'll enjoy varying the pace of the day.

27 DECEMBER

This is a good day to be practical about your aims and goals. Avoid allowing delays, difficult talks and miscommunications to get in the way. Be patient.

28 DECEMBER

A development or news is likely to surprise you. A disruption in your plans is best navigated carefully to avoid impulsiveness.

29 DECEMBER

There are benefits to looking after yourself and those you love, and you'll appreciate the chance to invest time and energy in your home or someone special.

30 DECEMBER

The new moon in Capricorn will kick-start a fresh phase in your domestic, family or home life. Look for stability and security, which you may find in unusual ways.

31 DECEMBER

Happy New Year! A guest or being a guest in someone else's house will prove relaxing. Your help may be required, and if you need a little help it will be available. Just ask for it.

LIBRA

22 September – 22 October

FINANCES

Be prepared to innovate and step into new territory financially in 2024. A shared concern such as communal family duties or finances may be subject to change. As someone else's circumstances will change during the year your joint investments will require a rethink as a result. Be sure to set aside part of your budget for your health and well-being so that you can logistically plan to maintain strong health through such means as sports or active holidays. Be prepared to cover your bases financially and avoid a hole in the money bucket.

HEALTH

Your health and well-being have been put to the test over previous years with Chiron, the celestial wounded healer, transiting your health sector and bringing out your vulnerabilities health-wise. As Chiron now transits your relationship sector you will gain the opportunity to bring inspiration and potentially new health and well-being treats into your life. Look out for clever collaborations and treatments that will help improve your vitality. It's an excellent year to be innovative with your health on all fronts: mental, spiritual, emotional and physical.

LOVE LIFE

Chiron, the celestial body associated with healing and health, will influence your romantic life and collaborations for several years to come. This means your love life will be undergoing a health check; in other words, this will be a good year to make sure your relationships are healthy. If you have fallen into negative behavioural patterns in your love life this will be an excellent year to correct these and seek expert advice if necessary. It's a year of healing, which means singles may increasingly enjoy your single life or, on the contrary, will meet someone you wish to commit to if this is what you prefer. Couples can find healing if relationships have fallen on rocky ground. Key turning points will be in March, April, September and October, when you'll be in a position to welcome someone new into your life if you're single and make positive changes in your relationship if you're a couple.

CAREER

There is so much focus in 2024 on your personal and home lives that your attention may not be specifically on work, yet as you make changes in your personal and family lives you'll see the knock-on effect in your work life and your career potential moving forward. You may be ready to turn a corner already in January at work as you'll gain an option to make changes to your usual workday around the full moon on 25 January. At the end of March, around the lunar eclipse in your own sign on the 25th, a chapter comes to a conclusion that will again encourage you to make changes at work and within your general direction. Early October will be another time to rearrange aspects in your career as your actions will be effective.

HOME LIFE

You'll gain the chance to make changes in your usual domestic circumstances early in 2024. If you miss the opportunity then, rest assured you will gain another chance to make extensive changes at home, with family or concerning property at the end of the year so there's no need to feel under pressure to make changes in a short amount of time. You will be able to plan ahead and at your leisure. Mid-year, the going will be good to make changes that are remedial such as renovation, DIY projects or improving domestic interpersonal dynamics among family members and those you live with.

January

1 JANUARY

Happy New Year! The peace and harmony you're looking for is within reach but it will depend on good communication skills, as someone's views differ from yours.

2 JANUARY

This is a good day for a mini financial review, especially if you overspend during the festive season and new year.

3 JANUARY

Your aims and goals are likely to differ from those of someone else, but you will nevertheless manage to overcome differences and find positive common ground.

4 JANUARY

The next four weeks are ideal for injecting a little more stability in your relationships. Travelling Librans will enjoy feeling more grounded.

5 JANUARY

You'll feel more passionate about your activities, and this is a good time to look at some of your joint investments to ensure you're on track.

6 JANUARY

Someone close may require your advice or help. This is a good day to seek expert help at home and, if you're travelling, to unwind. Just avoid delays by planning ahead.

7 JANUARY

An adventurous approach to your engagements and activities will pay off. Find time to anchor your ideas and plans to ensure success.

8 JANUARY

You'll appreciate the chance to discuss important aspects of your work and health care, so reach out to experts, someone special and colleagues.

9 JANUARY

You may experience delays and communication mix-ups, so plan extra time for travel and be patient. Back up computers for the best results. A vehicle may require fixing.

10 JANUARY

Keep an eye out for a lovely opportunity to enjoy a get-together or improvement at home.
You may receive surprise news.

11 JANUARY

The Capricorn new moon will kick-start a fresh phase at home, with family or a property.
If you're back from holiday you'll enjoy feeling at home. There are healing aspects to the day.

12 JANUARY

This is a good time for talks at home and at work, as you could make great progress. A trip will
be enjoyable.

13 JANUARY

You'll enjoy a short trip and meeting friends or family at your home or theirs.

14 JANUARY

Be prepared to look outside the box at some relationships and interactions as someone quirky
may simply be just that.

15 JANUARY

A creative and intuitive approach at work will work wonders. You'll enjoy being inspired but must
avoid forgetfulness.

16 JANUARY

You'll enjoy being with like-minded people and both work and your home projects can thrive,
especially if you're creative and inspired. It's a good day for spiritual work and self-development.

17 JANUARY

You're communicating well and can make solid progress with your efforts and ventures.

18 JANUARY

This is a good day for serious talks about money, family and personal investments. Just focus
on facts and avoid distractions.

19 JANUARY

Be prepared to think big but avoid forgetfulness, making assumptions and being easily led.

20 JANUARY

You'll enjoy looking at your home life or domestic and family situation from a fresh perspective.
A key get-together or project could be transformational.

21 JANUARY

This is a good time to consider something new at home. Think laterally for the best results.

22 JANUARY

You're inspired and ready to implement new ideas. However, you must avoid being rash or impulsive, especially at work and on the roads.

23 JANUARY

A positive approach to talks and negotiations will be productive. Base your decisions on facts and above all be practical.

24 JANUARY

The lead-up to a full moon can be intense, so be prepared to have short breaks if necessary.

25 JANUARY

The Leo full moon will spotlight your career, status and general direction, bringing matters to a head. Be proactive and avoid taking the random comments of other people personally.

26 JANUARY

You may experience delays and communication glitches, so be patient and prepared to sort out a conundrum. Avoid minor bumps and scrapes and erratic drivers if you're driving.

27 JANUARY

You like to seek peace and harmony but not everyone is the same. A difference of opinion is best looked at from a fresh perspective. Avoid making rash decisions.

28 JANUARY

This is a good day to discuss personal matters with someone special. Aim to find common ground as otherwise you may talk at cross purposes.

29 JANUARY

This is a good day for talks and putting forward new ideas. You'll enjoy a trip or get-together. Romance could thrive as long as you haven't recently argued.

30 JANUARY

You may be sensitive to other people's opinions of you, which will provide you with insight into their thoughts, but you must maintain perspective rather than being influenced by them.

31 JANUARY

Be prepared to see someone else's point of view or meet them halfway. If you feel vulnerable, find an expert who can offer advice or help. Your expertise may be in demand.

February

1 FEBRUARY

It's a good day to set up meetings and important talks for tomorrow if possible. If they're today at work, be prepared to be super clear and look for balance.

2 FEBRUARY

This is a good day to connect with colleagues, employers and those you rely on at home.

3 FEBRUARY

You'll feel passionate about your work and chores and are likely to want to spread your wings and do something a little different. Just avoid overspending if you're shopping.

4 FEBRUARY

You'll appreciate the opportunity to focus a little more on yourself, someone special and those you love. Just avoid allowing a difference of opinion to become an issue.

5 FEBRUARY

You'll enjoy certain discussions and meetings; however, others may become a little intense unless you're clear about wishing to create an even playing field.

6 FEBRUARY

You'll enjoy some upbeat interactions, but if some discussions and people in your environment are difficult avoid taking this personally. You may be asked for help.

7 FEBRUARY

Someone's news may surprise you, and you'll enjoy an impromptu get-together. This is a good day for improving your environment and relationships.

8 FEBRUARY

Be prepared to be flexible and adaptable, as unexpected news or developments may arise.

9 FEBRUARY

The Aquarian new moon supermoon will kick-start a fresh chapter, for some in your personal, family and home lives and for others at work or health-wise. Be innovative.

10 FEBRUARY

Be prepared to think laterally as you may be surprised by an unexpected disagreement or change of plan.

11 FEBRUARY

The Pisces moon will bring out your romantic and idealistic sides. You'll enjoy indulging in romance, the arts and the company of favourite people.

12 FEBRUARY

It's a good day to consider how you might improve your domestic and professional relationships and adopting a can-do attitude in this regard.

13 FEBRUARY

Be prepared for quirky or unusual news and developments. The more spontaneous and innovative you are the better it will be for you. Romance could thrive.

14 FEBRUARY

Happy St Valentine's Day! You'll enjoy doing something different for Valentine's Day and may be drawn to creating a little domestic bliss. Just avoid arguments with someone special.

15 FEBRUARY

A practical, realistic approach to your projects and chores will reap rewards. If you must make long-range changes, be sure to keep an open mind to avoid feeling stuck.

16 FEBRUARY

Venus, your sign's ruler, enters Aquarius and will bring a new dynamic to your home life and also potentially to one particular relationship. Keep an open mind.

17 FEBRUARY

This is a romantic day but things may also be feisty. You'll enjoy a meeting at home or making changes in a new domestic arena or environment.

18 FEBRUARY

A trip, meeting or event that brings your light-hearted and active sides out will be enjoyable. Just avoid forgetfulness.

19 FEBRUARY

Someone may reveal their vulnerable side and you may be asked for help. A meeting with a teacher, mentor or employer will be significant. If you need advice it will be available.

20 FEBRUARY

Trust your instincts as you gain insight into your best way forward, especially regarding your career, general direction and daily schedule.

21 FEBRUARY

The next two days will involve important personal developments that may take your mind off your chores, so be sure to focus when you're at work.

22 FEBRUARY

A key meeting or news concerning your home, family or property will be significant. The Leo moon brings out your feisty side and you may surprise someone with your outlook.

23 FEBRUARY

Mercury in Pisces for the next few weeks will bring out your romantic, idealistic and creative sides. You'll be drawn to the arts, music and dance more than usual.

24 FEBRUARY

The full moon in Virgo spotlights the end of a key cycle, for some September Librans in your work and health lives and for most Librans in your social and personal lives. It's time for something new!

25 FEBRUARY

This is a good time for get-togethers and making a commitment to a particular person or routine. However, you must avoid idealising circumstances.

26 FEBRUARY

Strong emotions are likely to be bubbling under the surface, so be prepared to keep your professional hat on while at work and to channel your feelings into something pleasant.

27 FEBRUARY

Your discussions will be successful with a view to creating a balanced outlook but your ideas will not necessarily sit well with everyone, so be prepared to negotiate.

28 FEBRUARY

This is a good time to seek direction at work and concerning your family and someone special, as you could make some long-standing agreements.

29 FEBRUARY

You'll enjoy a get-together with someone special. Romance could truly thrive, so singles may meet someone special!

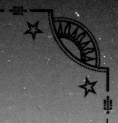

March

1 MARCH

This is a good day for making commitments, so take the initiative if you're looking for a commitment from someone such as an employer. There are healing aspects to the day.

2 MARCH

You'll enjoy doing something you love, so be sure to schedule in a treat.

3 MARCH

You may be surprised by someone's news or an abrupt change of plan. Find out more before jumping to conclusions.

4 MARCH

A proactive approach to your communications and general interactions will be productive, especially if developments delay or frustrate you.

5 MARCH

This is a good day for meetings, both at work and in your personal life, and for building bridges if you've recently argued with someone.

6 MARCH

This is a therapeutic day, especially in your personal life, as you'll gain the opportunity to overcome differences. It's a good day for a health or beauty treat.

7 MARCH

Take the initiative to bring a more proactive and upbeat feel to your day, both at work and at home, as your efforts will pay off.

8 MARCH

A key talk at work or regarding health will be productive and illuminate your best way forward.

9 MARCH

You'll enjoy a change of pace or of place. Romance, the arts, music and dance will thrive under these stars, so be inspired.

10 MARCH

The Pisces new moon supermoon will kick-start a transformative chapter in a work or health routine and, for some Librans, in your personal life.

11 MARCH

Be prepared to dream a little and take the initiative with your creative and personal endeavours, as you could make positive changes in these areas at work and home.

12 MARCH

You may find some people are a little feisty and others may find you more outspoken than usual, so be prepared to give and take for the best results.

13 MARCH

This is a lovely day for get-togethers and romance in particular. You may be drawn to zhuzhing up your domestic life with a DIY project or fresh décor.

14 MARCH

The Taurean moon will encourage you to be practical to reach your goals while adding a little spice and variety into the mix for a twist of fun.

15 MARCH

You'll appreciate spending time on your favourite activities and with the people you love, so be sure to organise something you'll enjoy.

16 MARCH

If you're working you're likely to be productive, and if you're clearing chores at home you'll be similarly industrious. It's a good day to make a commitment.

17 MARCH

You'll enjoy spending time on self-development, spirituality and finding a new look such as a fresh outfit. Just avoid being super idealistic if you're making a commitment.

18 MARCH

The moon in Cancer puts your heart on your sleeve and you may need to focus extra hard at work.

19 MARCH

You're likely to get on with those at work as long as you're realistic and practical. You may tend to be a little idealistic, so be sure to stay grounded.

20 MARCH

The sun will shine on your relationships over the coming weeks, improving dynamics. However, a delicate topic may require focus.

21 MARCH

This is a lovely day for a sociable get-together and romance. You may be prepared to make a commitment to a project or person.

22 MARCH

You'll feel increasingly drawn to looking for projects and work that are inspiring but must be sure to be realistic about the viability of some of your ventures.

23 MARCH

A larger-than-life character may prove particularly inspiring. A teacher, mentor or collaborator will prove beneficial.

24 MARCH

The lead-up to a full moon eclipse in your sign can be super intense, so be sure to pace yourself and take short breaks if necessary.

25 MARCH

The lunar eclipse in Libra signals a fresh chapter in your personal life, especially if you were born at the end of September. Those born in October will begin a fresh health or work routine.

26 MARCH

This is a good day for a health or beauty appointment. Someone close may ask for your help, and if you need help it will be available.

27 MARCH

You'll feel motivated by some of your higher ideals and desires, many of which you can bring to fruition. However, you must avoid daydreaming.

28 MARCH

An impromptu or spontaneous get-together will be enjoyable. You may receive surprise news from a colleague or collaborator. Some Librans will receive good financial news.

29 MARCH

It's another good day to be inspired by your favourite activities and consider adventurous and fun plans for the weekend.

30 MARCH

An outgoing and upbeat approach to activities such as sports and shopping will be productive. Just avoid overtiring yourself.

31 MARCH

You will appreciate the help of someone you admire and a short trip or meeting will be enjoyable. Just avoid forgetfulness and overspending as you may regret it.

April

1 APRIL

It's a good day to be practical with your projects, especially to do with arrangements during the week, paperwork and family.

2 APRIL

You may receive key news from someone close such as a personal or business partner. Try to get important decisions on the table to avoid delays further down the road.

3 APRIL

This is a perfect day to focus on health, beauty and well-being. You may be drawn to a new look and may receive key news at work. Just avoid forgetfulness.

4 APRIL

Important news is on the way unless you already received it from someone close such as a colleague, employer or partner. You will enjoy a reunion.

5 APRIL

As Venus enters your seventh house the focus over the coming weeks will go on collaborations and partnerships, giving you the chance to improve these areas.

6 APRIL

This is a lovely day to focus on your home and family and improving your usual daily or weekend routine to bring more of what you love into your life.

7 APRIL

The lead-up to the new moon is an ideal time to make a wish. Someone close is likely to take up much of your focus. This is a good day to discuss new ideas and make changes.

8 APRIL

The total solar eclipse signifies a change in a key personal or work relationship. Be prepared to be adaptable and see another person's point of view. A teacher or expert's opinion will be valuable.

9 APRIL

You'll feel drawn to pressing ahead with your various ventures and plans but must avoid rushing them before they're ready to be implemented.

10 APRIL

An unexpected meeting or news will buoy your mood. This is a good time to make a valid commitment either at work or to someone special.

11 APRIL

A reunion with someone special and the opportunity to review paperwork and agreements will be useful.

12 APRIL

This is a good day for talks, making agreements and meeting new people. However, you must avoid gossip and distractions at work.

13 APRIL

A trip and favourite activity will grab your attention and you'll enjoy a sense of freedom. Just avoid idealising a situation or person if you're making key decisions.

14 APRIL

You'll find the time to create a relaxed and romantic atmosphere involving the arts, music and the chance to focus on yourself. However, you must avoid arguments.

15 APRIL

Someone close will have important news and may request your help. You may need to ask for expert advice or support yourself, and it will be available.

16 APRIL

You can progress at work with a tactful and diligent approach. This is a good day for a health or beauty appointment and one on which you'll need expert advice. Just avoid rushing.

17 APRIL

You'll enjoy a reunion and romance could thrive. If you were born after mid-October you may receive key work or health news.

18 APRIL

As an air sign you like to be analytical, yet sometimes you must trust your intuition and you certainly can today!

19 APRIL

As the sun enters Taurus your plans can take shape, especially with shared ventures, legal matters and improving relationships. You'll enjoy a get-together or surprise.

20 APRIL

Today's Virgo moon adds to your ability to be methodical and practical, especially regarding health, well-being and chores. You'll enjoy sports and self-development.

21 APRIL

Someone special or a situation you share will catch your focus, perhaps unexpectedly or pleasantly. However, you must be careful to avoid a battle of egos.

22 APRIL

This is an excellent day to be outgoing and spontaneous, especially with those you share duties or space with.

23 APRIL

Your sign looks for balance and harmony in life and this is an excellent day to do exactly that. Avoid being caught up in other people's dramas.

24 APRIL

The Scorpio full moon will spotlight your values and principles and also, for some Librans, finances. Be prepared to discuss your plans financially and at work.

25 APRIL

It's a good day to talk as the Mercury retrograde phase ends. You may need to review certain agreements, either with someone special or at work and concerning health.

26 APRIL

A more adventurous outlook will raise your spirits and you'll appreciate the opportunity to consider new ideas and potentially even travel.

27 APRIL

You'll enjoy being with like-minded people and being active and outgoing, engaging in sports, for example.

28 APRIL

It's a lovely day to invest both in yourself and someone you love. Romantic comedy, the arts and music will raise your spirits.

29 APRIL

As Venus enters Taurus you'll appreciate the opportunity to indulge more in life's luxuries. However, you must avoid being stubborn and idealistic, especially at work.

30 APRIL

This is a good time to consider a beauty or health boost. You may enter fresh territory at work.

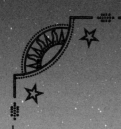

May

1 MAY

These are intense skies that could promote similar emotions, so be prepared to adopt a calm approach and avoid conflict.

2 MAY

Key developments at home, for some with family or a property, will precipitate long-term change, so choose your actions wisely.

3 MAY

This is a good day for making changes at home and at work and improving your daily routine so it suits you better.

4 MAY

Upbeat, proactive activities such as sports will boost your mood. You may be drawn to transforming your domestic realm or close relationships; just avoid pushing your own agenda.

5 MAY

An enjoyable meeting will flourish and this is a good day to make a commitment to someone or a plan of action.

6 MAY

Consider other people's feelings, especially concerning family and domestic matters, as you may otherwise experience resistance to your ideas or actions.

7 MAY

This is an excellent day to work on a strategy that will provide you with a solid base from which to grow, both at work and at home.

8 MAY

The Taurus new moon will kick-start a fresh chapter in a key collaboration or business or personal partnership.

9 MAY

You will enjoy bringing your admirable communication skills to the table both at home and at work and can as a result forge positive relationships.

10 MAY

You'll appreciate improved relationships and the opportunity to be more outgoing. However, not everyone will see things your way so be prepared to be tactful, especially at work.

11 MAY

This is a therapeutic day, especially in your relationships, as someone or a group or people prove to be good company at the least and supportive if necessary. Romance could thrive.

12 MAY

Find time to devote caring attention to someone close and to indulge in your favourite activities. It's a good day for self-development.

13 MAY

You may receive unexpected news. It's a good day to make a commitment to someone or to a financial agreement.

14 MAY

You have a natural empathy with people and a buoyant approach will certainly resonate with others.

15 MAY

You'll gain fresh perspective about the people you associate with at work and at home and will find a more grounded, earthy approach to communication beneficial.

16 MAY

The moon in Virgo helps you get organised, and this is a good time to consider your priorities at home and with someone special.

17 MAY

Certain interactions may be delayed or complex, so be sure to be patient. Avoid rushing and pressuring others.

18 MAY

Shared matters such as finances and responsibilities will demand your focus as you work together as a team to produce positive results. You may be surprised by news.

19 MAY

This is a romantic day, so plan a date! It's also a super-creative time, so artistic Librans will feel inspired. It's a good day for spiritual development.

20 MAY

Over the next four weeks your collaborations and relationships will take much of your focus. Be prepared to make changes. A meeting may have swift repercussions.

21 MAY

The next two days are ideal for making changes at home and within shared agreements or commitments. A loving relationship could positively transform.

22 MAY

This is a good time to make changes at home and in other areas you share such as communal space at work. A financial matter may be reviewed.

23 MAY

The full moon in Sagittarius will spotlight a fresh phase in a key relationship for some Librans and a fresh chapter financially for others.

24 MAY

An outgoing, upbeat approach to your ventures, especially at home, will be productive. However, tact will still be a useful skill set.

25 MAY

This is another good day to positively transform domestic, family and personal relationships. A trip or visit will be refreshing.

26 MAY

As Jupiter enters Gemini the focus for you over the coming year will be on good communication skills and boosting your finances, beginning now.

27 MAY

You'll achieve a great deal even if you feel things are a little stuck. Be prepared to discuss your ideas in optimistic ways with those they concern.

28 MAY

This is a good day to discuss long-term plans at work and in your personal life. You may make an agreement or key financial decision.

29 MAY

Someone close such as a business or personal partner may require help and they may appear a little vulnerable or rushed. If you need advice it will be available.

30 MAY

It's an excellent day to discuss shared concerns, including finances. A trip or meeting may be particularly therapeutic.

31 MAY

Be inspired, as your ideas are both creative and practical. You'll enjoy an impromptu get-together or unexpected news.

June

1 JUNE

You'll be pleasantly surprised by news or a get-together. You'll love doing something different; just avoid making rash decisions.

2 JUNE

A partner or someone close will prove to be motivational and you'll enjoy being outgoing and upbeat with your favourite activities. Just avoid being bossed around if possible!

3 JUNE

More light-hearted communications will thrive, and you'll appreciate the opportunity to touch base with family or friends and make changes at home.

4 JUNE

A trip or meeting will be enjoyable. It's a good day for key financial matters and for get-togethers with those you admire.

5 JUNE

The lead-up to a new moon is a good time to consider what you'd like to improve in your life, especially regarding collaborations, joint finances and areas you share.

6 JUNE

The new moon will help you initiate plans. For some Librans these will be to do with favourite activities – for example, a trip – and for others to do with finances and/or love.

7 JUNE

You may feel a little vulnerable. If so, be prepared to take things one step at a time.

8 JUNE

The key to happiness is being prepared to give and take and careful planning.

9 JUNE

Be practical and adaptable, as certain activities may be delayed and someone may be stubborn. Avoid a Mexican stand-off and focus on relaxation and nurturance.

10 JUNE

The Leo moon will bring out your assertive and proactive sides, which will help you achieve goals and especially at work.

11 JUNE

There are therapeutic aspects to the day, and you'll appreciate the help and support of like-minded people and experts. Your expertise may be in demand.

12 JUNE

Your diplomacy will be in demand as certain projects and plans may need to be reviewed and communications are likely to be delayed.

13 JUNE

You'll enjoy the chance to be spontaneous and do something different. It's a good day for an impromptu get-together, and someone's news may surprise you.

14 JUNE

You may receive unexpectedly good news to do with a project or collaboration. A personal partner may surprise you.

15 JUNE

You'll enjoy being spontaneous and spending time with like-minded people. A trip somewhere different will be fun. You might like to pay a compliment to someone you admire.

16 JUNE

The moon in your sign will encourage you to look for peace and balance and chat with those who understand you best.

17 JUNE

A get-together or trip will prove to be nurturing. However, you must double-check details and plans to avoid delays and misunderstandings.

18 JUNE

You may be surprised by someone else's or your own emotions and will benefit from taking things one step at a time to avoid feeling under pressure.

19 JUNE

A passionate approach to your ventures will pay off but you must avoid appearing intense or zealous. Pace yourself.

20 JUNE

The solstice is a lovely time to review how far you've come this year. A project can progress, but you must once again focus on facts to avoid mix-ups.

21 JUNE

You'll enjoy a trip or get-together with favourite people. However, you may need to alter your plans or discuss tense topics so you must avoid arguments.

22 JUNE

The full moon in Capricorn will spotlight your relationships and finances. It's a good time to reconfigure agreements if necessary.

23 JUNE

You may discover that your priorities are different from someone else's and must alter your plans for the day accordingly. Delays are possible, so plan ahead.

24 JUNE

You'll appreciate adopting a bright, innovative approach to your home life and chores as you'll find matters advance better.

25 JUNE

Be prepared to take the initiative with your various chores, projects and work. Just avoid making rash decisions.

26 JUNE

This is a good day for discussions and meetings at work and improving interpersonal dynamics. However, certain matters will merit tact to avoid arguments.

27 JUNE

You'll enjoy making progress with your projects and at work. An inspired approach to communications and collaborations will pay off.

28 JUNE

You're communicating well but someone may be vulnerable, so be tactful. Your help will be required, and if you need assistance it will be available.

29 JUNE

You'll enjoy a favourite activity and the arts, self-development and sports will thrive. Romance could also appeal.

30 JUNE

An unexpected or unusual get-together or fun trip will be enjoyable.

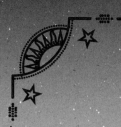

July

1 JULY

A slow but steady approach to relationships will work wonders, especially with someone who can be stubborn.

2 JULY

You'll feel more outspoken over the coming weeks. You may receive key news. Remember that you can't please everyone all the time, so avoid feeling you should.

3 JULY

It's a good time to make a work or financial agreement. You may receive important news from someone at home or family.

4 JULY

The lead-up to the Cancerian new moon is an ideal time to take stock of how you spend your time today and how you wish to proceed over the coming weeks and months.

5 JULY

The Cancerian new moon is a good time to kick-start a new career cycle and, for some, to begin a fresh activity or project. You could make a valid agreement.

6 JULY

You're in a strong position, so avoid feeling the opposite and especially at work. Someone may need your help, and if you need advice it will be available.

7 JULY

The Leo moon brings out your proactive and dynamic sides, so if you feel a little restless this an excellent time to channel energy into sports and other upbeat activities.

8 JULY

Key work meetings are likely to go well and you may be surprised by unexpected news.

9 JULY

Your approachable attitude to others will reap rewards, but you must avoid feeling limited by the expectations of others.

10 JULY

An eye for detail and practicalities at work and play will pave the way to a productive and fulfilling day.

11 JULY

And inspired yet down-to-earth approach at work and to your extracurricular activities will be productive. Someone may need your help, and if you need advice it is available.

12 JULY

If you'd like to make changes at home or at work this the day to do so. However, some interactions may be super intense so keep things on an even keel.

13 JULY

The Libran moon puts you at ease and helps you see your path clearly, so be sure to consider how you'd like to move forward in real terms. You'll enjoy a change of pace.

14 JULY

You may be surprised by news today or tomorrow. This is an excellent day to look after your own health and that of someone you love.

15 JULY

Someone who can be unpredictable will behave true to form. Be prepared to help if necessary and ask for advice if it's needed, especially at work.

16 JULY

A difference of opinion is best managed with a balanced approach to avoid unnecessary arguments.

17 JULY

As an air sign you like to think before you speak, but sometimes that's impossible and especially when you're busy. Be prepared to avoid misunderstandings.

18 JULY

A pleasant surprise or unexpected development will put a smile on your face. Be prepared to take the initiative at work.

19 JULY

This is a good day to mend bridges with anyone you've argued with recently. It's also a lovely day for get-togethers in your personal life and at work.

20 JULY

A situation that has been stuck will move forward again, giving you a little wiggle room.

21 JULY

The full moon in Capricorn will spotlight changes at home, with family or a property. Avoid misunderstandings and welcome something or someone new.

22 JULY

This is a good time to transform your home life or environment. You'll be feeling more positive about your situation and status – if not now, then in the coming weeks.

23 JULY

Key changes at home or within your status, career or direction will merit focus. Avoid intense interactions as these could escalate quickly.

24 JULY

Certain conversations may be a little difficult, so be prepared to be patient and have the facts at your fingertips to avoid confusion.

25 JULY

The key to success revolves around being super clear with facts and figures to avoid mix-ups and misunderstandings.

26 JULY

A meeting and developments at work or with someone special will buoy your mood. You may enjoy an impromptu get-together.

27 JULY

This is a good time to be inspired about your future at work and home. If you see obstacles you'll overcome them through research and discussion.

28 JULY

The Taurus moon will bring to the surface your love of luxury and a slower pace and sensuality, so find time to relax.

29 JULY

You'll attain your goals one step at a time, and as the day goes by you'll feel more in sync with those you collaborate with.

30 JULY

There are therapeutic aspects to the day. It's a good day to work collaboratively with colleagues, and if you need to delegate work to do so. An expert will prove helpful.

31 JULY

A meeting or chat will be significant. You could make progress at work and with your projects. September-born singles may meet someone alluring.

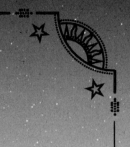

August

1 AUGUST

You're wearing your heart on your sleeve, so be professional at work and avoid taking things personally. Trust your instincts.

2 AUGUST

You may be surprised by developments that will require you to be flexible. You'll appreciate the support of someone who has your back.

3 AUGUST

The lead-up to the new moon in Leo will be a good time to consider how best to revitalise your work life and be discerning about your long-term choices.

4 AUGUST

The Leo new moon spotlights your career, status and big-picture direction. Someone special will house positive news or provide support. Trust your intuition if a mystery surfaces.

5 AUGUST

This is a good time to get your paperwork shipshape to avoid having to retrace your steps in the coming weeks. You may hear significant news from a friend or organisation.

6 AUGUST

Now that Mercury is retrograde you'll gain the chance to review recent affiliations and carefully choose who you bring into your inner circle.

7 AUGUST

A fun colleague or friend will prove supportive. This is a good time to broaden your skill sets and horizons.

8 AUGUST

You'll enjoy a reunion and may receive key news from a friend or organisation. This is a good day to review some of your agreements.

9 AUGUST

Trust your intuition, especially regarding big-picture plans including such ventures as travel, study and self-development.

10 AUGUST

It's a good day to clear a backlog of chores at home and get paperwork shipshape. Take things one step at a time and your productivity may surprise you.

11 AUGUST

You'll be drawn to only engaging with people and activities you enjoy, so you may need to compromise over a planned event.

12 AUGUST

You'll gain ground at work and with your chores but must be careful to avoid a battle of egos.

13 AUGUST

As the day goes by your mood will improve, which will allow you to reach your goals at work and in your personal life.

14 AUGUST

Be optimistic and your efforts will succeed. However, you must avoid a battle of wills and making rash decisions.

15 AUGUST

There are therapeutic aspects to the day. It's a good day to organise a healing treat, and if you feel you must improve communications with someone this is the day to do it.

16 AUGUST

Be sure to base your communications and decisions on facts as opposed to assumptions, and avoid impulsiveness and making hasty comments for the best results.

17 AUGUST

You'll enjoy spending time at home or in a favourite place and may appreciate focusing on your own health or that of someone else.

18 AUGUST

You may receive unexpected news so be prepared to be flexible, as a change of plan or surprise will merit a patient approach. Avoid misunderstandings.

19 AUGUST

The Aquarian full moon will spotlight a change in your personal life or creative project. A review or news you've been waiting for will arrive.

20 AUGUST

You have the direction or information you've been looking for, which provides you with the ability to make informed decisions.

21 AUGUST

An inspired, creative approach to developments will put you in a strong position. If a project is delayed, find ways to overcome obstacles through research.

22 AUGUST

The sun in Virgo over the next four weeks will spotlight your daily routine, health and well-being. Be practical and you could transform your everyday schedule.

23 AUGUST

You'll discover support and help in all the right places even if certain people are less friendly or amenable.

24 AUGUST

It's a great weekend to engage in activities you've had on the back-burner. Some communications may be tense, so engage in these carefully.

25 AUGUST

This is a lovely day to spend with someone special who is deeply in your bond.

26 AUGUST

The subtle art of good communication will be useful and you may be surprised by good news.

27 AUGUST

You'll enjoy a fun get-together. If you've been waiting for news from a friend or organisation it will be on its way.

28 AUGUST

You may receive news concerning your career or a health matter, which will provide you with insight. You must avoid being idealistic.

29 AUGUST

As Venus enters your sign your focus will gradually go on romance and socialising. A close relationship may enter fresh territory.

30 AUGUST

Your response to events may be purely emotional, so avoid making impulsive decisions.

31 AUGUST

You'll enjoy being spontaneous and the company of someone fun. You may be surprised by someone's news.

September

1 SEPTEMBER

This is a lovely day to forge strong relationships with those you care about. Just avoid tense topics, as these could ignite.

2 SEPTEMBER

You may need to review certain agreements at work or home. It's a good day for a health appointment.

3 SEPTEMBER

This new moon is a good time to embrace a fresh daily and work routine, especially in connection with those you prefer to keep in your inner circle.

4 SEPTEMBER

You'll appreciate gaining the chance to be more self-nurturing and conscious of the effects your communications have on others. A get-together will boost self-worth.

5 SEPTEMBER

The moon in your sign will encourage you to be more assertive and your emotions are likely to well up. A little tact will go a long way at work.

6 SEPTEMBER

You'll find more balance in your day and will be more productive, but you must be conscious of the sensitivities of someone close and avoid taking offence over minor matters.

7 SEPTEMBER

As you'll feel motivated to enjoy your weekend with upbeat and outgoing activities it's a good time for self-development and self-nurture.

8 SEPTEMBER

You'll make a great deal of progress with clearing a backlog of chores. It's a good day to make a commitment to a person or plan.

9 SEPTEMBER

As Mercury enters Virgo key talks and transactions could become intense, so be prepared to focus on details but avoid obsessing over them.

10 SEPTEMBER

An adventurous approach to communications and work will reap rewards. Just avoid taking other people's insensitivity personally but be mindful of their vulnerabilities.

11 SEPTEMBER

A diligent approach to chores and sensitive topics will be beneficial, as you could make great progress even if obstacles arise.

12 SEPTEMBER

Be prepared to think on your feet as it's likely to be a busy day. Talks will be productive; just avoid crossing swords with someone insensitive.

13 SEPTEMBER

A constructive and methodical approach to communications and travel will work well. It's a good time to consider logistics and strategy.

14 SEPTEMBER

You will not always agree with everyone and may need to find the middle ground. You may need to help someone, and if you need help it will be available.

15 SEPTEMBER

An original and fresh approach to your home life and favourite activities will revitalise relationships.

16 SEPTEMBER

Some of your interactions will require patience, especially at work and for September-born Librans in your personal life, so be prepared to take things carefully.

17 SEPTEMBER

Be inspired and prepared to discuss a fresh arrangement or agreement. The lead-up to a lunar eclipse can be intense, so pace yourself.

18 SEPTEMBER

The partial lunar eclipse supermoon in Pisces spotlights your agreements and relationships. You may make or break a commitment or a work or financial agreement.

19 SEPTEMBER

You'll appreciate a breath of fresh air and a change in your usual routine. You may experience a surprise.

20 SEPTEMBER

Your values and beliefs may not coincide with everyone else's, so be prepared to be flexible with some of your arrangements. Avoid overspending if you're in debt.

21 SEPTEMBER

This is a romantic day and you'll enjoy creativity and being with someone you admire. Self-development will appeal. Just avoid forgetfulness and misunderstandings.

22 SEPTEMBER

As the sun enters Libra you'll increasingly focus on love and investing in yourself. It's a good day to enjoy your home. Avoid tense topics if possible as arguments could ignite.

23 SEPTEMBER

Your sign's ruler, Venus, in Scorpio will bring out your motivated and passionate sides. Just avoid arguments and focus on positive developments.

24 SEPTEMBER

A change of pace or of place will be enjoyable. You may be surprised by good news involving someone else.

25 SEPTEMBER

Key communications and discussions may merit further research. Romance and the arts could thrive, so organise a date! Just avoid forgetfulness.

26 SEPTEMBER

This is a good day for discussions, meetings and communications. You may enjoy a reunion.

27 SEPTEMBER

The moon in Leo over the next two days will motivate you to get things done, so this is a super-productive phase. Take the initiative!

28 SEPTEMBER

This is an excellent weekend for deepening your relationship with someone you love. You'll appreciate the chance to be physically active, enjoying sports, for example.

29 SEPTEMBER

This is an excellent day for get-togethers and important discussions and changes at home, and also for forward planning. A trip will appeal.

30 SEPTEMBER

This is a good day for get-togethers and making a commitment to someone special or to a favourite project.

October

1 OCTOBER

During the dark of the moon, this is a good day to place your intentions for the future, especially regarding work, your personal life and long-term financial goals.

2 OCTOBER

The solar eclipse in Libra will help you turn a corner financially and in your personal life. It's a good time to put in place goals that will provide more balance.

3 OCTOBER

This is a good day for discussions, meetings and organising your work and finances.

4 OCTOBER

This is an excellent time to get ahead with work, financial and personal matters, so take the initiative in building a strong foundation.

5 OCTOBER

You'll feel motivated to invest in yourself and spending quality time with favourite people. You may be drawn to making a large investment.

6 OCTOBER

You're a good communicator but you won't always agree with everyone, so be prepared for some give and take to avoid arguments. Be patient.

7 OCTOBER

The Sagittarian moon will prompt you to be outgoing and upbeat, although your approach may surprise others.

8 OCTOBER

A focus on health and well-being will be rewarding. You may be asked for help and an expert will help you if necessary. This is a good time to plan a holiday and for favourite activities.

9 OCTOBER

Be practical with your various projects and you'll make great progress. Expert financial advice will be available if needed.

10 OCTOBER

You're seen as being amenable and charming but must avoid relying on this image if you feel under stress. The Capricorn moon helps you to take things one step at a time.

11 OCTOBER

Someone's unpredictable or erratic behaviour may test your mettle, so be prepared to be tactful.

12 OCTOBER

This is a good day for research and basing decisions on facts, as otherwise a conundrum, delay or frustrating developments will test your resilience.

13 OCTOBER

You'll feel increasingly passionate about your viewpoint, ideas and plans. However, someone may disagree, so be prepared for discussion and negotiation.

14 OCTOBER

A sensitive circumstance is best handled very carefully. Be prepared to see another person's point of view. You may receive surprise news. It's a good day for a health appointment.

15 OCTOBER

You have a strong empathy for someone close and must trust your intuition and avoid making rash decisions. Financial transactions will require focus.

16 OCTOBER

This is a lovely day for romance, the arts and engaging in activities you love, so take the initiative!

17 OCTOBER

The full moon supermoon in Aries will spotlight a relationship and, for mid-October Librans, a health or work situation. Be prepared to step into new territory.

18 OCTOBER

Be practical with financial and personal matters and avoid entering a stalemate in discussions if possible.

19 OCTOBER

Your ability to find common ground, peace and balance will be in demand as developments will require you to be a mediator or peacemaker.

20 OCTOBER

Distractions may lead to the sense that your day is slipping through your fingers, so be prepared to focus on favourite activities and goals.

21 OCTOBER

A chatty, busy day will keep you on your toes. A mentor, adviser or teacher will be particularly helpful.

22 OCTOBER

As the sun enters Scorpio the next four weeks will reconnect you with a sense of purpose and passion. However, communications may be tense today.

23 OCTOBER

This is a lovely day for a get-together with someone you love or admire in your personal life and work, so take the initiative!

24 OCTOBER

You may the thinking emotionally rather than objectively, so if you have important decisions ensure you double-check the facts and trust your intuition.

25 OCTOBER

Unexpected news or a change of focus will keep you on your toes. Be spontaneous, as you may enjoy a surprise or impromptu event. Avoid rushing.

26 OCTOBER

This is an excellent weekend for socialising and networking. You can build bridges in relationships you have let slide. Just avoid minor misunderstandings.

27 OCTOBER

A healing, therapeutic atmosphere will be restorative. If you're shopping avoid overspending, as you'll regret it.

28 OCTOBER

This is not a day for speculation, so avoid emotional and financial gambling as you may be inclined to overestimate your hand.

29 OCTOBER

The moon in your sign will increase your intuitive insight, so be sure to trust your instincts.

30 OCTOBER

Be prepared for unexpected news. It's a good time to discuss finances, but if you're making significant investments ensure you carefully check the details.

31 OCTOBER

Happy Hallowe'en! You may tend to take circumstances personally, so be sure to remain objective at work. Organisational skills will work wonders.

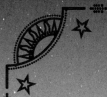

November

1 NOVEMBER

The Scorpio new moon will kick-start a fresh phase in your finances and, for some, in a personal relationship. Take the initiative in making changes at work.

2 NOVEMBER

You'll enjoy the opportunity to engage in your pet activities with favourite people. You may also enjoy a health or beauty treat.

3 NOVEMBER

This is a lovely day for get-togethers, and a trip or adventure will be enjoyable. Just avoid arguments as they could become fiery.

4 NOVEMBER

This is a good day to create a strong foundation at work and financially. It's also a good day to make a commitment or agreement in your personal life.

5 NOVEMBER

A positive, proactive approach to communications and relationships will be productive. You will need to be adaptable with collaborations.

6 NOVEMBER

A grounded, realistic approach to communications, travel and work will be productive. It's a good day to tee up for tomorrow a meeting such as an interview.

7 NOVEMBER

An outgoing, upbeat approach to work meetings and finances will be productive. It's a good day for get-togethers.

8 NOVEMBER

Be prepared to look outside the box at various options and opportunities. If an obstacle arises, think laterally for the best results.

9 NOVEMBER

You'll discover whether you've over- or underestimated a situation and will gain the opportunity to change course.

10 NOVEMBER

The moon in Pisces will encourage you to relax and indulge in the arts, music and romance, which you'll enjoy.

11 NOVEMBER

Communications and transactions are best approached from a practical, realistic point of view to gain the best results.

12 NOVEMBER

Certain communications and financial transactions may be subject to delays or confusion. Avoid financial and emotional gambling.

13 NOVEMBER

The Aries moon over the next two days will encourage you to be proactive and outgoing with colleagues and at work. However, some people may appear feistier than usual.

14 NOVEMBER

The lead-up to the Taurus full moon can be intense. This is a restless or changeable time, so be ready to anchor your projects and avoid losing sight of your goals.

15 NOVEMBER

The full moon in Taurus spotlights a shared financial circumstance, space or duty and you may be surprised by developments.

16 NOVEMBER

Someone who can behave unpredictably will do so again, so be prepared for the unexpected.

17 NOVEMBER

A little give and take is the recipe for success, especially if some communications are intense.

18 NOVEMBER

A trip, meeting or transaction will be a focus. If a disagreement arises, be prepared to find common ground.

19 NOVEMBER

This is a good day to overcome differences and experience a positive outcome, especially regarding finances and at work. You may deepen a key relationship.

20 NOVEMBER

As Pluto re-enters Aquarius you're ready to turn a corner with a domestic, family or property matter. Be prepared to see another person's point of view.

21 NOVEMBER

Over the next four weeks you'll feel more confident about your finances and self-esteem but you must avoid overspending. You'll enjoy a trip or a visit.

22 NOVEMBER

It's a good day to make a commitment to a plan that will create more stability and possibly abundance in your life.

23 NOVEMBER

This is a good day to be in touch with someone you know can help you along the way such as an adviser or mentor.

24 NOVEMBER

You'll enjoy spending time with like-minded people in a group, for example, or via a trip that takes you somewhere you enjoy.

25 NOVEMBER

Trust your intuition and your first impressions as they are spot on. You may meet someone you feel an inexplicable connection with.

26 NOVEMBER

You may receive key news or take a significant trip that brings you in touch with a like-minded character. You may make progress at work through good teamwork.

27 NOVEMBER

You may receive a financial or ego boost and can certainly advance your status or career path, so take the initiative.

28 NOVEMBER

You or someone close may feel a little sensitive, so be sure to take things one step at a time. Your help may be needed, and if you need advice it will be available.

29 NOVEMBER

You'll enjoy a reunion or return to an old haunt. Some Librans will enjoy a financial or ego boost.

30 NOVEMBER

The lead-up to the new moon is perfect for considering a fresh financial budget and ways to boost your self-esteem.

December

1 DECEMBER

The Sagittarian new moon signals the start of a more adventurous phase in your communications and relationships. You may consider a trip or will wish to update a device or vehicle.

2 DECEMBER

This is a good time for discussions, especially those that revolve around tricky topics.
You may experience a pleasant surprise.

3 DECEMBER

A practical approach to communications, colleagues and people you must interact with will reap rewards.

4 DECEMBER

This is a good day for a reunion and reviewing paperwork. Be open-minded and willing to see another person's point of view. You'll enjoy sprucing up your home or appearance.

5 DECEMBER

An innovative approach to people's involvement in your domestic or family life will be beneficial. Avoid making snap judgements.

6 DECEMBER

You may be ready to turn a corner at work and will receive news about a change of pace.
A trip or reunion may have a therapeutic quality.

7 DECEMBER

You'll enjoy a change of environment either through a trip or visit. Strong emotions may emerge. It's a good time to focus on DIY projects and improving domestic dynamics.

8 DECEMBER

You'll discover whether you've underestimated your circumstances, which will enable you to set things right.

9 DECEMBER

You'll be inspired by certain activities and topics, so ensure you find time to schedule something special you'll enjoy.

10 DECEMBER

It's a good day for a health or beauty boost and to schedule meetings with someone you find uplifting.

11 DECEMBER

Someone close may express their need for assistance, which you're in a strong position to provide. If you need advice or support it will be available.

12 DECEMBER

A key meeting or news will provide perspective, for some at work and for others at home. Certain relationships will thrive.

13 DECEMBER

Despite this being Friday the 13th it's a good day for get-togethers and a short trip. You'll appreciate the opportunity to spend time at home or at someone else's home.

14 DECEMBER

This is a good weekend for a DIY project and improving home décor. You may be drawn to reviewing your financial circumstances.

15 DECEMBER

The full moon will spotlight your interactions and relationships. You'll gain insight into a trip, study or particular venture.

16 DECEMBER

The moon in Cancer brings into focus your nurturing aspects, making this a good day to find time for a little self-care.

17 DECEMBER

You'll enjoy being more outgoing as they get day goes by, especially at work and with your long-term projects. Avoid intense discussions if possible by remaining calm.

18 DECEMBER

You may discover a mystery and will gain the opportunity to research circumstances. Misunderstandings and traffic delays are possible, so be patient.

19 DECEMBER

It's a good day for talks with family and friends and concerning a domestic or family matter. You may make a valid commitment to a project or person.

20 DECEMBER

This is a lovely day to be adventurous with your friends and projects. You have a wonderful ability to make people feel at ease.

21 DECEMBER

This is the solstice. You'll appreciate the sense that your projects and plans will gain a more even keel over the coming weeks.

22 DECEMBER

This is a good time to makes changes at home and within your environment. A trip is likely to be transformative.

23 DECEMBER

Some communications and potentially travel may be a little tense, so it's in your interest to choose your words carefully. Tact and patience will be very useful.

24 DECEMBER

There are therapeutic aspects to the day, and a focus on domestic and family matters and a change of routine will benefit you. Avoid idealising someone for the best measure.

25 DECEMBER

Merry Christmas! You'll enjoy the romance around Christmas and the peace that comes with it, especially if you avoid arguments and making rash comments.

26 DECEMBER

A trip, meeting or talk will be significant. This is a good time for a mini financial review or to benefit from the Boxing Day sales. Just avoid overspending and gambling.

27 DECEMBER

Certain conversations are likely to be off the table as you know already they will cause arguments. This is another day to be careful with your finances.

28 DECEMBER

Someone who tends to be irrational may surprise you. A change of environment will require a little adaptation.

29 DECEMBER

You'll appreciate the opportunity to focus a little on your health and well-being or that of someone else, but you will still need to be tactful.

30 DECEMBER

The new moon in Capricorn will kick-start a fresh phase in your communications, relationships and environment. You'll appreciate the chance to find stability.

31 DECEMBER

Happy New Year! There are therapeutic aspects to your New Year's Eve as certain relationships and activities will be uplifting. Your help and advice may be in demand.

♏

SCORPIO

22 October – 21 November

FINANCES

You'll be drawn to finding new ways to earn money in 2024, which will mean changes at work and in your career or status. For example, if you've been working as an employee in recent years you may be drawn to becoming self-employed or to developing new skills and embarking on a fresh career. As you make changes to how you earn your money the task will be ensuring you do adequate research and prepare for all eventualities. Luckily, you have a clean sweep in the first quarter in 2024 financially that will provide you with a strong platform to create stability for the rest of the year. Later in 2024 you must avoid speculating with the money you have already made.

HEALTH

As you'll be liable to burn the candle at both ends in 2024, the key to health and happiness will revolve around finding a balance between hard work on the one hand and peace and harmony in your spare time on the other. This aside, health and well-being will be of considerable focus for you in 2024. If you already work in a health-related field you will be drawn to working increasingly in a healing capacity. If you don't work in the health field, this year you'll feel motivated to engage your abilities in healing and supporting yourself or someone close.

LOVE LIFE

The focus will be very much on your personal life and daily existence in 2024, which will provide an ideal opportunity to nurture yourself and those you love. Romantically, you'll need to balance your own needs with those of someone close to the extent that you must perform a balancing act. This is largely because the behaviour of someone close may appear unpredictable on occasion, as will yours to others. Luckily, in 2024 you'll be stepping into a new phase in which a more broad-minded understanding of yourself and others will help you to navigate any ups and downs, which will in turn help you create a balanced scenario.

CAREER

For many Scorpios your work life will sync well with your home life in 2024, especially in the first quarter. As the year progresses you'll gradually gain more time for work as your home life takes less focus. For example, you may decide to work more hours or will be less focused on the complexities of your home than in previous years. Developments in April will demand that you anchor your career in order to find ways to balance your work with your home life a little more. At the end of August you'll once again need to carefully consider your priorities and to reinstate a sense of work/life balance if it eluded you mid-year.

HOME LIFE

Saturn in your domestic realm will bring a sense of stability and security and the need to find more balance in your home. If you have overinvested in a property or have underestimated domestic or family expenses you may need to tighten your belt or find ways to overcome high overheads. However, you must beware of taking short cuts and seeking peace at all costs, and also limiting your domestic options. If you discover there are limitations regarding your home life towards the last quarter of the year, be prepared to think open-mindedly in practical terms to find peaceful and viable options for improving your domestic circumstances.

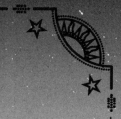

January

1 JANUARY

Happy New Year! The rest and recuperation you want is possible, so make space for it. Be prepared for some give and take with someone who disagrees with you.

2 JANUARY

This is a good day for a tidy up and to get various financial and personal plans on the table for discussion.

3 JANUARY

Approach a difference of opinion tactfully, as you may be surprised by the progress you can make.

4 JANUARY

The next four weeks are ideal for stabilising finances. Be prepared to discuss long-term plans.

5 JANUARY

You'll be drawn to creating a relaxed and supportive environment and avoiding sensitive topics.

6 JANUARY

Your help and advice will be required; however, you will need to be tactful to avoid arguments. A little retail therapy will appeal.

7 JANUARY

You'll be drawn to engaging in your favourite activities, and self-development, music and the arts will thrive.

8 JANUARY

You may surprise yourself with your proactive and outgoing approach to your ventures as your charming personality wins over minds and hearts.

9 JANUARY

Your charm can only go so far and you may experience delays and communication mix-ups, so plan extra time for travel and be patient. Avoid financial and emotional gambling.

10 JANUARY

You'll enjoy a surprise or impromptu get-together. You may experience a financial or ego boost.

11 JANUARY

The Capricorn new moon will kick-start a fresh phase in your communications. You may be drawn to a new environment or updating your communication device or car. There are healing aspects to the day.

12 JANUARY

You may experience a financial or work improvement. A change of routine or environment will boost spirits.

13 JANUARY

You'll enjoy a short trip and get-together or chats. You'll also be drawn to a little retail therapy.

14 JANUARY

A practical, grounded approach to finances and relationships will be beneficial. You may be surprised by developments.

15 JANUARY

Be prepared to see another person's point of view. A creative and intuitive approach at home well help you relax and enjoy your downtime.

16 JANUARY

You'll enjoy bringing more beauty and comfort into your home zone and may receive news from a family member. A get-together will be enjoyable.

17 JANUARY

You'll enjoy being proactive about your goals and ventures even if you feel a little vulnerable. You will enjoy the results of your hard work.

18 JANUARY

This is a good day for serious talks about responsibilities and finances as you are likely to reach an arrangement or agreement.

19 JANUARY

You may receive good news from work and/or receive a financial boost. Just avoid forgetfulness and overspending.

20 JANUARY

You'll appreciate the opportunity to go somewhere new and enjoy a beautiful place. Some interactions may be intense.

21 JANUARY

If you feel some relationships have become stale, consider a fresh approach. Think laterally for the best results. A new communications device or environment will be inspiring.

22 JANUARY

Be prepared to venture into new territory with your communications and relationships. A financial matter may require attention.

23 JANUARY

A positive approach to finances and negotiations will be productive. Base your decisions on facts and above all be practical.

24 JANUARY

The lead-up to a full moon can be intense. You may be feeling more sensitive than usual so be prepared to take short breaks if possible.

25 JANUARY

The Leo full moon will spotlight your ventures, travel and communications, bringing matters to a head. Avoid taking the random comments of others personally, but be prepared to stand up for yourself.

26 JANUARY

You may experience delays and communication mix-ups, so be prepared to sort out a conundrum. A financial mistake is possible, so be super careful.

27 JANUARY

This is a good time to review your finances and, if you're shopping, to avoid overspending. Avoid making rash decisions and financial and emotional gambling.

28 JANUARY

This is a good day to discuss personal matters and finances. Avoid making assumptions, as you may be talking at cross purposes.

29 JANUARY

Meetings are likely to go well even if some are unexpected. Be prepared to take the initiative. You may experience a financial or ego boost.

30 JANUARY

A fair-minded, balanced approach to your work and ventures will be successful. Avoid taking other people's issues personally.

31 JANUARY

You can decide whether you'll take sides in an argument or sit on the fence. The latter may be preferable for now.

February

1 FEBRUARY

This is a good day to channel your energy into work and find time for someone special.

2 FEBRUARY

There is a sense of excitement at the end of the week as you know you'll get more time for your favourite activities and people, so make plans!

3 FEBRUARY

While you have a go-ahead attitude to the weekend, someone may be feeling a little sensitive and will require some of your focus.

4 FEBRUARY

This is a lovely day to indulge in your favourite activities including music, dance and self-development. A trip will be enjoyable.

5 FEBRUARY

There are therapeutic aspects to the day and you could build bridges with someone you tend to argue with. Be prepared to discuss sensitive topics. You'll enjoy a trip.

6 FEBRUARY

A little give and take will be necessary to ensure the smooth running of certain potentially delicate discussions. Communications and travel may be delayed, so be patient.

7 FEBRUARY

Someone may surprise you with their news and you'll enjoy an impromptu get-together. Romance could thrive, so take the initiative!

8 FEBRUARY

Intend on being adaptable as a change of plan is likely and may come at short notice.

9 FEBRUARY

The Aquarian new moon supermoon will kick-start a fresh chapter in your communications and/or a relationship. You may consider upgrading a phone or vehicle or consider travel.

10 FEBRUARY

While you'll appreciate spending time at home or with someone whose company you enjoy, misunderstandings and travel delays are likely so plan ahead.

11 FEBRUARY

The Pisces moon will bring out your romantic and relaxed sides. You'll enjoy home comforts and spending time with people you love.

12 FEBRUARY

It's a good day for creative and family-based activities. However, you may be slightly idealistic and forgetful so you must focus while at work.

13 FEBRUARY

You'll be drawn to approaching a situation from a fresh perspective. Romance could thrive, and you'll enjoy home improvements.

14 FEBRUARY

Happy St Valentine's Day! This will be a busy or intense day, so be prepared to pace yourself and avoid arguments with someone special.

15 FEBRUARY

The Taurus moon will bring to the table your practical abilities, which will be useful at work and home.

16 FEBRUARY

You'll enjoy going somewhere new and doing something different. A holiday plan can take shape.

17 FEBRUARY

This is a romantic day but things may also be feisty. You'll enjoy a change of environment and the chance to meet a new circle of people.

18 FEBRUARY

You'll enjoy socialising, and a trip, meeting or event will bring out your light-hearted side. Just avoid speaking without forethought.

19 FEBRUARY

A personal or health matter will require a little focus. Be prepared to think outside the box regarding domestic and personal matters.

20 FEBRUARY

Look for the most viable way forward, as you may tend to be a little sensitive. Trust your intuition.

21 FEBRUARY

Developments over the next two days will encourage you to be outgoing, proactive and positive. It'll be a good time to reach out to people you know have your back and can help you.

22 FEBRUARY

A key meeting or trip will open doors for you. Consider a new way to look at your projects, relationships and a trip.

23 FEBRUARY

Mercury in Pisces for the next few weeks will bring inspiration your way. Be prepared to learn about new ideas and plan ahead.

24 FEBRUARY

The full moon in Virgo spotlights the end of a key cycle, for many to do with a learning curve, favourite pastime or relationship. Consider fresh, meaningful ventures.

25 FEBRUARY

This is a good time for meetings and to make a commitment to a particular person or idea, but you must do your research first to avoid idealism and making mistakes.

26 FEBRUARY

You'll have an eye for details, so this is a good day to focus on positive results at work and in your plans for the future.

27 FEBRUARY

You'll get good results for your hard work but some projects may be more difficult than usual, so focus on good communication skills and avoid delays.

28 FEBRUARY

You may receive key news that puts you in a position of knowledge, enabling you to plan ahead. You'll be inspired by travel.

29 FEBRUARY

This is a good day for talks and meeting like-minded people. Romance could thrive.

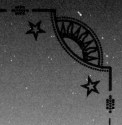

March

1 MARCH

What you say and do can make a difference. You may be ready to make a commitment to someone or a property. It's a good day to talk.

2 MARCH

There is a feeling of excitement around you, although not everyone will feel the same. You'll enjoy a reunion or return to an old haunt.

3 MARCH

Someone close may have unexpected news or behave out of character. Think laterally to overcome a conundrum.

4 MARCH

You have a reason to be enthusiastic about your projects and ventures but may need to be tactful to avoid hurting someone's feelings.

5 MARCH

You'll enjoy the opportunity to get together with someone you admire or who can be helpful.

6 MARCH

It's a good day for a health or beauty treat. A teacher, mentor or employer may have important news for you.

7 MARCH

This is a good day to build bridges with people you have recently argued with. It's also a good teaching and learning day.

8 MARCH

You'll enjoy being artistic and creative. This is a good day for self-development and romance. Just ensure you're on the same page with someone when you're making plans for the future.

9 MARCH

You'll enjoy being spontaneous and may appreciate an impromptu invitation. It's a lovely day for the arts, romance, music and self-development.

10 MARCH

The Pisces new moon supermoon will kick-start a transformative chapter in your personal life and also an appreciation of the importance of a happy home life.

11 MARCH

You'll discover over the next two days whether you've underestimated a particular project or person, giving you the chance to put things right.

12 MARCH

This is a good day for being productive at work and getting chores done. You may enjoy a get-together or short trip.

13 MARCH

This is a lovely day to change aspects of your environment either by improving your home décor or taking a short trip. You may be drawn to upgrading a vehicle.

14 MARCH

The Taurean moon will encourage you to focus on the needs of those close to you. It's a good time for romance.

15 MARCH

You're communicating well and will appreciate the opportunity to connect with like-minded people, but you may need to be patient.

16 MARCH

This is a good day to organise your home and environment and to make a commitment.

17 MARCH

This is one of the most romantic days of the year for you, so be sure to organise a treat or date. You'll enjoy music, dance and romance.

18 MARCH

The moon in Cancer brings out your intuitive abilities, so be sure to trust your gut and especially regarding domestic matters. Avoid taking other people's circumstances personally.

19 MARCH

You can make a great deal of progress with domestic and personal matters, and this is a lovely day for romance. You may wish to update or improve décor at home.

20 MARCH

The sun will shine on your work life and health over the coming weeks, improving these important areas of your life. It's a good day for a health or beauty appointment.

21 MARCH

This is another good day for domestic improvements, including décor and interpersonal dynamics. A visit or trip will be enjoyable.

22 MARCH

You'll feel increasingly drawn to investing emotionally and financially in your home and/or family over the coming few weeks.

23 MARCH

You'll enjoy a get-together, and a business or personal partner has news for you.

24 MARCH

The lead-up to a lunar eclipse can be super intense, so be sure to pace yourself. You'll enjoy taking things easy and spending time with like-minded people.

25 MARCH

The lunar eclipse signals a fresh chapter in your social life or affiliation with a particular group or organisation. Be prepared to carefully choose your company.

26 MARCH

This is a good day for get-togethers, especially with family or at home.

27 MARCH

The Scorpio moon will bring your feelings to the surface and your intuition will be stronger, so trust your gut instincts.

28 MARCH

You'll enjoy being spontaneous and may receive good news from someone special.

29 MARCH

You'll gain a deeper insight into someone close. Plan for an upbeat and outgoing weekend, which you'll enjoy.

30 MARCH

You may be drawn to retail therapy but must avoid overspending if you're already in debt. Sports and team-based endeavours will be productive.

31 MARCH

This is a good day to get on top of household chores and tie up loose ends with paperwork such as bills.

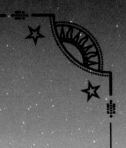

April

1 APRIL

This is a good day to organise your work and schedule for April to ensure everything is in order. Consider putting important matters on the table for discussion.

2 APRIL

A change regarding work such as a fresh schedule or new opportunities will arise. If a health matter has been on your mind, this is a good day for an appointment.

3 APRIL

This is an excellent day for the arts, romance and domestic improvements. Romance will thrive, so organise a date!

4 APRIL

A special meeting or get-together may be more significant than meets the eye. You'll enjoy a reunion.

5 APRIL

As Venus enters your sixth house your focus over the coming weeks will be on work, health and well-being. You'll be drawn to improving your appearance.

6 APRIL

This is a lovely day to focus on creative projects, family and someone special. You'll enjoy a get-together or trip somewhere different.

7 APRIL

The lead-up to a new moon eclipse is a potent time to make a wish. A change of pace or of place will catch your attention. This is a good day to focus on health and well-being.

8 APRIL

The total solar eclipse signifies a change in a daily work or health schedule. You may receive key health or personal news.

9 APRIL

Be practical and prepared to work towards specific goals at work and home, as your efforts are likely to succeed.

10 APRIL

Someone may have unexpected news for you. This is a good time to create a solid base in a project or venture, especially one involving your home or someone special.

11 APRIL

A review at work or reunion will clarify your circumstances and loyalties. It's another good day for a health or beauty appointment. Your advice may be sought.

12 APRIL

You're communicating well, so be prepared to engage in discussions that may require tact and diplomacy.

13 APRIL

You'll appreciate the opportunity this weekend for a change of pace and to focus on building strength and resilience. Sports and outdoor activities will appeal.

14 APRIL

This is the perfect day for self-nurturance and looking after those you love. You may be asked for help, and if you need help it is available.

15 APRIL

A health or work review will prove to be enlightening. Your help will be sought after and you'll appreciate the advice of an expert.

16 APRIL

There are therapeutic aspects to your discussions and meetings and you'll progress well as a result. Just avoid rushing.

17 APRIL

You'll enjoy a reunion and romance could thrive. Artistic, creative and spiritual Scorpios will find this a particularly inspiring time.

18 APRIL

The moon at the zenith of your chart puts your heart on your sleeve, so maintain a professional approach at work. However, you can be sure to trust your intuition.

19 APRIL

As the sun enters Taurus your focus will turn to business and personal partners over the coming weeks. You may already receive unexpected news or an invitation.

20 APRIL

You'll appreciate the company of like-minded people and for this reason will choose your company carefully.

21 APRIL

A clash of schedules may mean that you must reorganise your day at short notice. Someone will surprise you, so be prepared to be flexible. Avoid a battle of egos.

22 APRIL

A pleasant surprise will raise spirits. You may again need to alter your usual schedule.

23 APRIL

You'll be looking for balance and harmony in life yet some people will be feisty or argumentative, so prepare to be patient.

24 APRIL

The Scorpio full moon will spotlight a fresh chapter in your personal life, especially if it's your birthday on or before 6 November. Scorpios born later will turn a corner at work or with health.

25 APRIL

It's a good day to talk as the Mercury retrograde phase ends. You may need to review personal matters or a creative project.

26 APRIL

You'll enjoy that Friday feeling and planning exciting and upbeat adventures for the weekend.

27 APRIL

Be sure to channel your energy into active and outgoing projects as otherwise you may tend to feel a little frustrated or feisty.

28 APRIL

You'll enjoy a home DIY project or adding some luxury to your living arrangements. Romance, the arts and a little pampering will appeal.

29 APRIL

As Venus enters Taurus you'll appreciate the opportunity to indulge more in life's luxuries and will be drawn to expressing your values more at work. Romance could thrive.

30 APRIL

This is another good day to channel excess energy into positive outcomes, as you may otherwise feel feisty. Home improvement, the arts, romance and music will all appeal.

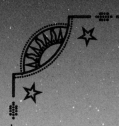

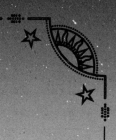

May

1 MAY

Once again, be sure to channel frustrated energy into constructive pursuits or you'll feel argumentative and feisty. Be patient with communications and travel.

2 MAY

Key news or discussions will provide you with direction, enabling you to plan better ahead at work and home.

3 MAY

You'll enjoy a lovely get-together or trip. Some Scorpios will appreciate a visit at home and the chance to improve your environment.

4 MAY

You'll feel inspired by your surroundings and favourite people. Artistic and spiritually minded Scorpios will find this an uplifting day.

5 MAY

A change of pace or of place will involve someone special, making this a good day for get-togethers and doing what you love.

6 MAY

Your viewpoints may differ from those of someone in a position of authority, so be prepared to find common ground and at the least to avoid a Mexican stand-off.

7 MAY

You'll find direction and support if necessary. It's a good day for a health appointment and making a commitment and overcoming differences.

8 MAY

The Taurus new moon will kick-start a fresh chapter in a key business or personal partnership and, for mid-November–born Scorpios, to begin a fresh daily health or work schedule.

9 MAY

A chatty, outgoing, light-hearted approach to those close to you will work wonders. However, some serious matters will require a down-to-earth approach.

10 MAY

Clear focus and attention to detail will pay off at work, then you'll enjoy being with like-minded people later in the day.

11 MAY

Someone close will have a healing, supportive or therapeutic effect. A fun get-together will raise spirits. Romance could thrive.

12 MAY

This is a lovely day to focus on favourite activities and invest more in your well-being and domestic bliss.

13 MAY

Someone close will surprise you, and if you've been looking for a commitment or agreement this is a good day to reach out although you must be realistic.

14 MAY

Upbeat, outgoing and active interests such as sports and gardening will appeal. Someone who can be unpredictable may behave true to form.

15 MAY

This is a good day to put adventurous, upbeat ideas on the table for discussion with those your plans concern.

16 MAY

Be practical and think of the best-case scenario with your plans and projects as you're in a realistic frame of mind.

17 MAY

You will not agree with everyone and certain communications may be misunderstood. Schedule extra time for travel as there may be delays.

18 MAY

This is a good time to share ideas with someone special, but you must avoid expecting them to agree with everything. You may be pleasantly surprised by domestic developments.

19 MAY

This is a good day for get-togethers, romance and improving your surroundings and domestic circumstances. It's also a good day for spiritual development.

20 MAY

Over the next four weeks your collaborations and investments will take much of your focus. Be prepared to make changes. A meeting may have swift repercussions.

21 MAY

You're prepared to see another person's point of view but you must avoid compromising your plans purely for the sake of peace. Be prepared to find common ground.

22 MAY

This is a good time for meetings, discussions and a short trip.

23 MAY

The full moon in Sagittarius will spotlight key personal and financial investments. Someone will have surprising news. It's a good day for romance, the arts and music.

24 MAY

A positive, uplifting outlook will reap rewards. Avoid falling prey to someone's bad moods.

25 MAY

This is a good day to transform your environment by taking a trip or investing in your surroundings. You'll enjoy the company of someone you love. Romance can thrive.

26 MAY

As Jupiter enters Gemini you'll gain a deeper understanding of those close to you. Relationships and partnerships will be a focus over the next 12 months.

27 MAY

A practical and realistic approach to someone who can be unpredictable will reap rewards.

28 MAY

This is a good day to make plans with someone special at work or home. A commitment or agreement can be made.

29 MAY

You may receive news or developments will quickly arise that encourage you to act on impulse. If you need advice it will be available.

30 MAY

If you need information it is available, so be sure to reach out. There are therapeutic aspects to the day that will help you improve circumstances.

31 MAY

You'll find out whether you've over- or underestimated circumstances at home or with someone special, which will enable you to move ahead with more insight.

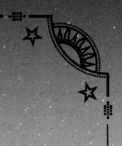

June

1 JUNE

News and developments may be a surprise, and you'll enjoy doing something fun and different.

2 JUNE

The Aries moon will contribute to an active and upbeat day and you'll enjoy a trip or change of environment at home.

3 JUNE

You'll appreciate people you associate with appearing to have a lighter mood and being more approachable. This is a good day for meetings and discussions.

4 JUNE

Someone close has news for you. This is a good day to get closer with someone you love and for creative projects and self-development.

5 JUNE

The lead-up to a new moon is a good time to consider your business and personal associations. It's also a good time to turn a corner in a relationship.

6 JUNE

The new moon will help you kick-start a fresh phase in a key relationship. This is a prime time for romance.

7 JUNE

The Cancerian moon will put your heart on your sleeve, providing you with insight into key matters, but you must avoid taking other people's moods personally.

8 JUNE

Be prepared to take other people's viewpoints into account, especially if their plans are different from yours. A favourite activity or event will be rewarding.

9 JUNE

Be practical and adaptable, as your plans may clash with someone else's. Avoid a Mexican stand-off and focus on relaxation and nurturance.

10 JUNE

The Leo moon helps you be proactive and dynamic and enables you to reach your goals, so take the initiative.

11 JUNE

There are therapeutic aspects to the day, so this is a good day to mend bridges if you've recently argued with someone. Your expertise may be in demand.

12 JUNE

Tact is a skill that will be very useful, especially as your viewpoints are likely to differ from those of someone else. Be diplomatic to find a solution.

13 JUNE

A change of pace or surprise event will provide you with the chance to break a stalemate or routine. You'll enjoy doing something different.

14 JUNE

A meeting or news from someone special will shine a light on your best options moving forward. Be prepared to think laterally.

15 JUNE

You'll enjoy being spontaneous and spending time with original thinkers. Consider new ways of spending your spare time with someone you love.

16 JUNE

The moon in Libra will encourage you to look for peace and balance and look after your health and that of someone close. You will manage to catch up on chores.

17 JUNE

You'll gain insight into someone you collaborate with, but if you still feel there is a mystery or you're receiving mixed messages then consider deeper research.

18 JUNE

The moon in your sign puts you in a strong position emotionally, but you must strive to see a mystery or misunderstanding from another person's point of view.

19 JUNE

You can learn a little more about how best to proceed with a joint responsibility or collaboration. Just avoid appearing intense or demanding.

20 JUNE

The solstice is a lovely time to review how far you've come this year. A project or relationship will progress, but you must focus on facts to avoid mix-ups.

21 JUNE

You may need to discuss thorny topics, so be prepared to overcome negotiations. A relaxed and friendly demeanour will be successful. Romance could thrive.

22 JUNE

The full moon in Capricorn will spotlight your relationships, collaborations and finances. It's a good time to talk and review agreements if necessary.

23 JUNE

Be prepared to make arrangements based on everyone's preferences. A difference of opinion is best navigated tactfully.

24 JUNE

You'll feel motivated to overcome interpersonal differences and simply get on with the job at hand. This approach points to success.

25 JUNE

Someone you admire will be helpful. Your expertise and skill sets will be in demand.

26 JUNE

You're communicating well. A trip or change at home will prove uplifting; however, certain matters will merit tact to avoid arguments.

27 JUNE

A creative and inspired approach to family and domestic matters will be successful. Combine practicalities with a sense of nurturance.

28 JUNE

Someone who can be sensitive or take the wrong end of the stick may take exception to some of your ideas, so be prepared to explain them more deeply. Avoid rushing.

29 JUNE

This is a lovely day for get-togethers, meetings and favourite activities. Romance could thrive, so take the initiative!

30 JUNE

You'll enjoy being spontaneous and may hear unexpected news or undertake a surprise trip.

July

1 JULY

Be prepared to work at a steady pace with someone who can be a little unpredictable.

2 JULY

You'll feel more outgoing over the coming weeks and may be drawn to travelling and expanding your horizons in other ways. This is a good day to research your options.

3 JULY

It's a good time to make a domestic or financial agreement. A trip or key news could be transformational.

4 JULY

The lead-up to the Cancerian new moon is an ideal time to take stock of your shared responsibilities and relationships. Consider ways of building more stability.

5 JULY

The Cancerian new moon is a good time to begin a more nurturing way of building a sense of security at home and financially. Be prepared to take action in this regard.

6 JULY

If you need rest this is the ideal day to look after yourself. Someone may need your help, and if you need advice it will be available.

7 JULY

The Leo moon brings out your sociable, proactive and dynamic sides. You'll enjoy upbeat activities and will appreciate the chance to be spontaneous.

8 JULY

Key meetings and projects are likely to go well and you may be surprised by unexpected news.

9 JULY

It's a good day to pay attention to details at home and work even if it means questioning someone else's plans or ideas. Just be prepared to be tactful.

10 JULY

You'll make progress with your projects and activities but must take into account someone else's viewpoints, which may differ from yours. Back up your ideas with facts.

11 JULY

This is a good day to make agreements with people you must collaborate with. It's also a good day for romance and self-improvement.

12 JULY

This is a passionate and feisty day that is ideal for getting things done, but you must avoid arguments. A key meeting or financial development is likely.

13 JULY

The Libran moon motivates you to look for balance. It's a good time to look after your health and for self-development.

14 JULY

Someone has surprising news for you today or tomorrow. Be prepared to be adaptable and helpful but avoid taking other people's problems or issues personally.

15 JULY

Unexpected news is on the way unless you received it yesterday. Be prepared to help if necessary and ask for advice if it's needed, especially in your personal life.

16 JULY

You'll see more deeply into circumstances than others. For this reason you may be misunderstood, so be discerning about who you share your insights with.

17 JULY

An upbeat, outgoing approach will be successful but you must avoid appearing gung ho. Be prepared to be clear without being blunt.

18 JULY

Pleasant or unexpected news will put a smile on your face. Be prepared to be adaptable and flexible.

19 JULY

There is a healing quality to the day's events. You may enjoy a change of environment or trip, and a get-together will bring you closer with someone you admire or love.

20 JULY

You'll enjoy a chatty, sociable time. Someone who can seem stuck in their ways will be more flexible.

21 JULY

The full moon in Capricorn will spotlight the need to consider fresh ways to communicate, including updating a device or vehicle. A change of plan may be necessary.

22 JULY

The next few weeks will be ideal for planning travel and enjoying a change of environment. Today's news or developments will be encouraging.

23 JULY

A meeting or news may be significant, and you must avoid intense interactions as they will escalate quickly to arguments. A new communications strategy will appeal.

24 JULY

Trust your intuition, as it is spot on. Be prepared to be brave with communications.

25 JULY

The key to success revolves around being adventurous and upbeat but also super clear with your facts and figures to avoid misunderstandings.

26 JULY

You'll enjoy an impromptu get-together and favourite activities such as sports and socialising.

27 JULY

This is a good time to meet friends and family members, but you must be careful with some interactions to avoid tense moments.

28 JULY

The Taurus moon will bring to the forefront your love of creature comforts and romance, making this an ideal day to find time to relax.

29 JULY

You'll manage interactions and communications one step at a time and will feel more in sync with those you collaborate with as the day goes by.

30 JULY

There are therapeutic aspects to the day as you'll gain the insight, information and guidance you need for a work or personal project to proceed.

31 JULY

A meeting or chat will be significant. A teacher, mentor or manager will prove helpful and your skill sets will be in demand.

August

1 AUGUST

You'll be seeing the world through intuitive and emotional eyes, so be prepared to maintain a professional outlook at work. Trust your instincts.

2 AUGUST

Someone special will prove their weight in gold. However, someone else may prompt a need to be careful with your responses.

3 AUGUST

The lead-up to the new moon in Leo will encourage you to re-evaluate your extracurricular activities, especially if some aspects no longer resonate.

4 AUGUST

The Leo new moon spotlights long-term plans such as travel, study, self-development and, for some, legal matters. Trust your intuition if a mystery surfaces.

5 AUGUST

Key news from a friend, mentor or organisation may cause you to rethink some of your plans and projects. Be prepared to invest in yourself.

6 AUGUST

Now that Mercury is retrograde you'll gain the chance to review recent decisions. You may like to return to an old haunt. Attention to detail is paramount.

7 AUGUST

A fun colleague, teacher or friend will prove supportive. This is a good time to reach out to experts and helpful people.

8 AUGUST

You'll enjoy a reunion and/or trip somewhere familiar. This is a good day to review some of your long-term plans and for self-development.

9 AUGUST

A calm, balanced approach to developments will be beneficial. You'll enjoy socialising and spending time with someone special.

10 AUGUST

The key to happiness lies in collaboration and compromise, as you may need to concede to someone else's point of view in an activity such as sport or at home.

11 AUGUST

You'll enjoy creature comforts and relaxation along with the chance to reconnect with someone special such as a family member. Just avoid sensitive topics.

12 AUGUST

Focus on building a strong work ethic and stay focused on your goals. You must be careful to avoid a battle of egos.

13 AUGUST

You will not suffer fools gladly, and while this will help you to focus on priorities you must avoid appearing blunt.

14 AUGUST

A work or personal partner has news that may surprise you. Avoid jumping to conclusions and consider your options carefully.

15 AUGUST

There are therapeutic aspects to the day. It's a good day to research your options. Tactful discussions will reap rewards.

16 AUGUST

You will not always agree with everyone, and today is a day to carefully avoid arguments and making rash decisions.

17 AUGUST

Consider what would make you happy and pursue your goals. If you're diligent you'll be happy with the outcome, but you must avoid assuming others have the same goals.

18 AUGUST

A patient approach to communications and interactions will be beneficial, as you may be surprised by developments. Travel may be delayed. Avoid misunderstandings.

19 AUGUST

The Aquarian full moon will spotlight the necessity to reconsider certain agreements and arrangements. A travel plan or domestic matter may need to be discussed.

20 AUGUST

You have a strong intuitive ability, so be sure to trust your instincts. Avoid arguments, as these could lead to a stalemate.

21 AUGUST

Be prepared to be practical with domestic, work and collaborative efforts and ready to go over old ground if necessary.

22 AUGUST

The sun in Virgo over the next four weeks will spotlight your career, status and general direction. Be practical with communications and prepared to make changes.

23 AUGUST

Meetings and discussions are likely to go well. Even if disagreements arise you can find ways to work together for the meantime.

24 AUGUST

It's a great weekend to engage in activities you love such as sports. It's a good day for a health or beauty treat. Some communications may be complex, so be clear.

25 AUGUST

You'll enjoy an unexpected or different experience by remaining adaptable and flexible and carefully choosing your company.

26 AUGUST

Be prepared to see another person's point of view, especially with long-term decisions and your career.

27 AUGUST

You'll enjoy a fun get-together or change in your usual routine. If you've been waiting for news from a friend, partner or organisation it will arrive.

28 AUGUST

Travel will be a focus. You may receive news concerning study or legal matters and may return from a trip. This is a lovely time for romance and domestic improvements.

29 AUGUST

You'll enjoying socialising or a trip somewhere beautiful. You may turn a corner in a close relationship.

30 AUGUST

You have deeper insight into your circumstances then you may believe, so make time to consult your own feelings and intuition to gain guidance.

31 AUGUST

You'll enjoy being spontaneous and the company of someone fun. You may be surprised by someone's news. If you're shopping, avoid impulse buys.

September

1 SEPTEMBER

You'll appreciate time spent with like-minded people and to relax. Just avoid tense topics, as these could be unpredictable.

2 SEPTEMBER

You may need to review certain arrangements such as financial or personal agreements. It's a good day for a health appointment.

3 SEPTEMBER

The new moon is a good time to turn a corner at work. This may have repercussions at home or you'll need to make a tough call.

4 SEPTEMBER

Be sensitive to other people's feelings for the best results. A work or social meeting will merit putting your best foot forward.

5 SEPTEMBER

You'll gain insight into a personal or health matter, enabling you to create more peace and balance in your life over the next two days.

6 SEPTEMBER

Be prepared to consider an understanding approach to someone who may appear vulnerable or weak-willed.

7 SEPTEMBER

The Scorpio moon will motivate you to be physically active and upbeat even if you do feel at times as though you're under pressure. Find ways to disperse your frustrations constructively.

8 SEPTEMBER

A change at home or with family can produce more stability, but you must avoid misunderstandings. It's a good day to make a commitment to a person or plan.

9 SEPTEMBER

As Mercury enters Virgo you'll be drawn to focusing on extracurricular activities. If you're a student, the next three weeks will be ideal for study. Avoid ego battles.

10 SEPTEMBER

A proactive and upbeat approach to communications and work will reap rewards. Be adventurous!

11 SEPTEMBER

You could make great progress in clearing a backlog of work and chores even if obstacles arise.

12 SEPTEMBER

Talks will be productive. Just avoid crossing swords with someone who can be insensitive. Avoid making assumptions socially and in meetings.

13 SEPTEMBER

You have your practical hat on, which will enable you to work constructively. However, you must avoid taking random comments personally.

14 SEPTEMBER

You risk overworking or overtiring yourself if you're tempted to burn the candle at both ends. Aim to take breaks and relax, and if you need support it will be available.

15 SEPTEMBER

You'll enjoy socialising and get-togethers but, again, you must avoid overspending and overindulging.

16 SEPTEMBER

This is a good day for a health or beauty appointment and for circulating your résumé if you're looking for work. However, not everyone will understand you, so avoid arguments.

17 SEPTEMBER

Be inspired and prepared to discuss a fresh arrangement or agreement, especially at home or with family. The lead-up to a lunar eclipse can be intense, so pace yourself.

18 SEPTEMBER

The partial lunar eclipse supermoon in Pisces spotlights your personal relationships and creative projects. You may make or break a commitment or work or financial agreement.

19 SEPTEMBER

You'll appreciate the chance to meet with like-minded people. Someone may surprise you with their news.

20 SEPTEMBER

While some relationships will blossom others may be slightly tense, so be sure to focus on your goals to avoid distractions.

21 SEPTEMBER

This is a lovely day for socialising. However, where you're already aware of sensitive topics you'll be wise to avoid them. Also avoid making assumptions.

22 SEPTEMBER

As the sun enters Libra you'll increasingly focus on your social life and health and well-being. You'll enjoy socialising again but must once again avoid tricky topics.

23 SEPTEMBER

Venus in your sign will bring your focus on love and money and how to increase both these areas in your life over the coming weeks.

24 SEPTEMBER

This is a sociable day that is ideal for work and personal talks, but care must still be taken to avoid intense topics if possible.

25 SEPTEMBER

A domestic or work matter will require focus and you may need to research circumstances further. Romance and the arts could thrive, so organise a date! Just avoid forgetfulness.

26 SEPTEMBER

This is another good day for discussions, meetings and communications. You may receive good news or enjoy a trip.

27 SEPTEMBER

The moon in Leo over the next two days will bring out your competitive and outgoing qualities, prompting you to enjoy sports and socialising. Take the initiative!

28 SEPTEMBER

You'll enjoy a reunion or trip and socialising. This is a good time for self-development and creative projects.

29 SEPTEMBER

This is an excellent day for get-togethers and important discussions and changes at home. A trip or visit at home will appeal.

30 SEPTEMBER

You may receive news from the past or get the green light you've been waiting for. This is a good day to take the initiative with collaborative and domestic matters.

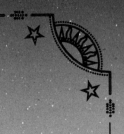

October

1 OCTOBER

This is a good day to set your intentions for the future, especially regarding your social life and your aims and goals.

2 OCTOBER

The solar eclipse in Libra will help you turn a corner, bringing more balance into your life.
A fresh association with a group of friends or the end of an agreement will arise.

3 OCTOBER

This is a good day for work and health discussions and meetings and planning.

4 OCTOBER

This is an excellent time to get ahead at work and home. Take the initiative in building strong relationships, as your efforts will succeed.

5 OCTOBER

You'll feel motivated to invest in yourself and your health and well-being. Your relationships could thrive, so take the initiative. Just avoid sensitive topics if possible.

6 OCTOBER

While in general relationships are going well someone or an issue may be the exception, so be prepared to find common ground. Avoid making rash decisions.

7 OCTOBER

You're sensitive to other people's moods, which will provide insight into relationships, but you must avoid seeing the bad problems of others as being your problems.

8 OCTOBER

A focus on health and well-being will be rewarding. You can make a great deal of progress at work and with your personal ventures.

9 OCTOBER

Be practical with your finances. Avoid financial and emotional gambling for the best results.

10 OCTOBER

The Capricorn moon helps you to take things one step at a time, but you must avoid being stubborn and unable to see another person's point of view.

11 OCTOBER

The key to success revolves around good communication skills and managing an unpredictable or mysterious circumstance.

12 OCTOBER

This is a good day for research and to base your decisions on facts, as otherwise delays and frustrating developments will test your mettle.

13 OCTOBER

As Mercury enters your sign you may uncover information that requires further research. Avoid misunderstandings and traffic delays.

14 OCTOBER

You may be feeling sensitive, tired or frustrated but you must be on your toes and prepared for a surprise. It's a good day for a health appointment.

15 OCTOBER

A sensitive and understanding approach to someone close will reap rewards, as you will gain insight into their feelings.

16 OCTOBER

This is a lovely day for romance and the arts and for engaging in activities you love, so take the initiative! A development at home will be enjoyable or nurturing.

17 OCTOBER

The full moon supermoon in Aries will spotlight a professional or personal relationship. Be prepared to step into new territory or help someone. If you need help it will be available.

18 OCTOBER

You'll feel ready to complete the week's chores in the most practical way possible, which will provide time to enjoy the end of the week.

19 OCTOBER

Someone who can be unpredictable will behave true to form. Nevertheless, you will enjoy an outgoing day.

20 OCTOBER

A misunderstanding or conundrum needn't get in the way of an enjoyable and upbeat day.

21 OCTOBER

You'll enjoy socialising and networking but must avoid distractions.

22 OCTOBER

As the sun enters your sign your attention will go to looking after yourself and those closest to you. You must avoid arguments and delays.

23 OCTOBER

A lovely connection with someone you love and admire such as a family member will be enjoyable.

24 OCTOBER

You may be tempted to speak before you have adequately thought things out, so be prepared to consider your words.

25 OCTOBER

You'll enjoy an impromptu get-together or surprise. Be spontaneous but avoid rushing.

26 OCTOBER

An active, outgoing and upbeat day is excellent for self-development, sports and creative endeavours. You could mend a bridge if you have argued with someone recently.

27 OCTOBER

A healing, therapeutic atmosphere will be restorative. However, you may need to clear a space for yourself as you will be in demand.

28 OCTOBER

Developments will gain their own momentum, so be sure they're heading in the direction you like. Otherwise you may need to make a tough call.

29 OCTOBER

You'll appreciate the wisdom and experience of someone loyal, especially if you have a difficult decision to make.

30 OCTOBER

Someone will surprise you and you may in turn have surprising news. Avoid making rash decisions.

31 OCTOBER

Happy Hallowe'en! Be prepared to find common ground, especially at work if you feel under pressure. You may be able to delegate some chores.

November

1 NOVEMBER

The Scorpio new moon will kick-start a fresh phase in your daily routine and, for October Scorpios, in a personal relationship. Take the initiative to make any changes effective.

2 NOVEMBER

You may enjoy a health or beauty treat. It's a good day for get-togethers. If you're considering an investment, avoid overcommitting.

3 NOVEMBER

This is a lovely day for get-togethers and a trip or adventure. It's also a good day for self-development and relaxation. Avoid arguments, as they could become fiery.

4 NOVEMBER

You'll feel motivated by your interests and projects and a personal or domestic matter can progress. Once again, avoid arguments as they will ignite.

5 NOVEMBER

You must be prepared to see another person's point of view. A practical approach to communications and relationships will be productive.

6 NOVEMBER

Consider who the most important person in your life is and be sure to check in on them.

7 NOVEMBER

It's a good day for get-togethers, especially with family and someone special.

8 NOVEMBER

You may be surprised by someone's news or developments. Avoid allowing distractions to take your focus off your goals.

9 NOVEMBER

Be careful with financial and emotional investments. Be sure to do your research, and avoid gambling and overspending.

10 NOVEMBER

The moon in Pisces will encourage you to relax and invest in your home life and those close to you.

11 NOVEMBER

It's a good day to focus on details at work and to maintain positive relationship dynamics. Be practical.

12 NOVEMBER

Be prepared to consider someone else's opinions. Certain communications and financial transactions may be delayed of confused. Be patient.

13 NOVEMBER

The Aries moon over the next two days will bring out your upbeat and feisty sides, encouraging you to be outgoing. Avoid appearing rash.

14 NOVEMBER

The lead-up to the Taurus full moon can be intense. Avoid impulsiveness and be practical if you're making long-term decisions.

15 NOVEMBER

The full moon in Taurus spotlights a personal or business partnership and, for mid-November Scorpios, a work or health situation. Look for ways to create stability.

16 NOVEMBER

You will be surprised by someone's news and will do well to be adaptable, but you must avoid gambling and putting other people's needs above your own to your own detriment.

17 NOVEMBER

Someone will want to talk. A trip or financial transaction will be significant.

18 NOVEMBER

A trip, meeting or financial transaction will be a focus. Be prepared to look at your situation from all perspectives.

19 NOVEMBER

This is a good day to consider making changes at home, such as interpersonal dynamics and improving domestic décor. Romance could thrive.

20 NOVEMBER

As Pluto re-enters Aquarius you're ready to turn a corner with a relationship or commitment. A work or personal arrangement will progress. Be prepared to think laterally.

21 NOVEMBER

Over the next four weeks you'll feel more confident about your personal situation, finances and self-esteem. You'll enjoy a trip or a visit.

22 NOVEMBER

It's a good day to make a commitment to a domestic or personal investment.

23 NOVEMBER

You'll appreciate being with someone whose company you enjoy. It's a good day for a trip, adventure and get-togethers.

24 NOVEMBER

This is a good day to plan ahead with long-term goals and get paperwork and your environment in order – and then to relax!

25 NOVEMBER

Trust your instincts both at work and home. Tact and diplomacy will work in your favour.

26 NOVEMBER

You may receive key news financially or in your personal life. It's a good day to review finances. You'll enjoy a get-together or visit.

27 NOVEMBER

A positive and proactive approach to your projects and ventures will be successful; just avoid appearing aggressive.

28 NOVEMBER

You or someone close may feel a little sensitive, so avoid taking random comments personally. Your help may be needed, and if you need advice it will be available. Avoid gambling.

29 NOVEMBER

This is a good day for a financial or work review and you'll enjoy a reunion.

30 NOVEMBER

You'll appreciate the opportunity to be active and outgoing and, equally, will enjoy home comforts.

December

1 DECEMBER

The Sagittarian new moon signals the start of a more adventurous phase. You may consider a trip or will make a fresh agreement with someone you admire. Just avoid overinvesting.

2 DECEMBER

This is a good day for a health or work review. You may experience a financial or ego boost. Someone has a surprise.

3 DECEMBER

Be practical with personal and domestic matters and avoid being stubborn if you disagree with someone.

4 DECEMBER

Financial matters will deserve careful focus, especially in connection with your home or a family member. Be prepared to invest in ventures that are close to your heart.

5 DECEMBER

You're thinking outside the square, which will be useful, but you must avoid alienating those who do not understand your ideas. Avoid making snap judgements.

6 DECEMBER

A particular idea or venture such as a trip may need to be reviewed. A key financial or personal agreement will be open for discussion.

7 DECEMBER

You'll enjoy a change of environment either through a trip or visit. Be prepared to consider new ideas, as discussions may otherwise be intense.

8 DECEMBER

You'll wish to emotionally invest in a relationship or domestic situation but may need to first come to a financial or personal agreement.

9 DECEMBER

Consider the most therapeutic and beneficial way ahead and base your actions on this. Someone special will be a true sounding board if you have a conundrum.

10 DECEMBER

This is a good day to build bridges if you've argued with someone, so take a moment to organise a get-together or chat.

11 DECEMBER

You'll enjoy being proactive and outgoing at work and could accomplish a great deal.

12 DECEMBER

A key meeting or trip will be significant. Certain relationships will thrive and romance, the arts and music will appeal.

13 DECEMBER

Despite this being Friday the 13th it's a good day for talks and improving relationships, so take the initiative!

14 DECEMBER

You'll be inclined to reach out to friends and someone special as this is a chatty, sociable time.

15 DECEMBER

The full moon will spotlight your personal relationships and finances. If you need to adjust your budget this is a good day to do so.

16 DECEMBER

Trust your intuition regarding shared duties, responsibilities and finances. Avoid financial and emotional gambling.

17 DECEMBER

You prefer to take things at an even pace but if you're doubtful about your circumstances this is difficult, so be sure to do adequate research.

18 DECEMBER

A mystery or unexplained message is best approached matter of factly. Misunderstandings and traffic delays are possible, so be patient.

19 DECEMBER

It's a good day for a change of environment at home and in your usual routine. You may make a valid commitment to a project or person.

20 DECEMBER

This is a lovely day to enjoy the company of fun people. Romance could thrive, so plan a date!

21 DECEMBER

This is the solstice. You'll appreciate the sense that your financial plans and potentially relationships will gain a more even keel over the coming weeks.

22 DECEMBER

Be prepared to make changes within particular agreements or in your environment. You'll enjoy a trip or meeting.

23 DECEMBER

You won't automatically get on with everyone, but if you take things one step at a time you will get on as well as possible.

24 DECEMBER

There are therapeutic aspects to the day, and a focus on a change of environment and/or family matters will benefit you. Avoid sensitive topics with a stubborn character.

25 DECEMBER

Merry Christmas! You'll enjoy the romance of Christmas and the peace that comes with it. However, some of your principles and ideas will not mix with everyone's so be tactful.

26 DECEMBER

Some of your interactions may be intense, so be prepared to concede if necessary to avoid arguments. The Boxing Day sales will appeal; just avoid overspending.

27 DECEMBER

Someone or a circumstance will be hard to budge, so be prepared to give and take a little to avoid arguments that will lead to a stalemate.

28 DECEMBER

A surprise may lead you to reassess someone's loyalty to you. Avoid impulsiveness and give yourself time to consider your thoughts.

29 DECEMBER

This is a good time to formulate a wish for the new year, especially regarding finding more stability in life.

30 DECEMBER

The new moon in Capricorn will kick-start a fresh phase in your finances and personal relationships; you'll appreciate the chance to experience more stability.

31 DECEMBER

Happy New Year! There are healing aspects to your New Year's Eve, as you'll find the time to establish a little peace.

SAGITTARIUS

21 November – 21 December

FINANCES

You'll be drawn to adopting a fresh approach to your finances in 2024 unless you already did so to a large degree in 2023. If you did, this year will provide the opportunity to consolidate what you've already learned and gained in 2023 and make further progress. Considerable opportunities to boost your finances will arise in February. Aim to focus on how your domestic life impacts your finances during the first quarter of the year, as you'll gain insight into how best to manage household expenses as a result. It's important you find ways to secure wealth in 2024, as you can be prone to financial and emotional gambling. You want to avoid losing your security, especially in the final quarter of the year.

HEALTH

You'll be drawn to being proactive and very busy in 2024, both in your personal life and at work, so be sure to create a strong health regime to support your well-being as otherwise you'll risk depleting your energy levels. Jupiter in your health sector will help you forge a steady routine, and you're best to put this in place early in the year so you can rely on it during times of stress. If you don't, your hard work ethic and tendency to burn the candle at both ends will mean you simply run on empty and could jeopardise your health and what makes you happy: being active and outgoing.

LOVE LIFE

Your relationships will precipitate some degree of soul searching in 2024, so it's an excellent year to boost your relationship and communication skills. Your search for the ideal relationship may tend to see-saw this year from being proactive and dynamic on the one hand to being quiet and seeking peace on the other. During times of stress this may be a source of confusion for those close to you. Consider finding balance in your self-expression to avoid misunderstandings, especially during the intense eclipse seasons in March, April, September and October.

CAREER

This will be a busy year and you'll be liable to take on large workloads. Accordingly, be prepared to slow the pace if you feel overwhelmed at any point but most notably during the stress points in April and August. You may be surprised by developments during these months in particular, as they will bring change to your work life or finances. As you'll be drawn to innovating and finding new ways to earn money, you must maintain a realistic and practical foundation from which to grow your ideas and career. It'll be in your interest to have a contingency plan in 2024 that provides a supportive fallback option.

HOME LIFE

The conjunction of Chiron and the moon's north node early in 2024 suggests there will be developments in your home life that could be life changing. Some of these you may already anticipate, while others will arise in line with the activities you undertake at home. You'll get an inkling at the end of January and in February of areas you could improve on at home, with family or domestically. You will be drawn to bringing more healing and well-being in your home, both in the shape of relaxing décor and improved interpersonal dynamics.

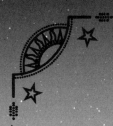

January

1 JANUARY

Happy New Year! You know what you want but other people have their own ideas and plans, so you may need to practise a little give and take for the best results.

2 JANUARY

A proactive approach to plans will be successful even if you need to be practical at the same time about some of your movements.

3 JANUARY

A slight difference of opinion will stem from different expectations and values. You'll overcome obstacles but must avoid gambling.

4 JANUARY

The next six weeks are ideal for strategising, planning and stabilising your finances. Be prepared to discuss long-term plans with those they concern.

5 JANUARY

You'll be drawn to looking beyond the obvious and researching a little into matters you're unsure of.

6 JANUARY

You may receive news to do with finances. A domestic or family matter will require tact and diplomacy.

7 JANUARY

A little down time will appeal and a change of routine will add some variety and spice.

8 JANUARY

The moon in your sign over the next two days will bring your proactive, fun frame of mind into the mix. Be positive.

9 JANUARY

Be prepared to see another person's point of view to avoid misunderstandings. Some travel or communications may be delayed, so be patient.

10 JANUARY

A fun or unexpected development will boost your mood. You may experience a surprise.

11 JANUARY

The Capricorn new moon will kick-start a fresh financial or personal chapter in your life. There's likely to be a healing or therapeutic aspect to this new chapter.

12 JANUARY

Plans you've undertaken are likely to produce positive results. Just avoid impulsiveness and the tendency to push your agenda. A personal matter will thrive.

13 JANUARY

Certain get-togethers and meetings will be informative or transformational. It's a good day to make an investment that can improve aspects of your life.

14 JANUARY

The next few weeks are ideal for investigating good ways to invest in your financial options and personal life, beginning today.

15 JANUARY

You'll find out whether you've missed important details in a personal or work matter. If you have you will get the opportunity to set things right.

16 JANUARY

A get-together or trip somewhere beautiful will be enjoyable. You may experience an ego or financial boost.

17 JANUARY

You'll enjoy being assertive in your communications, which will produce results, but you must avoid appearing bossy.

18 JANUARY

Meetings are likely to go well, especially those that could produce an agreement. A financial matter may be a focus.

19 JANUARY

You'll appreciate the opportunity to invest in your personal and/or home life. Just be sure to avoid misunderstandings and delays by planning ahead.

20 JANUARY

Key news or a get-together may be more intense than expected. A financial matter merits focus. Be sure to think laterally over the coming weeks.

21 JANUARY

You may be aware that you're stepping into fresh territory. For some this will be in your financial life and for others your personal life. Think outside the box for the best results.

22 JANUARY

An upbeat, chatty tone will put you in a positive position with friends and colleagues. Avoid misunderstandings by being super clear.

23 JANUARY

This is a good time to consider how to build more stability and security, especially financially and in your personal life.

24 JANUARY

The lead-up to a full moon can be intense. Someone close may appear moodier or needier than usual, so be prepared to think carefully.

25 JANUARY

The Leo full moon will spotlight shared responsibilities and, for some, joint finances, bringing matters to a head. Avoid knee-jerk reactions to developments and be prepared to help.

26 JANUARY

You may need to console someone. Be careful if you're considering an emotional or financial investment, as mistakes and misunderstandings are possible.

27 JANUARY

Key meetings and discussions will merit diplomacy. Avoid making rash decisions, erratic drivers and minor scrapes and bumps.

28 JANUARY

This is a good day to discuss personal matters and finances. If you can't come to an agreement, avoid feeling under pressure and continue the discussion tomorrow.

29 JANUARY

Discussions and meetings are likely to go well even if some have unexpected elements. Be prepared to take the initiative. You may experience a financial or ego boost.

30 JANUARY

Be prepared to come to the party with communications and meetings as you may be surprised by the outcome.

31 JANUARY

A fair-minded and balanced approach to communications will be beneficial to avoid a stalemate.

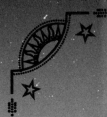

February

1 FEBRUARY

Be prepared to find the middle ground, especially if you see the potential for arguments to arise. You'll enjoy relaxing this evening.

2 FEBRUARY

You'll enjoy the chance to catch up with someone special and may also appreciate a financial or ego boost.

3 FEBRUARY

A little indulgence is always a good way to relax, but you must avoid overspending and overindulging as you'll regret the results.

4 FEBRUARY

This is a lovely day for socialising, as you'll enjoy a change of company and scenery.

5 FEBRUARY

You can make great progress with certain relationships and communications but you must avoid making unintentional social gaffes and taking other people's random comments personally.

6 FEBRUARY

You have your own views and values, and where these don't coincide with other people's then try looking for common ground if possible and, if not, tactfully move on.

7 FEBRUARY

You'll appreciate the opportunity to spend time with like-minded people. You may also enjoy a surprise or impromptu get-together.

8 FEBRUARY

You may be surprised by a sudden change of schedule or plans. An amenable approach will work in your favour. Avoid being stubborn.

9 FEBRUARY

The Aquarian new moon supermoon suggests that a little lateral thinking will benefit you, especially in relation to personal and financial matters.

10 FEBRUARY

You may be drawn to retail therapy but must avoid overspending, especially if you're already in debt. Think laterally about how to improve relationships. Avoid gambling.

11 FEBRUARY

The Pisces moon will bring out your idealistic side. You'll enjoy the arts and a short trip but must avoid unrealistically high expectations.

12 FEBRUARY

You are known for your optimistic and adventurous qualities, which will seek expression. Just avoid being super blunt if someone annoys you.

13 FEBRUARY

You'll be drawn to approaching a situation from a fresh perspective. Romance could thrive, and you'll enjoy the arts, music, a trip somewhere beautiful or a fun get-together.

14 FEBRUARY

Happy St Valentine's Day! There are intense aspects to the day, so be sure to organise your St Valentine's treat early so you get to relax and enjoy the day.

15 FEBRUARY

A practical approach to someone close who can be unpredictable well help earth the relationship and open the doors to understanding.

16 FEBRUARY

A financial or personal matter will grab your attention, and you'll be drawn to seeing a circumstance from a fresh perspective.

17 FEBRUARY

This is a romantic day but things may also be feisty. If you're shopping you're liable to invest in something special but you must avoid overspending.

18 FEBRUARY

You prefer to act fast and think later, but currently a little forethought will work in your favour.

19 FEBRUARY

Domestic, family or property-related circumstances will merit focus. A DIY project may appeal. It's a good day to mend bridges with someone close.

20 FEBRUARY

A nurturing and supportive approach to someone close will be particularly effective.

21 FEBRUARY

Trust your instincts, especially in relation to someone you care about. Be prepared to offer a helping hand, and if you need help be sure to reach out.

22 FEBRUARY

A financial or personal matter will require focus and perhaps restraint. Avoid financial and emotional gambling.

23 FEBRUARY

Mercury in Pisces for the next few weeks will enhance your intuition, so be sure to trust your instincts.

24 FEBRUARY

The full moon in Virgo spotlights certain agreements and arrangements and you may be ready to vary some of these.

25 FEBRUARY

You'll enjoy a trip or fun get-together but must avoid assuming everyone is on the same page.

26 FEBRUARY

It's a good day to get down to the nitty-gritty with certain communications. A travel agenda or vehicle will require a little more focus.

27 FEBRUARY

A fresh approach to your personal and financial investments will be productive. However, you must again avoid financial and emotional gambling.

28 FEBRUARY

This is a good day to make an agreement or commitment in personal and financial areas.

29 FEBRUARY

A communication, text or email will bring you in touch with someone you admire or love. This is a good day for get-togethers and romance.

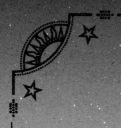

March

1 MARCH

It's a good day to talk and for making financial and personal commitments. Be sure, nevertheless, to double-check financial arrangements.

2 MARCH

You'll enjoy socialising and networking and may also appreciate a trip somewhere beautiful.

3 MARCH

A little retail therapy will appeal but you must avoid overspending. Someone has unexpected news. Be prepared to look outside the box.

4 MARCH

An active, dynamic day will contribute to you reaching your goals, so think big and take action.

5 MARCH

Take the initiative, especially if you require information or would like to get together with someone you admire or love.

6 MARCH

It's a good day to improve your domestic and personal circumstances. You may be drawn to adding a little luxury to your décor or improving domestic dynamics.

7 MARCH

This is a good day to build bridges with people you have recently argued with. It's also a good time to discuss financial strategy and for a lovely get-together.

8 MARCH

You'll enjoy a trip somewhere beautiful or a romantic get-together. It's a good day for the arts and self-development. You may receive a financial or personal reward.

9 MARCH

You'll enjoy a surprise or the chance to do something different. However, you must avoid overspending and overindulging as you'll regret it.

10 MARCH

The Pisces new moon supermoon will spotlight your ability to think big, especially in relation to your personal plans. Dream a little but anchor your ideas in practicalities.

11 MARCH

Your imagination and creativity are sparking on all cylinders. The next three weeks will be ideal for self-development and spirituality.

12 MARCH

Be prepared to channel a sense of restlessness into productive outlets, as you may otherwise feel a little feisty or appear bossy.

13 MARCH

This is a lovely day to change aspects of your circumstances you no longer like and, at the least, set the ball rolling. Romance could thrive.

14 MARCH

The Taurean moon will encourage you to focus on the needs of those close to you and create a lovely, relaxed feeling at home or with someone special.

15 MARCH

You'll enjoy a chatty, upbeat aspect to the day and will feel on top of changes, which will enable you to get through the day. You'll also enjoy socialising after work.

16 MARCH

This is a good day for a fun get-together and for reviewing your budget. It's also a good day to make a commitment.

17 MARCH

This is a romantic day, so be sure to organise a treat or date. You'll enjoy music, dance and the arts. Just avoid forgetfulness and idealising someone.

18 MARCH

The moon in Cancer brings out your ability to see other people's viewpoints. Trust your intuition.

19 MARCH

This is another intuitive day, so be sure to trust your instincts. You may be prone to overspending and overindulging, which you'll regret.

20 MARCH

The sun will shine on your personal life, especially your home, family and property, so it's a good time to improve these areas.

21 MARCH

You'll enjoy a visit or trip. It's a good day for get-togethers and talks, especially regarding finances and travel.

22 MARCH

An interest in travel, self-development and interpersonal dynamics will draw your attention towards improving communications over the coming weeks.

23 MARCH

A fun or creative event will be enjoyable. You may meet up with someone you admire or love.

24 MARCH

The lead-up to a lunar eclipse can be super intense, especially when the eclipse will fall in a key area of your chart: your learning curve in life, communications and relationships.

25 MARCH

This lunar eclipse signals it's time to explore new ways to invest, both emotionally and financially, in your well-being and that of those you love. A trip or learning opportunity will appeal.

26 MARCH

This is a good time to consider ways to improve your home, family and domestic arrangements.

27 MARCH

Be adventurous and prepared to consider new ideas both at work and home.

28 MARCH

You may hear unexpectedly good news that boosts your mood. You'll enjoy being spontaneous and may appreciate an impromptu get-together.

29 MARCH

Trust your gut instincts in connection with someone special. Be prepared to look for intuitive ways to get along.

30 MARCH

The moon in your sign will bring out your outgoing, adventurous qualities. You'll enjoy sports, a trip and get-togethers.

31 MARCH

This is a good day to invest your time in fun events. It's also a good time to clear a backlog of chores and focus on good health.

April

1 APRIL

It's a good day to get organised for the week, especially regarding domestic matters and travel and paperwork. Consider writing up a list.

2 APRIL

As Mercury turns retrograde you may receive key news from someone close such as a family member or at home. The next few weeks will be ideal for reviewing your personal duties.

3 APRIL

Romance is in the air. This is an excellent day for the arts and domestic improvements. You may enjoy a trip somewhere beautiful or a lovely get-together.

4 APRIL

It's an excellent day for a get-together, for some at home and with family and for others socially. Singles may meet someone seemingly familiar but nevertheless a stranger.

5 APRIL

Venus contributes to a more proactive and dynamic phase, especially in your love life, domestically and with family.

6 APRIL

This is a lovely day to focus on someone special, and your relationship could transform for the better. You may be drawn to a considerable investment.

7 APRIL

The lead-up to a new moon eclipse can be intense. A lot of focus will be on someone special, your home or family. It's a good time to overcome past differences.

8 APRIL

The total solar eclipse signifies a fresh chapter in a domestic, family or property circumstance and, for some, the chance to reinvent your personal life. You may receive key health news.

9 APRIL

Make the most of the chance to gain a sense of perspective and proportion, especially if circumstances are still intense.

10 APRIL

You may receive unexpected news or will need to make an unplanned trip. Be prepared to be adaptable but avoid making rash decisions and erratic drivers.

11 APRIL

You'll enjoy a reunion, so why not organise a get-together if you haven't already? You may need to review a domestic situation.

12 APRIL

A light-hearted approach to circumstances will put you in a strong position, but you must avoid appearing flippant to someone in authority.

13 APRIL

Someone close such as a family member may need your help or reassurance. You'll enjoy a change of pace and the chance to build stronger relationships.

14 APRIL

You'll appreciate the support and loyalty of someone who gets you. Just avoid needless arguments with someone whose presence is unavoidable.

15 APRIL

This is a good day for improving domestic and personal relationships, a DIY project and simply relaxing at home. If you're working trust your intuition, as it's spot on.

16 APRIL

Conversations, emails and texts may come thick and fast so you'll do well to be on your toes. Avoid rushing and taking someone's random comments personally.

17 APRIL

This is a good day for making changes at home, with family or in your environment. You may enjoy a reunion or get-together with an expert. Romance could thrive.

18 APRIL

Focus on fair play, diplomacy and tact as these qualities will help you navigate through the day's developments. You may experience an impromptu change of plan.

19 APRIL

As the sun enters Taurus your focus will turn to work and health over the coming weeks. You may already receive unexpected news or will enjoy a trip or domestic get-together.

20 APRIL

The moon at the zenith of your chart will take you where you want to be. You'll enjoy indulging a little in life's pleasures but must be sure to avoid overspending, which you'll regret.

21 APRIL

You may experience an intense or unexpected development and will appreciate the help of a family member or friend. Avoid gambling and a battle of egos.

22 APRIL

Someone will unexpectedly prove to be worth their weight in gold, and you may receive surprisingly good news.

23 APRIL

Be prepared to see both sides of an argument or issue as this will avoid conflict.

24 APRIL

The Scorpio full moon will shine a light on your social and networking circles and encourage you to turn a corner. It's a good day for talks, but you must avoid drama.

25 APRIL

It's another good day to talk as the Mercury retrograde phase ends, especially in connection with family, a trip or someone special.

26 APRIL

You'll feel motivated to get ahead but must avoid distractions.

27 APRIL

You'll find out whether you've over- or underestimated someone. You'll also enjoy the opportunity to take a trip or receive a visitor.

28 APRIL

You'll enjoy a short trip or receiving a visitor and in the process will appreciate improving your immediate environment. Romance could thrive.

29 APRIL

As Venus enters Taurus you'll enjoy bringing a little touch of luxury into your home life and creating more of a sense of security and stability.

30 APRIL

Mars in Aries for the next few weeks will bring out your more outgoing qualities, which will provide more opportunities for get-togethers, but you must avoid appearing feisty.

May

1 MAY

You're unlikely to agree with everyone, so to avoid arguments be prepared to be patient with communications and especially at home.

2 MAY

A personal or financial matter is best approached carefully and with a view to moving forward in due course.

3 MAY

This is a lovely day for a get-together or trip. Some Scorpios will enjoy a financial or ego boost.

4 MAY

You'll appreciate the opportunity to take to the road and be a little more flexible and outgoing with your communications and relationships.

5 MAY

A reunion and relaxing will boost your mood, relationships and sense of well-being. You'll enjoy a catch-up by phone.

6 MAY

This is a good day to set the ball rolling in the direction of long-term change, especially within your personal life and financially.

7 MAY

Someone may need your help and reach out for a chat or get-together. If you need advice or support be sure to ask for it, as it will be available.

8 MAY

The Taurus new moon will kick-start a fresh chapter in a personal or family situation. For some, this is an excellent time to make changes at home.

9 MAY

The Gemini moon adds to your charm, providing you with a witty and upbeat demeanour, so rest assured you'll be seen in a positive light.

10 MAY

If you're unsure of someone's feelings towards you be prepared to ask for clarity but also for the answers you receive.

11 MAY

A trip or meeting will be therapeutic. This is a good time to improve your environment and domestic circumstances. Romance could thrive.

12 MAY

Someone close may be in need of support or encouragement, and if you need some words of wisdom they will be available so be sure to reach out.

13 MAY

This is a good day to look at facts and figures, especially domestically. You may experience a surprise or unexpected guest.

14 MAY

You'll enjoy being able to discuss your favourite topics. A short trip or conversation will prove constructive.

15 MAY

You're looking for more stability and security in certain relationships and are likely to find it, but the next couple of days may be a little tense so avoid pushing for results.

16 MAY

You're thinking in practical terms and can make well-informed and realistic decisions, so be prepared to work towards your goals.

17 MAY

While you're generally a good communicator on occasion you can appear blunt, so to avoid misunderstandings it's best to be super diplomatic.

18 MAY

A change in your usual routine will bring a more balanced, stable feeling your way, but you may nevertheless be surprised by some developments.

19 MAY

This is a lovely day for a change of scenery and a short trip somewhere beautiful. It's also a good day for spiritual development.

20 MAY

Over the next four weeks your relationships and/or someone special will take much of your focus. Be prepared to make changes at home, with a property or family.

21 MAY

This is a sociable, upbeat time but you must avoid assuming you'll get on with everyone. Be prepared to make mutually agreeable arrangements.

22 MAY

This is a good time to suggest making changes financially and in your daily routine, such as work and health matters.

23 MAY

The full moon in Sagittarius will spotlight your work and health lives. If you were born in November you may experience a change in a key relationship.

24 MAY

This a good time to consider how to improve your daily routine and bring more variety and spice into your life.

25 MAY

You'll enjoy forging positive relationships and a change of routine. A new look may appeal. If you're working you may be particularly busy.

26 MAY

As Jupiter enters Gemini your focus will go towards a close business or personal relationship over the next year. If you're single you may find someone whose company you adore.

27 MAY

You'll manage to get your feet on the ground with your various chores and projects and may be pleasantly surprised by your progress.

28 MAY

This is a good day for a short trip and get-togethers. You can make realistic plans that will work.

29 MAY

You can make rapid progress with a domestic or personal matter but must avoid rushing and feeling under pressure. Avoid minor scrapes and bumps.

30 MAY

You may be surprised by news or developments. A health or personal situation will benefit from unexpected circumstances.

31 MAY

The Pisces moon will bring out your idealistic side, so be sure to also be practical.

June

1 JUNE

News and developments at home or with family will represent a pleasant change, and you'll enjoy doing something fun and different.

2 JUNE

The Aries moon will encourage you to get things done at home and spruce up your domestic circumstances, either in your environment or with domestic dynamics.

3 JUNE

This is a good day for meetings and discussions. You'll find over the next few weeks that communications improve, especially at work and in your personal life.

4 JUNE

You'll receive key news at work, through someone close or regarding your health. It's a good day to boost your well-being and appearance.

5 JUNE

A financial matter may require a little more focus to ensure you're on the same page as someone close.

6 JUNE

The new moon in Gemini will help you kick-start a fresh phase in a key relationship and at work or health-wise if you were born in mid-June.

7 JUNE

Someone close may require more focus and attention. This is a good time to treat yourself to a special reward.

8 JUNE

You may feel forgetful or have a misunderstanding. Avoid taking mix-ups personally and look for solutions to problems.

9 JUNE

You will not always agree with everyone and certain conversations may seem to get stuck, so look for practical ways to make progress.

10 JUNE

The Leo moon helps you see the lighter side of life. However, you must avoid making unnecessary mistakes, especially at work and financially.

11 JUNE

This is a good day to mend bridges if you've recently argued with someone. If you're looking for advice it will be available, so reach out.

12 JUNE

Be tactful as otherwise someone might see you as being blunt or thoughtless. Be careful with financial transactions to avoid making mistakes.

13 JUNE

Someone close such as a partner or work colleague may suggest an impromptu event or get-together, which you will enjoy. You may receive good news.

14 JUNE

This is an excellent day for a get-together and talks. Just be sure to adopt a serious tone if it's called for, as you may otherwise appear a little flippant.

15 JUNE

A change of scenery will be revitalising. You may be drawn to bringing a breath of fresh air into your domestic circumstances.

16 JUNE

The moon in Libra will encourage you to engage in activities that bring a sense of peace and harmony into your life and that of someone close.

17 JUNE

You will gain insight into someone close as they're likely to reveal some of your plans or feelings in more detail.

18 JUNE

The moon in Scorpio is motivational for you, enabling you to get on top of chores and projects. Combine your intuition with a realistic stance for the best results.

19 JUNE

You may be surprised to experience unexpected feelings towards a particular project or person but may be advised to wait until tomorrow before making decisions.

20 JUNE

The solstice is a lovely time to review how far you've come this year. A relationship will progress, but you must focus on facts to avoid mix-ups.

21 JUNE

While this is a good day for discussions, you must keep an open mind about other people's values and principles to avoid arguments.

22 JUNE

The full moon in Capricorn will spotlight your relationships and finances. You may be prepared to make a commitment but to do so you will need all the facts.

23 JUNE

Avoid taking a fundamental difference of opinion or personality clash to heart.

24 JUNE

It's an excellent day to think outside the box about your various options, especially regarding your work and finances.

25 JUNE

Projects and ideas will move forward quickly and you may be super inspired.

26 JUNE

This is a good day for a short trip and for business and personal meetings, but you must avoid assuming everyone is on the same page as you.

27 JUNE

The moon in Pisces will bring out your sensitive side and you'll gain insight into a collaborator or someone close. Trust your intuition.

28 JUNE

You or someone close may be feeling a little sensitive, so avoid tense topics. A health or personal matter will require a delicate approach.

29 JUNE

Romance could thrive, so take the initiative! You're imaginative and creative, so this is an ideal day for the arts and self-development.

30 JUNE

You may hear unexpected news or will enjoy an impromptu get-together, adding some variety to your usual Sunday.

July

1 JULY

You'll enjoy the company of someone who can be a little eccentric. Just avoid taking developments personally if they're not to your liking.

2 JULY

Communications are about to become livelier, so prepare for a busy few weeks. You or someone close may need a little extra space just for the day.

3 JULY

Certain conversations are likely to be animated or intense. It's a good day for a financial transaction as long as you've done your research.

4 JULY

It's a good day to make a wish and in so doing decide where your loyalties lie, both at work and in your personal life.

5 JULY

The Cancerian new moon will kick-start a fresh phase in a key business or personal relationship. It's a good day to make a financial agreement or personal commitment.

6 JULY

A fundamental difference in values may spark disagreements. Avoid taking other people's criticism personally unless it's merited.

7 JULY

The Leo moon brings out your proactive and dynamic qualities. You'll appreciate get-togethers and investing in people and activities you enjoy.

8 JULY

Particular meetings or a trip may be more relevant than meets the eye. It's a good day to reach out if you need information. You'll enjoy an impromptu get-together.

9 JULY

The next two days are excellent for deepening your connections with those you love, so be sure to organise something special.

10 JULY

This will be a passionate and busy time, a good opportunity to bond with someone close. However, you or someone close may be emotional.

11 JULY

You will gain a degree of balance and peace of mind by taking the time to engage in favourite activities.

12 JULY

This is another passionate and feisty day on which romance could soar but so, too, could arguments. A key meeting or financial development is likely.

13 JULY

You'll again establish a degree of balance that may come through being spontaneous and enjoying something different. It's a good time to look after your health and for self-development.

14 JULY

You may be called upon to be a mediator and, at the least, find balance in your day, as otherwise this may be a restless time.

15 JULY

A surprise change of routine or unexpected development will ask that you be helpful and supportive. Avoid impulsiveness.

16 JULY

You may surprisingly feel emotions bubbling under the surface. You'll appreciate the opportunity to discuss some of your feelings with someone who understands you.

17 JULY

The moon in your sign will encourage you to be positive about recent developments. If you're unsure of your position, this is a good time for research.

18 JULY

Be prepared to alter some of your plans, as a pleasant surprise or unusual event is on the way.

19 JULY

This is a good time to mend bridges with someone who is close to your heart. Romance could thrive. It is also a good time for a DIY project.

20 JULY

A busy, fun and upbeat activity such as sports will draw your attention. You'll enjoy socialising.

21 JULY

The full moon in Capricorn will spotlight the need to review shared areas, for example, joint finances and duties. You'll enjoy a get-together but must be prepared for a last-minute change of plan.

22 JULY

As the sun enters Leo it opposes Pluto and could spark differences of opinion. However, you will manage to move ahead with projects but must be tactful.

23 JULY

You'll appreciate the opportunity to discuss shared projects and ventures. A financial matter may require focus. Avoid a battle of egos.

24 JULY

Your idealism may be stronger than usual, so ensure you're not seeing someone or circumstances through rose-coloured glasses.

25 JULY

Be prepared to consider details very carefully, especially if you're considering a fresh agreement. Avoid misunderstandings.

26 JULY

This is likely to be a busy day. Avoid rushing and feeling under pressure by taking adequate breaks.

27 JULY

The key to a happy weekend lies in good communication skills and planning. Avoid feeling pressured into activities you know you won't enjoy.

28 JULY

You'll enjoy slowing down the pace if possible and taking time out with only the best of company.

29 JULY

You have the ability to feel motivated and excited yet at the same time be grounded, all of which spells the ability to overcome obstacles.

30 JULY

There are therapeutic aspects to the day and you'll manage to find ways to communicate with those you sometimes find difficult to get along with.

31 JULY

This is a lovely day for a get-together or short trip. A meeting or news will be uplifting.

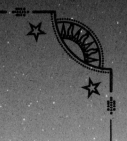

August

1 AUGUST

You have a deeper understanding of others than usual so may feel more sensitive and take other people's random comments personally, so maintain perspective.

2 AUGUST

Be prepared to make time and space for someone special as they may have unexpected news for you. If you experience a setback, rest assured it will set you on a better path.

3 AUGUST

The lead-up to the new moon in Leo is a good time to consider how you would prefer to move forward with the various shared matters in your life.

4 AUGUST

The Leo new moon spotlights shared matters and duties such as joint finances. If you're making long-term decisions, ensure you have all the facts.

5 AUGUST

News and developments are best approached from a factual point of view, especially in relation to financial and personal investments.

6 AUGUST

Now that Mercury is retrograde you'll gain the chance to review recent decisions. You'll then appreciate looking out from a new perspective.

7 AUGUST

This will be another busy day that you're likely to enjoy, but you must avoid taking on too much.

8 AUGUST

Financial and personal investments will be in the spotlight. A particular relationship could blossom. News or a reunion will be significant.

9 AUGUST

You'll enjoy dreaming a little and imagining travel and extracurricular activities becoming full time. You'll appreciate a change of pace, so organise a treat.

10 AUGUST

Certain responsibilities will take your focus even if you would prefer to throw caution to the wind. You'll find time for both work and play by being well organised.

11 AUGUST

You'll enjoy the company of like-minded people but will need to first clear chores or paperwork. If you're travelling, avoid delays by planning well ahead.

12 AUGUST

You'll appreciate a diverse schedule, so be sure to plan a fun event.

13 AUGUST

You may wonder 'Is it me or is it them?' as there is a chance of misunderstandings, so ensure you're extra clear.

14 AUGUST

Someone is likely to bring matters to a head and may also be insistent about their viewpoint. A lack of research could lead to mistakes, so be sure to work with facts.

15 AUGUST

There are healing aspects to the day, so it's a good one on which to invest time and energy in people close to you and your home and family.

16 AUGUST

A difference of opinion needn't lead to conflict if you can find common ground. Avoid feeling pressured into making an agreement.

17 AUGUST

You may feel more emotionally charged than usual and will be prone to impulse buys when shopping, so avoid overspending. A change of routine will require you to be adaptable.

18 AUGUST

Be prepared to be flexible with arrangements as you may need to reschedule some plans. Avoid misunderstandings.

19 AUGUST

The Aquarian full moon will illuminate where in your financial and personal lives you could make progressive changes. Be prepared to discuss matters to avoid arguments.

20 AUGUST

You'll find out whether you've over- or underestimated someone or your circumstances, which will enable you to set things right. Avoid forgetfulness.

21 AUGUST

A philosophical, fair-minded and practical approach to communications and plans will be most successful.

22 AUGUST

The sun in Virgo over the next four weeks will spotlight your extracurricular ventures and activities such as sports, making this is a good time to plan ahead.

23 AUGUST

You may need to play a mediatory role or reach a fair-minded decision with someone you must get along with.

24 AUGUST

You'll enjoy a reunion and spending some time reorganising and cleaning your home and environment.

25 AUGUST

A change of scenery and pleasant environment will prove to be uplifting. You'll enjoy feeling more grounded and rested.

26 AUGUST

You have good communication skills and will appreciate the opportunity to show them off.

27 AUGUST

An upbeat, fun development will raise your spirits. You may be surprised by the beneficial outcome of a project.

28 AUGUST

Key news or developments concerning a joint venture will be poignant. You may be ready to move forward with a financial plan.

29 AUGUST

A lovely trip or activity could be transformative, so take the initiative with your ventures. You'll be drawn to the arts, beauty and self-development.

30 AUGUST

A caring and nurturing approach to someone close will prove effective. You may enjoy kicking up your heels this evening.

31 AUGUST

Someone close may suggest a change in your usual weekend routine, which you'll enjoy. A change of pace will be uplifting.

September

1 SEPTEMBER

This is a good day to discuss delicate topics, but you must be prepared to hear someone else's point of view. A trip or meeting will be therapeutic.

2 SEPTEMBER

A return to an old haunt or the chance to remedy a situation domestically or in your personal life will appeal.

3 SEPTEMBER

The new moon in Virgo will kick-start a fresh appreciation of your abilities, especially in your projects, studies and long-term plans. It's a good day to make a commitment.

4 SEPTEMBER

Someone close may be more expressive of their feelings than usual. A meeting or get-together will illuminate your best path forward.

5 SEPTEMBER

A balanced and peaceful approach to work and your various projects will pay off.

6 SEPTEMBER

Your compassion and insight will be in demand at work and home.

7 SEPTEMBER

The Scorpio moon will provide you with deeper insight into someone else's feelings, enabling you to move forward with more foresight.

8 SEPTEMBER

It's a good day to make a commitment to a person or plan. However, if you need more information before making the commitment it's a good day for research.

9 SEPTEMBER

As Mercury enters Virgo you'll be drawn to focusing on the details of your various commitments and duties. Avoid power plays and concentrate on what must be done.

10 SEPTEMBER

You'll be motivated to pursue your goals but must avoid being stubborn about certain ideas and principles, especially if obstinacy will compromise your position.

11 SEPTEMBER

You may need to work a little harder at your goals than usual, but rest assured your efforts will be rewarded.

12 SEPTEMBER

This is a good day for talks, especially regarding shared ventures or collaborations. However, you must avoid a personality clash or battle of wills.

13 SEPTEMBER

Be practical, as you could truly make great progress with your various plans. Be sure to take someone else's views into account.

14 SEPTEMBER

A sensitive topic or development will mean you must be more focused on your goals. If you need support or guidance it will be available.

15 SEPTEMBER

A lucky break or lovely event will raise morale, so if you have nothing planned yet ensure you organise a trip, visit or event.

16 SEPTEMBER

You'll appreciate the opportunity to discuss some sensitive topics with an expert or adviser. You can make great progress at home and with interpersonal dynamics.

17 SEPTEMBER

Be prepared to dream a little as your dreams could come true. Just be careful what you wish for.

18 SEPTEMBER

The partial lunar eclipse supermoon in Pisces spotlights your communications and relationships. You may be drawn to updating a communications device or to travel. You may make or break a financial agreement.

19 SEPTEMBER

You'll enjoy an uplifting change of pace. Creative and romantic Sagittarians may appreciate an unexpected development.

20 SEPTEMBER

You are drawn to all things beautiful and luxurious. You may surprise yourself with some of the recent goals you'd like to attain, but avoid unnecessary upheaval in doing so.

21 SEPTEMBER

You'll enjoy a trip somewhere beautiful such as the ocean. This is a lovely time for self-development, but you must be prepared to enter uncharted territory and avoid making assumptions.

22 SEPTEMBER

You as the sun enters Libra you'll increasingly focus on ways to broaden your horizons and enjoy life more. Just avoid alienating those you love in the process.

23 SEPTEMBER

Venus in Scorpio will bring your focus over the coming weeks on how to attain a better circumstance in your life such as via work or status.

24 SEPTEMBER

This is a good day for get-togethers and doing something different in your spare time such as joining a new club or changing your usual timetable.

25 SEPTEMBER

Romance and the arts could thrive, so organise a date! Certain communications and travel may be a little delayed or confusing. Just avoid forgetfulness.

26 SEPTEMBER

The next few weeks will be ideal for finding more fair play and harmony in your collaborations. A trip, news or meeting could be transformative.

27 SEPTEMBER

The moon in Leo over the next two days will bring out your fun-loving and adventurous qualities, prompting you to spend time with like-minded people.

28 SEPTEMBER

Sharing good times with people you love makes you happy, so if you haven't already organised something special then consider doing so now!

29 SEPTEMBER

You'll enjoy the opportunity to return to a favourite place or meet someone whose viewpoints and experience you admire.

30 SEPTEMBER

A friend, partner or family member may be feeling particularly feisty and/or positive. If you're drawn to retail therapy avoid overspending, as you may regret it!

October

1 OCTOBER

The dark of the moon is a good time for you to set your intentions for the future, especially regarding existing agreements, travel and relationships.

2 OCTOBER

The solar eclipse in Libra will help you turn a corner, bringing more balance to your life and especially in connection with your work life, career, general direction and status.

3 OCTOBER

This is a good day for socialising, networking and planning ahead, especially at work and regarding your status.

4 OCTOBER

You'll enjoy a trip or get-together. If you're looking for a personal or financial commitment this could be the day to do it, so take the initiative!

5 OCTOBER

You'll feel motivated to spend time with like-minded people. It's a lovely day for socialising and group efforts such as teamwork.

6 OCTOBER

Certain agreements and plans may need to be rearranged. Someone who can be feisty may voice their opinions and you'll need to find middle ground. Avoid erratic drivers.

7 OCTOBER

The moon in your sign brings out your bold and adventurous qualities. Just be sure to avoid appearing blunt by being tactful.

8 OCTOBER

A trip or meeting will be therapeutic. You may need to assert yourself to gain the outcome you want. It's a good day for agreements, especially at work and with projects.

9 OCTOBER

You will temper your upbeat, optimistic traits with a view to being practical, as this will help you overcome a difference of opinion or challenge.

10 OCTOBER

The Capricorn moon helps you to be realistic, especially if you must juggle various chores, enabling you to prioritise activities.

11 OCTOBER

Be prepared to discuss your ideas with those they concern, even if you feel there may be opposition. You will be able to find common ground.

12 OCTOBER

You may experience confusing communications or even traffic delays, so be prepared to be patient and adaptable. Once you are, you'll enjoy socialising and favourite events.

13 OCTOBER

As Mercury enters Scorpio you'll feel more passionate about your beliefs and activities over the coming weeks, but today you must avoid miscommunications and overspending.

14 OCTOBER

Developments will ask that you choose between priorities, which may come about in unexpected ways. Avoid impulsiveness.

15 OCTOBER

You'll feel inspired to move your projects and ideas forward but must remain realistic and avoid distractions.

16 OCTOBER

A reunion or work meeting could be ideal. Romance could blossom, so be sure to organise a date!

17 OCTOBER

The full moon supermoon in Aries will spotlight a domestic or personal matter. You may need to choose between loyalties or work and domestic duties. Reach out if you need advice.

18 OCTOBER

You are fortunate in being able to juggle various duties, enabling you to reach goals and targets, but you must avoid needless arguments.

19 OCTOBER

You'll enjoy today's change of pace even if it means a little upheaval. Be sure to check your itinerary and plans to make the day a smooth one.

20 OCTOBER

This is a good day to find out the facts, especially if you've recently experienced a misunderstanding. You will unravel a mystery; just avoid being forgetful.

21 OCTOBER

It's likely to be a busy and at least chatty start to the week, which will enable you to complete many of your tasks, so be proactive.

22 OCTOBER

As the sun enters Scorpio your attention will go to ways of improving your daily routine, including your health and work schedule. Just avoid power plays, especially today.

23 OCTOBER

This is a good day to deepen your connection with someone special, so if you have nothing planned yet organise something you'll enjoy!

24 OCTOBER

An upbeat, positive approach to relationships and collaborations will be productive. Just avoid needless arguments.

25 OCTOBER

You'll enjoy a surprise and being spontaneous. You may be ready to approach someone with a clearer understanding of your relationship. Avoid impulsiveness.

26 OCTOBER

A little retail therapy will appeal but you must avoid underestimating the costs of a certain investment. A fun event could be ideal.

27 OCTOBER

Some communications may be a little tense or complex, so be prepared for some give and take. You'll enjoy a therapeutic or healing event.

28 OCTOBER

Be prepared to take the initiative even if you feel you're leading from the back foot. Rest assured that with a little courage your efforts will succeed.

29 OCTOBER

The moon at the zenith of your chart will put your heart on your sleeve, so be prepared to focus at work. A diverse schedule will keep you busy.

30 OCTOBER

You may be surprised by sudden news or a change of schedule that will require you to be adaptable and patient. Avoid making rash decisions.

31 OCTOBER

Happy Hallowe'en! This is a good time to decide on your priorities and which group or people to put at the top of your list. Trust your intuition.

November

1 NOVEMBER

The Scorpio new moon will kick-start a fresh phase in your social life and commitments to various groups and people. You'll enjoy get-togethers and meetings.

2 NOVEMBER

There are therapeutic aspects to the day. You'll enjoy self-development and being with people who make you feel good.

3 NOVEMBER

This is another lovely day for spending time with like-minded people, but you must avoid a battle of wills. An investment could be transformative. Romance will thrive.

4 NOVEMBER

You'll feel motivated by someone you find inspiring and will experience positive results in some of your plans and projects.

5 NOVEMBER

This is a good time to invest in the people and communications at the top of your to-do list. A proactive, upbeat approach will soon see you reaching your goals.

6 NOVEMBER

You have a truly visionary and positive approach to life but must avoid appearing zealous or even stubborn about your views.

7 NOVEMBER

You'll enjoy a reunion or trip somewhere beautiful. This is a good day for a catch-up with someone you love.

8 NOVEMBER

A quirky approach to developments will help you overcome any obstacles that arise. Be persistent but avoid appearing pushy.

9 NOVEMBER

You like to see the best in people, and when you're unsure of someone it's important you find out more. Some communications and travel may be delayed, so be patient.

10 NOVEMBER

The moon in Pisces will encourage you to be idealistic and, at the least, inspired, but you must also remain practical to avoid making mistakes.

11 NOVEMBER

Venus will put your attention on finances and love over the coming weeks. Maintain a positive outlook at work and you will overcome any potential obstacles.

12 NOVEMBER

You may wonder if it's you or if it's someone else who is seeing things from a complex point of view. Be clear and avoid mix-ups. Be patient with travel delays.

13 NOVEMBER

The Aries moon over the next two days will encourage you to be more proactive, especially in your home life and with family. Just avoid appearing rash.

14 NOVEMBER

The lead-up to the Taurus full moon can be intense, so be sure to maintain perspective and especially with personal and creative projects.

15 NOVEMBER

The full moon in Taurus spotlights a personal, family or domestic matter, and you may be surprised by developments. It's a good time to look for ways to create stability.

16 NOVEMBER

A change of pace or a surprise will see you on your toes. A difference of values or priorities could be at the root of a disagreement, so be prepared for give and take.

17 NOVEMBER

A busy day will be ideal for clearing a backlog of chores and improving health and well-being.

18 NOVEMBER

Meetings, a trip or news will be significant. It's a good day to talk, especially with a view to finding solutions and common ground.

19 NOVEMBER

This is a good day for socialising and networking. You'll enjoy a trip somewhere therapeutic. It's a good time for a health or well-being appointment and romance could thrive.

20 NOVEMBER

As Pluto re-enters Aquarius you're ready to advance with a financial or personal venture or commitment. You may receive unexpected news. Be prepared to think laterally.

21 NOVEMBER

Over the next four weeks you'll gradually feel more adventurous, uplifted and positive. You may already enjoy a lovely event or development today.

22 NOVEMBER

It's a good day to make a personal or financial commitment. You'll appreciate the opportunity to meet someone you admire.

23 NOVEMBER

Your relationships with people you feel motivated by and happy to be with can blossom, so be sure to meet up with friends or someone special.

24 NOVEMBER

This is a lovely day to discuss your exciting plans with those they concern and engage in activities that boost your self-esteem.

25 NOVEMBER

You'll appreciate the opportunity to connect with someone you admire such as a mentor or teacher. If you need information you'll uncover it.

26 NOVEMBER

Avoid making rash decisions, especially regarding key work or health news. Ensure you have all the information you need before committing to a plan.

27 NOVEMBER

You'll appreciate seeing your projects and activities take shape. If you need extra direction, someone will prove to be helpful. Just avoid rushing.

28 NOVEMBER

A difference of opinion needn't derail an agreement or relationship. Some news will require you to perceive circumstances in a new light. Avoid erratic drivers and minor scrapes.

29 NOVEMBER

You'll enjoy a reunion or the opportunity to review your personal and/or financial circumstances.

30 NOVEMBER

The moon in your sign will add a lovely sense of potential and possibility, especially regarding your personal life and long-term projects. Be positive.

December

1 DECEMBER

The Sagittarian new moon signals the start of a more adventurous phase in your personal life and, if you were born later this month, at work and health-wise.

2 DECEMBER

You'll enjoy a therapeutic event, for some at home and for others at work. You will experience a financial or ego boost.

3 DECEMBER

Recent developments are likely to provide you with more direction, enabling you to better focus on your goals.

4 DECEMBER

If you're diligent and careful with communications you can make great progress with your activities. However, you must avoid being super idealistic and stubborn.

5 DECEMBER

It's a good day to put your back into your projects and get new ideas on the table, even if you feel they may need to be reviewed at a later date.

6 DECEMBER

You will receive the news you've been waiting for. You may enjoy a reunion or the chance to improve your health and well-being.

7 DECEMBER

This is likely to be an intense day, especially with communications. It's a good day to review finances, especially those you share. Romance could blossom but could also be fiery.

8 DECEMBER

Be prepared to be realistic about your communications and plans, as you may otherwise lose perspective. Focus on the facts to avoid arguments.

9 DECEMBER

Be inspired by those you meet as you may appreciate the opportunity to learn something new.

10 DECEMBER

Certain meetings and get-togethers are likely to go well. If you wish to improve domestic circumstances or dynamics this is the day to take the initiative.

11 DECEMBER

Certain people may still appear to be antagonistic, so if you feel this may be the case ensure you're positive and avoid arguments. Instead, channel your energy into productive pursuits.

12 DECEMBER

This is potentially a romantic time, making it ideal for a lovely date. However, someone may be feisty so avoid crossing swords.

13 DECEMBER

Despite this being Friday the 13th you'll enjoy a financial or ego boost. You may appreciate the option to return to a favourite haunt.

14 DECEMBER

A busy and chatty time will make a productive day unless you tend to be easily distracted, in which case you must focus a little bit harder.

15 DECEMBER

The full moon will spotlight an important business or personal relationship. This is a good time to be clear about your arrangements, especially if grey areas arise.

16 DECEMBER

A sympathetic, nurturing approach to someone close will reap rewards. You may need to clarify some aspects of a travel plan or personal arrangement.

17 DECEMBER

If you're still unsure of where you stand with someone this is a good time to reach out and get a little more information. Avoid travel delays and confusion by organising your day well.

18 DECEMBER

You may experience delays or miscommunications so be sure to be super clear, and if you work with computers then back them up.

19 DECEMBER

You'll appreciate a personal or ego boost. This is a good day to make a personal or financial commitment. If you're shopping you're likely to find something special.

20 DECEMBER

This is a good day for a change of schedule and to truly enjoy a Christmas festivity. If you're shopping, avoid overspending. You'll appreciate a financial or ego boost.

21 DECEMBER

This is the solstice. Over the next four weeks you'll appreciate slowing down a little, but you must be careful today to avoid difficult topics so there are no arguments.

22 DECEMBER

This is a lovely time to transform and improve close relationships and discuss changes you'd like to implement in the new year.

23 DECEMBER

You are known as an honest and straightforward person but sometimes being tactful will grease the wheels of relationships, such as today.

24 DECEMBER

You'll enjoy connecting with those you love and being in a different or healing environment. However, you may need to avoid overindulgence as you'll regret it tomorrow.

25 DECEMBER

Merry Christmas! A practical, realistic approach to your many chores and interactions will be successful. Be patient with someone who can be feisty to avoid conflict.

26 DECEMBER

You'll enjoy a change of pace. You may be drawn to travelling or connecting with someone fun.

27 DECEMBER

Sometimes the least said the better, and this may be the case today to avoid arguments. If you're travelling, be sure to plan ahead.

28 DECEMBER

An unexpected development or change of pace needn't put a spanner in the works if you sidestep a knee-jerk reaction. Avoid financial and emotional gambling.

29 DECEMBER

You'll feel motivated to be more outspoken but must avoid indiscretions. Your support and help in the home or with family will be appreciated.

30 DECEMBER

The new moon in Capricorn will kick-start a fresh phase financially and, for some, at work and in your daily routine. Be prepared to find more stability and security.

31 DECEMBER

Happy New Year! There are healing aspects to your New Year's Eve so you may be drawn to spending more time at home, in someone else's home or with family.

CAPRICORN

21 December – 20 January

FINANCES

Financial security is particularly important for you, and this year your focus will be on building stability in relation to your home. The entry of Pluto into Aquarius in January (the sign it will be in for the next 20 years) signals that you are on track for major financial changes over the next two decades. You'll gain deeper acknowledgement in 2024 of the new ways in which you could potentially save and budget moving forward, so be prepared to venture into fresh financial territory. The supermoons in February, March, September and October will spotlight how viable your plans are and whether you must rearrange them so you can provide that all-important stability for those you love and yourself.

HEALTH

You may be liable to overdo things in January, so it's important you put in place a solid health regime early in the year so you're set health-wise for this eventful year. Be careful with decisions during the eclipse phases in April, September and October, as you may otherwise feel overwhelmed by developments. Find the time to unplug and reconnect with your true priorities and principles throughout 2024 or your ability to think objectively may be overridden. It will be as important to look after your mental, spiritual and emotional health as it is to look after your physical health and especially so in the last quarter of the year, when you may feel that things are going backwards when on the contrary you'll gain the chance then to refuel and reconnect with those you love.

LOVE LIFE

Expect the unexpected in your love life in 2024 as you'll be drawn to fresh experiences. For example, if you've been single for a long time you'll be ready to commit to someone special or at least to alter some of your relationship parameters. You may be drawn to reviewing certain commitments and may even consider reuniting with an ex, especially during the last quarter of the year. Couples will appreciate the opportunity to deepen relationships in new ways and perhaps consider experiencing fresh arrangements concerning how you nurture family and those you care about. Mid-year will be a particularly romantic time, so you'll be drawn then to finding time to celebrate love.

CAREER

The changes you experienced in 2023 will continue to have repercussions during 2024, as you embrace new projects and ideas you wish to develop. March, April and October are going to be particularly transformative in your career, and if you would like to make considerable changes within your direction these are good months to do so. You will be drawn to exploring new avenues and the tech world is likely to figure prominently in the decisions you make, particularly in September. The more adventurous and willing you are to discover fresh avenues the better it will be for you, especially in the first quarter. Be prepared to take a leap of faith – as long as it is financially sound.

HOME LIFE

Uranus in your fourth house of home, family and property points to considerable changes in these key areas of your life, especially in the first quarter and November. Be innovative, as this mindset will lead to the stability and security you love in the home. Bountiful Jupiter in your home sector until the end of May indicates an abundant opportunity that could involve such options as a bigger living space or even adding to the family. You may be tempted to overspend this year, and particularly on your home and family. At the end of April you'll get the heads-up whether this is likely to be the case for you.

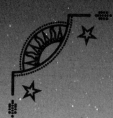

January

1 JANUARY

Happy New Year! You'll appreciate the opportunity to turn a corner and embrace something new in 2024. You may need to compromise over a commitment or finances.

2 JANUARY

This is a good day to get organised, especially with shared ventures and collaborations. Once again, you may need to be fair-minded about areas of contention.

3 JANUARY

If you're travelling ensure you leave extra time to avoid delays. Communications may also require a little extra effort to avoid grey areas.

4 JANUARY

You'll appreciate a sense of increased energy and vitality over the next six weeks, but today you must avoid impulsiveness and making assumptions.

5 JANUARY

You'll be drawn to spreading your wings, either through travel or simply enjoying learning something new and meeting different people.

6 JANUARY

Be prepared to see a matter from someone else's point of view, especially if delays and misunderstandings arise.

7 JANUARY

You'll be drawn to activities you're passionate about. It's a good day to spend some time on yourself, on self-nurturance and perhaps to consider a new look.

8 JANUARY

Mars in your sign can signal a busy time but also a time when you feel under pressure. Be sure to take breaks, especially if you're back at work after a break.

9 JANUARY

You may encounter a mystery or will need to look a little more deeply into a financial or personal matter to avoid confusion.

10 JANUARY

A fun development will boost your mood. You may experience a surprise, go somewhere different and refreshing or receive an unexpected guest.

11 JANUARY

The Capricorn new moon will kick-start a fresh chapter in your personal life. If you were born mid-January, expect a fresh development at work or regarding your health.

12 JANUARY

You'll enjoy a return to an old haunt or hearing from someone you admire. It's a good day for meetings, but you must avoid rushing.

13 JANUARY

This is a lovely day for socialising, and if you've been planning to make changes they are likely to take. You may be drawn to a beauty or health appointment.

14 JANUARY

Your communications and interactions will be a focus over the next few weeks. You may be surprised by news or a change of plan.

15 JANUARY

A proactive approach to chores and communications will be productive. Just avoid idealism and be realistic.

16 JANUARY

This is a lovely day for the arts, romance and music. You may enjoy a financial or ego boost.

17 JANUARY

You'll feel outgoing and upbeat, especially socially. Just avoid taking some circumstances personally and remain level-headed.

18 JANUARY

This is a good day to make a commitment, especially financially and at work. It's also good time to put a solid health regime in place.

19 JANUARY

A short trip or visit will be uplifting, but you must double-check arrangements to avoid making mistakes. Retail therapy may be effective but be wary of overspending.

20 JANUARY

Strong emotions are likely to arise and it's a good day to make changes, especially in your personal life and financially.

21 JANUARY

Be prepared to step into new territory but ensure you retain a sense of stability. Think outside the box for the best results.

22 JANUARY

Your efforts will be effective, especially if you must organise and tidy up your environment and complete paperwork. A beauty or health treat will appeal.

23 JANUARY

As Venus enters your sign, prepare to focus increasingly on love, the arts, beauty and organising finances over the coming two weeks.

24 JANUARY

The lead-up to a full moon can be intense. Someone close may appear moodier or needier than usual, so be prepared to be tactful and think carefully.

25 JANUARY

The Leo full moon will spotlight key agreements and collaborations. You may not agree with someone else's values but must be prepared to look at matters from a fresh perspective.

26 JANUARY

Your help will be in demand, and if you need advice or support it will be available. Be prepared to be patient, as there may be delays or mix-ups.

27 JANUARY

The key to success lies in good communication skills. Avoid taking criticism personally unless it's merited. Avoid making rash decisions and minor scrapes and bumps.

28 JANUARY

You'll appreciate the value of a financial or personal investment but you must avoid making rash decisions in your personal life and financially.

29 JANUARY

You may be surprised or delighted by news. This is a good day to take the initiative with your plans and at work. You'll enjoy a trip or visit.

30 JANUARY

Look for balance, peace and fair play, as all are possible. Just avoid being super idealistic.

31 JANUARY

Think outside the square about your various options. Once again, a fair-minded and balanced approach to communications will be beneficial.

February

1 FEBRUARY

Your ability to be level-headed when under pressure will be useful; just avoid obstinacy.

2 FEBRUARY

It's a good day for meetings and discussing financial and personal matters. You'll be drawn to music, the arts and film.

3 FEBRUARY

You're feeling passionate about life and will appreciate the opportunity to engage in favourite pastimes such as sports. It's a good day for self-development.

4 FEBRUARY

A little adventure, trip or fun get-together will raise spirits.

5 FEBRUARY

There is a healing aspect to the day, and your expert advice will be in demand. If you need advice it will be available.

6 FEBRUARY

Be diplomatic, as you may need to undertake talks regarding sensitive topics. Avoid taking offence where none is intended.

7 FEBRUARY

This is a better day for communications, but you must avoid assuming others have the same values as you. You may be drawn to overspending. Romance could thrive.

8 FEBRUARY

You may receive unexpected news or will need to take an unscheduled trip. Be prepared to be adaptable. Keep an eye on erratic drivers.

9 FEBRUARY

The Aquarian new moon supermoon points to a fresh chapter in your personal life and, for some, financially. It's a good time to begin something fresh in both of these areas.

10 FEBRUARY

As you consider new ideas and options some communications may require more patience and tact. If you're travelling, be prepared for delays.

11 FEBRUARY

The Pisces moon will bring out your dreamy, philosophical sides, which is ideal for relaxing and spending time with like-minded people.

12 FEBRUARY

You're thinking creatively and imaginatively while keeping your feet on the ground, which is perfect for making progress on a Monday morning.

13 FEBRUARY

You'll be drawn to approaching a situation from a fresh perspective. If you're contemplating an investment, ensure you have all the details. Romance could thrive.

14 FEBRUARY

Happy St Valentine's Day! There are intense aspects to the day, so be sure to maintain perspective as strong emotions may arise.

15 FEBRUARY

Feelings may still be strong, so be prepared to keep your professional hat on when you're at work. Be practical for the best results.

16 FEBRUARY

As Venus leaves your sign you'll begin to see a personal or financial matter in a new light.

17 FEBRUARY

Strong feelings will arise once again and this will be a passionate time. Romance will thrive but so, too, could conflict.

18 FEBRUARY

You'll enjoy the company of like-minded people and favourite activities but you may need to be super tactful with someone's feelings.

19 FEBRUARY

This is a good day for a health appointment. You may hear from an old friend or someone who needs your advice or support. If you need guidance it will be available.

20 FEBRUARY

Someone will prove to be supportive towards you, and if someone requires your help a nurturing and supportive approach will be particularly effective.

21 FEBRUARY

You're better known for your reliability, trustworthiness and patience but you're also a dynamic character and will display some of these characteristics.

22 FEBRUARY

Key developments will merit an innovative approach. A romantic, personal or financial matter will be a focus.

23 FEBRUARY

Mercury in Pisces for the next three weeks will encourage you to consider new ways to approach matters that have become stale. Be prepared to discuss your ideas.

24 FEBRUARY

The full moon in Virgo spotlights certain relationships. You may be ready to see these in a new light as you look for more stability and security.

25 FEBRUARY

This is a good day to make a commitment to a new financial or personal arrangement.

26 FEBRUARY

You are known for being reasonable and practical, and these qualities will be useful for you.

27 FEBRUARY

Certain ideas and feelings may be magnified, so be prepared to be the voice of reason. Avoid making rash decisions and be patient with communication or travel delays.

28 FEBRUARY

You may receive key news if you didn't already yesterday, either financially or in your personal life. It's a good day to make a commitment.

29 FEBRUARY

Romance could thrive, so organise a date if you didn't already. Business and financial meetings will provide clarity.

March

1 MARCH

It's a good day for talks and making financial and personal commitments. Avoid making rash decisions. Some communications may be erratic, so be patient.

2 MARCH

You'll enjoy a trip somewhere beautiful or a visit at home. Retail therapy will be enjoyable but you must avoid overspending.

3 MARCH

You may be surprised by someone's news or developments. Be prepared to look outside the box and be flexible if you must alter your plans suddenly.

4 MARCH

Your behind-the-scenes help is always appreciated, but you must avoid seeming to meddle with other people's personal matters.

5 MARCH

You'll gain a sense of purpose and appreciation by following through with some of your plans, especially with someone you love or admire.

6 MARCH

There are therapeutic aspects to the day. You may receive news that boosts morale; just avoid making rash decisions.

7 MARCH

Communications, meetings and news are likely to be busy, and you can make great headway at work and in your personal life.

8 MARCH

A financial or personal matter will take your focus. If you are making a large investment, ensure you have the full facts. You may enjoy an ego boost.

9 MARCH

Most interactions are likely to go well and this is certainly a good time to enjoy doing something different. However, you must be prepared for the unexpected.

10 MARCH

The Pisces new moon supermoon will spotlight your hopes and plans, especially in your personal life and finances. Be positive but also realistic, both emotionally and financially.

11 MARCH

You'll appreciate a change of pace and the opportunity to put some of your clever ideas and plans in action.

12 MARCH

A positive and upbeat approach to communications and interactions will be beneficial. You may reconnect with someone special. If you need advice it will be available.

13 MARCH

This is a good day to make changes in key areas such as your personal life or finances. Just avoids talks becoming intense and focus on common ground.

14 MARCH

A practical approach to developments, communications and your home life will be productive, especially if changes must be made.

15 MARCH

You'll enjoy a sense of freedom and the chance to be a little more light-hearted, especially in connection with creative or domestic or personal matters.

16 MARCH

You'll appreciate the opportunity to get down to brass tacks with chores. You may also be drawn to reviewing your finances and considering a special purchase.

17 MARCH

This is a lovely day for get-togethers, including for romance. It's also a good time to consider a large outlay or commitment.

18 MARCH

The moon in Cancer will bring someone's emotions to the surface, and you may be surprised by what they have to say or offer you.

19 MARCH

Be sure to act on your instincts and follow your intuition. This is a good day to make a personal or financial investment.

20 MARCH

The sun will shine on your relationships and communications over the next four weeks, so be prepared to improve these areas. Travel or communications maybe delayed, so be patient.

21 MARCH

It's a good day to make changes and a financial or personal commitment.

22 MARCH

The next five weeks will be inspiring and may take you into uncharted territory, so be prepared to be adaptable and embrace change starting today.

23 MARCH

You'll enjoy a get-together or short trip. You may meet someone you admire or love.

24 MARCH

The lead-up to a lunar eclipse can be super intense, so be sure to look for a calm, peaceful and balanced approach to your day.

25 MARCH

This lunar eclipse signals it's time to explore new ways to find balance and peace of mind in your collaborations and duties and responsibilities.

26 MARCH

You may discover your Achilles heel or that of someone else. This is a therapeutic day that is ideal for a beauty or health trip. You may receive a compliment or ego boost.

27 MARCH

The moon at the zenith of your chart will encourage you to look for viable, strategic ways to make this a happy day. You may enjoy a treat.

28 MARCH

A surprise will take you somewhere new, and you may enjoy an unexpected trip or visit.

29 MARCH

A passionate, adventurous approach to the day will be revitalising. It's a good day for self-development and to enjoy favourite activities.

30 MARCH

An upbeat and outgoing approach will open doors. You'll enjoy being with like-minded people.

31 MARCH

An active interest in your work and environment, such as your domestic surroundings, will encourage you to get up to date with chores and paperwork.

April

1 APRIL

It's a good start to the week as the moon in Capricorn for the next two days will help you get things shipshape. Try to get loose ends of paperwork tied up.

2 APRIL

As Mercury turns retrograde you may receive key news or will undertake a trip. The next few weeks will be ideal for updating communication methods or devices.

3 APRIL

Romance is in the air and it could thrive. A key financial or personal decision is likely; just avoid daydreaming.

4 APRIL

You'll appreciate the help or advice of someone special. It's a good day to reconfigure or review your finances and personal life.

5 APRIL

Venus in Aries for the next few weeks will contribute to a more proactive and dynamic phase, especially in your communications, relationships and for some with travel.

6 APRIL

This is a lovely day to take a short trip or change aspects of your environment. You'll enjoy get-togethers and may be drawn to romance.

7 APRIL

The lead-up to a new moon eclipse can be intense. Luckily, you'll gain the opportunity to dream a little and focus on your priorities.

8 APRIL

The total solar eclipse signifies a fresh chapter in your personal circumstance and the chance to improve a relationship. A new vehicle or trip may appeal and you may receive key health news.

9 APRIL

You're better known as someone who takes things one step at a time. Currently you may be uncharacteristically outspoken, so choose your words carefully.

10 APRIL

You'll gain the opportunity to make an informed yet inspired commitment. Unexpected news or an impromptu get-together will be uplifting.

11 APRIL

You'll enjoy a reunion or the chance to review a personal financial investment.

12 APRIL

Be adaptable and spontaneous as you'll enjoy doing something different, and developments at home will create a fresh atmosphere.

13 APRIL

A light-hearted approach to family and/or domestic circumstances will be motivating, especially if you're looking for ways to improve your environment or relationships.

14 APRIL

You have the green light to focus a little on your well-being, so this is a good day for self-development and self-nurturance.

15 APRIL

Be prepared to focus further on communications and travel, as mix-ups and misunderstandings are possible. Avoid taking someone's random comments personally unless you deserve criticism.

16 APRIL

This is a good day to take the initiative to improve relationships and fix communication devices or a vehicle. Just avoid rushing.

17 APRIL

This is an excellent day for a get-together with someone you love or admire. You may be drawn to reviewing finances or paying off a bill. Romance could thrive.

18 APRIL

You'll enjoy the sense that the weekend is almost here and will be happy to start making plans. Meanwhile, certain financial and work details will require detailed focus.

19 APRIL

As the sun enters Taurus you'll gain a sense of progress and feel more grounded over the coming weeks. You may receive financial news. It's a good day to make changes at home or with family.

20 APRIL

A practical approach to domestic and personal matters will be effective. It's a good day for a mini financial review.

21 APRIL

You may be surprised by developments. This is a good time to make long-term changes at home even if they are a little disruptive. Just avoid a battle of egos.

22 APRIL

Surprising news or a change of plan will be enjoyable. Your help may unexpectedly be sought after.

23 APRIL

You will be the voice of reason and may need to mediate or prove your knowledge. Be resourceful and innovative.

24 APRIL

The Scorpio full moon will shine a light on your chores, activities and favourite ventures, enabling you to more clearly see the path ahead. You may experience a financial or ego boost.

25 APRIL

As the Mercury retrograde phase ends you may enjoy a lovely get-together or reunion. This is a good time for seeking expert financial help.

26 APRIL

An adventurous and outgoing approach to work and your social activities will pay off, as your enthusiasm will be hard to miss.

27 APRIL

This is a lovely day to beautify your home and environment and for health or beauty appointments. Romance could thrive.

28 APRIL

You may be drawn to retail therapy but must avoid overspending. The arts, romance, music and creativity will thrive.

29 APRIL

As Venus enters Taurus you'll enjoy bringing a sense of stability into your daily life and communications, which will produce better relationships over the coming weeks. Avoid impulse buys.

30 APRIL

Mars in Aries for the next few weeks will bring out your assertiveness but could also predispose you to stubbornness, so avoid appearing obstinate if you encounter obstacles.

May

1 MAY

A difference of opinion needn't cause arguments if you maintain a fair-minded outlook and a view towards finding common ground.

2 MAY

A progressive approach to finances and relationships will help you avoid emotional or dramatic interactions. You may reconsider an important issue.

3 MAY

You'll begin to see positive outcomes to your patient approach and efforts to change important aspects of your life.

4 MAY

You'll enjoy taking the initiative with events and will see positive results. You'll be drawn to investing in yourself and those you love.

5 MAY

A short trip or get-together will be enjoyable as it will reconnect you with your sense of self and love of life.

6 MAY

This is a good day to set the ball rolling in the direction of long-term change, especially financially and within your personal life.

7 MAY

Someone may need your help and reach out for a chat or get-together. If you need advice or support be sure to ask for it, as it will be available.

8 MAY

The Taurus new moon is conducive to considering a fresh approach to a personal situation. You may be drawn to updating a communications device or planning a trip.

9 MAY

The Gemini moon provides an ideal opportunity to discuss your ideas in a relaxed manner, especially to do with your personal life, family or home.

10 MAY

You'll enjoy being flexible with arrangements, especially with your personal life and extracurricular activities, but you must avoid making waves.

11 MAY

There is a therapeutic feel to the day that makes it ideal for a mini health or beauty treat and a trip somewhere beautiful. You'll relish a reunion. Romance could thrive.

12 MAY

The Cancerian moon brings out your nurturing side, making this a good day for self-care and self-development and reconnecting with those you love.

13 MAY

An unexpected or unusual development will keep you on your toes. This is a good day to make a commitment or agreement financially and in your personal life.

14 MAY

An upbeat, fun character will add a little variety and spice to your day and encourage you to be more adventurous and outgoing.

15 MAY

Your communications will attain a more even and level-headed quality, enabling you to make informed, rational decisions.

16 MAY

Some communications are likely to be slightly intense over the next two days, so be careful to represent the facts and research details if necessary.

17 MAY

Be prepared to be patient but, equally, to take the initiative when necessary and think on your feet. Avoid misunderstandings and plan ahead to avoid travel delays.

18 MAY

Key developments at home or in your personal life may be unexpected or out of the ordinary. It's a good day to embrace something new such as taking a trip and thinking laterally.

19 MAY

This is a lovely day to invest in your home, family and those you love, including yourself. Romance could thrive. It's also a good day for spiritual development.

20 MAY

Be prepared to be more adaptable and flexible over the next four weeks. You may hear unexpected news from someone special or will need to think fast.

21 MAY

Combine your passionate, inspired attitude with the willingness to go the distance to make things happen to achieve your goals.

22 MAY

This is a good time make changes at home and in your personal life, so take the initiative. You're communicating well, so be inspired and inspire others.

23 MAY

The full moon in Sagittarius will spotlight your career, general direction and the people you associate with. You'll appreciate the sense that change can be for the better.

24 MAY

You can work towards an ideal while being practical to keep things on an even keel. Your personal life and creativity will flourish.

25 MAY

A creative project will blossom. Romantic Capricorns will love seeing your interests in music, dance and all things beautiful thrive.

26 MAY

As Jupiter enters Gemini your focus will go towards personal and financial investments over the next year. This is a good time to invest in yourself and someone special and also in a home or property.

27 MAY

Think laterally for the best results and be prepared to make inspired yet well-researched changes that you know will bring long-term happiness.

28 MAY

Rest assured you can make realistic plans that will work. Be prepared to make a commitment. This is a good day for get-togethers and a short trip.

29 MAY

You may be prone to making a rash decision or investing in a financial or personal matter without forethought, so be sure to research circumstances. Avoid minor scrapes and bumps.

30 MAY

This is a good day for discussions, but you must avoid taking random comments personally. You can remedy or overcome past mistakes or misunderstandings.

31 MAY

The Pisces moon will bring out your idealism and your love of the arts and romance, so be sure to also be practical.

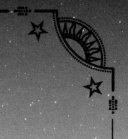

June

1 JUNE

You'll appreciate a change of pace at home and the opportunity to do something different. A spontaneous or impromptu get-together will be enjoyable.

2 JUNE

The Aries moon will encourage you to be active and take the initiative with talks, discussions and arrangements. You may enjoy a trip or visit.

3 JUNE

You have the gift of the gab over the next few weeks, especially where personal matters are concerned, so be prepared to initiate change if you feel it's necessary.

4 JUNE

This is a lovely day for romance, the arts and enjoying the company of someone special. It's also a good day for a health or beauty appointment.

5 JUNE

The lead-up to the Gemini new moon is a good time to consider how to spruce up your regular daily timetable and communications and to plan for travel.

6 JUNE

The new moon in Gemini will help you to turn a corner, especially in a romantic or close relationship and within a creative or financial matter.

7 JUNE

The Cancerian moon will bring your focus on someone special and how best to look after their interests and also your own.

8 JUNE

Take a break, especially if you feel some matters are simply too intense. Avoid misunderstandings and financial and emotional gambling.

9 JUNE

It's a good day to take the pressure off and engage in activities you love. You will not always agree with everyone, so look for practical ways to make progress.

10 JUNE

The Leo moon brings to the forefront your dynamic and proactive qualities, helping you to attain your goals and work collaboratively with others.

11 JUNE

There are therapeutic aspects to the day, making this a good time for a beauty or health appointment. If you need expert advice it will be available.

12 JUNE

Some communications will go very well, especially those in your personal life. However, other communications, for example regarding your finances or work, will require extra tact.

13 JUNE

You'll enjoy a surprise development or unexpectedly good news, for some at work and for others at home. You'll enjoy being spontaneous adding a little spice to your life.

14 JUNE

Key news will catch your attention. This is a good day to initiate talks with someone important such as an employer or financial expert.

15 JUNE

You may again receive unexpectedly good news. You may enjoy a short trip somewhere different or being spontaneous with your activities.

16 JUNE

A level-headed and fair-minded approach to communications and shared duties will pay off. Be careful with financial and personal decisions, as a little more planning may be necessary.

17 JUNE

You're prepared to see a work or personal matter in a new light, and to gain the information you need you must research situations more deeply. Avoid misunderstandings.

18 JUNE

You prefer to have a purpose in your activities rather than simply undertaking them mechanically, so you'll appreciate the chance to engage in a favourite activity.

19 JUNE

You're wearing your heart on your sleeve, which is uncharacteristic for you, so be sure to put your professional hat on at work.

20 JUNE

Your work, health and well-being will deserve focus over the coming weeks, beginning now with the opportunity to unravel a mystery or gain direction.

21 JUNE

While this is a good day for discussions, be sure to be mindful of other people's values and principles to avoid arguments.

22 JUNE

The full moon in Capricorn will spotlight your work and health. You must avoid pushing yourself too hard over the coming weeks. You may receive good news that is motivational.

23 JUNE

It's important that you see eye to eye with someone close, so looking for common ground is a good place to start if a difference of opinion arises.

24 JUNE

It's an excellent day to think laterally, especially about your personal life and chores and how to attain them.

25 JUNE

You'll enjoy catching up with someone special and feel motivated as a result. However, you must avoid making rushed decisions.

26 JUNE

This is a good day for meetings and discussions at work and regarding finances but you must avoid making assumptions, so be sure to discuss goals or values.

27 JUNE

The moon in Pisces will provide you with insight, so be sure to take a moment to reconnect with your goals and wishes to ensure you're still on the right path.

28 JUNE

You or someone close may be a little sensitive, and your help may be needed. You may find it best to avoid delicate topics or approach someone carefully or at least tactfully.

29 JUNE

This is a lovely day for meetings and discussions, so be sure to organise something special in your personal life. If you're working, this will be a productive day.

30 JUNE

You may hear unexpected news or will enjoy an impromptu trip or visit. It's a good day to brighten up your surroundings and relationships.

July

1 JULY

You'll appreciate the feeling that you can get your back into your projects and work, and as the day goes by communications are likely to get busier.

2 JULY

Someone you collaborate with such as a business or personal partner will have news. A key work or personal matter will require attention to get things on track if they go awry.

3 JULY

Key talks will be productive but you must avoid arguments, and you must also be realistic and willing to see another person's point of view.

4 JULY

This is a good day to make progress at work and home, and to decide where you'd like to initiate change in time to make a wish on the new moon tomorrow.

5 JULY

The Cancerian new moon will kick-start a fresh phase in a key relationship if you were born in December and at work if you were born in January. It's a good day for talks or a meeting.

6 JULY

Someone close may be feeling a little vulnerable or sensitive, so be sure to take things one step at a time. Avoid taking comments personally unless criticism is merited.

7 JULY

The Leo moon will encourage you to be sympathetic to someone else's feelings. You'll develop a deeper understanding of someone special.

8 JULY

You may receive good news. Be prepared to make unscheduled changes to your itinerary, as an impromptu trip or meeting will appeal or demand a change of plan.

9 JULY

The next two days are excellent for research and analysis and for grounding your plans and ideas.

10 JULY

This is a good day for discussions, and for looking forward to being more adventurous and making plans for the future.

11 JULY

An upbeat, outspoken approach to a business or work partner will be productive. This is a romantic day, so take the initiative!

12 JULY

Key talks and meetings will merit an open mind, so be sure to think outside the box. Romance and passion will ignite; just avoid arguments.

13 JULY

You'll be looking for a little piece and balance this weekend. However, scheduled activities will require you to fulfil various obligations beforehand.

14 JULY

You'll enjoy engaging in favourite activities such as sports and you may enjoy making changes at home. A mini financial review may be beneficial moving forward.

15 JULY

A change or sudden development at home or with family will merit a little focus. Avoid taking someone's comments personally unless you know what they say is true.

16 JULY

You'll be expressing your passionate side and will enjoy spending time with someone special. Aim to de-escalate intense circumstances if possible.

17 JULY

A sociable and proactive approach at work and in your personal life will bring you closer to your goals, so be positive.

18 JULY

You may hear unexpected news. Be prepared to be adaptable, especially regarding your home life or personal relationships. You may enjoy a change of pace.

19 JULY

This is a good time to mend bridges with someone who is close to your heart. Romance could thrive. You may experience a financial boost or compliment.

20 JULY

You'll enjoy a change at home or in your environment, but you must be well prepared to avoid unnecessary disruption.

21 JULY

The full moon in your sign signals the start of a fresh chapter in your personal life. Be careful with communications and travel to avoid misunderstandings and delays.

22 JULY

As the sun enters Leo important communications and meetings are likely. Be prepared to innovate and think laterally. Change will be positively transformative.

23 JULY

Key discussions and meetings will be productive but you must avoid power struggles. Be inspired and base your decisions on facts.

24 JULY

You may be seeing life through rose-coloured glasses, so be sure to check the facts and avoid making assumptions.

25 JULY

You have an analytical mind but may feel a little unsure of your decisions, so double-check details and avoid misunderstandings.

26 JULY

An upbeat, outgoing atmosphere will be productive and you may make positive changes at home and within a special relationship. You may enjoy an impromptu get-together.

27 JULY

Good communication skills and planning will lead to a better understanding of someone. Avoid a battle of wills; it's better to find common ground and work together.

28 JULY

Creature comforts and a treat will certainly boost your mood, so take time to indulge a little in life's pleasures.

29 JULY

A little effort goes a long way, so if you're experiencing Mondayitis consider breaking your tasks down into bite-sized pieces to achieve your goals.

30 JULY

This is a healing day that is ideal for a health or beauty treat and for building bridges with someone you find difficult to get along with.

31 JULY

This is a lovely day for a get-together or short trip. You may experience an uplifting event and compliment. If you're single and looking for a partner, this could be the day for it!

August

1 AUGUST

You'll gain a deeper understanding of a personal or work matter and, as a result, will find some direction.

2 AUGUST

You may be surprised by developments. If you experience a setback, rest assured you will at least gain insight into the best way forward. Avoid impulsiveness.

3 AUGUST

The lead-up to the Leo new moon is a good time to consider how you might improve certain relationships and collaborations.

4 AUGUST

The Leo new moon spotlights a key relationship. It's a good time to set an intention to be more outgoing and dynamic and also to tie up loose ends with paperwork.

5 AUGUST

You may receive key news to do with a shared investment, relationship or commitment. If you encounter an obstacle, rest assured you'll overcome it although you must avoid making assumptions.

6 AUGUST

Now that Mercury is retrograde you'll gain the chance to review a particular collaboration or investment. You'll be able to rethink recent decisions.

7 AUGUST

The day has an upbeat, dynamic quality and you'll enjoy being creative and outgoing. It's a good day for romance, music and the arts.

8 AUGUST

You'll enjoy a reunion or news from the past. This is a good day for a financial review and planning.

9 AUGUST

You may need to play a mediatory role or to find the best path forward within an existing agreement. You'll enjoy relaxing with someone special.

10 AUGUST

You'll be drawn to retail therapy and must decide the relative value of a purchase. If a disagreement arises, consider agreeing to disagree and move on from there.

11 AUGUST

Very little will take you out of your comfort zone as you'll be drawn to spending your free time doing what you love. It's another good day for a mini financial review.

12 AUGUST

A dedicated approach to your work and chores will pay off. Just be sure to research long-term decisions to avoid making mistakes.

13 AUGUST

You'll achieve a sense of progress as you move through the day. This is a good time to invest your time and energy into activities you love.

14 AUGUST

Significant developments involving someone special will bring your focus on your values and principles. Avoid allowing intense discussions to become arguments.

15 AUGUST

There are therapeutic aspects to the day. Talks and meetings will be progressive, and you may discover important information that dispels a mystery.

16 AUGUST

Your views will not always coincide with those of other people. Be prepared to see another person's point of view and avoid making rash decisions and financial and emotional gambling.

17 AUGUST

You'll enjoy the benefits of creature comforts and spending time investing in your well-being. A shopping spree may appeal.

18 AUGUST

You may be drawn to leaving your comfort zone but are best to avoid misunderstandings. You'll enjoy being spontaneous but must avoid pushing boundaries.

19 AUGUST

The Aquarian full moon will illuminate where in your personal life you could make changes. News from someone close will encourage you to do so, but you must avoid making rash decisions.

20 AUGUST

The Pisces moon brings to the surface your idealistic qualities over the next two days, so be philosophical but inspired and remember to keep your feet on the ground. Avoid forgetfulness.

21 AUGUST

A positive, outgoing approach will be fruitful, especially if some communications or developments are stressful. Be prepared to think laterally.

22 AUGUST

The sun in Virgo over the next four weeks will spotlight your collaborations, partnerships and relationships, enabling you to make solid progress in all areas.

23 AUGUST

This is a lovely day for get-togethers and meetings, but you must keep an open mind. You may experience a financial boost or compliment. Avoid financial and emotional gambling.

24 AUGUST

Your activities and get-togethers will be uplifting. It's likely, however, that a financial or personal matter will need to be reconfigured or rethought, although it will be to your advantage.

25 AUGUST

You are well known for your ability to be practical and realistic, and these qualities will be in demand.

26 AUGUST

A flexible and adaptable approach, especially to domestic, creative, personal and family matters, will be productive. You have the gift of the gab.

27 AUGUST

You may be surprised by news or developments that could improve your personal, domestic and financial circumstances, so take the initiative.

28 AUGUST

You may receive key news from a personal or business partner. This may be ideal, especially financially, but if not be sure to research your circumstances a little more.

29 AUGUST

Developments have a transformative aspect that could open doors for you and bring more your way of what you love in life.

30 AUGUST

Someone close may need your care and attention. This is a good time to consider a fresh way to approach someone special.

31 AUGUST

You'll appreciate the opportunity to do something different and be a little more spontaneous. You may enjoy a visit or surprise guest.

September

1 SEPTEMBER

Someone close with an upbeat, outgoing attitude will bring out the best in you. This is a good day to self-nurture and enjoy a trip somewhere beautiful.

2 SEPTEMBER

You'll be drawn to reconsidering certain personal matters that will create more transparency and dynamism in your personal life, and today is a good day to begin.

3 SEPTEMBER

The new moon in Virgo will kick-start a fresh phase in a personal or business agreement. Be prepared to reconfigure financial or legal matters. It's a good day to make a commitment.

4 SEPTEMBER

You'll begin to feel more energetic, but if you feel restless be sure to channel your energy into constructive pursuits. A key financial or personal matter may be decided upon.

5 SEPTEMBER

A balanced, peaceful approach to colleagues and partners will be productive, even if you feel a little emotional.

6 SEPTEMBER

Your ability to see two sides of a story will be in demand. However, you may need to make a tough call.

7 SEPTEMBER

The Scorpio moon will encourage you to invest in your favourite activities. This is a good day for self-development and spending time with someone you love or admire.

8 SEPTEMBER

A personal or financial commitment is likely to take, especially if you've already researched circumstances. Rest assured you will overcome a minor misunderstanding.

9 SEPTEMBER

As Mercury enters Virgo you'll be drawn to focusing on communications and verbal agreements. Be sure to avoid a clash of priorities and stick with a schedule.

10 SEPTEMBER

This is likely to be a busy, sociable and networking day. Once again, double-check priorities to avoid a conflict of interest.

11 SEPTEMBER

You won't always agree with everyone and disagreements may simply come down to different values. Avoid overspending, especially if you're already in debt.

12 SEPTEMBER

This is a good day to talk, especially at work and regarding shared chores, but you must avoid a personality clash or battle of wills.

13 SEPTEMBER

The moon in your sign will encourage you to be practical, hands-on and efficient, so be proactive and positive.

14 SEPTEMBER

A shared matter or agreement will deserve careful focus, especially if you'd like to alter some of the conditions of your arrangement.

15 SEPTEMBER

You'll enjoy a trip, get-together or favourite activity with someone special. This is a good day for self-development.

16 SEPTEMBER

A productive day may involve frustration or a disappointment, but if you stick with your goals you will achieve them. Be tactful. A bill may need to be paid.

17 SEPTEMBER

You may benefit from being more realistic about your finances, personal obligations and debt to avoid overspending. It's a good day for a mini financial review.

18 SEPTEMBER

The partial lunar eclipse supermoon in Pisces spotlights your finances and personal life. It's a good day to discuss important obligations. You may make or break a financial agreement.

19 SEPTEMBER

You'll enjoy a surprise or doing something different, such as a trip or get-together.

20 SEPTEMBER

You may leave your comfort zone and will be drawn to looking for balance and harmony, which you'll find by being innovative and outgoing.

21 SEPTEMBER

You'll find out whether you've overestimated a circumstance, especially regarding your finances and personal life. This is a good time for research and being realistic.

22 SEPTEMBER

As the sun enters Libra you'll be drawn to looking for peace and harmony, especially in your shared ventures and duties. Just avoid a battle of wills in the process.

23 SEPTEMBER

Venus in Scorpio will bring into being a passionate and potentially feisty phase, and you'll enjoy feeling motivated at work but must avoid arguments.

24 SEPTEMBER

A pleasant if surprising development will raise your spirits. This is a good day for communications and making changes within shared ventures, including your home.

25 SEPTEMBER

You may receive sensitive or important news, for some to do with money and for others in your personal life. Just avoid forgetfulness.

26 SEPTEMBER

Tact and diplomacy will work in your favour over the next three weeks. You'll enjoy a get-together or news that improves your mood.

27 SEPTEMBER

The moon in Leo over the next two days will bring fun activities your way, prompting you to spend time with like-minded people.

28 SEPTEMBER

This is an excellent weekend to spend time with someone close and for a reunion. The arts, romance, music and creativity will appeal.

29 SEPTEMBER

You'll enjoy a trip or get-together with someone special. This is a good time to trust your intuition and for self-development.

30 SEPTEMBER

You can make headway at work and financially, so take the initiative. It's a good time to make a commitment to someone special but avoid making rash decisions.

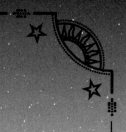

October

1 OCTOBER

The days in the run-up to an eclipse can feel intense, making this a good day to take things one step at a time to avoid fatigue and feeling overwhelmed.

2 OCTOBER

The solar eclipse in Libra will help you kick-start a fresh venture, for example, a favourite interest, trip, study course, spiritual development class or even legal matter.

3 OCTOBER

This is a good day for get-togethers, meetings and a trip. If you need expert advice it will be available.

4 OCTOBER

This is another good day for meetings and talks, especially those concerning work, finances and romance.

5 OCTOBER

You have your heart on your sleeve, and if you channel emotions into upbeat and inspiring pursuits you will enjoy your day.

6 OCTOBER

Be prepared to meet someone halfway, especially if you find that you have very different agendas. Avoid impulsiveness, as you may regret it.

7 OCTOBER

The moon in Sagittarius can bring back memories and this can be motivational, but if you find it distracting then be prepared to focus at work.

8 OCTOBER

This is a good day for a health or beauty appointment. Some conversations may be ideal and others stressful, so be adaptable. You may enjoy a visit or trip. Romance will thrive for some lucky Capricorns.

9 OCTOBER

The key to success at the moment is to keep an open mind and be sensitive to the feelings of other people. Avoid stubbornness in yourself and others by being approachable.

10 OCTOBER

The Capricorn moon keeps your feet on the ground and helps you to get things done without rushing or making hasty decisions.

11 OCTOBER

You may experience strong emotions, but if you keep your professional hat on at work you will overcome obstacles. You'll enjoy a change of pace later in the day.

12 OCTOBER

Be prepared to consider meeting someone halfway, especially if obstacles arise or communications are complex. You may manage to unravel a mystery.

13 OCTOBER

As Mercury enters Scorpio you'll feel passionate about your activities. However, not everyone will have the same motivation, so be prepared to find common ground to avoid arguments.

14 OCTOBER

Tact will go a long way in smoothing over surprising communications or developments. Someone may need your help, and if you need advice it will be available.

15 OCTOBER

An inspired and philosophical approach to developments will be beneficial, but you must avoid financial and emotional gambling.

16 OCTOBER

You may encounter ideal elements in your day that will boost not only your self-esteem but potentially also your status and direction. Avoid overspending if you're shopping.

17 OCTOBER

The full moon supermoon in Aries will spotlight a decision that is best approached carefully with a view to experiencing more harmony and balance in your life.

18 OCTOBER

A practical, measured approach to communications and developments will put you in a strong position. You'll enjoy treating yourself to a little luxury.

19 OCTOBER

A guest or surprise development may take you out of your comfort zone but needn't take you off track. Rise to the challenge and you'll enjoy your day.

20 OCTOBER

If you're unsure of someone's motives this is a good day to find out by asking them, although you must be prepared for the answer. Avoid being absent-minded.

21 OCTOBER

You're communicating well even if you can at times be forgetful. Leave yourself reminders or write a list to ensure you stay on top of your schedule.

22 OCTOBER

As the sun enters Scorpio your attention will go to activities you're passionate about such as extracurricular interests. You must avoid a battle of wills.

23 OCTOBER

This is a good day for meetings and broadening your horizons by, for example, improving your work schedule or status.

24 OCTOBER

You'll feel motivated by people close to you who take a positive approach to life. Just avoid needless arguments.

25 OCTOBER

Someone close has unexpected news for you and a change at home or work is likely to be beneficial in the long term. Avoid impulsiveness.

26 OCTOBER

While you prefer to take things one step at a time, someone close such as a partner or colleague may wish to put pressure on you. Rest assured you will rise to the occasion.

27 OCTOBER

You have a lot to say, and the key to success lies in choosing your words carefully. You may need to plan travel ahead to avoid delays. Avoid misunderstandings.

28 OCTOBER

A little give and take goes a long way, especially if you and someone close have different expectations. A financial matter will require focus. Romance will thrive.

29 OCTOBER

You'll gain insight into someone's deeper feelings, which will encourage you to overcome disagreements or make changes to your arrangements.

30 OCTOBER

News and developments are likely to surprise you or be a little unpredictable, so be on your toes over the next two days. Avoid making rash decisions.

31 OCTOBER

Happy Hallowe'en! You'll enjoy interacting with all kinds of different people and may experience an unexpected development unless you recently already did.

November

1 NOVEMBER

The Scorpio new moon will kick-start a fresh venture or interest. You'll enjoy get-togethers and meetings and may experience a financial or personal boost.

2 NOVEMBER

This is an excellent weekend to focus on your health and well-being and spend time with like-minded people, as you could boost important relationships.

3 NOVEMBER

This is a lovely day for therapeutic, creative and uplifting activities. Romance could thrive, but you must avoid arguments as someone could be feeling feisty.

4 NOVEMBER

You'll appreciate the sense that you're making progress with your projects. You'll gain the collaboration of someone whose presence you admire.

5 NOVEMBER

An upbeat, outgoing approach to friends, groups and organisations will be productive, but you must avoid assuming everyone is on the same page as you.

6 NOVEMBER

You have a motivational quality and people will look up to the example you set, but you must avoid putting pressure where it's not needed.

7 NOVEMBER

You may experience deeper emotions than you're comfortable with, so be prepared to pace yourself. You'll enjoy a reunion or good news.

8 NOVEMBER

You may receive unusual or unexpected news at home or from a friend or organisation, and you may need to organise your timetable or a response carefully.

9 NOVEMBER

This is a good weekend to look after your health and well-being and take things one step at a time to avoid mix-ups. Avoid overindulging and overspending.

10 NOVEMBER

The moon in Pisces will create a dreamy atmosphere and you may be prone to forgetfulness and idealism, so be careful with long-term decisions.

11 NOVEMBER

Venus will put your attention on your finances, work and love life over the coming weeks. You must take careful consideration of your goals and direction.

12 NOVEMBER

This is a good day for a mini financial review, especially if you're in debt. It's also a good time to avoid mix-ups and misunderstandings with a friend or organisation. Be patient.

13 NOVEMBER

The Aries moon over the next two days will be motivational, enabling you to accomplish your goals, but you must avoid arguments and appearing reckless.

14 NOVEMBER

You'll feel more grounded, which will enable you to action some of your plans and ideas.

15 NOVEMBER

The full moon in Taurus spotlights a personal matter, and for some this will be due to a trip or changes at work and in your general direction or status. You may be surprised by news at home.

16 NOVEMBER

Be prepared to think on your feet as a surprise is likely, unless you already experienced one recently. If disagreements arise these will stem from a difference in values.

17 NOVEMBER

You're communicating well and will feel more adaptable, especially with friends and groups. Just avoid arguments over minor or petty matters.

18 NOVEMBER

This is a good day for a short trip and meetings. Discussions are likely to go well even if they are animated.

19 NOVEMBER

You may experience a boost in your work or financial circumstances. It's a good day to reach out if you're looking for financial support or help from a friend or organisation.

20 NOVEMBER

As Pluto re-enters Aquarius, be prepared to approach someone special or relationships in general from a fresh perspective. You may be surprised by news or a change of pace.

21 NOVEMBER

It's a good time over the next four weeks to focus on your work and improving your status, and also for investing in favourite activities.

22 NOVEMBER

You may experience a financial improvement and a debt may be repaid. It's a good day to make a commitment. You may enjoy a reunion.

23 NOVEMBER

This is an excellent day for get-togethers in your personal life and at work. You could forge some truly unbreakable bonds.

24 NOVEMBER

This is a good day to clear a backlog of chores and paperwork and to discuss serious matters with people they concern, as you're likely to reach an agreement.

25 NOVEMBER

You'll appreciate the opportunity to collaborate with someone whose work you admire. However, time is likely to be short so be prepared to work hard.

26 NOVEMBER

This is another good day for collaborations and reaching goals. You may receive key work or health news.

27 NOVEMBER

This is an excellent day again for pursuing your work and personal goals, even if you need to review or adjust some of your aims.

28 NOVEMBER

Your sensitivities may come out, so be prepared to be methodical and especially if you're under pressure. Avoid taking people's comments personally unless criticism is merited.

29 NOVEMBER

Discussions and meetings are likely to go well, especially if you need to put some matters straight or review agreements. It's a good day for a health or beauty appointment.

30 NOVEMBER

You'll be motivated to engage in your favourite activities, and those who wish to share your time will appreciate your focus.

December

1 DECEMBER

The Sagittarian new moon signals the start of a more adventurous phase in your work life and within your status and direction. You may be drawn to socialising more.

2 DECEMBER

A meeting, get-together or news will have a therapeutic if unexpected effect, so this is a good time to mend bridges if you've argued with someone.

3 DECEMBER

The moon in your sign will encourage you to be practical, hands-on and realistic. You may need to take the reins.

4 DECEMBER

Be prepared to work hard for the outcome you desire. Getting communications right is what will take you towards the results you want.

5 DECEMBER

It's a good day to be proactive but also to think laterally to achieve your goals. However, it's also important to be realistic and avoid overt idealism.

6 DECEMBER

Key talks and meetings will merit special attention. Avoid feeling pressured by someone while also embracing something new.

7 DECEMBER

Emotions may be intense, so a measured approach to developments will balance this out. Avoid getting caught in someone else's drama and look instead at the most positive way forward.

8 DECEMBER

You'll find out whether you've over- or underestimated a situation, which will give you the green light to set things straight – for yourself, at least.

9 DECEMBER

This is a good time to adopt a fresh approach to someone, which will enable you to move ahead in a more matter-of-fact way.

10 DECEMBER

You'll reap the rewards of facing situations in a measured, calm and nurturing way. You may enjoy a reunion and at the least a confidence boost.

11 DECEMBER

A proactive and dynamic approach to meetings, news and travel will give you the upper hand. Once the moon enters Taurus you'll feel more grounded and productive.

12 DECEMBER

Romance could truly thrive; however, so too could conflict, so be prepared to avoid sensitive topics unless you truly feel they need to be aired. If this is the case, tact will be a useful tool.

13 DECEMBER

Despite this being Friday the 13th it's a lovely day for get-togethers at work and socially. You may receive good feedback for work well done.

14 DECEMBER

A busy, chatty day will be enjoyable, and you'll make progress in your favourite fields and activities in your spare time.

15 DECEMBER

The full moon will spotlight the chance to kick-start a fresh creative project and change major aspects of your career or personal life.

16 DECEMBER

You may receive key news to do with your career, status or general direction that will encourage you to be adventurous in these areas.

17 DECEMBER

It's a good day to be sensitive to someone else's feelings but not to allow them to distract you from your goals and chores.

18 DECEMBER

Certain matters, including finances and your personal life, may require more focus than usual to avoid misunderstandings. Avoid daydreaming.

19 DECEMBER

This is a good day for a mini review of your finances and personal commitments. You'll enjoy a get-together but may need to be conscious of certain boundaries.

20 DECEMBER

You'll enjoy a trip or lovely get-together with family or friends and making changes at home. Some lucky Capricorns will also enjoy a financial boost.

21 DECEMBER

As the sun steps into your sign, this is the solstice. Over the next four weeks you'll feel more in your element and enjoy a slower or at least more grounded pace.

22 DECEMBER

You'll appreciate meeting a new circle of people and, at the least, a change of routine.

23 DECEMBER

Your reliable and stable approach to life will be an asset over the next two days as you'll certainly enjoy the seasonal spirit, but you must be careful to avoid tense interactions.

24 DECEMBER

There is a lovely calm, therapeutic aspect to the day, but if you're working or changing aspects of your domestic life you'll need to be patient and then find time to relax.

25 DECEMBER

Merry Christmas! Being a traditionalist, you'll enjoy the day's proceedings. However, not everyone sees life the same as you do, so a little tolerance on both sides may be needed.

26 DECEMBER

A get-together will be enjoyable. However, once again, recognising you may have different viewpoints will prevent arguments. A trip may be delayed.

27 DECEMBER

Tact and diplomacy will be useful to avoid arguments. If you're shopping, be prepared to curtail excessive expenses to avoid overspending.

28 DECEMBER

A change of circumstance at home or with someone special may be unexpected. Avoid making rushed decisions and be prepared to be adaptable.

29 DECEMBER

You'll feel ready to change the pace as you head towards New Year's Eve and will appreciate the opportunity for a little self-nurturance.

30 DECEMBER

The new moon in Capricorn will kick-start a fresh phase in your personal life if you were born in December and at work or in your daily routine if you were born in January.

31 DECEMBER

Happy New Year! A get-together or visit will be therapeutic. You may be asked to help or be a volunteer, and if you need assistance rest assured it will be available.

AQUARIUS

20 January – 19 February

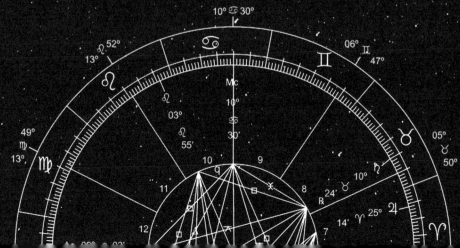

FINANCES

The first quarter of the year will offer the chance to improve your finances. The end of January is particularly favourable for making new financial arrangements that could be beneficial in the long term. Once Jupiter enters Gemini at the end of May you could be more drawn to considering investing in your home and/or family. Entrepreneurial Aquarians will find the period from May to August productive and could find ways to improve finances then. Times to avoid making rash decisions will be during the eclipse phases: the first from March to April and the second from September to October. The key is to focus on secure investments, as otherwise you risk gambling with your hard-earned profits.

HEALTH

You'll appreciate the opportunity to move on from niggling health worries, but in the process some health matters may demand your attention. See this as an opportunity to tailor-make a supportive health routine that suits your constitution. Seize the first quarter of the year to begin a fresh schedule, as otherwise symptoms or niggling health concerns could resurface in September and October. The end of January will be a good time to gain a sense of purpose in life, and this will lead to better motivation and self-esteem. If you already have a strong, healthy approach to supporting your mind, body and spirit you'll again get the opportunity by the year's end to let go of old health concerns.

LOVE LIFE

The re-entry of Pluto into your sign, where it will remain for the next two decades, will take ideas and relationships you formed in 2023 to another level. If you decided to make considerable changes in your love life in 2023 you'll find you gain ground with the changes you instigated, especially during the first quarter and in November. However, if during 2023 you merely considered fresh relationship dynamics or even a change in an existing relationship, 2024 will be the year you actually put your ideas and plans into action. The year begins with Venus at the zenith of your chart, encouraging you to follow your heart. Just be sure during 2024 that you don't sacrifice your romantic life for your work, status or career.

CAREER

You'll find the time and motivation to turn a corner in your career in 2024, and you may be surprised by the year's end with the twists and turns in your career. Be prepared to diversify and learn new aspects of your existing career, and if you truly feel you must leave an old career behind this is the year to do so and especially if you were born at the end of January. Be prepared to re-imagine yourself and your role in your own life; you'll be glad you did. In September and October a period of reflection or potentially backtracking to remedy past circumstances will prepare the ground later in 2024 and in 2025 to consolidate your place in fresh territory. You won't look back.

HOME LIFE

You'll have the opportunity to invest more time, energy and money into your home and/or family, and if you wish to fully place your attention on these important areas of your life this year could see a brand new chapter begin domestically that creates a sense of renewal and revitalisation. June and July will be particularly conducive for DIY projects, improving domestic dynamics or even a move. You may once again be drawn to making considerable changes at home towards the end of the year. And, finally, if you've been considering bringing another family member into the household, the period from the end of May until early October will be a particularly fertile/abundant time!

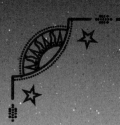

January

1 JANUARY

Happy New Year! You'll appreciate the opportunity to relax, but if you're working or feel pressured then rest assured you'll gain the chance to unwind in due course.

2 JANUARY

While on the one hand you'll enjoy being outgoing and upbeat, on the other hand you're aware of chores and paperwork and will need to find the middle ground.

3 JANUARY

The secret to happiness lies in being willing to be outgoing and learn something new while also keeping your feet on the ground.

4 JANUARY

The next six weeks may dredge up feelings of nostalgia and memories. You may be drawn to revisiting an old haunt. It will be a good time to boost your health and well-being.

5 JANUARY

You may need to play a mediatory role and find peace and the middle ground, especially if arguments arise.

6 JANUARY

Finding the fine line between what others want and what you want will keep you occupied. You may need to consult an expert or adviser.

7 JANUARY

An adventurous and outgoing approach to activities will be rewarding. You'll enjoy sports, socialising and favourite ventures.

8 JANUARY

Mars in your 12th house can bring up unexpected feelings and frustrations, so be sure to take things in your stride and retain perspective.

9 JANUARY

You can be both realistic and inventive, so you may need to decide what the most feasible path to take is. Avoid misunderstandings.

10 JANUARY

This is a good time to consider your priorities and be open to new and different things. You may experience a fun surprise or social event.

11 JANUARY

The Capricorn new moon will kick-start a fresh chapter in your daily schedule; you may be ready to alter your routine. A healing and well-being event and self-development will appeal.

12 JANUARY

This is a lovely day to take the initiative, especially at work. You'll enjoy meeting with friends and also networking.

13 JANUARY

You're in a strong position to take the lead with a work or health initiative, so be prepared to discuss your ideas with those they concern.

14 JANUARY

You'll appreciate the sense that your communications and interactions gain a more even keel over the coming weeks. However, today you may be surprised by developments.

15 JANUARY

An inspired approach to your ventures and finances may open your eyes to new options such as investment strategies.

16 JANUARY

A reunion or return to an old haunt will be inspiring, but you must avoid absent-mindedness.

17 JANUARY

Your unique ability to encapsulate both a realistic and idealistic attitude means you're able to inspire others and are a born leader. These qualities will be useful.

18 JANUARY

It's a great day for work and social get-togethers, as you'll enjoy the company of like-minded people and could make valid agreements.

19 JANUARY

This is a good day for a trip and meetings. However, you must be clear about your aims or misunderstandings will occur. It's a good day for financial discussions.

20 JANUARY

Be prepared to turn a corner over the coming days. This may be an intense time but also a good time to make changes, either at work or in your personal life.

21 JANUARY

This will be a transformative year and there's no time like the present to put your plans in motion.

22 JANUARY

A chatty, light-hearted approach to potentially complex matters will oil the wheels of change, but you must avoid appearing flippant.

23 JANUARY

As Venus enters Capricorn you'll look for an increased sense of stability in your daily routine, work, health and well-being over the coming weeks.

24 JANUARY

The lead-up to the full moon could be intense, so be prepared to work intuitively and avoid stepping on someone's toes if possible.

25 JANUARY

The Leo full moon will spotlight key agreements and work duties. It's a good time to consider devising a fresh daily work or health schedule. Your help may be required. Avoid making rash decisions.

26 JANUARY

A group, friend or organisation may have news for you. You'll enjoy socialising. It's a good time to consider your options carefully and avoid knee-jerk reactions.

27 JANUARY

You have many original and inventive ideas, but some people think differently and you may need to avoid arguments. You'll enjoy an impromptu get-together.

28 JANUARY

This is a good day to make a commitment in your personal life or financially, but you must avoid making rash decisions. It's better to do your research.

29 JANUARY

You may be surprised by news or developments. This is a good day to make solid progress at work and financially. If you're shopping, avoid overspending.

30 JANUARY

A balanced and thoughtful approach to others will be productive, and if you feel pressured take short breaks when possible.

31 JANUARY

Be prepared to establish common ground and work collaboratively to avoid making rash decisions.

February

1 FEBRUARY

Look for innovative and positive ways to move forward, especially if you feel a stalemate or bad habit will repeat itself.

2 FEBRUARY

A reunion or return to an old haunt will be enjoyable. A debt may be repaid. This is a good day to improve your appearance or well-being.

3 FEBRUARY

Take time out to enjoy life; you'll be glad you did. Be positive. It's a good day for self-development.

4 FEBRUARY

Travel, sports, spirituality and the arts will all appeal, encouraging you to leave your comfort zone. You'll find being active relaxing.

5 FEBRUARY

There is a healing aspect to the day. You'll enjoy returning to an old haunt or a reunion and also a little retail therapy. Just avoid overspending as you'll regret it.

6 FEBRUARY

Your values will not always align with those of other people, so avoid allowing a difference of opinion to upset the status quo. Research options carefully if you're making a financial investment.

7 FEBRUARY

You'll enjoy an impromptu get-together and the chance to enjoy indulgences in life. Just avoid overspending and overindulging as you'll regret it.

8 FEBRUARY

You may be surprised by developments, so be prepared to think on your feet and avoid making snap decisions.

9 FEBRUARY

The Aquarian new moon supermoon points to a fresh chapter in your personal life if you were born on or before today and, if you were born after, in your work or health life.

10 FEBRUARY

Be sure to investigate a personal or financial investment carefully to avoid mistakes and misunderstandings. You may need to alter your plans at short notice.

11 FEBRUARY

The Pisces moon will encourage you to attain your goals. Break your plans down into small stages and work one step at a time to avoid feeling overwhelmed.

12 FEBRUARY

It's possible you're seeing the world idealistically, so keep your feet on the ground while also reaching for the stars. Avoid forgetfulness.

13 FEBRUARY

Mars in Aquarius for the next five weeks will boost your energy levels and encourage you to be positive and physically active. Just avoid appearing aggressive. Romance could thrive.

14 FEBRUARY

Happy St Valentine's Day! You may be particularly nostalgic. You may hear from someone from the past or will be drawn to expressing yourself as strong feelings emerge.

15 FEBRUARY

You may be surprised by your feelings and by developments, so take things one step at a time. A practical and realistic approach will be productive.

16 FEBRUARY

As Venus enters your sign you'll begin to see a personal, work or health matter in a new light. This is a passionate and potentially volatile time, so pace yourself.

17 FEBRUARY

Strong feelings will arise, so be prepared to channel excess energy into constructive pursuits. A reunion may be poignant. It's a good time for a health and well-being treat.

18 FEBRUARY

Be prepared to discuss your feelings with those they concern. This is a good time to consider long-term financial and personal aims.

19 FEBRUARY

As the sun enters Pisces your attention will go to values, principles and finances. You'll enjoy a reunion and may be asked for help. If you need advice it will be available.

20 FEBRUARY

Trust your instincts, as you'll gain deeper insight into a personal or work situation. Avoid taking someone's random comments personally unless criticism is merited.

21 FEBRUARY

An intuitive approach to your work and chores will get things done. You'll be drawn to enjoying music and the arts. A reunion may be on the cards.

22 FEBRUARY

This is potentially one of the most romantic days of the year, especially if you were born at the end of January. If you were born in February you may receive key work or health news.

23 FEBRUARY

Mercury in Pisces for the next three weeks will encourage you to consider a compassionate and sympathetic approach to someone who can appear vulnerable.

24 FEBRUARY

The full moon in Virgo spotlights a personal or business relationship. Be prepared to think carefully about how you wish to continue. You may be prepared to make a commitment.

25 FEBRUARY

A reunion or return to an old haunt will be enjoyable, but you must double-check details to avoid forgetfulness and misunderstandings.

26 FEBRUARY

A practical, realistic approach to situations that are outside your control will be beneficial.

27 FEBRUARY

While you'll be happy to be proactive, not everyone is moving at the same pace as you so you'll need to be patient to attain your goals.

28 FEBRUARY

News or a development could be ideal, especially if you're considering a financial or personal investment. Ensure you do your research.

29 FEBRUARY

This is a good day for talks and meetings at work and in your personal life. Romance could thrive. You may be drawn to retail therapy but must avoid overspending.

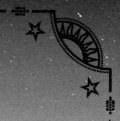

March

1 MARCH

This is a good day to make a commitment in your personal life and at work, and also to overcome personal or financial hurdles.

2 MARCH

You'll appreciate the opportunity to spend time doing what you love with people you love, so take the initiative if you have nothing planned yet.

3 MARCH

You may be surprised by developments. A personal, business or travel arrangement may need to be reconfigured at short notice. Think laterally.

4 MARCH

You'll manage to accomplish your goals by being inspired and proactive. A positive team mentality will work wonders.

5 MARCH

You'll enjoy meetings and get-togethers at work and in your personal life. Be prepared to take the initiative.

6 MARCH

There are therapeutic aspects to the day. Just avoid rushing and putting pressure on yourself and others. It's a good day for a beauty or health appointment.

7 MARCH

This is an excellent day to build bridges with anyone you've argued with and to improve all relationships. It's also a good day to discuss finances.

8 MARCH

You may receive key financial or personal news. It's a good day for romance, the arts, inspiration and self-development.

9 MARCH

You'll enjoy doing something different this weekend and being spontaneous. However, you must be prepared for the unexpected such as delays and mix-ups.

10 MARCH

The Pisces new moon supermoon will spotlight your long-term personal and financial plans. It's a good time to instigate changes in these areas.

11 MARCH

You may be drawn to expressing your deeper feelings with someone close as you both experience a change of focus in your relationship.

12 MARCH

You'll appreciate the opportunity to be proactive and dynamic but may need to choose your words carefully with someone who is sensitive.

13 MARCH

This is a good day to make changes in your daily routine to include more focus on your health and well-being and the people you love.

14 MARCH

A practical approach to your personal life, finances, investments and goals will be productive. Avoid making rash decisions.

15 MARCH

This will be a chatty day and you'll enjoy being able to connect with people whose company you enjoy.

16 MARCH

A mini work or financial review will be productive. This is a good day to make a commitment to a person or plan.

17 MARCH

A financial or personal matter will be a focus. Romance, the arts and self-development can all thrive.

18 MARCH

Trust your intuition, especially in connection with someone special. If you feel emotional, keep your professional hat on at work.

19 MARCH

You are inspired and perceptive, especially today, so be sure to act on your impressions as you could accomplish a great deal.

20 MARCH

The sun will shine on your productivity and ability to get on with others over the next four weeks. Key financial, personal or health news will merit focus.

21 MARCH

This is a good time to improve your daily routine and also to make a financial or personal commitment.

22 MARCH

The next five weeks will encourage you to follow your instincts and invest in activities, people and inspiration that light up your life.

23 MARCH

News, trip or a get-together could broaden your horizons or increase your finances. A teacher or expert will be helpful.

24 MARCH

The lead-up to a lunar eclipse can be super intense. A partner or friend will help you find balance.

25 MARCH

The Libran lunar eclipse signals it's time to experience more of the things you love in your everyday life. A business or personal partner may have news.

26 MARCH

This is a good day to talk and also to improve your appearance and health. You may be drawn to undertaking a mini financial review.

27 MARCH

Teamwork and collaboration hold the key to success. You'll appreciate the opportunity to really get stuck into your projects.

28 MARCH

A pleasant surprise or trip will be enjoyable. Be adaptable, as you may receive an unexpected invitation.

29 MARCH

You have strong instincts, so be sure to trust these. You may enjoy a trip and, at the least, will deepen your understanding of a venture or person.

30 MARCH

Your adventurous, outgoing qualities will seek expression. You'll enjoy sports, travel and exploration.

31 MARCH

A lovely sociable atmosphere will encourage you to get in touch with like-minded people. You may experience a confidence boost.

April

1 APRIL

This is a good day to get loose ends at work and paperwork tied up. It's also a good time to get important conversations on the table.

2 APRIL

As Mercury turns retrograde you may receive key news from a friend, at work or financially. The next few weeks will be ideal for a mini financial review and to update gadgets.

3 APRIL

This is an excellent day for romance, the arts, music and self-development. You may be drawn to investing in a new look. If you're shopping, avoid overspending.

4 APRIL

You'll enjoy a reunion. If you need help or advice from an expert this is a good day to find it.

5 APRIL

Venus in Aries for the next few weeks will motivate you to stay on top of financial and personal commitments and duties. You may be drawn to reviewing some of your principles.

6 APRIL

You'll enjoy a reunion or return to an old haunt. You may also be drawn to updating your wardrobe or changing your appearance.

7 APRIL

You'll appreciate the opportunity to relax, dream a little and invest time, energy and money in yourself and someone special.

8 APRIL

The total solar eclipse signifies the chance to bring a revitalising and healthy chapter into being. Be prepared to look outside the square at your options.

9 APRIL

You can be determined, and while this frequently gets the job done today you'll need to avoid appearing dogmatic.

10 APRIL

This is a good day to make a commitment in your personal life or financially. You may be surprised by developments or news.

11 APRIL

You'll enjoy a reunion and the chance to pay off a debt or have a debt repaid. You may hear from an old friend from out of the blue.

12 APRIL

A chatty, sociable end to the week will be enjoyable. You may enjoy a trip or meeting somewhere different.

13 APRIL

This is a good weekend to invest in your home or family, and if you're travelling to invest in yourself and some self-nurturing.

14 APRIL

You'll enjoy being outgoing and upbeat. A change of pace or unexpected guest or visit will be revitalising.

15 APRIL

Be prepared to review matters at work, and if you've overspent in a budget it's time to review your finances. An expert or adviser will be useful, especially health-wise.

16 APRIL

There are therapeutic aspects to the day. Be sure to look after yourself and your health. Avoid taking other people's random comments personally.

17 APRIL

This is a romantic day ideal for a treat. If you're single you may meet someone new who is strangely familiar.

18 APRIL

An optimistic approach to difficult or unpredictable circumstances will work in your favour and pave the way for better communications.

19 APRIL

The next four weeks will be ideal for establishing more stability financially and in your personal life. Key news or a get-together may be unexpected.

20 APRIL

You'll enjoy adding a little variety and spice to your weekend but may also be surprised by circumstances, so take things one step at a time.

21 APRIL

Your help and advice will be needed, and you may be surprised by developments or a change of scenery. Avoid a battle of wills.

22 APRIL

This is a good day for talks and/or get-togethers, despite circumstances being out of the ordinary.

23 APRIL

A calm, peaceful approach to circumstances will work well for you. Be prepared to take the initiative.

24 APRIL

The Scorpio full moon will shine a light on your collaborations and joint duties. This is a good day to discuss financial and personal commitments.

25 APRIL

As the Mercury retrograde phase ends you may receive key financial or personal news. It's a lovely day for a reunion.

26 APRIL

An optimistic outlook to your ventures at work and in your own time will be productive, and you'll be happy with the result.

27 APRIL

It's a good day to invest in yourself and those you love. You may be drawn to a little retail therapy but must avoid overspending. Romance could thrive.

28 APRIL

You'll enjoy indulging in creature comforts, the arts and romance. The spiritually minded may reach an epiphany.

29 APRIL

As Venus enters Taurus communications will become steadier. You'll be drawn to the arts and romance and may be a little forgetful.

30 APRIL

Mars in Aries for the next few weeks will bring out your assertive and proactive sides, which will help get things done, but you must avoid appearing bossy.

May

1 MAY

You or someone else may be seeing things emotionally. Be calm and patient for the best results, although you may need to stand your ground but without becoming aggressive.

2 MAY

You're likely to change your mind about a personal or financial investment. Consider your options and obtain expert help if necessary.

3 MAY

You're powerful and dynamic at the moment but risk appearing rash and domineering, so be sure to maintain perspective.

4 MAY

Trust your instincts and be prepared to invest in projects and people that make sense to you.

5 MAY

A lovely relationship can blossom. If you're hoping to improve your finances or position this is a good day to take the initiative.

6 MAY

Your work and projects are likely to succeed but you must be prepared for hard work, especially if you wish to change some aspects of what you do.

7 MAY

Someone you rely on and trust will prove their loyalty. This is a good day for a mini health or financial review. Your help may be in demand.

8 MAY

The Taurus new moon is a good time to turn a corner with a significant relationship and put it on a firmer footing. You may be drawn to updating a communications device or vehicle.

9 MAY

The Gemini moon brings out your independent and fun-loving qualities, and you'll enjoy a reunion or favourite activity.

10 MAY

A social get-together or the chance to spend more time with friends and family will appeal, and you'll enjoy a short trip.

11 MAY

There is a therapeutic feel to the day that makes it ideal for revitalising your health and appearance. You'll relish a reunion. Romance could thrive.

12 MAY

The Cancerian moon brings your appreciation of your friends and family and time to relax into the frame.

13 MAY

A surprise or change of plan could work out to be beneficial. You may experience a financial or confidence boost.

14 MAY

A productive, busy day will see you in your element. You may need to hold the reins more than usual at work.

15 MAY

You'll gain a more even keel in certain relationships and communications, which you'll appreciate over the coming three weeks.

16 MAY

A colleague, friend or partner will prove to be helpful, especially if you need to bounce some ideas around.

17 MAY

Pluto in your sign is encouraging you to make changes in your life, but you must avoid rushing. Plan ahead to avoid travel delays and mix-ups.

18 MAY

A change of pace or of place brings unusual circumstances. You're likely to be pleasantly surprised but must avoid making rash decisions.

19 MAY

This is a romantic day ideal for a trip somewhere beautiful and enjoying romance, the arts and creativity. It's also a good day for spiritual development.

20 MAY

You'll be drawn to getting in touch with someone special. Some get-togethers will be unavoidable. You'll enjoy pleasant company but must not give in to impulsiveness.

21 MAY

This is a good time to forge ahead with positive plans to alter aspects of your life you'd love to improve, so take the initiative.

22 MAY

This is an excellent time to make changes as your efforts are likely to take, even if you need to cover old ground.

23 MAY

The full moon in Sagittarius will encourage you to broaden your horizons. You may be drawn to travelling and at least to booking a trip. Be inspired and aim for your goals.

24 MAY

An active, adventurous approach to life will encourage you to be outspoken and positive. A trip or meeting will spotlight your good communication skills.

25 MAY

A change of environment and the chance to revisit an old haunt will be appealing. Romance with an ex may be rekindled. The arts, music and creativity will thrive.

26 MAY

As Jupiter enters Gemini your focus will go increasingly towards exciting ways to brighten up your communications, relationships and travel options.

27 MAY

Be prepared to collaborate with a friend, group or organisation. You have good communication skills right now that will prove useful if you're under pressure.

28 MAY

This is a good day for negotiations, meetings and financial discussions. You may be prepared to make a commitment.

29 MAY

You may be prone to impulse buys if you're shopping. Avoid taking the random comments of other people to heart and minor scrapes and bumps caused by rushing.

30 MAY

If you need expert advice or help it will be available, so be sure to reach out. Your help and advice may also be in demand.

31 MAY

The Pisces moon will bring out your idealistic side and you may wish that things were different. However, you are also realistic and will find ways to work with the positives in your life.

June

1 JUNE

You'll appreciate a change of environment or pace, and you may be drawn to spontaneity in your activities. Just avoid impulse buys as you may regret them!

2 JUNE

You have certain duties and responsibilities and will fulfil these, enabling you to enjoy relaxing afterwards.

3 JUNE

A chatty or busy day could be super productive and meetings are likely to go well, so take the initiative.

4 JUNE

Developments at home or due to a change of environment will be uplifting. It's a good day to take a short trip and for a DIY project and to enjoying a treat. Romance could thrive.

5 JUNE

Be prepared to be practical with various arrangements, especially regarding travel and work.

6 JUNE

The new moon in Gemini will help you turn a corner, especially with a domestic or personal matter. You may be drawn to updating a communications device or repairing a vehicle.

7 JUNE

The Cancerian moon will bring out your nurturing qualities, and you'll appreciate the opportunity to self-nurture and spend time with someone you love.

8 JUNE

You'll discover whether you've overestimated someone. A domestic expense or personal commitment may require focus. Avoid overspending. Look for peaceful ways ahead if conflict arises.

9 JUNE

Be practical with finances and look for ways to budget and plan ahead, especially domestically.

10 JUNE

The Leo moon signals a productive day. Be inspired and avoid rushing.

11 JUNE

This is a good day to mend bridges with someone, especially if you've argued recently. You may need to pay a debt or have one repaid.

12 JUNE

Be prepared to be tactful, especially at work and regarding finances. Avoid traffic and communication delays by planning well ahead.

13 JUNE

An unusual trip or guest will provide a reason to pull out all the stops. You may receive an unexpected compliment or financial boost.

14 JUNE

Key news at home or to do with family will be worth focusing on. Be prepared to consider the big picture.

15 JUNE

You'll enjoy being spontaneous and spending time with like-minded people. You may be drawn to making changes at home or in your environment.

16 JUNE

Think laterally, especially if you would like to bring more variety and spice into your life.

17 JUNE

A creative, more self-nurturing phase is about to begin, so be prepared to look after yourself and your interests. Just avoid financial and emotional gambling.

18 JUNE

You may be prone to misunderstandings and mistakes, so be sure to double-check details and avoid making rash decisions.

19 JUNE

You may be inclined to be reactive to other people's feelings, although your reliable and steadfast input may be what is needed.

20 JUNE

You'll appreciate the opportunity to devote more time to friends, family and creative projects in the next four weeks. Avoid forgetfulness today.

21 JUNE

You'll appreciate the opportunity to review your finances and get back on track with someone whose points of view you admire.

22 JUNE

The Capricorn full moon will spotlight your social life and the groups and friendships you invest in. You may need to choose between priorities as a trip or visit will take some focus.

23 JUNE

Fundamental agreement may be needed, especially in a family or personal circumstance, so be sure to look for common ground as opposed to entering into conflict.

24 JUNE

The Aquarian moon brings out your inventive and resourceful qualities. Just avoid feeling pressured into certain decisions but, equally, avoid being stubborn.

25 JUNE

Someone you admire or feel close to will have a positive influence over some of your decisions and may be able to help with a personal or financial matter.

26 JUNE

This is a good day to make a commitment to a work or financial plan. However, you must double-check that you're not crossing any lines regarding your principles.

27 JUNE

The moon in Pisces will be inspiring as it will make your intuition stronger, enabling you to make careful decisions and invest in people and projects you admire.

28 JUNE

Be prepared for a little give and take, especially at work and regarding finances. Someone may need your help, and if you need advice it will be available.

29 JUNE

This is a productive and upbeat day that is ideal for taking the initiative with chores. You may be prone to overspending or overindulging, which you'll regret.

30 JUNE

Being spontaneous will take you somewhere new. You may enjoy an unexpected trip or visit, or bump into or hear from an old friend.

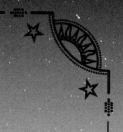

July

1 JULY

A practical, methodical approach to work and chores will be productive, especially as some developments may be unexpected.

2 JULY

Look for the middle ground and find ways to collaborate. Check whether any disagreements or mysteries that arise can be solved with a little research.

3 JULY

You may feel strongly about certain matters that could make a meeting feel intense. Bear in mind that this is a constructive, productive day and be positive.

4 JULY

This is a good day to decide how you could improve your personal life and creative input. It's also a good day for research. Avoid gambling.

5 JULY

The Cancerian new moon will kick-start a fresh phase in a personal, creative or family circumstance. It's a good day to take the initiative to create more stability and security.

6 JULY

Be adaptable about your plans as you may need to change them. Someone may need your help, and if you need expert advice it will be available.

7 JULY

The Leo moon will encourage you to be positive and proactive, prompting activities such as sports, self-development and the improvement of your appearance.

8 JULY

This is a good day to talk and for meetings. If you're single you may meet someone who seems familiar even if you don't know them. Be adaptable for the best results.

9 JULY

The next two days are excellent for collaborations and being proactive with your chores and favourite activities.

10 JULY

The Virgo moon may bring out your inner critic, so be sure to avoid appearing critical of someone when in reality you wish to support them.

11 JULY

This is a super industrious day, so be sure to work hard as you're likely to gain the results you're looking for. You may enjoy a financial or confidence boost.

12 JULY

There are passionate aspects to the day, and key developments could signal long-term change. Just avoid arguments.

13 JULY

A fair and equal approach to chores and activities this weekend will ensure everyone gets to do what they want without major stress.

14 JULY

This could still be a fiery or intense time, so be sure to avoid igniting contentious topics if possible.

15 JULY

You may be surprised by news or an abrupt change of plan. Be prepared to pitch in or ask for help if necessary.

16 JULY

Trust your intuition. A change of pace or of place will mean you must be a little more instinctive than usual.

17 JULY

The moon at the zenith of your chart will encourage you to be adventurous. Just avoid going too far outside your comfort zone to avoid disappointment.

18 JULY

You'll enjoy a pleasant change of pace. A trip somewhere may involve a surprise or impromptu get-together.

19 JULY

There are therapeutic aspects to the day. You'll enjoy being somewhere beautiful or being with someone you admire or love.

20 JULY

A trip or get-together will bring out your chatty and sociable sides. You may enjoy a reunion or return to an old haunt.

21 JULY

The full moon in Capricorn suggests a fresh daily routine, work or health schedule will appeal. Avoid misunderstandings and delays by planning ahead.

22 JULY

As the sun enters Leo your relationships and communications will become a focus. This is a good day for a short trip or get-together.

23 JULY

This is a good time to make changes in your usual work or health routine. Some developments may be intense, so be prepared to take things one step at a time.

24 JULY

Be inspired and guided by your intuition. Just ensure you keep someone you must get along with in the loop to avoid mix-ups.

25 JULY

Double-check you're on the same page as someone else, especially if confusion or misunderstandings arise.

26 JULY

You're likely to be productive and achieve your goals as long as you avoid rushing and pressuring someone.

27 JULY

Be prepared to go the extra mile and you will achieve goals even if you seem to encounter obstacles. Be super clear to avoid misunderstandings.

28 JULY

You'll appreciate the opportunity to relax and enjoy good company or a lovely environment.

29 JULY

A quirky outlook and lateral thinking will help you overcome any minor hurdles, so think outside the box.

30 JULY

There are therapeutic aspects to the day that make it a good one to try something uplifting. You may experience a financial or confidence boost.

31 JULY

A social or work get-together will get you in touch with someone who can be very supportive or helpful. You may reach a goal.

August

1 AUGUST

Be prepared to self-nurture, especially if you feel a relationship has been complex. Avoid raking over old coals.

2 AUGUST

You may be surprised by developments. Avoid pressuring someone and be prepared to take the pressure off yourself.

3 AUGUST

The lead-up to the Leo new moon is a good time to consider how you might be more proactive to achieve the outcome you wish for both in your personal life and at work.

4 AUGUST

The Leo new moon spotlights a new chapter in a personal relationship for January Aquarians and at work for February Aquarians. Take the initiative but avoid mix-ups.

5 AUGUST

Someone close such as a work colleague may have news for you regarding work or finances. Be prepared to research circumstances.

6 AUGUST

Now that Mercury is retrograde you'll gain the chance to review circumstances in more detail and, if necessary, rethink recent decisions.

7 AUGUST

You'll enjoy spending time with upbeat, active people and doing what you love. A work, domestic or family situation could thrive.

8 AUGUST

You'll enjoy a reunion and may receive news from a business or personal partner.

9 AUGUST

Your analytical and perceptive qualities will be useful, especially if you're unsure about a decision. Be practical.

10 AUGUST

Hard work may be required with a commitment to someone else or with chores. Rest assured: you will reach your goals.

11 AUGUST

This is a good day for relaxation and spending time with those you love. You may be drawn to self-development, the arts, music and romance.

12 AUGUST

You like to be inspired by your ventures and will appreciate the opportunity to take some time out for your extracurricular activities.

13 AUGUST

An optimistic, dynamic approach at work and in your personal life will be infectious and could even overcome minor obstacles.

14 AUGUST

Be prepared to review recent decisions open-mindedly. You may experience a sudden development at home or with family. Avoid impulse spending.

15 AUGUST

There are therapeutic aspects to the day. You'll benefit from discussing matters with those they concern and must avoid contributing to a mystery.

16 AUGUST

While some domestic matters will require swift action, Rome wasn't built in a day so you will need to be patient. Avoid minor bumps and scrapes.

17 AUGUST

A grounded, practical and earthy approach to accomplishing chores and getting on top of meetings and paperwork will be productive.

18 AUGUST

Someone is likely to surprise you or may be surprised by your news. Avoid misunderstandings and traffic delays by planning ahead.

19 AUGUST

The Aquarian full moon will illuminate where you could make constructive changes in your life, as news from someone close or a meeting will be significant.

20 AUGUST

Consider the most practical path forward while maintaining open communication channels and not making rash decisions.

21 AUGUST

Be prepared to dream a little but avoid seeing circumstances through rose-coloured glasses and being impulsive.

22 AUGUST

The sun in Virgo over the next four weeks will spotlight your shared duties and space and finances. Be prepared to be super clear about your intentions in these areas.

23 AUGUST

If you have fundamental differences with someone you collaborate with you'll find this out. This aside, it's a good day for improving relationships.

24 AUGUST

You'll enjoy sprucing up your home and spending time with friends and family. However, you must avoid contentious topics if possible. Your help may be required.

25 AUGUST

You'll enjoy spending time with like-minded people and could build a solid basis for your relationship. Just avoid arguing over minor matters.

26 AUGUST

You'll be ready to move ahead with certain domestic decisions. It's a good time to be thinking laterally about your various projects and investments.

27 AUGUST

A friend, colleague or partner may surprise you. It's a good day to be spontaneous, enjoying a trip or adding a little variety to your usual schedule.

28 AUGUST

This is potentially a super-romantic day, but it is also conducive to forgetfulness. You may receive key news from someone important.

29 AUGUST

If you'd like to make changes within an agreement either in your personal life or with a group or organisation, this is the day to do it!

30 AUGUST

An intuitive approach to what needs doing will be successful; you will be in the right place at the right time. You may experience a second wind this evening.

31 AUGUST

A spontaneous visit or get-together will be fun. You may enjoy investing in your home, family or domestic décor.

September

1 SEPTEMBER

You'll appreciate the opportunity to take some time out to do something that improves your self-esteem, confidence, sense of self and a relationship.

2 SEPTEMBER

It's a good time to reconsider how you go about your daily life so that it brings maximum options for better health and vitality.

3 SEPTEMBER

This new moon in Virgo will kick-start a fresh phase in your shared commitments, such as duties and financial responsibilities. Be prepared to commit to a pragmatic plan.

4 SEPTEMBER

You'll enjoy a lovely reunion or the chance to reconfigure some of your duties and plans. This is a good time to focus on self-nurturing, creativity and family.

5 SEPTEMBER

You have an analytical mind and currently this will be useful, but you must avoid overanalysing and lead from the heart a little.

6 SEPTEMBER

You'll appreciate the chance to connect with someone you prefer to see eye to eye with, even if on occasion your views differ.

7 SEPTEMBER

You'll need to feel passionate about what you do otherwise you may feel lacklustre. Take the cue from someone who is motivational and follow their example.

8 SEPTEMBER

It's a good day to make a commitment, so look carefully into your options. However, some communications may be confusing, so be sure to go with the facts.

9 SEPTEMBER

As Mercury enters Virgo you'll be drawn to focusing on someone close and your relationship with them. Avoid a power struggle.

10 SEPTEMBER

A positive, dynamic and optimistic approach will do you credit and could serve to create a breakthrough in a stuck circumstance.

11 SEPTEMBER

Consider shared finances and ventures carefully and work together towards a common goal. Just to be sure your goals are the same.

12 SEPTEMBER

Some of your deeper thoughts and feelings may break through, surprising you. Someone may seem critical or antagonistic, so be sure to avoid arguments.

13 SEPTEMBER

Today's moon encourages you to take things one step at a time, which is fortunate, as making rash decisions and speaking without forethought could land you in hot water.

14 SEPTEMBER

It's an ideal day to take the weight off your feet and encourage someone close to relax as well. However, sporty Aquarians will benefit from activities you love.

15 SEPTEMBER

This is a lovely day for get-togethers in your personal life and at work. You may be drawn to retail therapy but must avoid overspending.

16 SEPTEMBER

This is a good day for a mini financial review and to double-check whether you're on track with your financial and emotional investments.

17 SEPTEMBER

You'll discover whether your expectations have exceeded reality, in which case you'll gain the opportunity to set things right over the coming days and weeks.

18 SEPTEMBER

The partial lunar eclipse supermoon in Pisces spotlights your personal and financial investments. Be prepared to make realistic commitments to a solid plan of action.

19 SEPTEMBER

You'll enjoy a spontaneous get-together or the chance to go somewhere different. Someone close may surprise you.

20 SEPTEMBER

Think laterally about your financial and personal circumstances, as you may find a fresh way to share time or resources.

21 SEPTEMBER

On the one hand romance could thrive, but on the other you must be prepared to see someone else's point of view to avoid misunderstandings. Avoid overspending.

22 SEPTEMBER

As the sun enters Libra it's a lovely time to make changes in your daily routine that better support you and those you love. Be sure you all agree on arrangements.

23 SEPTEMBER

Venus in Scorpio will bring your way a passionate and potentially feisty phase, but it will be a good time to focus on shared ventures and investments.

24 SEPTEMBER

Someone close is likely to surprise you, and you may enjoy an impromptu get-together or a trip.

25 SEPTEMBER

This is a lovely day for self-development and introspection. A colleague or partner is likely to have news for you. Avoid forgetfulness and being easily influenced.

26 SEPTEMBER

You'll be drawn to looking for balance in your life and relationships and this is certainly a good time to discuss your ideas, both at work and in your personal life.

27 SEPTEMBER

The moon in Leo over the next two days will motivate you to be optimistic and outgoing, which is ideal for extracurricular activities such as sports.

28 SEPTEMBER

You'll enjoy the company of upbeat and positive people. You'll be drawn to any activity that improves your self-confidence, such as changing your appearance.

29 SEPTEMBER

A reunion or news from the past could be ideal. However, if it causes confusion be sure to carefully research your options.

30 SEPTEMBER

This is a good time to kick-start a venture such as a work project. If you need advice from an expert, for example a lawyer, this is a good day to reach out.

October

1 OCTOBER

The days in the run-up to an eclipse can feel intense, and this is certainly a good day to set an intention to find more peace and balance in your relationships.

2 OCTOBER

The solar eclipse in Libra will help you turn a corner, especially in your personal life and shared responsibilities and finances. Look for the most balanced option.

3 OCTOBER

Meetings and communications are likely to proceed relatively well, especially if you're looking for direction from someone who has your back.

4 OCTOBER

You'll appreciate the opportunity to consider and put in place inspired yet fun plans that will enable you to thrive.

5 OCTOBER

You'll feel passionate about your activities and the people you associate with. Trust your intuition and avoid making rash decisions.

6 OCTOBER

This is an excellent day for creativity, self-development, music and the arts. However, you must avoid complex or angry talks as they could quickly escalate to conflict.

7 OCTOBER

The moon at the zenith of your chart will bring out your adventurous side, enabling you to accomplish your goals.

8 OCTOBER

You'll enjoy get-togethers and progress with your various ventures. It's a good day for a mini financial review. Avoid taking the random comments of other people personally.

9 OCTOBER

A progressive, upbeat approach at work will be effective. Your ventures will succeed, but you must avoid overinvesting both financially and emotionally. Be practical.

10 OCTOBER

The Capricorn moon helps you keep your feet on the ground and will support your efforts to create a balanced outlook in your personal life and at work.

11 OCTOBER

The combination of your innovative and practical abilities produces your unique outlook on life. You may need to persuade someone of the merits of your ideas.

12 OCTOBER

You may be easily led, so be sure to determine what you want. If you encounter delays, rest assured you will nevertheless accomplish tasks.

13 OCTOBER

As Mercury enters Scorpio you'll feel expressive in the coming weeks and may be surprised by the thoughts and feelings that arise today. Avoid arguments.

14 OCTOBER

A surprise needn't put you off your stride, but you must steer clear of making rash decisions. Avoid taking someone's feelings personally unless criticism is merited.

15 OCTOBER

You're in a position to help someone, but if initially they don't want your help it's important you be available as support should they reach out. Avoid daydreaming.

16 OCTOBER

This is an excellent day to dream a little and pursue your goals. You may enjoy a trip or favourite activity and could boost your finances.

17 OCTOBER

The full moon supermoon in Aries will spotlight a decision that is best approached with those your choices affect in mind. An adventure or trip is likely to appeal to you.

18 OCTOBER

You'll be drawn to enjoying a little luxury or a treat. If you do encounter a difference of opinion, avoid stubbornness.

19 OCTOBER

A lovely change of pace or of place will be enjoyable, and if you encounter an obstacle then rest assured you can overcome it.

20 OCTOBER

You'll feel inspired by a person or activity, and if you're unsure of your decisions then trust your intuition. Avoid overspending as you'll regret it.

21 OCTOBER

You'll appreciate the opportunity to get your feet on the ground at home, with family or in your personal life. Just avoid crossing swords over minor matters at work.

22 OCTOBER

As the sun enters Scorpio your attention will go to collaborations and relationships over the next four weeks. Avoid arguments as they could quickly escalate.

23 OCTOBER

It's a good day for talks or a meeting with someone special such as a mentor, teacher, adviser or romantic partner.

24 OCTOBER

This will be a productive day, especially if you channel strong feelings into work as opposed to unnecessary arguments or discord.

25 OCTOBER

Be prepared to take the lead and be productive. You'll enjoy a change of pace or of place. Avoid impulsiveness.

26 OCTOBER

An optimistic approach, especially to someone close, will put you in a strong position, but you must avoid appearing zealous.

27 OCTOBER

While you may feel expressive and wish to connect on a deeper level with someone you care about they may feel sensitive, so avoid misunderstandings.

28 OCTOBER

You'll enjoy music, the arts and romance but may be a little idealistic, so be sure to avoid assuming everyone is on the same page as you. Avoid arguments.

29 OCTOBER

A view to maintaining a balanced outlook, especially towards someone you share duties or commitments with, will go far.

30 OCTOBER

A trip or meeting may take you somewhere new. Plan ahead to avoid delays. You may be surprised by unexpected news. Avoid making rash decisions.

31 OCTOBER

Happy Hallowe'en! You'll enjoy a fun event and a change in your usual routine. The arts, romance and music will thrive.

November

1 NOVEMBER

The Scorpio new moon will encourage you to consider better ways of improving communications and relationships, starting today. You'll enjoy a productive or inspiring day.

2 NOVEMBER

This is an excellent weekend to focus on mending bridges with someone you've argued with. A trip or visit may be therapeutic.

3 NOVEMBER

You may be drawn to a little retail therapy but must avoid overspending. A new look may be therapeutic. A change of routine may be tense, so avoid arguments.

4 NOVEMBER

You're beginning a more upbeat, adventurous phase at work in which collaborations and teamwork will signal success.

5 NOVEMBER

A step-by-step approach to work and your projects will be productive. Avoid rushing.

6 NOVEMBER

The next two days are ideal for working collaboratively with other people, so if you need advice be sure to look for it. Your wisdom and experience will also be in demand.

7 NOVEMBER

This is a good day for get-togethers and for travel somewhere different or adventurous. Be positive.

8 NOVEMBER

A change of pace or news at work will require an adjustment. Be persistent and you will achieve your goals. Double-check your finances to avoid making mistakes.

9 NOVEMBER

You'll find out whether you've overestimated a particular circumstance, which will enable you to set things right. Avoid overindulging and overspending.

10 NOVEMBER

The moon in Pisces will encourage you to take time out to relax and enjoy favourite activities, but you must avoid seeing things idealistically.

11 NOVEMBER

Venus will put the attention on your work, health and well-being. Take a little time to focus on what makes you tick.

12 NOVEMBER

A financial, personal or work matter will require extra attention to avoid misunderstandings and frustrations. Be patient and you will attain your goals.

13 NOVEMBER

This is a good time to focus on reviewing and repairing any past mistakes. Avoid feeling super sensitive about other people's opinions. Be positive.

14 NOVEMBER

The lead-up to a full moon can be intense so be sure to pace yourself and be practical, especially with communications and meetings.

15 NOVEMBER

The full moon in Taurus spotlights communications, travel and relationships. Consider whether being more flexible is constructive. You may be surprised by news or a meeting or trip.

16 NOVEMBER

A change of pace or of place will include some surprises. Be prepared to see matters from another point of view.

17 NOVEMBER

This is a good day for communications, especially with family or concerning your home or property. A trip may be significant.

18 NOVEMBER

A key decision concerning work and how this fits in with your home life may be necessary. A trip or news will require your full attention.

19 NOVEMBER

This is a good day for the arts, music and romance. It's also a good day for a health or beauty appointment. You may enjoy a financial or confidence boost.

20 NOVEMBER

As Pluto re-enters your sign you're ready to make considerable changes. Plan ahead. You may be surprised by news or a change of pace.

21 NOVEMBER

As the sun enters Sagittarius you'll enjoy a more adventurous and outgoing four weeks, starting today with an upbeat get-together or news.

22 NOVEMBER

This is a good day for a mini financial review. You may experience a financial improvement. It's also a good day to make a commitment to a friend, group or person.

23 NOVEMBER

A meeting, news or circumstances will proceed under its own steam, so if you're unhappy with developments be prepared to apply the brakes.

24 NOVEMBER

You'll appreciate the opportunity to spend time doing what you love. It's a good day to clear a backlog of chores and for gardening.

25 NOVEMBER

Be prepared to work towards your goals, as you can make progress despite some delays. Tie up loose ends today to avoid having to make changes over the next few weeks.

26 NOVEMBER

You may receive key news at work or from a friend or organisation. Be prepared to overcome misunderstandings. You'll enjoy a lovely get-together or development.

27 NOVEMBER

There is a dynamic quality to the day that makes it ideal for getting ahead at work and with your projects, so take the initiative.

28 NOVEMBER

This is a good day to push ahead with chores to get them done. However, you may encounter a difference of opinion that stems from contrasting values.

29 NOVEMBER

You'll appreciate the help or advice of a good friend or organisation. It's a good day for a health or beauty appointment.

30 NOVEMBER

You'll enjoy putting your back into your projects and ventures, feeling both adventurous and willing to step into new territory.

December

1 DECEMBER

The Sagittarian new moon signals the start of a fresh venture or interest such as study, travel or sports. Some January-born Aquarians may be turning a corner at work or in your status.

2 DECEMBER

This is a good day for talks that aim to remedy a past situation. It's also a good day for a mini financial review and a health appointment.

3 DECEMBER

You have your feet on the ground and are able to see your choices clearly, so be diligent with your decisions. Your realistic attitude is appreciated.

4 DECEMBER

You won't always agree with everyone, and a little give and take will be necessary at work or home or at both. You'll enjoy a reunion or the repayment of a debt.

5 DECEMBER

The Aquarian moon will encourage you to see life's peculiarities from a fresh perspective, enabling you to adopt a different approach to serious matters.

6 DECEMBER

You may experience a change of routine or focus at work. A review or reunion will be significant.

7 DECEMBER

Developments at home or work will encourage you to find the middle ground. A reunion or return to an old haunt will be significant or intense.

8 DECEMBER

Be prepared to focus a little more than usual on your health over the coming weeks and devise a supportive routine.

9 DECEMBER

A busy or motivated day keeps you engaged. You may enjoy a get-together at work or with someone special.

10 DECEMBER

This is a constructive day that is ideal for getting chores completed. There is also a therapeutic quality that is ideal for strategic thinking and overcoming obstacles.

11 DECEMBER

Be prepared to invest in yourself and your projects as your dynamic approach will take you far. Just avoid making rash decisions.

12 DECEMBER

Romance could truly thrive, especially if you were born at the end of January. Those born in February will find this a busy and potentially intense day, so pace yourself.

13 DECEMBER

Despite this being Friday the 13th you'll enjoy a reunion or may receive positive financial, health or work news.

14 DECEMBER

It's a lovely weekend for travel and visits. You may enjoy a reunion; just be sure to avoid sensitive topics.

15 DECEMBER

The full moon will spotlight personal and domestic matters. Be prepared for a change of plan or unusual developments. You may receive health news.

16 DECEMBER

Trust your instincts, as you will gain insight into someone special and devise a clever and constructive plan of action.

17 DECEMBER

Be prepared to see someone else's perspective but avoid allowing them to distract you from your goals and chores.

18 DECEMBER

As an adventurous and innovative person you like to entertain new ideas. However, today you must avoid daydreaming and being easily misled.

19 DECEMBER

This is a good day to make a commitment to a plan of action or person. You may experience a financial improvement or confidence boost.

20 DECEMBER

This is a good day to discuss domestic and personal matters, as reason can prevail. Some Aquarians will enjoy a trip to an old haunt or reunion.

21 DECEMBER

As the sun steps into Capricorn this is the solstice. Over the next four weeks you'll be drawn to being more practical about work, the past and health.

22 DECEMBER

A lovely reunion and the chance to kick up your heels a little and enjoy some festive cheer will be enjoyable. You may positively transform your environment.

23 DECEMBER

You can't expect to get on with everyone all the time. An unavoidable connection or relationship is best approached calmly.

24 DECEMBER

You may enjoy a little retail therapy; just avoid overspending. A trip or meeting may encounter delays, so be patient. Nevertheless, there is a therapeutic aspect to the day.

25 DECEMBER

Merry Christmas! Take the pressure off yourself and allow others to help you organise and enjoy the day. You'll appreciate the collaboration and support.

26 DECEMBER

A change of ambience at home or due to a trip will be exciting, but you must avoid delays by planning ahead. Some communications will require patience.

27 DECEMBER

You may be drawn to the sales. A short trip or meeting may be delayed or complex, so be ready to take things one step at a time.

28 DECEMBER

Be prepared to be adaptable with arrangements as you may have a sudden or unexpected change of schedule. Someone may surprise you.

29 DECEMBER

The Sagittarius moon at the zenith of your chart will encourage you to be outgoing and active. You'll be drawn to travelling, favourite interests and get-togethers.

30 DECEMBER

The new moon in Capricorn will kick-start a fresh phase in your social life and association with certain groups and organisations. You're ready to turn a corner in your daily routine.

31 DECEMBER

Happy New Year! Being health conscious will be one of your focuses as you place intentions for the New Year. A get-together or event will have an uplifting effect.

PISCES

19 February - 20 March

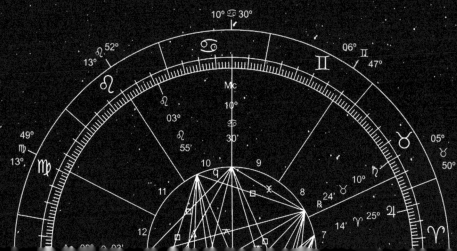

FINANCES

Secure your savings and be prepared to put your finances to work! Look for solid investments if possible, and avoid risking your hard-earned cash by gambling. The first quarter of the year and November are ideal times to seek out experts and advice, and to research how best to save and invest. In mid-April you may be tempted to overspend or invest indiscriminately, so be careful then to avoid making rash decisions. During the third quarter you may once again be tempted to let your finances take whichever road they want, so you must avoid potentially exposing yourself to loss. Be proactive about money management.

HEALTH

Saturn in your sign throughout the year will encourage you to stick to a strong, healthy fitness schedule, but you must avoid making your health routine too strict or you'll be tempted to break out of it and ruin all your hard work. You may also be tempted to overwork or overexercise, both of which could damage your health, so be prepared to see your health in a holistic framework and embrace tried and trusted regimes that suit you personally. The first quarter and November are the best months to focus on improving your health, as your efforts are likely to succeed then.

LOVE LIFE

Neptune in Pisces until March 2025 brings romance front and centre stage, making this a wonderful year to enjoy your love life. Saturn in your sign for the entire year indicates you're going to be looking for a stable and steady year in your personal life. Just ensure you don't forgo spontaneous and joyful developments in favour of living life safely in the hope of protecting yourself from disappointment. If you do you'll risk missing out on some of life's miracles and delights. Peak times for socialising include January, February, November and December, and romance will be on your mind in March, April, August, September and early December.

CAREER

You're ready to alter how you manage your daily routine, which will inevitably affect your career. You like to be adventurous, and this could be the year to step up to a fresh level career-wise. You may consider, for example, working from home or finding time to change track in your daily work schedule. Be prepared to look outside the box at your various options. You're also likely to embrace working with technology, devices or gadgets that require a little instruction or even a new skill set, so be prepared to study or learn different aspects of your existing career.

HOME LIFE

A great deal of focus will be on your home, family or a property from the end of May until early October. You may be drawn to a DIY project, renovating or even to a move. Be prepared to find the balance between home and work in 2024, otherwise you may feel you're not giving either area your full attention and this could lead to feelings of disappointment. Instead, find the time to arrange your home life so it suits you in your relaxation time. During the last quarter of the year you'll be in a position to review how you feel about your domestic commitments and your home life in general, which will enable you to move forward once again in 2025.

January

1 JANUARY

Happy New Year! You may be torn between your duties and favourite activities. Choose wisely, as this could be a theme for the year. Start the way you mean to carry on!

2 JANUARY

While you'd much rather dream a little your work, travel or other duties are likely to take your attention to more everyday pursuits.

3 JANUARY

A little give and take will certainly oil the wheels of relationships. This is a good day for a mini financial review, especially if you have the urge to splurge at the sales.

4 JANUARY

Be practical with your various plans, especially regarding your career and finances, for the best results.

5 JANUARY

This is a good time to consider your circumstances from a financial and practical point of view.

6 JANUARY

Be tactful, especially as someone in your midst can be sensitive. Avoid taking random comments personally unless criticism is merited.

7 JANUARY

You'll enjoy doing something different. Trust your instincts with the feelings of someone close. You'll also enjoy being creative. Self-development and spirituality will appeal.

8 JANUARY

The opportunity to expand your horizons and enjoy a trip or learning experience or simply to relax will appeal. This is a good time for study and self-development.

9 JANUARY

You'll find out whether you've over- or underestimated a circumstance. Watch out for misunderstanding and traffic delays.

10 JANUARY

You'll appreciate a coincidence or the chance to broaden your mind and meet new people. You may hear from someone unexpectedly.

11 JANUARY

The Capricorn new moon will kick-start a fresh chapter in your social and networking circles. You may join a new group. There are therapeutic and uplifting aspects to the day.

12 JANUARY

This is a productive day that is ideal for getting work done. You can make great progress with your projects and may experience a financial or confidence boost.

13 JANUARY

You'll enjoy a reunion and a chance to discuss important plans. It's a good day to boost your health, well-being and appearance.

14 JANUARY

You may encounter an unexpected hurdle at work or must consider a project from a new point of view, which in the long run will be advantageous.

15 JANUARY

The moon in your own sign brings out your artistic, creative qualities. However, you must avoid being idealistic and forgetful.

16 JANUARY

This is a good day for meetings, the arts, romance and socialising. You may receive good news from a group or friend.

17 JANUARY

You have strong intuition and may pick up on someone's vulnerabilities without realising it. You're in a strong position to take the lead at work or with a venture.

18 JANUARY

A meeting at work is likely to go well. If you're going to an interview you may make a solid agreement or arrangement.

19 JANUARY

It's another good day for meetings. You must avoid expecting perfect circumstances or you may be disappointed. Be realistic.

20 JANUARY

You'll enjoy focusing on your health, well-being and appearance and may enjoy a reunion.

21 JANUARY

You'll appreciate a constructive and progressive point of view moving forward, especially to do with health, well-being and domestic chores.

22 JANUARY

A talkative and busy day will merit a focused approach to avoid lateness and making mistakes.

23 JANUARY

As Venus enters Capricorn, over the coming weeks you'll adopt a down-to-earth, practical approach at work that will enable you to accomplish tasks.

24 JANUARY

The lead-up to the full moon could be intense, so be prepared to keep your professional hat on at work and avoid unnecessary arguments at home.

25 JANUARY

The Leo full moon will spotlight key personal and family matters. Avoid rushing, as minor accidents and mistakes could occur. Be prepared to seek clarity if some matters are unclear.

26 JANUARY

Once again, be prepared to avoid misunderstandings by being super clear. Avoid taking the random comments of other people personally. You may benefit from the help of an expert.

27 JANUARY

Key news and meetings are best met with an open mind. Be prepared to see another person's point of view.

28 JANUARY

This is a good day to make a commitment to a friend, group or organisation, as your plans are likely to go well as long as you've researched the variables.

29 JANUARY

An unexpected development will keep you on your toes. You may bump into an old friend or hear from someone from out of the blue.

30 JANUARY

A balanced, productive approach to relationships will encourage progress, especially with someone who can be a little exasperating.

31 JANUARY

You'll enjoy spending time with like-minded people but will not suffer fools gladly and must be prepared to be patient.

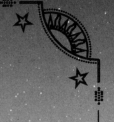

February

1 FEBRUARY

Teamwork and collaboration will be productive, so be sure to delegate chores if you need an extra pair of hands and to make compromises with colleagues.

2 FEBRUARY

This is a good day for talks, meetings, socialising and networking. You may be drawn to a new group or organisation.

3 FEBRUARY

Your intuition is in top form, so be sure to trust your gut. A social event will be enjoyable, but you must avoid overspending and rushing.

4 FEBRUARY

You'll enjoy a reunion and a chance to clear a backlog of chores. Some news may be intense, so be sure to consider the best way forward.

5 FEBRUARY

It's a good day for a health or beauty appointment and to look for common ground with someone whose views you dislike for the sake of peace.

6 FEBRUARY

A difference of opinion needn't get in the way of productivity, so be focused at work and avoid taking random comments personally.

7 FEBRUARY

A surprise development may be pleasant and will encourage you to be more outspoken and express your viewpoints. Be inspired.

8 FEBRUARY

An unexpected development is best approached carefully to avoid impulsiveness.

9 FEBRUARY

The Aquarian new moon supermoon points to a fresh chapter in your work or health life. It's a good day for talks, meetings and financial discussions.

10 FEBRUARY

Be prepared for a little give and take, especially if your plans clash with those of a friend or group. Avoid misunderstandings and delays by planning ahead.

11 FEBRUARY

You'll appreciate the opportunity to dream a little and indulge in music, the arts, creativity and romance.

12 FEBRUARY

Trust your intuition and be prepared for meetings and talks that ask you to offer inspired yet practical advice or information.

13 FEBRUARY

Mars in Aquarius for the next five weeks will encourage you to be innovative at work and with your health routine. You may enjoy a reunion and romance.

14 FEBRUARY

Happy St Valentine's Day! There is an intense quality to the day and strong feelings may emerge. You may hear from someone from your past.

15 FEBRUARY

The Taurean moon will bring out your practical side, but you will benefit from thinking outside the box.

16 FEBRUARY

As Venus enters Aquarius you'll place more attention on work, health and well-being over the next few weeks. Give yourself permission to have a break.

17 FEBRUARY

This is a lovely day for a health or beauty treat and considering a new look. You may hear key news from the past or return to an old haunt.

18 FEBRUARY

A chatty day may distract you from chores, but you will nevertheless find time to get things shipshape. Just avoid forgetfulness.

19 FEBRUARY

As the sun enters your sign your energy levels will begin to improve. You may need to help someone or focus on health. An expert's advice will be invaluable.

20 FEBRUARY

You'll appreciate the opportunity to spend time at home or with someone whose company you enjoy, so be sure to organise some downtime.

21 FEBRUARY

Your advice and ability to see beyond the obvious will be in demand. If you need help or support it will be available, so reach out.

22 FEBRUARY

You'll enjoy a meeting, get-together or news. You may need to leave your comfort zone, so be prepared to think laterally.

23 FEBRUARY

Mercury in your sign for the next three weeks will encourage you to be more expressive and reveal your true feelings.

24 FEBRUARY

The full moon in Virgo spotlights your daily health or work routine, enabling you to plan ahead more exactly to create the schedule you want.

25 FEBRUARY

This is a good day to make a fresh agreement at work or in your health routine. You may enjoy a reunion or return to an old haunt.

26 FEBRUARY

You may not agree with everyone's opinions, but being diplomatic will be more favourable for you than arguing.

27 FEBRUARY

With a little diligence you can attain your goals. However, you must avoid stubbornness on the one hand and rushing on the other.

28 FEBRUARY

This is a good day to make a valid commitment. You may receive news from the past, at work or regarding health.

29 FEBRUARY

You'll appreciate the opportunity to spend time with someone you love or admire. This is a good day to find ways of improving your appearance and health.

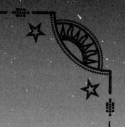

March

1 MARCH

You may be drawn to a little retail therapy. If you're working you're likely to make positive financial headway. It's a good day to make an agreement.

2 MARCH

You'll enjoy a return to an old haunt and being adventurous with activities such as sports and self-development.

3 MARCH

A change of plan will mean you must be on your toes. You may be surprised by a financial circumstance or news from the past. Think laterally.

4 MARCH

You'll enjoy feeling motivated to get things done but must avoid being idealistic about how much you can achieve in one day.

5 MARCH

A reunion or meeting may be more significant than meets the eye. This is a good day for a mini health review or appointment.

6 MARCH

There are therapeutic aspects to the day. It's a good time to mend bridges if you've argued with someone and also to improve finances and work circumstances.

7 MARCH

This is a good day for a mini financial review and to improve both your health and appearance. You may enjoy a reunion.

8 MARCH

The arts, creativity, music and film will appeal. Your romantic qualities may surface; just ensure you're realistic. It's a good day for self-development.

9 MARCH

A fun get-together will be enjoyable but you must avoid impulsiveness and rushing. You may experience a surprise.

10 MARCH

The Pisces new moon supermoon will kick-start a fresh phase in your personal life, especially if it's your birthday. If you were born later in March you'll begin a fresh work or health routine.

11 MARCH

As Venus enters your sign you'll be drawn to love, romance, the arts and creativity over the coming weeks.

12 MARCH

Be prepared to dream a little but also to keep your feet on the ground to avoid unrealistic expectations, especially of others.

13 MARCH

This is a good time to consider a new look or change your usual health and fitness routine. You may enjoy a reunion.

14 MARCH

Be practical and keep your feet on the ground, because in this way you'll attain your goals even if you must think a little laterally.

15 MARCH

A versatile approach to talks and meetings will be productive, but you must avoid trivialising serious work or health matters.

16 MARCH

This is a good day for financial and personal discussions, as you could come to a mutually agreeable arrangement. You may enjoy a get-together or trip.

17 MARCH

This is a super-romantic day, so be sure to organise a treat! You'll enjoy creativity, romance and spirituality. Just avoid forgetfulness and delays by planning ahead.

18 MARCH

The Cancerian moon will bring out your nurturing qualities and you may prefer spending time at home than at work. Trust your intuition with important talks.

19 MARCH

You may receive information connected with a past circumstance or at work. You'll find out whether you've over- or underestimated a situation or person.

20 MARCH

Key financial, personal or health news will merit focus. This is a good day to evaluate your expectations of someone else and find a clever way to move forward.

21 MARCH

Changes in your daily routine could be for the better. It's a good day to make a commitment to a particular path, person or work schedule.

22 MARCH

As Mars enters your sign for the next five weeks you'll gradually experience improved energy levels, but you must avoid appearing feisty or bossy.

23 MARCH

You may be drawn to a little retail therapy and this will be uplifting, but you must avoid overspending. You'll also enjoy getting together with someone special.

24 MARCH

The lead-up to a lunar eclipse can be super intense. You'll appreciate the opportunity to find ways to relax and unwind and enjoy a little domestic bliss.

25 MARCH

The Libran lunar eclipse spotlights a particular relationship. It may be time to find ways to relax more and enjoy company.

26 MARCH

This is a good day to present your compassionate, caring side, as your insight and help will be much appreciated.

27 MARCH

Trust your intuition as it is spot on, especially in relation to someone who may behave mysteriously or give mixed messages.

28 MARCH

You'll enjoy being spontaneous and may appreciate an impromptu meeting or news from someone you love.

29 MARCH

A decision may be best informed by your values and principles. Be prepared to trust your intuition as, once again, it is strong.

30 MARCH

You'll enjoy seeking like-minded company, and an interest in spirituality, the arts, creativity, music and study will all appeal.

31 MARCH

An outgoing, upbeat approach to your day will bring you in touch with similarly dynamic and upbeat people. However, you must avoid forgetfulness.

April

1 APRIL

It's in your interest to consider personal and financial matters from a practical perspective and to get the ball rolling if you wish to make changes.

2 APRIL

As Mercury turns retrograde you may receive key news that will help you to review a personal or financial matter, enabling you to move forward.

3 APRIL

This is a super-romantic day, so be sure to organise a treat. It's a good day for self-development, spirituality, the arts and music.

4 APRIL

You'll appreciate the opportunity to touch base with someone you love or admire. You may be drawn to making a valid financial decision.

5 APRIL

Venus in Aries for the next few weeks will motivate you to consider your principles and values and take action based on these priorities.

6 APRIL

This is a lovely day for a reunion or return to an old haunt. It's also a good day for improving your appearance, health and well-being.

7 APRIL

You'll manage to get a backlog of chores cleared. The lead-up to an eclipse can be intense, so be prepared to channel excess energy into productive activities.

8 APRIL

The total solar eclipse signifies the chance to revitalise your personal and financial arrangements. It's a good time to improve your health and well-being. You may enjoy an ego boost.

9 APRIL

A productive day may nevertheless be a little intense, so be sure to organise a relaxed evening. If an obstacle arises, rest assured you will overcome it.

10 APRIL

Be spontaneous and think on your feet, as a pleasant opportunity may arise. This is a good day to make a commitment, but you must ensure it aligns with your values.

11 APRIL

A reunion and the chance to reconsider a financial situation and review paperwork will be successful.

12 APRIL

You'll enjoy socialising and networking, and a short trip is likely to be pleasant.

13 APRIL

An outgoing, upbeat approach to your various activities will provide a sense of motivation and purpose. This is a good weekend for a health or beauty treat.

14 APRIL

You'll appreciate the opportunity to enjoy the comfort of your home or someone else's. Just be prepared to meet someone halfway should differences arise.

15 APRIL

This is a good day for a health appointment and to double-check finances to avoid making mistakes. Your expertise or that of someone else may be in demand.

16 APRIL

You may need to think on your feet, especially as someone may need your help. If you need support or advice it will be available.

17 APRIL

You'll enjoy a reunion, and romance and the arts could thrive. If you're single you may meet someone who is strangely familiar.

18 APRIL

A productive outlook will certainly see you reach your goals; just avoid cutting corners.

19 APRIL

The next four weeks will be ideal for gaining more stability and security in your life. You may receive key financial or personal news, some of which may surprise you.

20 APRIL

This is an ideal day to get on top of housework and gardening, and to schedule in a little relaxation time to unwind.

21 APRIL

A surprise encounter, get-together or news will take much of your focus. Just avoid overspending and overindulging and a battle of wills.

22 APRIL

Be prepared to be adaptable, as you may be surprised by developments or will experience something out of the ordinary.

23 APRIL

The lead-up to the Scorpio full moon can be intense, so be sure to pace yourself and look for balance.

24 APRIL

The Scorpio full moon will spotlight collaborations, shared duties and joint finances. This is a good time to reorganise a financial or personal arrangement.

25 APRIL

As the Mercury retrograde phase ends you may receive key financial or personal news. You'll enjoy a reunion, and communications will become easier over the coming days and weeks.

26 APRIL

There is an adventurous and upbeat quality to the day that you'll enjoy. You may appreciate socialising this evening.

27 APRIL

This is a good day for sports and pursuing any other favourite activity. You'll appreciate the opportunity to touch base with someone special.

28 APRIL

Romance and the arts can thrive. It's a good day for improving your appearance and shopping, but avoid overspending as you'll regret it.

29 APRIL

As Venus enters Taurus you'll increasingly be drawn to investing in your happiness and spending time with those you love. Romance will thrive, so organise a date!

30 APRIL

Mars in Aries for the next few weeks is motivational for you, giving you extra drive and the will to succeed. Just avoid appearing overzealous.

May

1 MAY

The key to success lies in realising you may have different values from others but also, nevertheless, have common ground so you must find the best outcome.

2 MAY

Key news from a friend, group or organisation will merit an even-minded approach. Avoid a power struggle.

3 MAY

This is a good day to take the initiative and make changes within your daily routine or health schedule.

4 MAY

You'll appreciate the opportunity to dream a little and indulge in some relaxation and luxury. You'll enjoy a change of pace or of place.

5 MAY

You'll enjoy investing in a lovely relationship and finding the time to allow it to thrive.

6 MAY

A little hard work will pay off. You must be prepared to make changes within your usual routine or in the way you approach someone in your circle.

7 MAY

It's a good day for meetings and a health or well-being appointment. You may make a solid agreement or find expert help supportive.

8 MAY

The Taurus new moon will help you turn a corner in a personal or financial context. It's a good time to plan ahead.

9 MAY

The Gemini moon brings to the day a chatty, light-hearted atmosphere. However, you may feel restless and if you're shopping you may overspend, which you'll regret.

10 MAY

A short trip, talks and meetings will bring out your sociable side, which you'll enjoy.

11 MAY

You'll enjoy relaxing, investing in your appearance and well-being and a reunion. Romance could thrive.

12 MAY

The Cancerian moon brings out your nurturing and creative sides. You'll appreciate time spent at your home or someone else's and will enjoy music, dance and relaxation.

13 MAY

This is a good day to be spontaneous but also to focus when necessary at work, otherwise you're likely to be easily distracted.

14 MAY

You like to feel motivated about your daily activities so you'll enjoy the day, especially as you'll appreciate the chance to express yourself.

15 MAY

You'll enjoy the sense that communications and relationships can regain a more even keel over the next few weeks, starting today.

16 MAY

Focus on the details of your various chores to avoid making mistakes, but avoid being overly analytical and critical as this will backfire.

17 MAY

A go-ahead attitude will certainly be productive. However, some communications and meetings may be fraught with misunderstandings and delays so be patient and clear.

18 MAY

You may enjoy a financial or confidence boost. Some developments may come from out of the blue, so be adaptable but avoid distractions if you're working.

19 MAY

You'll be drawn to a little retail therapy and may well discover a gem. It's a lovely day to indulge a little in life's luxuries. Romance and the arts will appeal.

20 MAY

A confident and knowledgeable approach will be productive; however, you must avoid making rash decisions. A meeting is likely to go well.

21 MAY

You're more in touch with other people's feelings when the moon is in Scorpio, enabling you to understand them a little better. Trust your intuition.

22 MAY

This is a good day for get-togethers and meetings as communications are likely to go well, especially if you wish to make changes.

23 MAY

The full moon in Sagittarius will encourage you to be adventurous and express yourself more fully. You may experience a confidence or financial boost. Romance could thrive, so make a date!

24 MAY

A proactive approach to your activities will give you the upper hand, as you'll feel motivated to succeed – which is often the secret to success!

25 MAY

You'll enjoy making changes, and whether these are due to a trip or a change in your appearance, for example, you're likely to be happy with the result.

26 MAY

As Jupiter enters Gemini your focus will increasingly go towards exciting ways to have more fun in your life and prospectively to plan a trip.

27 MAY

A practical, measured approach to your various chores and activities will be successful. Just avoid gambling and being stubborn.

28 MAY

This is a good day for planning, including scheduling a trip or financial mini review. It's also a good day to make a commitment.

29 MAY

Think before you speak, as you may unintentionally cause embarrassment. Avoid rushing and minor bumps and scrapes.

30 MAY

This is a good day to find out a little more about circumstances that may have caused concern. You may be drawn to retail therapy. Avoid rushing and impulse buys.

31 MAY

The Pisces moon will get you in touch with your deeper feelings, but you must avoid being overly sensitive. You'll enjoy being a little spontaneous.

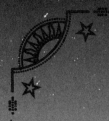

June

1 JUNE

You may be surprised by developments that will keep you on your toes. A little variety and spice will boost moods.

2 JUNE

A proactive, outgoing day will encourage you to reach out and meet someone and, at the least, connect by phone, which will raise spirits.

3 JUNE

Talks and meetings are likely to go well and some developments will gain their own momentum, so be sure you're happy with the direction they take.

4 JUNE

It's a lovely day for a get-together. Financial and personal matters may be on the table for discussion. Romance could thrive.

5 JUNE

You'll feel drawn to discussing some of your plans with those they concern, and you can certainly come to agreements.

6 JUNE

The new moon in Gemini will help you turn a corner in a relationship. You may be drawn to travelling or to updating a communications device or repairing a vehicle.

7 JUNE

The Cancerian moon accentuates your intuition and instinct, so be sure to trust your gut.

8 JUNE

You'll be drawn to the arts, relaxation and romance but must avoid overindulging, as you may be prone to disagreements.

9 JUNE

You may be suffering from Mondayitis and may prefer to stay at home or at least not go to work. However, it will be a productive day.

10 JUNE

You'll manage to accomplish a great deal of chores but you must remain focused on the details or you risk rushing or making mistakes.

11 JUNE

You'll enjoy sprucing up your home life and treating friends or family to something special. There is a healing aspect to the day.

12 JUNE

You won't always agree with everyone, and this is a day when patience will be a virtue. Plan ahead to avoid traffic delays.

13 JUNE

You'll enjoy being spontaneous and may do something different or will hear unexpectedly good news, financially so for some.

14 JUNE

It's a good day for a short trip and meetings. You may hear important financial or personal news.

15 JUNE

A little retail therapy will appeal and you may find an unexpectedly good deal. A trip or visit will be enjoyable.

16 JUNE

Someone you love or admire will have a calming or supportive approach, so be sure to reach out.

17 JUNE

A change of dynamic at home will encourage you to look for a more self-nurturing and supportive approach in the domestic arena.

18 JUNE

You'll gain the motivation you need to get things done but you must avoid unnecessary arguments that spring seemingly from nowhere.

19 JUNE

Trust your intuition, as it is spot on. Avoid taking other people's unreliable or erratic behaviour personally.

20 JUNE

You'll enjoy the opportunity to find time to rest and relax at home but must avoid misunderstandings and delays.

21 JUNE

You'll feel motivated to spend time with friends or family and plan for a DIY project or home visits and decoration over the weekend.

22 JUNE

The Capricorn full moon will spotlight your career, status and general direction. You may not agree with everyone about what this should be, but you will enjoy making plans.

23 JUNE

There are certain people you agree with and others you don't, and choosing who you spend time with will determine your level of happiness.

24 JUNE

An innovative, resourceful approach to your work schedule will bring positive results. Think outside the box.

25 JUNE

Your expertise and advice will be in demand, and if you need support or direction it will be available. Avoid making rash decisions.

26 JUNE

Communications and meetings are likely to go well. However, fundamental matters you disagree upon are worth careful discussion to avoid assumptions being made.

27 JUNE

The moon in your sign brings out your intuition and love of the arts, music and creativity. It's a good day to plan a fun or romantic evening.

28 JUNE

You may need to pay extra attention to interpersonal dynamics, as you or someone else will feel particularly sensitive about various matters.

29 JUNE

You'll appreciate the opportunity to create the domestic atmosphere you love. You'll enjoy improving domestic décor and interpersonal dynamics.

30 JUNE

A creative and upbeat mood will encourage you to reach out to people whose company you enjoy. Music, the arts and romance will appeal.

July

1 JULY

A mini financial review and the chance to get on track with your various projects will provide a productive start to the week.

2 JULY

Over the next few weeks you're likely to feel more expressive, starting today. Just ensure you have the full details to avoid making assumptions.

3 JULY

Some meetings will lead to the chance to make changes in your personal life. It's a good day for planning and for making a commitment.

4 JULY

The next two days are ideal for placing your attention on your home, family or a property, as you'll gain the chance to make invaluable changes there.

5 JULY

The Cancerian new moon will kick-start a fresh phase in a domestic capacity. This is a good time to take the initiative with work and financial matters.

6 JULY

Be prepared to focus on health and well-being, especially within your domestic arena or family. Avoid minor bumps and scrapes.

7 JULY

The Leo moon will encourage you to be more outspoken and creative. You'll enjoy spending time with someone special and investing in your well-being.

8 JULY

You may be surprised by the positive outcome of some developments. You may hear from a good friend.

9 JULY

A practical yet also dynamic approach to work and chores will ensure you meet your goals. Be prepared to make the extra effort.

10 JULY

Attention to detail and planning will be productive. Avoid taking someone's criticism personally unless it's merited. Avoid overanalysing someone.

11 JULY

The next few weeks are likely to be busy and you'll be productive. Romance could thrive, and you'll appreciate a therapeutic aspect to your day.

12 JULY

A work or social meeting is likely to be memorable, as emotions may emerge. It's a good day for romance and to make changes.

13 JULY

You'll appreciate the opportunity to establish a little peace and calm in your life and relationships and focus on your health and well-being.

14 JULY

Be prepared to re-evaluate some of your loyalties, especially if someone's behaviour surprises you or circumstances are out of the ordinary.

15 JULY

An unexpected development will merit a careful and attentive approach. Your help and support may be needed. Avoid impulse buys.

16 JULY

The Scorpio moon will bring out your passionate side, encouraging you to engage in favourite activities. Trust your intuition.

17 JULY

You'll enjoy being spontaneous over the next two days and will embrace the chance to do something different, so be adventurous!

18 JULY

A pleasant or surprising development will boost your confidence. You may enjoy a financial improvement.

19 JULY

This is a good day to mend bridges if you've argued with someone, and also for a health appointment. Romance could thrive.

20 JULY

You'll gain the opportunity to change the way you invest emotionally and financially in projects and people.

21 JULY

The full moon in Capricorn suggests you will be drawn to a fresh social circle or different group or organisation. Avoid misunderstandings.

22 JULY

As the sun enters Leo you'll be drawn to investing more in the people and activities you love over the next four weeks.

23 JULY

This is a good time to connect with different people, groups and organisations to deepen your experiences and influence in life.

24 JULY

Trust your instincts with the people you meet and the work you undertake, as you are intuitive.

25 JULY

You'll appreciate the opportunity to analyse or research circumstances that don't add up, enabling you to unravel a mystery.

26 JULY

This is a busy day and you'll appreciate getting on top of chores. You'll enjoy being spontaneous but must avoid rushing.

27 JULY

A change of pace or of place will require you to adapt to circumstances. Once you do, you'll enjoy the results. Your hard work will pay off.

28 JULY

A little luxury or treat will certainly appeal, and you'll enjoy indulging in creature comforts.

29 JULY

Be practical, especially with financial decisions and work, for the best outcome. Avoid being easily distracted.

30 JULY

This is a good day for a health or beauty treat and to consider a new look such as a fresh hairstyle or outfit.

31 JULY

You'll enjoy getting together with someone you love or admire. This is a good day to be dynamic with your projects and ventures.

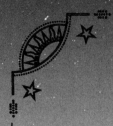
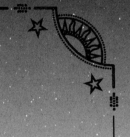

August

1 AUGUST

This is a good day to focus on your well-being and health and that of your family. You may be busy at work.

2 AUGUST

An unexpected change of plans or schedule will keep you on your toes. You'll appreciate the help of someone special and will enjoy a reunion.

3 AUGUST

The lead-up to the Leo new moon is a good time to consider how you might create a more dynamic daily schedule.

4 AUGUST

The Leo new moon spotlights a new chapter in a work or health schedule. Be prepared to research details if agreeing to something new. You'll enjoy a fun get-together.

5 AUGUST

Good communication skills will create a positive outcome in a situation that may include mixed messages, so be prepared to talk.

6 AUGUST

Now that Mercury is retrograde you'll gain the chance to review circumstances in more detail and rethink recent decisions if necessary, especially regarding work and health.

7 AUGUST

Attention to detail will be productive but you must avoid becoming overly analytical and self-critical. You may receive good news or enjoy a trip.

8 AUGUST

You'll enjoy a get-together and may receive key news at work, regarding health or from a personal partner.

9 AUGUST

You'll enjoy that Friday feeling as you look forward to planning events for this evening and the weekend.

10 AUGUST

It's a good day for clearing a backlog of chores at home and in the garden. If you overworked during the week you'll enjoy relaxing.

11 AUGUST

An intuitive approach to someone or a circumstance will be beneficial, so take time to look beneath the surface.

12 AUGUST

Once again, an intuitive approach to circumstances will be beneficial, especially if you feel that some discussions are difficult or complex.

13 AUGUST

You'll appreciate creating the space or time to enjoy a favourite activity such as sports or yoga. A positive outlook will overcome obstacles.

14 AUGUST

Your communication skills will be in demand and you may be rushed off your feet. A trip or unexpected meeting will benefit from a focused approach.

15 AUGUST

This is a good day for a health or beauty appointment. If you've been worried about circumstances at work they are likely to improve. Just be super clear.

16 AUGUST

A patient, open-minded approach to someone who can be changeable or demanding will be beneficial to avoid arguments or a stalemate. Avoid rushing.

17 AUGUST

You'll appreciate the opportunity to get down to brass tacks over a complex circumstance. This evening, you'll enjoy doing something different for a change.

18 AUGUST

A change of plan will require a patient approach and the key to success lies in good communication skills. Avoid arguments by looking for common ground.

19 AUGUST

The Aquarian full moon will spotlight the chance to change your usual daily or health routine. A meeting or news could lead to a valid commitment.

20 AUGUST

The moon in your sign for the next two days will provide you with extra insight into circumstances, so trust your intuition.

21 AUGUST

A creative yet also practical approach to your chores, personal relationships and work will be productive.

22 AUGUST

The sun in Virgo over the next four weeks will spotlight your collaborations and personal relationships. Be prepared to be super clear about your intentions in these areas.

23 AUGUST

This is a good day for talks and meetings, especially with a view to reviewing and improving circumstances. It's a good day for a health or beauty appointment.

24 AUGUST

This is an excellent time for remedial work such as sprucing up your environments at home and work. You'll enjoy get-togethers.

25 AUGUST

A trip and socialising will raise your mood, and you may enjoy a spontaneous gathering or bump into someone fun.

26 AUGUST

Be confident about your communication abilities, as you may surprise yourself and could make progress in your work and personal life over the next two days.

27 AUGUST

You'll appreciate the opportunity to spend time with someone upbeat and fun. If you're single you may meet someone you click with out of the blue.

28 AUGUST

You may receive key health news. It's an excellent day for romance and the arts, but you must avoid being forgetful and idealistic.

29 AUGUST

This is an excellent day for meetings, both socially and at work. Decisions and commitments made now are likely to succeed as long as you have carefully researched them.

30 AUGUST

You'll be drawn to spending time with like-minded people and enjoying music, dance and romance. You may bump into someone fun.

31 AUGUST

You'll enjoy an impromptu get-together or trip. Someone may have unexpected news. Just avoid overspending on something out of the ordinary.

September

1 SEPTEMBER

You'll appreciate the opportunity to take some time to focus on your health and well-being and find ways to bring more fun into your daily life.

2 SEPTEMBER

This is a good day for a beauty appointment. You may experience encouraging signs at work.

3 SEPTEMBER

The new moon in Virgo will kick-start a fresh phase in a personal or business collaboration and, if you were born later in September, a fresh daily routine at work or health-wise.

4 SEPTEMBER

Someone special will be particularly supportive, so be prepared to reach out if you need their help or guidance. You'll appreciate spending time at home or with family.

5 SEPTEMBER

This is a good time to be looking for peace and balance in relationships, as you're likely to find it and especially at home.

6 SEPTEMBER

A proactive approach to those you care about will be appreciated, although you may be feeling sensitive. It's a good time to look for balance and common ground.

7 SEPTEMBER

You'll find the motivation to make changes at home and improve your environment. You'll appreciate the results.

8 SEPTEMBER

This is a good day to unravel a mystery or do some research, especially in relation to work and health and for someone special. You may make a solid agreement.

9 SEPTEMBER

As Mercury enters Virgo your attention is likely to go on someone special as they become more communicative. It's important to avoid a power struggle.

10 SEPTEMBER

The Sagittarian moon brings out your adventurous qualities. You'll enjoy scheduling in a favourite or fun activity.

11 SEPTEMBER

You won't always get on with everyone, and a little extra care and attention will overcome any minor hurdles in communications.

12 SEPTEMBER

Be prepared to go the extra mile to ensure communications run smoothly to avoid arguments. Also be prepared for a travel delay by planning ahead.

13 SEPTEMBER

Be practical and realistic, especially with groups and organisations you must interact with, for the best results.

14 SEPTEMBER

You may be inclined to take random comments and other people's sensitivities to heart, so maintain perspective. You may be asked for help.

15 SEPTEMBER

This is a lovely day for get-togethers and romance could thrive, so be prepared to organise something special.

16 SEPTEMBER

You are once again more prone to pick up on other people's feelings and may tend to take this personally, so maintain perspective and avoid making rash decisions.

17 SEPTEMBER

If someone has disappointed you be prepared to consider a fresh approach to the relationship. You may be asked for help. If you need advice it will be available.

18 SEPTEMBER

The partial lunar eclipse supermoon in Pisces spotlights your personal life and for some a fresh work or health circumstance. Be prepared to make a solid plan of action.

19 SEPTEMBER

You may receive a surprise offer, or an unexpected development that is likely to be to your benefit will arise.

20 SEPTEMBER

Be prepared to discuss your options with someone special. If you feel under pressure, be sure to take regular breaks.

21 SEPTEMBER

Stick with the facts, as you must be prepared to see someone else's point of view to avoid misunderstandings. Romance could thrive, so plan a date!

22 SEPTEMBER

As the sun enters Libra it's a lovely time to look for balance and harmony in your relationships. You'll enjoy a get-together as long as you avoid a battle of wills.

23 SEPTEMBER

Venus in Scorpio for the next few weeks will bring a passionate and potentially feisty phase your way, so it's a good time for romance but also to focus on good relationship skills.

24 SEPTEMBER

You'll enjoy an impromptu get-together or will receive good news that could be potentially transformational.

25 SEPTEMBER

This is a lovely day for romance and the arts. A colleague or partner may have news. Avoid forgetfulness and being easily influenced.

26 SEPTEMBER

You'll find the right words in meetings and talks. If you wanted to make changes to an arrangement or even a relationship, this is the day to do it!

27 SEPTEMBER

An uplifting approach to chores, work and activities will be productive. Just avoid arguments with someone whose views are contentious.

28 SEPTEMBER

This is a good day to improve your health, well-being and appearance. You may enjoy a get-together with someone special over the next two days.

29 SEPTEMBER

You are likely to receive important news or will enjoy a lovely trip or meeting. If you're single and looking for a partner you may find them.

30 SEPTEMBER

You'll receive important news, for some do with work. This is a good time to make solid agreements at home and in your personal life, as they will bring stability.

October

1 OCTOBER

The days in the run-up to an eclipse can feel intense, and this is certainly a good day to set an intention to relax and avoid being critical and overly analytical.

2 OCTOBER

The solar eclipse is a good time to consider ways to be more measured in your response to others, even if others are the fiery ones. Look for the most balanced option.

3 OCTOBER

It's a good day to discuss personal matters and for work meetings. A financial matter can be remedied.

4 OCTOBER

It's another good day for socialising and networking and for work-related meetings, so be confident and take the initiative.

5 OCTOBER

You'll be motivated to enjoy activities you relish with people whose company you love, so be sure to reach out if you have nothing planned yet.

6 OCTOBER

You'll enjoy spending time with someone special. However, you must avoid complex or angry talks as they could quickly escalate to conflict.

7 OCTOBER

An adventurous and outgoing attitude will certainly see you reaching targets and obtaining goals, so be proactive.

8 OCTOBER

This is a good day for overcoming past disagreements, get-togethers and also romance. It's also a good day for financial planning.

9 OCTOBER

If you know what your goals are you will attain them. Be practical, and if you don't have any goals set for the day you must avoid being easily distracted.

10 OCTOBER

The Capricorn moon helps you get things done. Be sure to schedule important chores because you will succeed.

11 OCTOBER

The key to success relies on good communication skills; you may need to think on your feet. Avoid allowing a difference in values to derail your well-laid plans.

12 OCTOBER

Double-check plans, as there may be a misunderstanding or change at the last minute. You'll enjoy the arts and creativity but must avoid forgetfulness.

13 OCTOBER

As Mercury enters Scorpio you'll feel increasingly in tune with your intuition over the coming weeks. Mix-ups and misunderstanding are likely, so avoid arguments.

14 OCTOBER

Think on your feet, as developments will require you to react quickly yet be practical. Your help and advice will be in demand. A surprise is on the way.

15 OCTOBER

You have strong empathy for others, even if they don't understand you. You'll be drawn to the arts, romance and music but must avoid being easily influenced.

16 OCTOBER

This is an excellent day for romance, so why not schedule a date? If you're single you may meet someone charming. The arts, creativity and self-development will thrive.

17 OCTOBER

The full moon supermoon in Aries will spotlight a personal or financial matter that will require a patient and calm approach. Avoid making rash decisions.

18 OCTOBER

You'll enjoy a little retail therapy or indulging in a favourite pastime, food or activity. Just avoid overspending if you're already in debt as you'll regret it.

19 OCTOBER

Someone close may have unusual or unexpected news that merits a change of plan. Rise to the challenge and you'll enjoy your day.

20 OCTOBER

Further research into your options moving forward, especially regarding self-development and in your personal life, will be worthwhile. Avoid idealism.

21 OCTOBER

A short trip or meeting may at first seem intense, but if you rely on your good communication skills you may enjoy the day's developments.

22 OCTOBER

As the sun enters Scorpio your attention will go on your professional and personal relationships over the next four weeks as you look for more meaning and purpose in these areas.

23 OCTOBER

You'll appreciate the opportunity to spend time doing what you love, so be sure to schedule some me time. This is a good day to deepen your relationships.

24 OCTOBER

The Leo moon is motivational for you at work, so you'll be productive. If you're on a break you'll enjoy activities such as sports.

25 OCTOBER

A fun, spontaneous approach to the day will be productive, and you'll enjoy your favourite activities and being creative.

26 OCTOBER

Be inspired by your work and the people you spend time with and you'll enjoy your day.

27 OCTOBER

This is an excellent day to relax and enjoy the company of like-minded people, music, the arts and romance. Just avoid unnecessary arguments.

28 OCTOBER

You can tend to be a little idealistic, and when reality doesn't match you can be disappointed. Be practical, as hard work will help you attain your goals.

29 OCTOBER

It's another good day to aim for achieving your goals. Be prepared to think on your feet, though, as unexpected developments are likely. It's a good time to check your finances.

30 OCTOBER

You may receive unexpected financial or personal news. Avoid making rash decisions.

31 OCTOBER

Happy Hallowe'en! This is a good day to decide how you would prefer your relationships to develop and to make a wish on tomorrow's new moon.

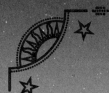

November

1 NOVEMBER

The Scorpio new moon will revitalise your relationships. It's a good time to aim for your goals and put a plan of action in place.

2 NOVEMBER

There are therapeutic aspects to the weekend. It's a good time to improve your health and appearance and for a short trip somewhere fun.

3 NOVEMBER

Travel or a visit will be enjoyable, but you must avoid arguments that arise due to tension or drama.

4 NOVEMBER

The next few weeks will be constructive as you gain an opportunity to build a solid platform for yourself in your personal life and at work.

5 NOVEMBER

A practical approach to your career and status will be productive. Be prepared to collaborate.

6 NOVEMBER

You'll enjoy meeting different groups of people or a new circle over the next two days.

7 NOVEMBER

You'll enjoy a favourite activity, trip or get-together. It's a good day to consult an expert or adviser.

8 NOVEMBER

Be prepared to think laterally regarding various options, especially at work and financially.

9 NOVEMBER

Research circumstances to ensure you haven't missed important details, especially work-wise and financially.

10 NOVEMBER

The Pisces moon will get you in touch with your intuition, although you may tend to misread someone's intentions so be sure to trust your gut.

11 NOVEMBER

Venus will put the attention on your status, career and general direction. Just ensure you have carefully researched circumstances before making key choices.

12 NOVEMBER

Be prepared to be tactful and take personal and work decisions one step at time. Be patient and you will attain your goals.

13 NOVEMBER

You'll be motivated by the people you admire, so remember to maintain sight of your goals.

14 NOVEMBER

The lead-up to a full moon can be intense and may feel slow or tough going, so be sure to pace yourself.

15 NOVEMBER

The full moon in Taurus spotlights financial and personal decisions. You may be surprised by news and developments. Maintain a level head.

16 NOVEMBER

You'll appreciate the chance to do something different, although you may need to adjust to an unexpected change of plan. Avoid needless arguments.

17 NOVEMBER

You'll enjoy a trip or meeting. This is a good day to discuss important matters; just avoid feeling overly emotional.

18 NOVEMBER

A key meeting or trip will be significant. Avoid allowing a difference of opinion to derail your day.

19 NOVEMBER

This is a good day for the arts, music and romance. You may drive to a beautiful place that has a healing effect.

20 NOVEMBER

As Pluto re-enters Aquarius you're ready to make considerable changes in your activities, social life and network. Be patient with an unexpected or complex matter.

21 NOVEMBER

As the sun enters Sagittarius you'll enjoy a more adventurous and outgoing four weeks, starting today with an upbeat project or venture.

22 NOVEMBER

You'll enjoy a productive get-together. A work matter could prove fortunate or lucrative. It's a good day to make a commitment.

23 NOVEMBER

A spontaneous activity, change in routine or impromptu get-together will be enjoyable. If you're single and looking for a partner you may bump into someone.

24 NOVEMBER

You'll enjoy an opportunity to discuss serious matters such as your work schedule moving forward and organising a trip.

25 NOVEMBER

Someone close may be feeling a little emotional, so be prepared to show support. You'll enjoy an upbeat and varied day.

26 NOVEMBER

It's a good day to get paperwork on the table and initiate important talks. You may receive keys work news. You'll enjoy a fun activity but must avoid delays and mix-ups.

27 NOVEMBER

You'll enjoy being busy and productive. There is a fun aspect to the day that you'll enjoy.

28 NOVEMBER

You'll manage to overcome any delays, and the advice or help of an expert will be useful. Avoid taking disappointing news personally and find ways to remedy issues.

29 NOVEMBER

This is an excellent day for talks, a reunion and a return to an old haunt.

30 NOVEMBER

This is an excellent day to make plans for travel and other adventurous activities.

December

1 DECEMBER

The Sagittarian new moon signals the start of a fresh venture or interest such as study, travel or sports. Some March-born Pisces may be turning a corner in a collaboration.

2 DECEMBER

This is a good day for a health or beauty appointment and to review and remedy any outstanding issues. You may receive a pleasant surprise.

3 DECEMBER

A practical, methodical approach to your chores and relationships will be productive.

4 DECEMBER

Work hard and you will attain your goals, especially at work. Key talks or a trip will be productive.

5 DECEMBER

The Aquarian moon will encourage you to think outside the box and this will be useful, especially at work and regarding your health.

6 DECEMBER

Be prepared to think on your toes as a trip or significant news brings change your way.

7 DECEMBER

You'll enjoy a reunion or return to an old haunt, even if it is intense. Travel, sports or study will take your attention. Think laterally for the best effect.

8 DECEMBER

The moon in your sign will be inspiring, and you'll appreciate an opportunity to slow down the pace. However, you may have pre-existing chores to complete first.

9 DECEMBER

Do you love what you do? If so, you'll enjoy cruising through events. If not, you'll be able to change what you dislike in the coming week.

10 DECEMBER

There are healing aspects to the day that make it ideal for improving your health and well-being. This is a lovely day for get-togethers and romance.

11 DECEMBER

Consider whether you're passionate about your life, especially your daily routine. If not, take slow steps to change things. You'll enjoy a treat.

12 DECEMBER

A serious talk or get-together will put your priorities into perspective. This is a wonderful day for romance for some Pisces, so go with the mood if it takes you.

13 DECEMBER

Despite this being Friday the 13th there are positive aspects to the day. You'll enjoy a reunion, socialising or good news financially or at work.

14 DECEMBER

It's a lovely weekend to do something different and for a short trip and socialising. However, if you're tired it's a perfect day to relax.

15 DECEMBER

The full moon will spotlight your home, family or a property. Some Pisces will be getting ready for a trip. Be prepared for the unexpected.

16 DECEMBER

Trust your intuition, especially regarding someone close such as a family member or partner.

17 DECEMBER

Pay attention to details, as you may be inclined to be slightly forgetful and absent-minded.

18 DECEMBER

You'll enjoy the wonder and spectacle of this festive time of year but must avoid being easily distracted and overindulging, which you'll regret.

19 DECEMBER

You'll be drawn to making a commitment to certain ideas, projects or people but you must avoid making assumptions.

20 DECEMBER

You'll enjoy a trip or return to an old haunt. There is a fun aspect to the day.

21 DECEMBER

As the sun steps into Capricorn it's the solstice. Over the next four weeks you'll be drawn to being more practical about your ventures, pastimes, relationships and planning.

22 DECEMBER

You'll appreciate the opportunity to improve your usual daily routine and will enjoy a reunion.

23 DECEMBER

Take things one step at a time, looking for peace and balance, even if some developments or people are annoying.

24 DECEMBER

There are equally enjoyable as frustrating aspects to the day. Be prepared to be patient, especially with travel and conversations.

25 DECEMBER

Merry Christmas! You'll be motivated to get right into the Christmas spirit but must avoid feeling under pressure to entertain. Relax and enjoy yourself.

26 DECEMBER

This is a chatty, busy day that is ideal for a trip and get-togethers. Just avoid feeling sensitive and enjoy the day. You may be drawn to the Boxing Day sales.

27 DECEMBER

If you've underestimated a circumstance you may experience a reality check. Travel and meetings may be delayed, so plan ahead.

28 DECEMBER

You may unexpectedly hear from someone from the past. A work schedule may need changing. Be prepared to be flexible and focus on good health.

29 DECEMBER

The Sagittarius moon will promote your adventurous qualities and you'll be drawn to sports, outdoors activities and ways to boost health and well-being.

30 DECEMBER

The new moon in Capricorn will kick-start a fresh phase in your career, status or general direction. Be prepared to think outside the box about your options.

31 DECEMBER

Happy New Year! You'll enjoy being outgoing and upbeat, and a trip or get-together will be food for the soul.